**hr**WORKS®

The Handbook of Canadian Pension and Benefit Plans
12th Edition

Revised by
Jennifer Greenan, B.Sc., LL.B.

Reviewed by the following professionals of **Morneau Sobeco**:

Michele Bossi	Wade Harding	Francine Proulx
David Burgess	Karen Kesteris	Joy Sloane
Greg Caines	Rick Kular	Gary Stoller
Jeff Clark	Fred Lewis	Ian Sullivan
Jason Eatock	Neil Narale	Jacqueline Taggart
Conrad Ferguson	Claire Ouellet	John Trieu
Greg Forbes	Marcel Poitras	Bethune Whiston
Cheryl Fullerton	Robin Pond	Fred Vettese

CCH CANADIAN LIMITED
90 Sheppard Avenue East, Suite 300
Toronto, ON M2N 6X1
Telephone: (416) 224-2248 Toll Free: 1-800-268-4522
Fax: (416) 224-2243 Toll Free: 1-800-461-4131
Internet: www.cch.ca

Published by CCH Canadian Limited

Important Disclaimer: This publication is sold with the understanding that (1) the authors and editors are not responsible for the results of any actions taken on the basis of information in this work, nor for any errors or omissions; and (2) the publisher is not engaged in rendering legal, accounting or other professional services. The publisher, and the authors and editors, expressly disclaim all and any liability to any person, whether a purchaser of this publication or not, in respect of anything and of the consequences of anything done or omitted to be done by any such person in reliance, whether whole or partial, upon the whole or any part of the contents of this publication. If legal advice or other expert assistance is required, the services of a competent professional person should be sought.

Edited by:

Nancy Turner, B.A. (Hons.)

www.cch.ca ®

Canadian Cataloguing in Publication Data

The National Library of Canada has catalogued this publication as follows:
    Main entry under title:
        The Handbook of Canadian Pension and Benefit Plans

    12th ed.
    Previously published under title: Mercer Handbook of Canadian Pension and Benefit Plans
Includes index.
ISBN 1-55141-061-3

1. Old Age Pensions — Canada. 2. Employee Fringe Benefits — Canada. 3. Social Security — Canada.
I. CCH Canadian Ltd. II. Title: The Handbook of Canadian Pension and Benefit Plans.

HD7129.G74 2002   658.3′25′0971   C2002-905566-0

ISBN 1-55141-011-7

© **2002, CCH Canadian Limited**

Typeset in Canada by CCH Canadian Limited.
Printed in Canada.

FOREWORD

This book is the result of the efforts of various individuals who assisted in the revision of the 12th Edition. I would like to express my sincere appreciation to the members of the Morneau Sobeco team, namely Bethune Whiston, Michele Bossi, David Burgess, Greg Caines, Jeff Clark, Jason Eatock, Conrad Ferguson, Greg Forbes, Cheryl Fullerton, Wade Harding, Karen Kesteris, Rick Kular, Fred Lewis, Neil Narale, Claire Ouellet, Marcel Poitras, Robin Pond, Francine Proulx, Joy Sloane, Gary Stoller, Ian Sullivan, Jacqueline Taggart, John Trieu and Fred Vetesse, who reviewed the content of the Handbook and provided corrections and numerous insightful comments.

Due credit must be given to the exceptional work of the original authors of the Mercer Handbook of Canadian Pension & Benefit Plans, 11th Edition, upon which this book is largely based and, in particular, Mr. Gordon Hall, Editor of the 11th Edition.

At CCH Canadian Limited, I would like to acknowledge Shirley Spalding, Developmental Editor, Human Resources, Legal & Specialized Markets, and I would like to thank Janet Kim, Acquisitions Manager, Human Resources, Legal & Specialized Markets for her unending support. Last but definitely not least, I would like to thank Nancy Turner, B.A. (Hons), Editor of the 12th Edition, whose outstanding editing skills have shaped the final version of this edition.

Jennifer A. Greenan

October 2002

TABLE OF CONTENTS

LIST OF ACRONYMS

The following acronyms are used in this publication:

ACPM	Association of Canadian Pension Management
AcSB	Accounting Standards Board
AD&D	Accidental Death and Dismemberment
AIR	Annual Information Return
ASO	Administrative Services Only
ASP	Application Service Provider
CANSIM	Canadian Socio-economic Information Management database. Statistics Canada, the Bank of Canada and Canada Mortgage and Housing Corporation maintain information contained in this database
CAP	Capital Accumulation Plan
CAPSA	Canadian Association of Pension Supervisory Authorities
CCRA	Canada Customs and Revenue Agency
CEIC	Canada Employment Insurance Commission
CFR	Claims Fluctuation Reserve
CHST	Canada Health and Social Transfer
CIA	Canadian Institute of Actuaries
CICA	Canadian Institute of Chartered Accountants
CLHIA	Canadian Life and Health Insurance Association
CPI	Consumer Price Index
CPP	Canada Pension Plan
DB	Defined Benefit
DC	Defined Contribution
DLR	Disabled Life Reserves
DPSP	Deferred Profit Sharing Plan
EAP	Employee Assistance Program
EDI	Electronic Data Interchange
EI	Employment Insurance
EPSP	Employees Profit Sharing Plan
ERISA	*Employee Retirement Income Security Act of 1974* (U.S.)

FASB	Financial Accounting Standards Board (U.S.)
FSCO	Financial Services Commission of Ontario
GAINS	Guaranteed Annual Income System (Ontario)
GIS	Guaranteed Income Supplement
GST	General Sales Tax
HCSA	Health Care Spending Account
HRDC	Human Resources Development Canada
IBNR	Incurred But Not Reported
IPP	Individual Pension Plan
ITA	*Income Tax Act* (Federal)
IVR	Interactive Voice Response
LIF	Life Income Fund
LIRA	Locked-In Retirement Account
LLP	Lifelong Learning Plan
LRIF	Locked-In Retirement Income Fund
LTC	Long-Term Care
LTD	Long-Term Disability
MIE	Maximum Insurable Earning
OAS	Old Age Security
OSFI	Office of the Superintendent of Financial Services
PA	Pension Adjustment
PAR	Pension Adjustment Reversal
PBGF	Pension Benefits Guarantee Fund (Ontario)
PBM	Pharmacy Benefit Manager
PBSA	*Pension Benefits Standards Act* (Federal)
PHSP	Private Health Services Plan
PIPEDA	*Personal Information Protection and Electronic Documents Act* (Federal)
PPN	Preferred Provider Network
PSPA	Past Service Pension Adjustment
QPP	Quebec Pension Plan
RAMQ	Régie d'assurance-maladie du Quebec
RCA	Retirement Compensation Arrangement
RPP	Registered Pension Plan
RRIF	Registered Retirement Income Fund
RRSP	Registered Retirement Savings Plan
RSF	Rate Stabilization Fund
SDA	Salary Deferral Arrangement
Section 3461	CICA Handbook, Section 3461, "Employee Future Benefits"

SERP Supplemental Executive Retirement Plan

SIN Social Insurance Number

SPPA *Supplemental Pension Plans Act* (Quebec)

SRI Socially Responsible Investing

SRP Supplementary Retirement Plan

STD Short-Term Disability

SUB Supplemental Unemployment Benefits

TPA Third Party Administrator

UI Unemployment Insurance

WC Workers' Compensation

WCB Workers' Compensation Board

YBE Year's Basic Exemption

YMPE Year's Maximum Pensionable Earnings, as defined under the Canada Pension Plan. Similarly, "MPE" refers to Maximum Pensionable Earnings under the Quebec Pension Plan

PART I
RETIREMENT INCOME
ARRANGEMENTS

OVERVIEW OF RETIREMENT INCOME ARRANGEMENTS

More than ever before, governments, employers, and employees are concerned about pension planning.

This chapter describes the changing environment within which pension arrangements operate, and looks at how governments, employers and employees view pension arrangements. The different types of government and employer pension arrangements are described, as are the issues that an employer might consider in choosing a pension arrangement that best meets its needs and the needs of its workforce.

The balance of the chapters in Part 1 describe the pension programs sponsored by government and the variety of plans sponsored by employers in more detail. The typical terms and conditions found in employer plans are described, as are the considerations, including legislation, that an employer will take into account when deciding on these terms and conditions. While the focus is on registered pension plans, Part I also reviews other supplementary plans for executives and other retirement income and savings arrangements.

Part I also looks at governance issues — the administration and financial management of pension plans and the investment of pension fund assets. Finally, since pension arrangements operate in a complex legislative environment, separate chapters are devoted to the taxation system in which retirement arrangements operate and to pension standards legislation.

History

Informal pension arrangements existed in Canada as early as the late 1800s to provide benefits to employees who were no longer able to work or to widows of former employees. In 1887, the federal government passed the *Pension Fund Societies Act*, which enabled employees to establish pension funds to which an employer might or might not contribute. A few of these Societies still exist. The federal government further encouraged the implementation of pension plans through income tax legislation introduced in 1919. This legislation allowed an employee to deduct from taxable income the contributions made to a pension plan. Further changes to income tax legislation, in later years, allowed employers to deduct their contributions to pension plans on behalf of their employees.

Pension arrangements were originally provided on a pay-as-you-go basis. In 1908, the federal government passed the *Government Annuities Act*, which provided a means of pre-funding pension benefits. Government annuities were discontinued in 1975. Canadian insurance companies introduced group annuity contracts for pension plans during the 1930s as an alternative to government annuities. In 1961, insurance companies were authorized to establish segregated pension funds, and since that time, group annuity contracts have largely been replaced by segregated fund and deposit administration contracts. Today, while over 64%[1] of pension plans are funded through insurance company contracts, these plans tend to be small (in terms of numbers of members) and account for only 15% of the total membership of all Canadian employer-sponsored pension plans. Large employers favour trusteed arrangements under which they assume responsibility for the investment of pension fund assets. Assets are generally held by a trust company or individual trustees and investment of these assets is delegated to a trust company or investment manager(s).

Canadian governments have also actively implemented broad-based retirement programs. Old Age Security (OAS) pensions were first introduced by the federal government in 1952. The Canada and Quebec Pension Plans were established in 1966 and the Guaranteed Income Supplement (GIS) was introduced in 1967. In recent years, these arrangements have been subjected to intensive scrutiny due to concerns over their long-term financial viability. In 1989, Old Age Security ceased to be a universal arrangement when benefits became subject to a clawback for high income earners. In the March 1996 budget, the Minister of Finance announced major changes to the

---

[1] Source: *Pension Plans in Canada* January 1, 2000, Statistics Canada.

program, whereby Old Age Security and the Guaranteed Income Supplement would be replaced in 2001 by a new "Seniors Benefit". The proposal was not well received and in July 1998, the federal government announced that the proposed Seniors' Benefits program would not be undertaken. Instead, the current program of OAS and GIS benefits would continue. The future of the Canada and Quebec Pension Plans (CPP and QPP) was somewhat uncertain in light of escalating contribution requirements and the changing demographics of the Canadian workforce. This prompted the government to review proposals for reform of the CPP/QPP to ensure it would be sustainable in the long run, without placing too much of a financial burden on future generations. In 1998, a variety of amendments were made to both the CPP and QPP to ensure both plans' financial sustainability, including a new schedule of contribution rates. Further details on government-sponsored arrangements are found in Chapter 3.

The first of the provincial pension benefits acts was introduced in Ontario in 1965, and it provided improved vesting and funding of benefits under employer-sponsored pension plans. Today, nine provinces plus the federal government have comparable legislation (referred to throughout this *Handbook* as pension standards legislation) in place.

Major reform of the legislation took place in the 1980s and early 1990s. Revisions were made to the minimum standards for employer-sponsored arrangements, covering such items as eligibility for plan membership, vesting of pensions for terminated employees and benefits for spouses of plan members, as well as administration and governance. Furthermore most provinces continue to adjust their pension legislation on a fairly regular basis and some provinces have since adopted a third set of reform-type legislation (Alberta, effective March 1, 2000 and Quebec effective, January 1, 2001).

In the early 1990s, the federal government introduced major changes to the *Income Tax Act*, which significantly changed the tax treatment of retirement savings arrangements. The government's stated purpose of this "tax reform" was to put members of all types of retirement arrangements on a "level playing field" and to eliminate the more favourable treatment previously enjoyed by members of employer-sponsored pension arrangements. In the 1997 federal budget, an adjustment known as a Pension Adjustment Reversal (PAR) was introduced to deal with concerns that some of these "equality" provisions introduced in 1992 were actually creating inequitable results for some plan members. Chapter 7 provides additional information on the taxation of retirement savings arrangements.

In the province of Quebec, legislation was adopted in 1997 to provide phased retirement provisions, permitting employees to receive an annual lump-sum payment from their pensions while continuing employment. Alberta subsequently enacted similar legislation. Phased retirement is discussed in more detail in Chapter 2.

Present Position

Canadians typically receive retirement income from three key sources: government-administered pension programs, employer-sponsored retirement savings programs, and personal savings. Each of these sources is sometimes referred to as one leg of a three-legged stool.

Government Pension Programs

Government-administered pension programs include two distinctly different programs:

- Old Age Security (OAS) and Guaranteed Income Supplement (GIS), which supply the base of the retirement income system and are financed out of general tax revenues; and

- Canada and Quebec Pension Plans (CPP/QPP), which are work-related arrangements with earnings-based benefits financed solely by employee and employer contributions.

Currently, all persons who have resided in Canada for a sufficient period are entitled to the Old Age Security benefit commencing at age 65. For those with sufficiently high individual incomes, however, Old Age Security benefits will be entirely taxed back. For those with small incomes, a Guaranteed Income Supplement and an Allowance (paid to spouses and common-law partners of pensioners) may also be payable. Old Age Security benefits are now taxable; in contrast, the benefits from the Guaranteed Income Supplement and the Allowance are tax-free.

In its March 1996 budget, the federal government proposed major changes to its benefit program. When it was to become effective in 2001, the "Seniors Benefit" was to replace the current system of Old Age Security and Guaranteed Income Supplement benefits, and the old age and pension tax credits were to be eliminated. The Seniors Benefit was to be income-tested, based on the family income of the pensioner and his or her spouse, and would be completely tax-free. However, it appears that the government ultimately bowed to pressure and in July 1998, the federal government announced that the proposed Seniors' Benefits program would not be undertaken.

In addition to these federally administered social security programs, some provincial programs, such as Ontario's GAINS program, also provide pension supplements, subject to an income test.

The CPP and QPP provide a basic level of earnings replacement on earnings up to the Year's Maximum Pensionable Earnings, which is linked to the average Canadian wage and is indexed annually. Virtually all employees and self-employed persons in Canada, other than those with very small earnings, must contribute to one of these Plans. Unlike the social security programs, which are income-tested, the CPP and QPP are universal and are financed solely by contributions from employees, employers and the self-employed, without any government subsidy. The benefits are payable in addition to Old Age Security and benefits from other income-tested programs. Benefits from the CPP and QPP are subject to income tax. Chapter 3 provides more details on government pension programs.

Employer-Sponsored Pension Plans

On January 1, 2000 there were 15,557 employer-sponsored pension plans in operation, covering over 5 million employee members. These include 1,276 plans for some 2.4 million federal, provincial, and municipal government employees, and a great variety of individual and multi-employer plans maintained by commercial, industrial and other private-sector organizations of all sizes. Their assets have grown over the last few decades and totalled almost $700 billion at of the end of 1999[2].

Personal Savings

Some people continue to earn income after they have reached normal retirement ages. Personal savings through Registered Retirement Savings Plans, profit sharing plans, and savings plans are often important sources of retirement income for older individuals. Others rely on personal resources in addition to pension income — investment income, personal savings and home ownership.

All Sources Needed

Except for lower income earners and the self-employed, all legs of the three-legged stool are necessary to accumulate sufficient retirement savings to maintain a comparable standard of living after retirement. However the ability of individuals to accumulate adequate overall retirement savings is obviously influenced by certain variables beyond the individual's control (i.e., government cutbacks such as the

---

[2] Source: *Pension Plans in Canada*, January 1, 2000, Statistics Canada.

implementation of the OAS clawback and employer's desires to reduce pension costs).

There has been increasing responsibility placed on individuals to save for their own retirement. Tax sheltering for retirement savings has been constrained somewhat by the federal government's actions and high personal income taxes have also reduced the amount individuals can divert to personal savings.

The changing nature of the three-legged stool has caused and will continue to cause the government, employers, and financial institutions to increase their focus on educating individuals on their role in saving for a secure retirement and making them aware of the relevant issues. Chapter 4 includes a more detailed discussion of the tools that can be used to educate employees about their retirement programs.

Establishing Pension Plans

An employer may pay pensions out of current revenue without setting up a pension plan. As long as retirement payments out of current revenue are reasonable, the employer may deduct them as an expense for income tax purposes, as if they were salary or wages.

However, if an employer formally commits to paying a group of employees a pension when they ultimately retire, and this commitment is sufficiently defined, the pension plan regulators may consider the arrangement to be a formal pension plan; that is, a plan "organized and administered to provide a pension benefit for employees". Implicit in this definition is that the primary purpose of a formal pension plan is to provide retirement income in the form of a lifetime annuity. So far, the authorities have not considered group Registered Retirement Savings Plans or supplementary arrangements for employees as falling within the definition of a pension plan.

A formal pension plan has two main features:

1. The plan contains provisions stating how the pension and other benefits are determined, together with the terms and conditions under which the benefits will be payable; and

2. Financial arrangements are made to provide the funds needed when benefits fall due, usually by building up assets in a trust fund or under an insurance contract.

As with most contracts, the employer and employees have latitude in negotiating the terms of the pension plan, subject to applicable legislation. In addition to deciding on the level of benefits, the employer will need to decide what group or groups of employees to cover. A small employer will typically have only one pension plan applying to all of its employees. A large employer may have a variety of pension plans — perhaps one plan for salaried staff and different plans for unionized groups. A large employer may also have special retirement arrangements for its executive group. A pension plan may also be established by a group of unrelated employers for their employees. Multi-employer plans are often established by trade unions or trade associations in certain industries.

Pension legislation does not mandate that an employer establish a pension plan; nor does it require that, if a pension plan is established, the plan cover all of the employer's employees. However, if a registered pension plan is established, all employees within a similar class must be eligible to join the plan. On the other hand, if pension benefits are being provided outside a registered pension plan, the employer has complete freedom to tailor the benefit structure to suit its needs.

The pension contract can be terminated by the employer if sufficient notice is provided to its employees. The termination of a pension plan can be precipitated by many different types of business events — divestitures, mergers, insolvency, or a change in the corporation's philosophy towards the provision of pension benefits. Sometimes, the termination of one type of pension plan may be followed by employee participation in a new type of retirement savings vehicle, which may or may not be a registered pension plan. Complex provincial rules and administrative policies govern the treatment of employees' accrued benefit entitlements when a plan is wound up, when a company or division is sold, or when a pension plan is converted to another type. Generally, these rules and policies establish minimum benefit levels that must be provided to employees in such situations.

Legislative Environment

Historically, the development of formal pension plans in Canada was encouraged by the favourable tax treatment that was provided under income tax legislation. In order for the employer and members of a formal pension plan to enjoy the tax shelter under the *Income Tax Act*, it is necessary to apply to the CCRA for registration of the pension plan.

Subject to certain conditions and limits, registration under the *Income Tax Act* allows employees and employers to deduct their pension contributions from their respective incomes for tax purposes. Registration also exempts the pension fund's investment income from taxation. However, all benefits paid out of the plan are taxable to the recipient with the exception of certain transfers. Details of legislation under the *Income Tax Act* are contained in Chapter 7.

In addition to registration under the *Income Tax Act*, a formal pension plan must be registered under pension standards legislation maintained by all provinces (except Prince Edward Island, which has prepared legislation but has not yet proclaimed it in force). A pension plan that covers employees in more than one province need only be registered in the province with the greatest number of employees. A pension plan must comply with the pension legislation of each province that has enacted pension benefits legislation with respect to any plan members who report for work in that province.

The federal government has enacted similar legislation that governs pension plans for businesses under federal jurisdiction (i.e., transportation, communications, banking). This legislation also applies to employees in the Yukon, Northwest Territories and Nunavut.

Pension standards legislation governs the terms and conditions of the formal pension plan, minimum funding requirements, and the investment of plan assets. The intent is to protect the interests of plan members. The pension commitments must be funded by advance payments under an accepted method. This means that pay-as-you-go and terminal funding are not allowed under the legislation. Pension standards legislation is examined in detail in Chapter 8.

Arguments For and Against Pension Plans

Government View

Private pension plans for employees are encouraged by governments because of their social utility. Government programs provide a reasonable minimum income for all seniors, but most employees look for more than the minimum and so are encouraged to save for their retirement. Pension plans are thought to foster the desirable qualities of independence and self-reliance. Employment pension plans reduce the pressure on government to increase income security benefits. Also, the contributions to pension funds, whether channeled through insurance companies or trust funds, generate large amounts of capital needed to develop Canada's resources and industry. Accordingly, the government encourages the development of pension plans by granting them special tax privileges.

The tax privileges provided to pension plans lead, of course, to lost tax revenues. For this reason, the federal government places a limit on the tax assistance provided to pension plans.

Employer's View

As a rule, it is the employer who decides whether or not to establish a pension plan, and if so, what its conditions and benefits will be. Sometimes, an employer agrees to establish a pension plan as a result of collective bargaining, or because its competitors provide pension benefits.

If a company decides to provide pensions, a registered pension plan delivers them at the lowest cost and in the most orderly manner. Here are some of the reasons.

- A registered pension plan allows for contributions of pre-tax dollars to be accumulated in a fund, with the earnings not subject to income tax until a benefit is paid to an employee.

  Consider a simple example where investments earn a before-tax return of 10% per year and the tax rate is always 50% (for employers and employees). For this illustration, we will ignore "bracket shifting", that is, any difference between the tax rates applicable when contributions are paid into the fund and when benefits are paid out.

  If the company were to place $1,000 into a registered fund, its cost would be the same as to set aside $500 in a non-registered fund. After one year, the registered fund would accumulate to $1,100, as interest is non-taxable. If the fund is then converted into a pension, the after-tax proceeds would be $550.

  The non-registered fund of $500 would earn $50 of investment income, on which $25 would be owed as tax. The after-tax proceeds would therefore be $525. Registration of the fund has effectively resulted in tax-free interest on the company's outlay. The results compound if the example were extended over several years.

- A registered pension plan allows a company to expense its pension costs in the years in which the pensions were earned by and credited to its employees. It is sound accounting and business practice to recognize liabilities as they arise and allow for them in the costing of the product or service provided by the business.

- The existence of a pension plan makes it easier for a company to retire employees in an orderly fashion as employees reach retirement age or as part of business restructuring.

- A good pension plan improves the employer's competitive position in bidding for labour, particularly labour with specialized skills. This will become more important in the future if labour shortages occur as the baby boomers retire.

- Certain types of retirement savings plans can be designed to improve the employees' interest in the profit objectives of the company. For example, the employer contribution can be tied to the level of company profit in a Deferred Profit Sharing Plan (DPSP), a group Registered Retirement Savings Plan (RRSP) or through innovative money purchase plan designs.

On the other hand, for valid reasons, some companies do not establish pension plans.

- Some employers may prefer to use these funds to re-invest in their own enterprises, where the potential return could be higher than in a pension fund.

- Some employers are discouraged by rising administration costs and the time and effort required to comply with federal and provincial legislation. Given the complex requirements of pension reform that emerged in the 1980s and 1990s, smaller employers may prefer a DPSP or group RRSP instead.

- Some social security benefits are "selective"; that is, subject to various forms of income tests. The Guaranteed Income Supplement and provincial pension supplements are examples. Income from company pension plans could reduce or eliminate social security benefits with the result that the employer is subsidizing the government rather than assisting the company's pensioners.

- Some employers feel that saving for retirement is the employee's responsibility and that RRSP limits and salaries are high enough for employees to accumulate adequate pensions through personal savings.

Employee's View

A formal pension plan can give an employee a retirement income which, together with government programs, is considered adequate. Funding of the plan gives the employee confidence that the promised pension will be paid because the pension assets are in the hands of a third party. Pensions should then be secure, even if the employer becomes unprofitable or the business is wound up.

A pension plan also permits an employee to save money on a tax-sheltered basis. While an employee could use a personal RRSP, this alternative is often less convenient and requires greater self-discipline.

The changing nature of the three-legged stool, changing demographics and economic events have created increased employee interest in pension plan issues and a greater demand by employees not only to establish pension plans, but also to have pension plans designed to meet their needs: tax-effective plans, plans with suitable termination as well as retirement benefits, and funded arrangements.

As the maximum earnings that can be pensionable under a registered pension plan have decreased from about six times the average wage in 1976 to just over two times the average wage today, there has been a dramatic increase in the number of employees for whom adequate pensions cannot be provided through registered pension plans. As a result, there have been increased employee expectations and demands for employers to provide top-up arrangements.

Types of Employer-Sponsored Retirement Income Plans

An employer who has decided to provide a pension plan for its employees must decide whether to establish a registered or a non-registered arrangement. A registered arrangement is one that is registered with the provincial or federal pension authorities and with the CCRA; it must comply with the requirements specified in the applicable pension standards legislation and with the *Income Tax Act*. Under a registered plan, employees are not taxed on employer contributions made on their behalf and investment earnings on plan funds accrue tax-free. In contrast, in a non-registered arrangement, employees are taxed on employer contributions made on their behalf and investment earnings on plan funds will generally be taxed.

This chapter deals with registered plans. Non-registered, supplementary arrangements are discussed in Chapter 9.

The employer needs to decide on the type of plan to enact. In other words, the employer must decide how the plan will deliver benefits. Most pension plans will fall into one of the following broad categories:

- Defined benefit plans;

- Defined contribution plans; and

- Combination or hybrid plans.

The following table provides a summary of these types of plans.

TYPES OF PENSION PLANS

Registered Pension Plans

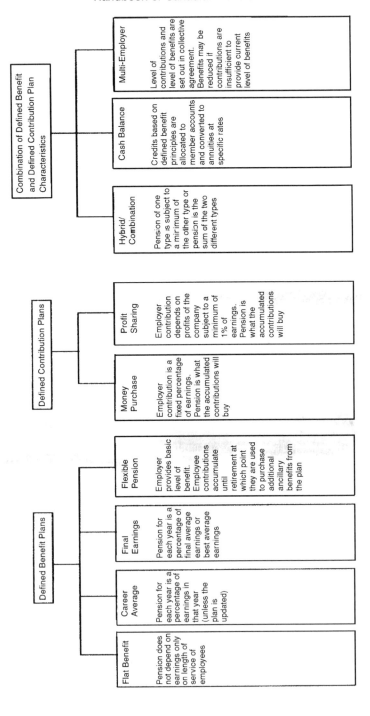

Defined Benefit Plans

Flat Benefit	Career Average	Final Earnings	Flexible Pension
Pension does not depend on earnings only on length of service of employees	Pension for each year is a percentage of earnings in that year (unless the plan is updated)	Pension for each year is a percentage of final average earnings or best average earnings	Employer provides basic level of benefit. Employee contributions accumulate until retirement at which point they are used to purchase additional ancillary benefits from the plan

Defined Contribution Plans

Money Purchase	Profit Sharing
Employer contribution is a fixed percentage of earnings. Pension is what the accumulated contributions will buy	Employer contribution depends on profits of the company subject to a minimum of 1% of earnings. Pension is what the accumulated contributions will buy

Combination of Defined Benefit and Defined Contribution Plan Characteristics

Hybrid/ Combination	Cash Balance	Multi-Employer
Pension of one type is subject to a minimum of the other type or pension is the sum of the two different types	Credits based on defined benefit principles are allocated to member accounts and converted to annuities at specific rates	Level of contributions and level of benefits are set out in collective agreement. Benefits may be reduced if contributions are insufficient to provide current level of benefits

Defined Benefit Plans

A defined benefit plan specifies the formula for determination of benefit entitlements and employees are promised a "defined" amount of pension. The cost of this type of plan is determined, on an actuarial basis, as the total amount of money required to provide the given level of benefit for all employees in the plan. The plan may specify that employees contribute a percentage of their earnings to help fund the benefit. The employer's contributions are not fixed and the amount contributed by the employer is based upon actuarial calculations. Statistics Canada reports that at January 1, 2000, defined benefit plans accounted for approximately 45% of all pension plans, but they cover almost 85% of employees belonging to employer-sponsored pension plans. The four most common types of defined benefit plans are described below.

Flat Benefit Pension Plan

The annual pension under a flat benefit or uniform benefit pension plan is a specified number of dollars for each year of service. For example, the benefit formula may be $20 per month for each year of service, so that a member of the plan with 10 years of service would receive an annual benefit of $20 × 10 × 12, or $2,400. The pensions are commonly integrated with CPP/QPP retirement benefits by providing bridge or supplemental benefits from retirement to age 65.

The flat benefit formula ignores differences in earnings. The flat amount of pension is established in terms of wage levels and dollar values at the time the benefit level is set, despite the fact that most of the pensions will not be paid until a future date when wage levels and dollar values are likely to have increased. For this reason, most flat benefit plans are subject to periodic upgrades in their benefit formula in an attempt to reflect increases in inflation and wage levels.

Approximately 16% of all defined benefit pension plans are flat benefit plans. These plans are prevalent in unionized environments, so part of the collective bargaining process often involves negotiating increases in the flat benefit accrual rate.

Flat benefit plans originally had the advantage of being simple and easily understood by employees. However, as a result of the collective bargaining process, many of these plans now contain complicated features, such as variable rates for different job classes or periods of service, minimum benefit levels, bridge benefits, and other special provisions.

Career Average Earnings Pension Plan

Under a career average earnings pension plan, the member's pension is calculated as a certain percentage of earnings in each year of plan membership. If a member earned $50,000 in 2001 and $55,000 in 2002, then under a 2% career average plan, the benefit accrued for 2001 would be 2% of $50,000 or $1,000 and the benefit accrued for 2002 would be 2% of $55,000 or $1,100 for a total accrued benefit of $2,100 at the end of 2002.

The career average earnings formula gives equal weight to employment earnings in each year of the employee's working lifetime, and therefore, may provide a low pension relative to employment earnings just prior to retirement. This is particularly evident in the case of an employee who has made significant advancements over his or her career, or for all members if inflation is high. This problem is often overcome by updating the earnings base that will produce results similar to those calculated under a final average earnings plan. (Final earnings plans are described below.) As an example, a plan may be improved such that, for all service accrued prior to 2002, the benefit is calculated as 2% of 2001 earnings, times years of service up to 2001. Thus, earnings for each year prior to 2001 are deemed to be equivalent to the earnings in 2001 for benefit calculation purposes.

Career average plans are frequently integrated with CPP/QPP by having a lower percentage benefit credit on earnings up to the CPP/QPP earnings ceiling and a higher percentage above the ceiling. If employees contribute to the plan, the contribution formula may also be integrated with CPP/QPP contributions.

Career average earnings plans account for approximately 32% of all defined benefit pension plans. Career average earnings plans are straightforward to administer and easily understood because the exact pension amount can be determined at any particular time. However, many such plans were converted to final average earnings plans because employers were constantly updating the plans due to high inflation in previous years. Nonetheless, they are still popular with certain employers because the cost is more manageable for them, since pensions already earned are not affected by an employee's future earnings and the employer can choose the timing of any upgrade.

Final Average Earnings Pension Plan

Under final average earnings pension plans, the member's pension is based upon the length of service and average earnings for a stated period before retirement. For example, the plan formula may be 1.5% of average earnings in the five years immediately prior to retirement, multiplied by the years of service accrued. Thus, for a member with final average earnings of $50,000 and 25 years of service, the annual benefit would be calculated as 1.5% × $50,000 × 25, or $18,750. In order to protect employees whose earnings decline as they approach retirement, some plans may use a best average earnings base in the benefit calculation. An example of this would be the five consecutive years of highest earnings in the last 10 years before retirement.

A final average earnings pension plan best meets the basic objective of providing continuity of income after retirement, such that the pensioner may maintain a standard of living after retirement comparable to the one he or she enjoyed while in active employment. It recognizes the long-term changes in the value of the dollar, up to the employee's retirement age, and the fact that most employees receive promotions during their working lifetime.

Most final earnings plans are contributory. Benefits and employee contributions are often coordinated with government pensions in the same way as career average plans.

Over half of all defined benefit pension plans are final average earnings plans. These plans are popular for salaried employees and have been adopted by many large and well-established Canadian employers, including those in the public sector.

Flexible Pension Plans

Flexible pension plans represent a new design alternative for plan sponsors. The first plan of this type was implemented in the early 1990s for a large private sector employer. Flexible pension plans offer a tax-effective means of providing enhanced retirement benefits to employees. A flexible pension plan is a defined benefit pension plan in which the employer pays for the basic pension benefit and the employees pay for additional ancillary benefits. This allows employees to enhance the value of their pensions without increasing their Pension Adjustments (explained later in this chapter) or reducing the amount of allowable RRSP contributions.

A front-end flex plan requires the employee to choose the ancillary benefits in advance in exchange for his or her contributions. Under a back-end flex plan, the employee makes his or her contributions, which accumulate, and the employee may then choose the ancillary benefits he or she desires upon termination or retirement. Examples of ancillary benefits include post-retirement spousal benefits, an enhanced definition of final average earnings, enhanced early retirement benefits, and indexing.

Aside from the tax advantages, a major advantage of the flexible pension plan is that it is tailored to meet the needs of each individual employee. If an employee is satisfied with the current level of benefits provided, he or she need not contribute to the plan. On the other hand, an employee may contribute the maximum each year, and thus ensure more generous retirement benefits. From an employer's perspective, this type of plan is administratively more complex than a regular defined benefit plan. In addition, its success requires a higher level of understanding on the part of members.

Defined Contribution Plans

A defined contribution plan specifies the level of contributions to be made to the plan by both the employer and the employee. Contributions accumulate with investment earnings until retirement. Thus, the amount of retirement income that may be purchased with the account balance is unknown until the actual retirement date. Defined contribution plans account for over 52% of all pension plans in Canada, but cover less than 14% of all members belonging to pension plans. The two basic types of defined contribution pension plans are outlined below.

Money Purchase Pension Plan

This is an employer-sponsored arrangement where employer and employee contributions are defined. They may be fully employer-paid, or require employee contributions as well. Contributions may be a fixed percentage of earnings, a fixed dollar amount, or a specified amount per year of service or per hour worked. An employee becomes vested in employer contributions made on his or her behalf after being a member of the plan for a specified period, but generally not more than two years. The vesting is subject to pension standards legislation. If an employee terminates prior to that date, the benefit received will be based on the employee's contributions only. (This is not applicable in Quebec as members vest immediately. See Chapter 8 for more details.) The employer contributions that are forfeited in this situation are usually used to reduce the employer's cost.

Profit Sharing Pension Plan

A profit sharing pension plan is a type of defined contribution plan where employer contributions are linked to the profitability of the company. The employer's total annual contribution is determined using a formula related to profits. The CCRA requires that employer contributions be at least 1% of employees' earnings, even in years of little or no profit. Allocation of profits among plan members may be based on a points system where points are assigned based on service, earnings or both. Investment earnings and forfeitures are allocated to employees in proportion to their account balances.

Although profit sharing plans are registered arrangements where employer contributions made on behalf of employees are not taxable to the employees, these arrangements have a significant drawback to employees if used for pension plan purposes. Contributions are linked to profit, and thus further increase the uncertainty associated with the level of retirement income provided by a defined contribution plan. From the employer's perspective, costs are linked to the company's ability to pay. In addition, this type of plan may act to motivate employees and lead to increased productivity.

Plans with Defined Benefit and Defined Contribution Characteristics

Hybrid Plans

Hybrid pension plans have defined benefit and defined contribution components. The most common type of hybrid plan provides the greater of a defined benefit pension and the pension that may be purchased with the member's defined contribution account balance. For example, the defined benefit may be calculated as 1.5% of final average earnings for each year of service. The employee may be required to contribute 5% of earnings to a defined contribution account in the plan and these contributions may be matched by the employer. At retirement, the member's account balance is converted to a pension. If this defined contribution pension amount is less than the defined benefit pension amount, then the defined benefit pension amount is paid. If the defined contribution pension amount is greater than the defined benefit pension amount, then the defined contribution pension amount is paid.

This type of plan essentially operates as a defined contribution plan. Its major advantage is that it alleviates some of the employee uncertainty associated with a defined contribution plan, since it guarantees a minimum level of retirement income.

Combination Plans

The combination plan offers a benefit that is the sum of the pension provided through the defined benefit component and the pension provided through the defined contribution component. Typically, the employer will provide a defined benefit of, for instance, 1% of final average earnings. Employees will contribute to the plan, and their contributions will be deposited in a defined contribution account that will accumulate until retirement. There may also be some employer matching of the employee contribution. At retirement, the member will receive the defined benefit pension in addition to the pension that can be purchased with his or her defined contribution account balance.

Hybrid and combination plans represent less than 2% of all pension plans in Canada. Most employers find these plans too complex to administer and too difficult to explain to employees.

Cash Balance Plans

A cash balance plan is another example of a plan that combines defined benefit and defined contribution characteristics. Like a defined contribution plan, the employer credits an amount based on a percentage of the employee's earnings (i.e., 5% of earnings), to a hypothetical account for each individual employee. This credited amount accumulates at a specified rate of interest until termination or retirement. The interest rate is a set rate and is frequently a rate linked to the Consumer Price Index. The fact, however, that the account is a "hypothetical" account is one of the reasons that a cash balance plan is a defined benefit plan. In a cash balance plan, it is the employer who makes the investment decision, takes the investment risk and ultimately is liable for a guaranteed benefit payment. Cash balance plans expose the employee to little investment risk and for the employer, as it is a defined benefit plan, a cash balance plan provides flexibility in setting the benefit level and also allows for a certain degree of funding flexibility. Cash balance plans provide higher benefits on termination than regular defined benefit pension plans. This is an attractive feature for a mobile workforce.

Cash balance plans became popular in the United States in 1980's. They have not, however, become as popular in Canada, and furthermore, may also not be permitted under the *Income Tax Act* provisions.

Multi-Employer Plans

A multi-employer pension plan is another example of a plan that combines characteristics of defined benefit and defined contribution plans. A multi-employer plan is usually established by union negotiation with two or more non-affiliated employers in a related industry. Typically, these plans are established in industries where employees frequently move between employers but remain part of the same trade union. Although the employee may work for several of the employers, he or she will remain a member of the plan and earn credits as if employed by only one.

Multi-employer plans specify both the contribution level and the level of benefits. For example, employer contributions may be determined as a certain number of cents for each hour worked by each employee. The benefit is generally determined using a flat benefit formula.

The level of contributions to the plan is typically determined through the collective bargaining process. Actuarial valuations are required to determine if the level of benefits is supportable by the contribution rate. Unlike plans for single employers, benefits may be reduced if they cannot be supported by the current level of contributions and if employers are unable or unwilling to increase their contributions.

Other Retirement Income Arrangements

There are several other retirement income arrangements an employer can establish in place of or to supplement pension plans. These include Registered Retirement Savings Plans, Deferred Profit Sharing Plans and other Employee Profit Sharing Plans. These arrangements are discussed in Chapter 10.

Plan Design Considerations

There are a number of fundamental issues that need to be considered when designing retirement income arrangements. The issues and their relative significance have changed over time. As well, pension and tax reform have resulted in major review and redesign of existing arrangements.

Employers who established pension plans in the early 1900s generally had a paternalistic culture. They were concerned about the well-being of their employees and were intent on ensuring they were financially secure in retirement. Often employees spent their entire careers with one employer and the pension plans were viewed as a reward for long service.

Times have changed. Few employers can now afford to continue this paternalism. Although employers may be concerned about the well-being of their employees, the environment is such that many employers must do what is necessary to remain competitive.

The changing environment has changed the focus of plan design. If an employer does not expect employees to work their entire career for the enterprise, this is an important consideration when designing the plan. If an employee does not expect to retire from the plan, retirement benefits may not be perceived as valuable. Employees will focus instead on the level of termination benefits.

In addition, there has been a shift in responsibility for ensuring that an employee has adequate retirement income. Increasingly, employers are not prepared to assume sole responsibility and encourage employees to share in the responsibility. In fact, many employers are actively involved in educating employees about the importance of saving for retirement.

The following comments highlight some of the principal issues in plan design.

Adequacy

The major goal of retirement income arrangements is to ensure that employees will have an adequate level of retirement income. While earlier vesting and locking-in and increased frequency of job changes have shifted more attention to benefits for terminating employees, the primary focus remains the retiring employee.

Most plan sponsors aim to provide an adequate level of retirement income at normal retirement. Generous early retirement provisions can be quite expensive. Consequently, if funds are limited, it may be preferable for an employer to provide a generous benefit formula and less generous early retirement provisions.

Adequacy is often measured as the ratio of an employee's retirement income from all sources to the level of earnings just prior to retirement. The resulting "net replacement ratio" of after-tax pension to the after-tax rate of pay just before retirement is seldom 100%. Income needs in retirement are usually less than in working years, for a number of reasons. No longer are there work-related expenses (i.e., travel or meals away from home). By retirement, the house mortgage has generally been paid off and the care and education of children is usually complete. Many goods and services are reduced in price for senior citizens as well.

As a rough guide, taking into account standard expenses and income tax deductions, most individuals believe they need approximately 60–70% of pre-retirement income (the percentage will be higher at lower incomes) to enjoy the same standard of living as they enjoyed prior to retirement. A middle-income individual will receive approximately 30–35% replacement from CPP and QPP benefits and Old Age Security as they currently exist. Hence, an employer plan that delivers 30–40% of pre-retirement earnings could be considered adequate by a middle-income employee.

Since the indexing of the maximum allowable pension has been deferred to 2005, employers have had to reassess the adequacy of pensions for higher income employees. When the current limit was initially introduced in 1976, only individuals with very high earnings were affected by the limit. This is no longer the case, and more and more employees are having their benefits capped by this limit. The impact of this change and employers' responses are discussed in Chapter 9.

Adequacy is a relative rather than an absolute concept. Hence, many employers will measure the adequacy of their retirement income plan not only against some accepted norm but also by comparing them to the industry standard or to the plans offered by their major competitors. It is not uncommon for an employer who is considering a redesign of its plan to conduct a survey of the benefits offered by other employers in competing companies or related industries.

Tax-Effectiveness

The current system of tax assistance for retirement savings is addressed in Chapter 7. The system of savings limits applies to all retirement income arrangements. This means that an individual's allowable RRSP contributions are reduced by the value of any benefits earned under registered pension plans or DPSPs. This value is known as a Pension Adjustment (PA). For money purchase plans, the PA is the sum of employer and employee contributions. For defined benefit plans, the benefit is converted to a value using the system's prescribed formula. The PA is nine times the amount of pension accrued in the year, minus $600.

This factor of nine is based on some key assumptions:

• The employee will remain to retirement; and

• The plan provides some valuable ancillary benefits (such as unreduced retirement at age 63, survivor benefits, indexing).

The factor of nine overvalues the pension accruals under all defined benefit pension plans, and particularly overvalues pension accruals for younger employees who most likely will not remain in the same pension plan for their full careers. Few plans other than those in the public sector provide all of the valuable ancillary benefits assumed in the PA calculation.

The 1997 federal budget introduced an adjustment known as a Pension Adjustment Reversal (PAR) to deal with concerns that the factor of nine was producing unfair results. The PAR effectively increases the RRSP contribution limit if an employee ceases (after 1996 and before retirement) to be entitled to a benefit under a DPSP or a benefit provision of a registered pension plan, and does not have a sufficiently large termination benefit.

If an employer's objective is to maximize tax-effectiveness — and employers will be under pressure from at least some employees to do so — the employer will need to modify the design of the plan to optimize the PA and/or reduce the RRSP contribution room taken up by the plan's benefits. To do so, the employer can:

- Reduce the defined benefit credit and add ancillary benefits while maintaining the same cost;

- Introduce a defined contribution component;

- Introduce flexible plans where employees can buy ancillary benefits; or

- Allow employees to opt out of the plan.

Tax-effectiveness is a relatively new design issue and has been responsible for much of the plan review activity of the 1990s and the search for new and innovative plan designs.

Changing Demographics

In the latter half of the 20th century, Canada experienced the baby boom followed by the baby bust. An extraordinary number of births occurred following the Second World War. Since then, birth rates have been declining. As a result, the Canadian population is ageing.

What impact does an ageing population have on pension plan design? To begin with, employees are probably more knowledgeable about pensions than they ever have been in the past. Baby boomers are concerned about their retirement income.

Employers are also concerned. Sponsors of defined benefit plans will see a definite increase in their annual cost as the workforce ages, and will need to consider cutting back benefit levels in order to control costs.

In addition to the ageing population, the second demographic change that has occurred is the diversity in the composition of the workforce — more two-income families, part-time employees, increased frequency of job change — with a companion diversity of needs. Employers face a greater challenge in defining plan objectives.

Equity

The pension plan should be equitable among members with different employment histories. The plan should also be seen to be equitable to employees in varying circumstances. Several different concepts of equity exist, sometimes in conflict. For instance, should pensions be equal in value or equal in amount? In defined benefit plans, pension standards legislation requires that the amount of pension to males and females with the same employment history be the same, although this treatment provides greater relative value to females who, on average, can be expected to live longer than males. On the other hand, in a defined contribution plan, the pensions of two individuals of different ages who are retiring now with identical work histories will not be of the same amount. These pensions, however, will have the same value.

While defined contribution plans provide equal value to all members regardless of age, defined benefit plans may provide equal pensions to two individuals of different age but the values will not be equal. This means that a young employee with the same years of service and earnings history as an older employee will have a pension of a lesser value. Many pension plans provide valuable ancillary benefits to employees who meet certain criteria. Plans may also impose constraints on service or earnings when calculating benefits. When these complications are introduced, equity can be an elusive ideal.

Pensions are frequently integrated with the CPP/QPP by providing a lower rate of benefits on earnings up to the CPP/QPP earnings ceiling, or by an offset of part of the government benefit. This integration may raise a question of equity between employees with high and low earnings, if the reduction to integrate is perceived to be excessive.

Cost and Cost Sharing

A fundamental question when establishing a pension plan is how much the employer is willing to spend. The employer needs to set cost parameters and examine alternative designs opposite these criteria. For example, a final earnings plan with a generous benefit formula and generous ancillary benefits will be very expensive relative to a modest career average plan.

For many employers, stability of cost is vitally important because of the nature of their businesses. Unforeseen cost increases or deficiencies could place the company in a precarious financial situation. These employers might prefer to implement a defined contribution plan where cost levels remain predictable and stable. On the other hand, defined benefit plans may offer funding flexibility not found in defined contribution plans.

Employers must also decide on the level of cost sharing. That is, do they want employees to contribute to the plan, and if so, at what level? This will depend, in part, on the employer's philosophy on who has responsibility for the delivery of retirement income. Also, employee contributions will help reduce employer cost, which in turn may allow the employer to offer a more generous plan. Pension standards legislation imposes limits on the extent that benefits may be funded through employee contributions.

Coordination With Government Pension Programs

When Canada's national pension system provided only a modest flat dollar benefit at age 70, government benefits were often ignored in designing the pension plan, although they may have influenced the amount of pensions. Today, CPP and QPP benefits are large enough that they cannot be ignored in the design of a pension plan. Employers with generous pension plans must coordinate or integrate the pension plan with these social security benefits.

A defined benefit pension plan can be integrated with the CPP/QPP in a number of ways:

- The "step rate" method, under which lower rates of benefits and contributions apply on annual earnings up to the CPP/QPP earnings ceiling (called the Year's Maximum Pensionable Earnings, or YMPE, this ceiling was $39,100 in 2002);

- The "direct offset" approach, in which the calculated pension is reduced by all or part of the government pension;

- The "ineligible earnings" method, under which integration with government benefits is achieved by ignoring a slice of earnings for both contribution and pension purposes (the ineligible earnings may be a fixed amount of say, $10,000, or may be a percentage of the YMPE of say, 30%).

Chapter 2 discusses alternative integration approaches in more detail. It should be noted that the ineligible earnings approach is now rarely used.

Human Resource Planning

In choosing a plan design, the employer will want to consider its staff planning objectives. For example, a pension plan can be used to attract and retain employees. Where labour is scarce, the pension plan could be structured to discourage early retirements. Or, it may even be used to support or even encourage early retirement programs through the provision of enhanced benefits to employees who voluntarily elect to retire early. An employer may also use the pension plan to facilitate the transfer of employees between locations or as a strategic element to the union negotiation process.

Compensation Philosophy

A pension benefit is only one part of an employee's total compensation. Some employers view pensions as a form of fixed compensation or deferred wage. These employers view pensions as a reward for long service and a way of providing employees with security. Other employers have a compensation philosophy geared more heavily towards variable compensation that rewards individual performance only; employees of these organizations may be expected to plan for their own retirement by saving through RRSPs. Other employers may combine elements of both compensation philosophies.

The key concept is that companies should look at the context in which pensions are designed and delivered. By examining and giving weight to each of the components of the total compensation package, with retirement income being just one of these components, companies are able to achieve an appropriate balance between providing incentives for individual and/or corporate performance, and providing employee security. Companies with different cultures and objectives will strike the balance differently.

Variations in Design for Different Groups

As mentioned earlier in this chapter, an employer may have different pension plans for its different employee groups. This can be driven by a variety of factors — differences in either the compensation structure (i.e., hourly, salaried, executive), union associations, the distribution of employees by age and pay, the level and predictability of profits, competitors' plans, and the demand for labour.

Pension plans for salaried and hourly staff are often designed to replace a target level of retirement income for employees who put in a full working career with the employer. For example, under a 2% integrated final average plan, a retiring employee with 35 years of service can expect to receive 70% of his or her pre-retirement income in the form of a pension.

The objectives in designing a top-up arrangement for executives can be very different. Tenure with the company is likely shorter, benefits are limited by the CCRA, and the relationship of pension benefits to other elements of compensation is likely of more significance for this group. Chapter 9 provides a more detailed review of executive retirement plans.

Legislation

Pension plans must comply with pension standards legislation in the jurisdictions where the employer has employees, and they must also qualify for registration under the *Income Tax Act*. They must satisfy requirements of other related legislation as well, including human rights, employment standards, family property and workers' compensation.

Location

Employers operating in different provinces must administer their pension plans subject to the provisions of pension standards legislation in several jurisdictions. In an attempt to minimize the administrative requirements, an employer can design a plan that, to the extent possible, meets the requirements of all jurisdictions instead of a plan with different provisions to satisfy each jurisdiction's minimum rules. While this increases the employer cost of funding the plan, this cost is offset by lower administration costs.

A "uniform" plan is also perceived by some employers to be more equitable, since it treats all employees of the company in the same manner. Despite these advantages, it is important to realize that it is not possible to develop a common set of rules respecting the provincial variations with respect to all terms of the pension plan. The best that can be accomplished is uniformity in a large number of the plan terms.

Setting Objectives

The key point to keep in mind in the design of pension arrangements is that no two situations are identical and the design must be tailored to the specific circumstances of the various employee groups, the employer, and the industry in which the employer operates. Plan sponsors need to establish the criteria, define and evaluate their alternatives, and then select the arrangement and design that best meets their objectives.

EMPLOYER PENSION PLANS — TERMS AND CONDITIONS

This chapter outlines the principal terms and conditions that must be included in a pension plan document, together with the choices and considerations involved in designing the plan. The considerations will vary, depending on whether the pension plan is defined benefit or defined contribution, whether the plan is single employer or multi-employer, and whether the employer is in the private sector or public sector. Certain plan provisions will be driven by the minimum standards in the provincial and federal pension standards legislation, which are discussed in more detail in Chapter 8. Other provisions are required by the registration rules of the *Income Tax Act*, described in Chapter 7.

The principal provisions for pension plans relate to:

- Eligibility;

- Pension formula;

- Pensionable service;

- Employee contributions (for contributory plans);

- Retirement age;

- Normal and optional forms of pension;

- Death benefits before retirement;
- Termination benefits;
- Disability benefits; and
- Inflation protection.

Each of these issues is discussed in detail below.

Eligibility Requirements

The eligibility requirements of a pension plan determine the date on which an employee may (or must) become a member of the employer's plan. Once an employee becomes a member, pension credits begin to accumulate. In a pension plan that requires the members to make contributions, the date the employee becomes a member also determines the date from which the member's contributions commence.

Most pension standards legislation requires that employees be eligible for membership on the completion of two years of employment, regardless of their age, if they belong to the class of employees for whom the plan was established. Some employers make membership in the pension plan compulsory. Compulsory membership ensures that all employees receive some pension benefit in respect of their period of employment with the plan sponsor.

Eligibility conditions based on age used to be common, but are now contrary to human rights legislation. Different eligibility conditions for females and males, while once common, are now prohibited for the same reason.

In most jurisdictions, part-time employees who are in the same class as eligible full-time employees, and who have earned at least 35% of the Year's Maximum Pensionable Earnings (YMPE), as defined under the *Canada Pension Plan*, for two consecutive years must be allowed to join the pension plan. Alternatively, the employer may set up a separate plan for part-timers if it provides reasonably equivalent benefits. Details of the pension standards legislation on eligibility can be found in Chapter 8.

Pension Formula

The pension formula defines how pension benefits will accumulate during years of plan participation to deliver the targeted retirement income. The employer will determine what is an acceptable level of income replacement in designing the plan.

Not long ago, a pension plan that ensured that the employee would receive a total retirement income, including that from all government sources, of about 50% of the employee's earnings at retirement after 30 or 40 years of service was considered quite generous. Today, the level of income replacement individuals believe they need is often somewhat higher, particularly at lower income levels — in the range of 70%.

The nature of the pension formula or promise varies with the type of plan (i.e., whether it is a defined benefit or defined contribution arrangement).

Defined Benefit Plans

As described in Chapter 1, a defined benefit plan specifies the formula to determine benefit entitlements. The specific formula will vary depending on the type of defined benefit plan.

Final Average Earnings Plans

In a final average earnings plan, a typical pension formula is 1.5% of average earnings for the last five or best five years prior to retirement, multiplied by years of service. For example, Jan Jones is an employee of "X" Co., where she has been employed for the last 35 years. Her plan has a pension formula, which is 1.5% of her average earnings for her last five years (being $65,000 in this case) prior to retirement. Jan's pension would be $34,125.00 (1.5% x 65,000 x 35).

If the plan is contributory (that is, if plan members are required to make contributions), the benefit credit is generally higher.

Often the benefit formula is integrated with CPP/QPP benefits to deliver a pension of about 70% of final average earnings at retirement for a long-service employee, inclusive of the government benefits. The CPP/QPP benefit is essentially 25% of average earnings covered by the CPP/QPP; that is, the Year's Maximum Pensionable Earnings (YMPE). For a working career of 35 years, this is equivalent to about 0.7% of the YMPE for each year of employment. It is therefore logical for a private pension plan to provide a step of 0.7%, for example, by a formula under which the pension per year of service is 1.3% of earnings up to the YMPE, and 2% of earnings in excess of the YMPE.

Example of Step-Rate Integration With CPP/QPP

Jan Jones has pensionable earnings of $65,000 and she is entitled to the maximum CPP retirement pension in 2002, which equals $9,465. Jan has worked for 35 years and retires at age 65. According to her pension plan, the pension formula is 2%. With no integration the following result would occur:

Pension plan

$65,000 × 2% × 35 .... $45,500

Canada Pension Plan $9,465

Total... $54,965

> As a result, Jan would actually receive approximately 85% of her pre-retirement income, which is more than the intended 70% of her final average earnings.
>
> As a result, Jan's employer's pension plan calls for a step-rate integration method to produce the intended 70% of final average earnings. The formula is 1.3% of earnings up to the YMPE and 2% of earnings in excess of the YMPE (the YMPE in 2002 is $39,100).

1.3% × $39,100 × 35 .... $17,790.50

2% × $25,900 × 35 .... $18,130

Canada Pension Plan $9,465

Total... $45,385.50

> As a result of the integrated model, Jan will receive approximately 70% of her pre-retirement earnings

Typically, in a final average plan with step-rate integration, the average YMPE would be used in the formula, where the YMPE is averaged over the same years that the earnings were averaged.

Another type of integration method is the direct offset method, in which a portion of the employee's CPP/QPP benefit is deducted directly from his or her pension benefit payable under the employer's pension formula.

While the amount of the Old Age Security (OAS) benefit may be taken into account in establishing the income replacement objectives of a private pension plan, it is generally prohibited in most provinces, to make an explicit reduction for the OAS in the pension formula.

Career Average Earnings Plan

In a pure career average earnings pension plan, a typical formula is a pension equal to 1.5% (or an integrated formula that credits 2%) of the employee's earnings in each year. This approach is equivalent to averaging the employee's earnings over his or her career, and multiplying this average by the employee's years of service and the formula rate. As noted in Chapter 1, such plans are usually updated from time to time to reflect increases in wages and salaries. If the updates are made regularly, the pension benefit approximates that of a final average earnings plan. Career average earnings plans that are not updated are not common; their design is not tax-effective, since a 2%

career average earnings plan produces the same reduction in RRSP contribution room as a 2% final average earnings plan.

Another variation in a career average earnings plan is to apply a final earnings minimum to the basic career average earnings plan. For example, the basic benefit may be 2% of career earnings, which will be supplemented, if necessary, up to a minimum level of 1.25% of the final five years' average earnings for each year of service.

Flat Benefit Plan

The pension formula in a flat benefit plan is normally expressed as a dollar amount for each year of service. Most flat benefit plans result from labour negotiations, in which case the benefit level is settled upon by the parties to the agreement.

Typical settlements in larger plans provide basic pensions of $30 to $50 per month for each year of service, paid for by the company. Different benefit levels may apply for employees in different wage classes and for past and future service. Many flat benefit plans include a supplement in the form of a "bridge benefit" payable from retirement until the age at which government pensions can be received. These bridge benefits can take the form of a dollar amount per year of service, subject to some dollar maximum, or they can be determined by reference to CPP/QPP and/or OAS benefits.

Defined Contribution (Money Purchase) Plans

Under a defined contribution pension plan (sometimes referred to as a money purchase pension plan), or a profit sharing pension plan, there is no pension formula that defines the pension benefit on retirement. Instead, the plan defines the amount of contributions to be made by the company and the employee. The plan also states how the income from investments will be allocated to individual member accounts. The pension, when the employee retires, is whatever can be purchased or provided by these fixed contributions and the investment income allocated to the member's account.

A common type of money purchase plan in Canada is one in which the employee and employer each contribute 5% of the employee's earnings, for a total contribution of 10% of earnings.

Uniformity in the Plan

As discussed in Chapter 1, an employer may cover one or all classes of employees in a plan. In the latter case, one may find different pension formulas for different classes of employees (i.e., a 2% benefit for executives and 1.5% for other employees). Legislation does not prohibit different benefit levels or qualifying conditions that depend on the employee's position in the company or salary level. However, there must be no discrimination by age, sex or marital status, and all employees in the same class must receive the same benefit.

Past Service Benefits

When a new pension plan is implemented by an employer who has been in business for many years, there are usually some long-service employees who are fairly close to retirement. These employees will receive inadequate pensions unless they receive pension credit for their employment before the effective date of the pension plan. Very few employees are able to make any significant contribution themselves towards these past service pensions.

Ideally, the past service pension formula would be the same as for future service. This way, the employee would be in the same position as he or she would if the pension plan had been in effect during the entire period of prior service. In practice, in order to reduce the employer's cost and in recognition of the fact that the employee made no contributions in respect of past service, the past service pension formula is often lower than the formula for future service.

For example, if the formula for future service is 2% of final average earnings, the employee might receive a pension equal to 1% for each year of past service that is credited.

Today, there are also tax implications for the employee when new benefits are provided for past service, since the employee must have enough RRSP contribution room to receive the benefits. This is explained in Chapter 7 under "Past Service Pension Adjustments".

Pensionable Service

The plan must define the period of service for which the employee will earn pension benefits, typically defined as "credited" or "pensionable service". Certain periods of absence are required by law to be included as pensionable service (i.e., maternity or parental leave).

The Income Tax Act Regulations limit the periods of service that can be recognized for pension purposes under a defined benefit plan. The related rules are explained in Chapter 7.

Employee Contributions

Pension plans may be either contributory (that is, the employees are required to contribute and the employer pays the balance of the cost), or non-contributory (that is, the employer pays the full cost). Traditionally, most union-negotiated pension plans have been non-contributory. Although only approximately half the members of private-sector pension plans have to make contributions to the plan, nearly all plans in the public sector are contributory.

Advantages of a Contributory Pension Plan

The advantages of a contributory plan from the employer's viewpoint are as follows:

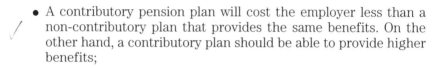

- A contributory pension plan will cost the employer less than a non-contributory plan that provides the same benefits. On the other hand, a contributory plan should be able to provide higher benefits;

- Employees will in theory take more interest in (and have a better understanding and appreciation of) a pension plan if they share in the cost.

Advantages of a Non-Contributory Pension Plan

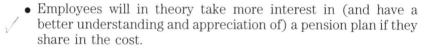

- A non-contributory pension plan is generally simpler and less expensive to administer than a contributory plan;

- A non-contributory plan ensures pension coverage for all eligible employees (in contrast to a voluntary contributory plan).

Required Employee Contributions

Contributory pension plans are more common in Canada than in the United States because pension plan contributions are tax deductible in Canada, unlike the United States.

The level of contribution will be governed by factors such as the level of benefits provided, and the employer's willingness and/or ability to pay. Employee contributions in private-sector pension plans tend to fall in the range of 3% to 5% of earnings. The large public-sector pension plans, including those for federal and provincial public servants and teachers, mostly require a basic employee contribution in the 6% or 7% of earnings range.

Where the pension plan benefits are integrated with CPP/QPP benefits, employees' contributions are nearly always reduced to integrate them with the contributions required for the CPP/QPP. Integration typically takes the form of step-rate contributions (i.e., 3.5% on earnings up to the CPP/QPP YMPE limit and 5% on earnings above the YMPE limit). Alternatively, there may be a direct reduction to contributions to the company plan by the amount of the CPP/QPP contributions, although this approach results in erosion of employee contributions to the pension plan as the rate of CPP/QPP contributions increases.

Additional Optional Contributions By Employees

Many contributory pension plans historically allowed employees to make extra "voluntary" contributions to increase the amounts of the pensions they would otherwise receive from the plans. However, most employees today prefer to use their personal Registered Retirement Savings Plans to make additional tax deductible contributions, since they are more flexible than the pension plan. As a result, voluntary contribution clauses in many pension plans are being eliminated.

Optional contributions are found in some plans to enhance the level of benefit. Flexible pension plans, which are emerging in response to tax limits on pension benefits, allow plan members to make tax-deductible contributions towards ancillary benefits (i.e., indexing) without losing RRSP contribution room. More details on flexible pension plans are found in Chapter 1.

Retirement Age

A pension plan needs to specify normal retirement age as well as the earliest retirement age and the conditions that apply when a pension commences early or is postponed.

Normal Retirement

Normal retirement age is the age specified in the pension plan text at which the employee has the right to retire on a full, unreduced pension. Nevertheless, accrued pensions payable on an unreduced basis are sometimes available before normal retirement age.

In the past, the normal retirement age was often 65 for men and 60 for women. This difference is now prohibited as discriminatory. Normal retirement age is the same for both men and women, usually age 65, which is the commencement age for unreduced benefits from the CPP/QPP. Pension standards legislation in several jurisdictions prohibits a pension plan from having a normal retirement date later than the attainment of age 65 or 66.

Early Retirement

Many employees retire before age 65, and some plans provide pensions without reduction for early retirement at ages younger than 65. The *Income Tax Act* permits pensions to be paid on an unreduced basis as early as age 60, when the number of years of age plus service total 80 "points", or after 30 years' service, regardless of age ("30 and out"). If the employee is employed in a public safety occupation (i.e., commercial airline pilot, air traffic controller, corrections officer, police officer or firefighter), the age 60 requirement above is reduced to age 55, the 80-point requirement is reduced to 75 points and the 30-year requirement is reduced to 25 years. In the early 1980s, when many companies were forced to reduce their staff, early retirement was encouraged by a variety of special early retirement incentives both within and outside the pension plan.

The trend to earlier retirement ages is anomalous, in view of the great advances in health and life expectancy that we have experienced over the past decades. Further, the population is ageing as a result of the 1950–1965 baby boom, followed by a period of low birth rates. This means that the ratio of those age 60 and over to those between the ages of 20 and 60 is rapidly increasing and suggests that retirement ages should not be reduced. However, retirement well before age 65 is popular with many employees, some of whom then find other paid work, and receive both pension income and earned income.

A pension plan will ordinarily allow the employee to retire at his or her own wish, up to 10 years before the normal retirement age. Pension standards legislation in most jurisdictions gives an employee the right to retire at any time within ten years of normal retirement age. The early retirement pension may be the actuarial equivalent (that is, of equal value on an actuarial basis) of the pension the employee has earned up to the date of early retirement, payable at normal retirement age.

Actuarial equivalents result in quite severe reductions to the accrued pension. For example, a pension of $1,000 a month that has been earned by age 60 can commence on an unreduced basis at age 65, or on a reduced basis immediately at age 60. The reduction on an actuarial basis would be about 35 per cent to account for the longer payout period.

Consider the following example for a member of a 2% final average earnings plan that compares the reduced pension at age 60 to the pension the individual would have received if he or she had remained employed to age 65.

	Retirement Age	
	60	65
Final average monthly salary	$3,000	$3,800
Years of service	20	25
Monthly pension before reduction	$1,200	$1,900
Monthly pension after reduction	$ 780	$1,900

A member who works the additional five years to normal retirement has a significantly greater pension than the early retiree for a number of reasons: five years of additional service, the higher final average salary, and the absence of any early retirement reduction factor.

A plan may reduce the pension by less than the full actuarial adjustment. Frequently the early retirement reduction factors are formula-based, such as a reduction of 3% or 6% for each year of early retirement. In the example quoted above, with a 3% reduction, the pension at 60 would be $1,020 (85% of $1,200) per month, instead of $780. The rationale for the lesser formula reduction is that the full actuarial discount is simply too severe. The cost of lowering the discount factor is a proper and necessary cost of the plan to encourage the orderly retirement of employees.

As noted earlier in this chapter, a plan may provide bridge benefits on early retirement. Depending on early retirement frequency, subsidies to early retirement reductions and bridge benefits can significantly increase plan costs.

Phased Retirement

Phased retirement generally refers to the gradual reduction of work by older employees transitioning into full retirement. Some older Canadian employees continue to work as a result of inadequate income following retirement. In addition, many employees consider the abrupt movement from full employment to full retirement to be stressful, often with too much time on their hands too soon. A properly designed phased-retirement program can assist older employees with the transition to full retirement, both financially and psychologically. Current trends in Canadian demographics and predictions of impending labour shortages may also provide incentives for employers to begin considering the implementation of a phased retirement program.

A phased-retirement program includes any program that provides employees with assistance or incentive in the transition from employment to retirement. It will almost always involve a gradual reduction of work time during a specified period immediately prior to some formal retirement date.

Since the concept is intended to gradually reduce the employee's work time, the employer must carefully structure a formal agreement to minimize the potential for any misunderstanding that might lead to litigation. Moreover, the phased-retirement program should not be imposed by the employer, but provided as an option to the employee.

The *Income Tax Act* and supporting regulations impose conditions and restrictions on the benefit accrual limits, contribution limits and the permissiveness and timing of distributions for registered pension plans.

The *Income Tax Act* currently prohibits the accrual of defined benefit pension credits while receiving a lifetime pension from the same registered pension plan. In addition, most provincial jurisdictions continue to defer discussions on the issue of phased retirement within a registered pension plan.

Currently, the only two jurisdictions that have formally implemented provisions to permit phased retirement are Quebec and Alberta. Conflict with the federal *Income Tax Act* has been avoided as a result of regulations under that Act that permit a lump-sum distribution from a registered pension plan. It would not be surprising to see other jurisdictions considering changes to their pension legislation.

Quebec Legislation on Phased Retirement

In the province of Quebec, legislation was adopted in 1997 to provide for income from a registered pension plan when employees and their employer agree to a phased-retirement arrangement. According to this legislation, active pension plan members who are within 10 years of the normal retirement age and whose hours of work are reduced through an agreement with their employer may request to receive an annual lump-sum benefit from their pension plan.

Such a lump-sum benefit may not be greater than the minimum of the following amounts:

- 70 per cent of the reduction in compensation;
- 40 per cent of the YMPE under the Quebec Pension Plan (i.e., 40 per cent of $39,100 or $15,640 in 2002);
- The value of entitlements under the plan.

The payment of such a lump-sum benefit will reduce the member's entitlements at full retirement.

During the period of phased retirement, the member continues to accrue pension benefits and to contribute to the plan, as the case may be. Such accruals and contributions are based on the reduced salary, or on the full salary as provided by the pension plan, and are subject to limitations as specified under the *Income Tax Act*.

Additionally, an employee who is at least age 55 but younger than 70, and whose compensation is reduced due to phased retirement, may arrange in writing with the employer to have all or part of the reduction added back for purposes of calculating QPP contributions. The employee and the employer would contribute on a non-reduced salary basis, which would allow the individual to include this deemed salary in the calculation of the average earnings used to determine their QPP retirement pension.

Using the non-reduced salary as a basis for QPP contributions will not always be to the employee's advantage, since some years where earnings are low or non-existent can be excluded from the contribution period.

Temporary Pension

Quebec also has provisions in its legislation regarding temporary pensions. A member or a member's spouse may elect to substitute all or part of his or her lifetime pension with a temporary amount from the pension plan until the time when the spouse or member is entitled to government benefits.

As a general rule, the member or spouse must be 10 years or less from normal retirement age as specified in the plan; however, eligibility is limited to no later than age 65. The member or spouse must specify the amount of pension benefit before payment begins. The amount of the pension benefit cannot be greater than 40% of the QPP maximum pensionable earnings in the year payment begins. This limit will be reduced by any other bridging benefit provided under the plan. The temporary pension must end by the end of the month following which the member or spouse turns 65 years of age. Basically, such temporary pensions permit a member to elect a bridging benefit from the plan, even where the plan does not specifically provide for one.

Postponed Retirement

Some pension plans allow the pension payments to commence at normal retirement age even though the employee continues to work and draw salary or wages. However, the employee cannot continue to accrue further pension credits in this event. This practice has been criticized as conflicting with the basic purpose of a pension plan, which is to provide an income when earnings cease. The practice has also been defended on the ground that pensions are essentially deferred pay, and that the payment of an employee's pension should not be suspended as the result of postponed retirement.

Another design for postponed retirement allows pension credits to continue to accumulate after the normal retirement date (the employee continuing to pay the required contributions, if any), so that when postponed retirement occurs a larger pension may commence. Alternatively, the pension, on postponed retirement, may be the actuarial equivalent of the pension that would have been paid at normal retirement age.

In Quebec, plans must actuarially adjust benefits to reflect the post-postponement period. Additionally members are allowed to receive payment of all or part of their normal pension during the postponement period. This amount cannot exceed the sum necessary to offset any permanent reduction in remuneration during the post-ponement period. However, a member may receive all or part of his or her pension, regardless of the limit, under an agreement with his or her employer, if the pension plan document permits. The amount of pension not paid out during the postponement period shall be adjusted at the end of the postponement period. An adjustment is made to ensure that the pension payable at the end of the postponement period is actuarially equivalent to the pension at the member's normal retirement date had that pension not been postponed.

Normal and Optional Forms of Pension

Normal Form of Pension

Every pension plan must define the normal form of pension that will determine what benefits, if any, an employee's beneficiary or estate will receive when the employee dies after retirement. In some plans, the normal form of pension will be different for members who do not have a spouse and those who do. (See discussion below on pre-retirement death benefits regarding the definition of spouse.)

Pensions are always payable for the lifetime of the retired employee. The plan may provide a minimum guarantee that if death occurs within a certain number of years, the pension will continue for the balance of the period. If the period is five years, this type of pension is known as a "life annuity guaranteed five years". In a contributory plan, there may be a guarantee that if death occurs before the pensioner has received payments equal to his or her contributions, with interest, up to the retirement date, the balance will be paid in a lump sum to the estate or beneficiary. This is known as a "refunding life annuity" or "modified cash refund annuity".

Another approach provides that the pension continue after the member's death to the surviving spouse for the spouse's lifetime. This form of pension is a joint and survivor annuity. The spouse's pension is usually 50% or 60% of the amount paid to the retired member and is more common today as a result of pension standards legislation. More specifically, if the normal form of pension is not joint and survivor, the pension standards legislation in all jurisdictions requires that the pension elected must be a joint and survivor annuity continuing to a spouse, unless a waiver is signed by the spouse. As a general rule, the pension payable after the first death of the member and spouse must not be less than 60% of the pension payable before the first death. Manitoba is the exception to this rule; its legislation requires a minimum of 66⅔% of the initial benefit to continue to the surviving spouse.

Typically, the joint and survivor pension is payable in a reduced amount to reflect the more expensive nature of this form of pension. As a result of legislation requiring joint and survivor pensions, some plans have changed their normal form for members with a spouse to a joint and survivor pension, so that these members do not have to bear full cost. This is discussed in more detail in the following section.

The *Income Tax Act* allows the normal form of the pension to be as generous as a joint and survivor annuity, which provides a survivor pension not in excess of 66⅔% of the member's pension, combined with a guaranteed period of five years. If a survivor annuity is not provided, the maximum guarantee period is fifteen years.

Optional Forms of Pension

Pension plans customarily allow the employee to elect a pension different from the normal form before pension payments commence. Hence, an employee can choose the form that best suits his or her needs at retirement, subject, of course, to the rules in pension standards legislation and the *Income Tax Act*. The amount of pension paid under the option is usually the actuarial equivalent of the normal pension, so that the election does not result in either a gain or loss for the pension fund.

The following are the usual optional forms of pension.

Pension Guaranteed For a Term Certain

Some pension plans allow the retiring member to elect a pension payable for his or her lifetime, and for a minimum guarantee period if the pensioner dies within this period. Common guarantee periods are five, 10 or 15 years. The *Income Tax Act* restricts the maximum guarantee period to 15 years. A pension with no guarantee period is known as a "life only annuity".

Joint and Survivor Option

After the member's death, a percentage of the member's pension will continue to the member's joint annuitant for that person's lifetime. Common percentages are 50%, 60%, 66⅔%, 75% or 100%. The pension may reduce only on the death of the member or on the first death.

Integrated Option

This option (sometimes called the "level income" or "notched" option) allows an employee who retires prior to age 65, at which time OAS and CPP/QPP benefits are normally payable, to take a higher pension from the employer's plan up to age 65 and a lower pension thereafter, so as to produce a roughly level total income from both sources. The calculation may reflect the fact that CPP/QPP payments are available prior to age 65 on a reduced basis. However, once the integrated pension has been calculated, the payments cannot be changed to allow for a change in the commencement date or the actual amount of CPP/QPP payments.

Some of the optional forms of pension discussed above can be combined. For example, a joint and survivor annuity can be paid with a guarantee of at least five years.

Commutation

Each jurisdiction has a provision allowing the value of a small pension to be paid in cash. In general, a "small" pension is one in which the annual pension due is less than 2%-10% of the YMPE, or, depending upon the jurisdiction, if the commuted value is less than 4%-20%. Each jurisdiction must be reviewed as the conditions for commutation vary from province to province. Pension standards legislation in some jurisdictions permit 25% of the value of an employee's pension benefit, earned before the legislation was revised, to be taken in cash if employment terminates before retirement, even if the termination occurs very shortly before normal retirement age.

In some jurisdictions, pension plans may also permit the transfer on retirement of the commuted value of an employee's pension to another locked-in arrangement (see "Termination Benefits"). However, the employee is still required to ultimately receive those benefits in some form of lifetime annuity or stream of income payments.

Death Benefits Before Retirement

Every pension plan must define what benefits, if any, an employee's spouse, beneficiary or estate will receive if the employee dies before retirement. These benefits are referred to as pre-retirement death benefits.

For purpose of the *Income Tax Act*, a "spouse" of an individual effectively includes a person of the opposite sex to whom the member is married or a common-law partner of the opposite or same sex who has been cohabiting in a conjugal relationship with the individual for at least 12 months, or who is a parent of a child whom the individual is also a parent. The registered pension plan should include a definition of "spouse", and that definition is subject to minimum provincial standards. Virtually all of the provinces have amended their pension benefits standards legislation to include same-sex spouses, either under the definition of "spouse" or "common-law partner".

The pension standards legislation in all jurisdictions requires pension plans to provide pre-retirement death benefits. Prior to legislated minimum standards in this area, death benefits were minimal. In a non-contributory pension plan, there was often no benefit payable on death before retirement. If the pension plan was contributory, the death benefit payable to the deceased employee's beneficiary or estate was generally a return of employee contributions with interest. Group life insurance plans were thought to meet the needs of most employees.

Some pension plans did provide, prior to pension reform, death benefits from the pension plan in the form of spouse's and children's pensions. A plan of this type might provide a deceased employee's spouse with one-half of the pension that had been earned for service up to the date of death, perhaps with a minimum amount. However, these spouses' pensions were somewhat restrictive. For example, the pension typically ceased if the spouse remarried, or the spouse's pension was paid only if the employee had been married for at least one year prior to death. The definition of spouse was usually limited to widows, and did not include widowers.

Changing social attitudes and the frequency of common law relationships prompted reform of pension plans in the area of pre-retirement death benefits. Pension standards legislation, as amended in the 1980s, now requires the payment of specific benefits to the surviving spouse if a plan member dies before retirement. The definition of spouse has continued to evolve (as discussed above).

Provincial legislation usually requires a minimum pre-reform benefit equal to a return of the member's own pre-reform contributions, if any, with interest. Beyond this, there is usually no specific requirement to provide a pre-reform, pre-retirement death benefit.

The minimum post-reform, pre-retirement death benefit, in some jurisdictions, that is payable to a spouse is the commuted value of the post-reform benefit that would have been payable to the plan member if he or she had terminated service at the date of death. The spouse does have the right to waive entitlement to this death benefit, in some jurisdictions.

Some jurisdictions require that only 60% of the commuted value of the post-reform benefit need be payable.

As well, a beneficiary who is not the member's spouse may not be entitled to the same benefits as the spouse. Some jurisdictions provide a commuted value to the spouse, but the beneficiary, who is not a spouse, is only entitled to contributions with interest.

Termination Benefits

Every pension plan must define the benefits and rights of the employee upon termination of employment other than by death or retirement. The employee is always entitled to his or her own contributions. An employee who is vested is entitled to his or her accumulated pension commencing at normal retirement age, or to an actuarially reduced pension at an earlier age. If a pension is locked-in, both the employee and employer contributions must be used to provide a pension at retirement, and cannot be withdrawn in cash.

Vesting, Locking-In and Portability

"Vesting" means the right of an employee who terminates employment to the portion of the pension benefit provided by employer contributions, as a result of achieving a certain age and/or length of service or plan membership. It is taken for granted that terminating employees have a right to their own contributions with credited interest.

"Locked-in" means that the employee cannot withdraw any contributions or portion of the benefit in cash. The benefit can only be received in the form of retirement income.

"Portability" means that the commuted value of a terminating employee's pension may be transferred on a locked-in basis to another Registered Pension Plan (RPP), or to a prescribed retirement arrangement.

Pension standards legislation has established minimum standards of vesting, locking-in and portability. These standards are detailed in Chapter 8 and vary across jurisdictions. Where existing pension standards legislation was amended in the 1980s, different standards may apply for pre-amendment date service. Locking-in of contributions typically occurs at the same time as vesting.

National employers, therefore, have had to decide whether to adopt the minimum vesting rules of each jurisdiction for employees in those jurisdictions, or a common vesting rule that meets the requirements of all jurisdictions. All employers have also had to decide whether the new vesting standard should be made retroactive to all service, or whether different treatment should be given to pensions accrued before and after the effective dates of the pension standards legislation. (This issue of uniformity is discussed in Chapter 1).

Pension standards legislation currently gives a terminating employee the right to transfer the commuted value of the vested pension to another retirement savings arrangement prescribed in the legislation. The institution receiving the transferred amount must agree to administer it on a locked-in basis as prescribed by legislation.

Interest on Employee Contributions

Employees who leave an employer before satisfying the vesting requirement are entitled to a refund of their own contributions accumulated at a prescribed minimum rate of interest, usually the investment return earned on the pension fund or the average of five-year personal term deposit rates. The rate to be credited on additional voluntary contributions is normally the same as for required contributions or the actual rate of return earned on the pension fund. Most pension standards legislation prescribes both the minimum rate of interest and the manner in which interest shall be credited. (See Chapter 8 for details.)

Reciprocal Transfer Agreements

The vesting requirements may be satisfied if a group of related employers (such as a group of Crown corporations) allows the transfer of an appropriate sum of money from the pension fund of one employer directly to the pension fund of another, on behalf of an employee who leaves the first employer and who finds employment with the second.

This procedure is actually portability in a literal sense; the paying and receiving pension plans need not be identical to accommodate these transfers.

Reciprocal transfer agreements between pension plans in the public sector are common. Since public-sector plans are generally similar in design, the amount to be transferred is often determined by a simple but arbitrary formula, such as twice the employee's contributions with interest. The employee is then credited with a number of years of credited service in the second employer's plan.

Today, more plans are using an actuarial-based formula. The commuted value of the employee's pension, as calculated by the actuary of the first plan, is transferred. The actuary of the second plan then calculates the amount of pension or the period of credited service that may reasonably be granted to the employee in respect of the transferred funds. The details of the calculation method are contained in the reciprocal transfer agreement or in the plans.

Arrangements may be made to transfer pension reserves or refunds of contributions to any other pension fund willing to receive them without a specific reciprocal transfer agreement. The transferred funds are then deemed to be additional voluntary contributions made by the employee.

Multi-Employer Pension Plans

In multi-employer pension plans, an employee may work for several employers in the industry for short periods of time and will continue to be a member of the industry-wide plan. Pension credits earned with various employers will accumulate as if the employee had worked for only one employer. These plans contain vesting and locking-in rules similar to those in single employer plans, except that the rules are usually based on participation in the plan or employment in the industry, rather than service with one employer.

Disability Benefits

A pension plan should specify what provisions are to apply to an employee who becomes disabled, and should contain a clear definition of disability for purposes of the plan.

A majority of employees are covered by their employers under some form of short- or long-term disability plan. These plans (see Chapter 16) provide for regular payments to the employee to replace a portion of the employee's wages or salary while the employee remains disabled. If such a plan is in place and delivers adequate benefits, there will be no need for the pension plan to provide disability pensions. However, as the payments from nearly all long-term disability plans stop at age 65, it is necessary to provide an appropriate pension after age 65. Hence a pension plan member who is receiving disability income usually continues to accrue pension credits so that the pension at age 65 will be based on service as an active employee plus deemed service while disabled. Under the Income Tax Act Regulations, an employee must satisfy prescribed definitions of disability to continue to accrue benefits under the pension plan. In contributory pension plans, it is usual to waive any required employee contributions during the period of disability.

If the employees are not covered or are not eligible for insured long-term disability benefits, the pension plan can be designed to provide an immediate unreduced pension. The pension is usually equal to the full pension accrued to the disability date with no adjustment for early commencement. Sometimes the pension is equal to the full estimated pension the employee would have earned had he or she remained at work until normal retirement. The *Income Tax Act* imposes limits on the qualifying conditions and the additional projected pension benefits that can be provided. These are described in Chapter 7.

Inflation Protection

Before Retirement

In the 1970s and 1980s, when the rate of inflation was high, considerable attention was given to ways of maintaining the purchasing power of pensions. Final average earnings plans generally provide inflation protection up to the point of retirement, although there may be some shortfall, since the last five-year-average salary can fall well below the salary at retirement date in periods of high inflation.

By contrast, career average earnings and flat benefit pension plans do not compensate for inflation that occurs prior to the employee's retirement age, unless they are updated from time to time.

With much earlier vesting and locking-in, a large number of vested deferred pensions will be created and these will lose their purchasing power unless they are updated during the period up to commencement date. A possible solution is the transfer of the commuted value to a locked-in RRSP/LIRA, where favourable investment earnings could compensate for inflation, as in a defined contribution pension plan.

In the province of Quebec, the legislation was modified, effective January 1, 2001, to provide for an additional benefit representing partial inflation protection between the date the employee ceases active membership in the plan until the date that is 10 years prior to the normal retirement date. The value of the additional benefit is determined as the difference in value, if any, between

- The plan's regular termination benefit; and

- The pension payable under the plan at age 65, indexed between the date the employee ceases active membership in the plan until the date that is 10 years prior to the normal retirement date at 50% of the Consumer Price Index (CPI), to a maximum of 2%.

The additional benefit is only calculated for years of service after January 1, 2001 (or later, if a collective agreement was in force on January 1, 2001).

Defined contribution pension plans automatically make some adjustment for inflation prior to retirement, provided that the investment return of the pension fund rises with the rate of inflation. Assuming, ideally, that the rate of interest consists of a basic real rate of return plus the rate of inflation, and that the pension fund is invested in short-term securities, then the defined contribution pension plan would be inflation-proof up to retirement.

After Retirement

Protecting against inflation prior to retirement is only part of the issue. Post-retirement adjustments are also necessary if the purchasing power of pensions is to be maintained. One can argue that the income needs of pensioners decline as they get older, and thus their purchasing power does not have to be fully protected against increases in the cost of living. This view is understandably unpopular with some employees and pensioners. Post-retirement inflation protection can take several forms.

Indexation

The obvious way to protect the pensioner from loss in time of inflation is to index pensions according to a wage or price index. Pensions that increase 1% for every 1% increase in the CPI maintain their purchasing power to the extent that the CPI is a good measure of the prices of goods and services that pensioners buy. Pensions that are increased in line with increases in the average industrial wage do more — they also give pensioners a share in the growing productivity, by keeping their pensions in line with pay rates of active workers.

A pension that is adequate at retirement and thereafter is adjusted for cost-of-living increases is ideal for the retired employee. However, private-sector employers usually regard it as too costly and risky to promise fully indexed pensions. Generally, automatic indexing after retirement is prevalent only among public-sector pension plans.

Mandatory Inflation Protection

To date, no pension standards legislation requires that pensions and deferred pensions be adjusted to provide inflation-related increases. Although the Ontario and Nova Scotia pension standards legislation provides for mandated increases in accordance with a pre-scribed method, neither province, as of 2002, has prescribed an index-ation formula and, therefore, inflation protection is not yet required in any jurisdiction.

Effective as of January 1, 2003, the above mentioned provision regarding inflation protection in the Nova Scotia legislation will be removed from the Act, thereby eliminating the possibility that indexing of pensions will be required in Nova Scotia.

Index-Linked Bonds

The government has issued index-linked bonds with the nominal amount of the coupons and capital repayments linked directly to the CPI. By investing in these bonds, a pension plan is able to provide index-linked pensions at a pre-determined cost.

Ad Hoc Adjustments

Ad hoc adjustments have been used by nearly all large employers in the private sector in recent years to compensate for post-retirement cost of living increases. Union groups often bargain for *ad hoc* pension adjustments on behalf of their retired members.

The amount of the *ad hoc* increase varies from plan to plan. It may be a percentage increase in all pensions that have been paid for a number of years or a percentage for each year since the last increase (or retirement if sooner). Other approaches include a flat addition of, say, $50 a month, or the introduction of a minimum pension or a combination of these approaches.

Ad hoc adjustments are made on a one-time only basis, with no promise of any future increases. A company may adopt a policy of regular review and upgrading, but without a firm commitment to future increases.

Ad hoc adjustments are popular with employers because the related costs are completely under the employer's control. Employers are reluctant to provide automatic indexation due to uncertain costs, but are often willing to make substantial *ad hoc* adjustments, as long as they are not committed to repeat the practice on a regular basis.

A second advantage of *ad hoc* increases is that all the circumstances — inflation, the company's financial position, changes in social security — may be taken into account. A company that has a good year or that has a surplus in the pension fund may tend to give larger increases and to give them more frequently. A company in a poor financial situation will tend to defer and to minimize the increase. Members who retired under a recently improved plan may be treated differently than those who retired before the improvements came into effect.

Limitations Under the Income Tax Act

The *Income Tax Act* permits defined benefit pensions to be adjusted for inflation both before and after retirement subject to certain limits. These rules are described in Chapter 7.

Variable Annuity Plan

In a variable annuity plan, the amount of pension at any point in time depends on the then-value of a portfolio of investments. Thus, the pension amount is directly related to the performance of the investments, in the hope that the value of the fund will roughly offset inflationary trends in prices.

A variable annuity plan generally takes the form of a money purchase pension plan. The contributions of employer and employee are invested in units of a mixed portfolio, or the employee may choose to direct the contributions to units of a fixed-income fund or equity fund. Interest and dividends are applied either to buy extra units or to increase unit values. On retirement, the pension of the retired employee is expressed in units, so that the amount the employee receives thereafter varies with the unit value of the fund.

GOVERNMENT PENSION PROGRAMS

Canada's retirement income system is made up of three tiers which, in combination, are designed to provide Canadians with the opportunity to accumulate adequate income in retirement:

1. Government-administered pension programs, which include Old Age Security (OAS), Guaranteed Income Supplement (GIS) benefits and the Canada/Quebec Pension Plan (CPP/QPP);

2. Employer-sponsored retirement income plans; and

3. Individual retirement savings.

This chapter focuses on the government-administered pension component of the retirement system: the OAS, the GIS and the CPP/QPP.

The Old Age Security benefit provides a flat monthly pension for Canadians aged 65 and older who meet certain residency requirements. The OAS benefit was originally designed as a universal benefit available to all Canadians who qualified. The universality of the program has since been eroded by the implementation of a "clawback" tax in 1989, which requires pensioners earning an income over a certain threshold ($56,968 in 2002) to pay back up to 100% of the OAS pension.

The Guaranteed Income Supplement is an income-tested benefit that provides additional monies over and above the OAS benefit. The GIS provides a flat monthly benefit, which is reduced by one dollar for every two dollars of any other income received — other than the Old Age Security pension and a few other excepted amounts, such as family allowance payments — to maintain the needs-based approach to the benefit.

The Canada and Quebec Pension Plans (CPP/QPP) were introduced in 1966. They are compulsory earnings-related plans that are financed solely through employee and employer contributions. The benefits available from the plans are designed to assist in providing retirement income for working Canadians, as well as disability, death and survivor benefits. The aim of the CPP/QPP retirement benefit has been to provide a pension approximately equivalent to 25% of the worker's average annual lifetime earnings up to the yearly maximum, which is adjusted to reflect current wage levels.

In the 1996 budget, the federal government proposed that the OAS and GIS benefits would be replaced on January 1, 2001 by a Seniors' Benefits program. This was the first major redesign of the social security income program since the plans were introduced. Under this proposal, the OAS and GIS benefits were to be replaced with a fully income-tested, tax-free Seniors Benefit. In July 1998, the federal government announced that the proposed Seniors' Benefits program would not be undertaken. Instead, the current program of OAS and GIS benefits would continue.

As the future sustainability of the Canada/Quebec Pension Plan came into question, the government was forced to contemplate some new solutions. Due mainly to Canada's ageing population, higher than expected disability benefit payments and lower-than-expected economic growth, pay-as-you-go contribution rates to the CPP were projected to increase to 14.2% of earnings by the year 2030 unless changes were implemented. This prompted the government to review proposals for reform of the CPP/QPP to ensure that it would be sustainable, fair and affordable in the long run, without placing too much of a financial burden on future generations.

In 1998, a variety of amendments were made to both the CPP and QPP. A new schedule of contribution rates for both plans was introduced, and the rate was structured to increase from the 1997 rate of 6.0% to an ultimate rate of 9.9% in 2003. Additionally, as a result of the amendments, the year's basic exemption (YBE) for both CPP and QPP was to be frozen at $3,500 and no longer indexed. Consequently, as the year's maximum pensionable earnings (YMPE) increases due to indexation, contributors will be paying more into the CPP/QPP as a greater portion of their earnings are subject to compulsory contributions. Furthermore, both plans lowered the maximum death benefit payout from $3,500 to $2,500, and it is frozen at that level.

The method for calculating combined benefits was also changed as a result of the 1998 amendments. Under the changes, the combined survivor/retirement benefits are lower for many new beneficiaries. As well, the changes mean lower combined survivor/disability benefits for all new beneficiaries.

One very significant change brought about by the 1998 amendments to the CPP was the establishment of the Canada Pension Plan Investment Board — a crown corporation that acts at arm's length from the government. The intent is that this independent professional body will not only be able to diversify the CPP assets, but also enhance the performance of such assets.

In July 2000, Parliament enacted most of Bill C-23, *An Act to modernize the Statutes of Canada in relation to benefits and obligations*. Bill C-23 amended more than 60 federal Acts, including the CPP and OAS, to provide same-sex partners with the same benefits and coverage as those already provided to common-law partners of the opposite sex. As a result, the term "common-law partner" has replaced the term "spouse" in the CPP and OAS.

On June 7, 2002, the Quebec National Assembly passed Bill 84, *An Act instituting civil unions and establishing new rules of filiation*. The intent of the Act is to enable the solemnization of gay and lesbian civil unions, although it is equally applicable to opposite-sex couples. The legislation defines a civil union as "a commitment between two persons eighteen years of age or over who express their free and enlightened consent to live together and to uphold the rights and obligations that derive from that status". Among various pieces of other legislation, the Act amends the QPP. The legislation affects the definition of a surviving spouse, in that same-sex partners who have entered into a civil union will automatically qualify as a surviving spouse. Even prior to Bill 84, a same-sex partner could qualify as a surviving spouse, but he or she had to meet the cohabitation period time specifications set out in the QPP (and these rules continue to be applicable for those who choose not to enter into a civil union). The definition of former spouses with regards to the division of unadjusted pensionable earnings has also been altered to reflect the new status of individuals who have entered into a civil union.

This chapter describes in detail social security benefits as they currently exist and provides, as well, an overview of the key issues facing the government-administered retirement program.

Old Age Security

The government-supported tier of Canada's income security system provides pensions through a combination of three programs:

- Old Age Security, which provides monthly benefits to all who reach age 65 after meeting residency requirements;

- Guaranteed Income Supplement, which provides monthly benefits to Old Age Security recipients subject to an income test and residence requirements; and

- Allowance and Survivor's Allowance (formerly referred to as Spouse's Allowance and Widowed Spouse's Allowance), which provide monthly benefits to the pensioner or deceased pensioner's spouse or common-law partner. These benefits are only paid out to those who are between the ages of 60 and 64, and it is subject to residence and income tests.

The Old Age Security Act

The federal *Old Age Security Act* came into force on January 1, 1952, and provided universal pensions as a right, without a means test. The original benefit of $40 per month pension payable from age 70 has been raised several times, and the criteria for qualification have also been made more favourable. When the Canada Pension Plan was enacted in 1965, Old Age Security benefits were changed in important respects. First, the Act was modified to provide a Guaranteed Income Supplement effective January 1, 1967. Second, the commencement age for benefits was progressively reduced to age 65, and the amount of the benefit was gradually raised. An income-tested Spouse's Allowance (now referred to as the "Allowance") was introduced October 1, 1975, payable to eligible spouses of OAS recipients aged 60 to 64. In 1979, legislation was introduced to allow recipients who became widowed to continue to receive benefits to age 65, and in 1985 the Spouse's Allowance was first payable to all widows and widowers from age 60–64 and in need.

Since 1972, Old Age Security benefits and Guaranteed Income Supplements have been indexed to the increases in the Consumer Price Index, the adjustments being made quarterly. The Spouse's Allowance has been indexed since inception.

The pension under the *Old Age Security Act* is paid in addition to that derived from the Canada or Quebec Pension Plan. The payment commences in the first month after the application has been approved. For those persons who are late applying for the Old Age Security benefit and apply after October 31, 1995, retroactive payments can be made for up to 12 missed monthly payments. Prior to October 31, 1995, late applicants could receive up to 60 missed monthly payments.

Qualifications for Old Age Security Benefits

To qualify for the pension benefit, a person must furnish proof of age and must have met a residence qualification.

Prior to July 1, 1977, the conditions were:

- 40 years of residence in Canada after age 18; or

- 10 years of continuous residence in Canada immediately prior to the date of application for the pension; or

- If the applicant did not have 10 years of Canadian residence between the ages of 55 and 65, the applicant could make up each missing year by three years of Canadian residence between ages 18 and 55, provided the applicant resided in Canada for the year immediately before applying for the pension.

All persons meeting one of the above conditions qualified for the full OAS pension.

New residence requirements were introduced for individuals who were under age 25 on July 1, 1977, and for people over age 25 who did not reside in Canada before July 1, 1977. A full Old Age Security pension is payable for 40 years of residence in Canada after age 18. A proportionate pension is payable for those with 10 to 40 years of residence after age 18. If the person is residing in Canada as of the date of attainment of age 65, a proportionate pension is payable if they have at least 10 years of residency in Canada. For example, someone with 14 years of residence would receive 14/40ths of the maximum amount. However, if the person is not residing in Canada at age 65, 20 years of residency after attainment of age 18 is required to be eligible for the proportionate pension.

A person over age 25 on July 1, 1977 and previously resident in Canada can qualify under the pre- or post-July 1, 1977 rules, whichever provides the more favourable benefit.

Portability of Old Age Security Benefit

Canada has negotiated reciprocal agreements with some countries so that social security benefits may be preserved when people emigrate or immigrate. Persons who have spent portions of their working lives in more than one country may receive partial social security benefits from each country.

Where there is no reciprocal agreement, the Old Age Security pension is payable for six months after the pensioner leaves Canada and may be resumed if the pensioner returns. If, however, the pensioner had 20 years' residence in Canada after age 18, the pension is not affected by the pensioner's absence from Canada.

Universality

Until 1988, the Old Age Security pension was universal; that is, it was paid to all qualifying applicants irrespective of their wealth or income. Beginning with the 1989 taxation year, however, a special tax or "clawback" on the Old Age Security pension was imposed by the federal *Income Tax Act*.

The tax was phased in over three years, so that by 1991 it was fully implemented. More details on the effect of the clawback are given in the section on Taxation.

Financing

Pensions under the *Old Age Security Act*, including the Guaranteed Income Supplement and the Allowance, are financed on a pay-as-you-go basis from Government of Canada general tax revenues.

An Actuarial Report on the Old Age Security Program at December 31, 1997 indicated that the ratio of total annual expenditures to GDP is expected to increase from 2.38% in 2010 to a high of 3.28% in 2030, driven largely by the retirement of the baby boom generation. The demographic changes will have a major impact on the ratio of retirees to workers. The ratio of the number of people over the age of 65 to those between the ages of 20 and 65 is anticipated to grow from approximately 20% in 1997 to 42% in 2050.

In 2001, more than $24 billion in Old Age Security, GIS and Allowance payments were made to 3.9 million recipients.

Taxation

The OAS pension is included in the income of a taxpayer for the purposes of taxation, and regular income tax is paid on these amounts.

Beginning with the 1989 taxation year, a special tax, or "clawback", on the OAS pension, GIS and Allowances was imposed by the federal *Income Tax Act*. The tax was phased in over three years, and by 1991 it was fully implemented. The clawback is achieved by a 15% surtax of a taxpayer's net income in excess of $56,968 in 2002 (including benefits). Thus the total amount of the OAS benefit is taxed away from taxpayers with high incomes (approximately $93,000 in 2002)

Effective July 1996, OAS benefits are paid on a net basis, after taking into account the anticipated clawback of benefits. The amount of benefits payable are estimated based upon the individual's income for the prior year. The actual clawback is still based upon the individual's actual income for the year, and any differences are settled upon the filing of a tax return.

Non-residents are subject to the clawback based on their world-wide income, rather than only on income taxable in Canada, as had been the case. Non-residents are required to file a form containing relevant tax data to avoid having any of their OAS benefits withheld at source on account of the clawback tax liability.

Guaranteed Income Supplement

The Guaranteed Income Supplement is available to all recipients of the Old Age Security pension, subject to an income test. The supplement is reduced by $1 for each full $2 of other monthly income over and above the Old Age Security pension. Income for this purpose is the individual's income for the previous calendar year as defined by the *Income Tax Act*, minus pension payments and allowances under the *Old Age Security Act*, payments under the *Family Allowance Act*, similar payments to either of these under provincial legislation, or death benefits under the CPP/QPP. For purposes of the GIS income test, income includes any income from the Canada or Quebec Pension Plans (other than death benefits), from private pension plans, from earnings and from investments.

The Guaranteed Income Supplement benefits are indexed quarterly in line with increases in the Consumer Price Index.

Benefit payments from the Guaranteed Income Supplement are not taxable income to the recipients.

The maximum amount of Guaranteed Income Supplement is the same for a single person and for a married person/common-law partner whose spouse or common-law partner does not receive either the Old Age Security pension or an Allowance. The GIS for a single person and for a person whose spouse or common-law partner does not receive an OAS pension or an Allowance is greater than the GIS received by a person whose spouse or common-law partner also receives an Old Age Security pension or an Allowance.

Allowance and Survivor's Allowance (formerly referred to as the Spouse's and Widowed Spouse's Allowance

The Allowance and the Allowance for the Survivor apply to pensioners' spouses and common-law partners, and to deceased pensioners' spouses and common-law partners. The applicant spouse or common-law partner of an Old Age Security pensioner may receive the Allowance or Allowance for the Survivor if he or she is between the ages of 60 and 64, and if the applicant qualifies under an income test as well as a residency test. The residency test requires that the spouse or common-law partner reside in Canada at least 10 years after attaining age 18; if the residence period is less than 20 years, the person must be resident in Canada when the application is approved.

The Allowance is reduced by $3 for every $4 of the couple's income from sources other than Old Age Security, until the amount of the reduction is equal to the Old Age Security pension. Above that point the reduction is $1 for every $4 of income.

The Allowance is payable to the earlier of the month of death or the month preceding attainment of age 65. Also, the Allowance ceases to be paid in the event of separation, or when the applicant ceases to be a spouse or common-law partner.

The Allowance for the Survivor is payable to the earlier of the month of death, the month preceding the attainment of age 65, or remarriage.

Maximum Monthly Pensions Under the *Old Age Security Act*

The following table shows maximum monthly pensions for the various components for selected years.

Date Effective	Basic OAS Pension	Guaranteed Income Supplement		Allowance	
		Single[1]	Spouse or Common-Law Partner of Pensioner (each)	Regular Allowance[2]	Survivor's Allowance
1/1/52	$40.00				
1/7/57	$46.00				
1/2/62	$65.00				
1/1/67	$75.00	$30.00	$30.00		
1/1/72	$82.88	$67.12	$59.62		
1/1/77	$141.34	$99.13	$88.03	$229.37[3]	
1/1/82	$227.73	$228.63	$176.27	$404.00	$404.00[4]
1/1/87	$297.37	$353.41	$230.17	$527.54	$582.42
1/1/92	$374.07	$444.54	$289.55	$663.62	$732.64
1/1/97	$400.71	$476.20	$310.18	$710.89	$784.82
1/1/00	$419.92	$499.05	$325.06	$744.98	$822.47
1/1/01	$431.36	$512.65	$333.92	$765.28	$844.88
1/1/02	$442.66	$526.08	$342.67	$785.33	$867.02

Source: Extracted from data prepared by Forecasting, Information and Results Measurement, Income Security Programs, Human Resource Development Canada.

(1) spouse or common law partner not receiving OAS or regular Allowance
(2) spouse or common-law partner must be a GIS recipient
(3) first paid in 1975
(4) first paid in 1979

The Spouse's Allowance (now referred to as the "Allowance") was first paid to married beneficiaries in 1975 at the level of $209.81 per month and the Widowed Spouse's Allowance (now referred to as the "Survivor's Allowance") in 1979 at the level of $281.36 per month (the same level as married Spouse's Allowance). The first time that the Widowed Spouse's Allowance was paid at a higher level than the married Spouse's Allowance was in 1985 ($536.26 versus $485.73 per month).

The table below shows the maximum OAS, GIS, and Allowance and Survivor's Allowance amounts payable at January 1, 2002 for married or common-law partners, single individuals and survivors of pensioners in the appropriate age categories. The table assumes:

- The pensioner is (or was) an Old Age Security Pension recipient over age 65, and

- The spouse or common-law partner is the spouse, common-law partner or survivor of the pensioner and is over age 60.

Benefit	Single person over age 65	Married Couple/ Common-Law Partners		Survivor age 60-64
		Spouse/ Common-Law Partner age 60-64	Spouse/ Com- mon-Law Partner over age 65	
OAS • Pensioner • Spouse	$442.66 n/a	$442.66 0	$442.66 $442.66	n/a 0
GIS • Pensioner • Spouse	$526.08 n/a	$342.67 0	$342.67 $342.67	n/a 0
Spouse's Allowance • Spouse	n/a	$785.33	0	$867.02
Total:	**$968.74**	**$1,570.66**	**$1,570.66**	**$867.02**

Provincial Supplements

Several of the provincial and territorial governments offer a variety of benefits to assist low-income seniors. These benefits range from income assistance to home heating subsidies. Examples of programs are:

- *Alberta* — Alberta Seniors Benefit;

- *British Columbia* — Seniors Supplement;

- *Manitoba* — 55 PLUS program;

- *Ontario* — Guaranteed Annual Income System (GAINS);

- *New Brunswick* — New Brunswick Low-Income Seniors' Benefit;

- *Newfoundland and Labrador* — Low-Income Seniors Benefit;

- *Northwest Territories* — Seniors' Home Heating Subsidy and Supplementary Benefit;

- *Nunavut* — (See N.W.T. above as many programs are currently the same);

- *Saskatchewan* — Saskatchewan Income Plan;

- *Yukon* — Yukon Income Supplement.

The Seniors Benefit

The March 1996 federal budget proposed replacing the Old Age Security, GIS and special tax benefits for the elderly with a new fully income-tested, tax-free benefit: the Seniors Benefit. However, on July 29, 1998, the federal government announced that it would not be proceeding with the proposed Seniors Benefit, which was to take effect in 2001 for anyone born after 1935. The proposed system would have moderately increased payments for seniors with below-average incomes and phased them out for better-off recipients. According to the government, the primary objectives behind the new Seniors benefit were to ensure a higher level of income for the poorest Canadian seniors and to ensure the future sustainability of the federally funded program. Critics, however, argued that the Seniors Benefit would effectively encourage individuals to lower their incomes through various mechanisms in order to obtain money from the program. After much criticism, the government deferred and the Seniors Benefit was shelved.

Canada and Quebec Pension Plans

Introduction

The Canada Pension Plan (CPP) and the Quebec Pension Plan (QPP) are government-sponsored plans designed to replace employment income in case of retirement, death or disability. They came into effect on January 1, 1966. The province of Quebec exercised its constitutional right to opt out of the federal plan and established the QPP, which is a provincial statute applying to workers in Quebec, while the CPP governs elsewhere in Canada. Members of the Canadian Forces and the RCMP stationed in Quebec belong to the CPP.

The CPP/QPP are compulsory and cover practically all employees and self-employed persons. The main exceptions are casual and migratory workers, and certain types of employment such as exchange teaching, employment as a member of certain religious groups (this exception was abolished under the QPP in 1998), the employment of a child by the parent without remuneration and, in the case of the CPP, employees of provincial governments, unless the province agrees to have its employees covered.

The CPP/QPP benefits are supported by contributions from employers and employees. There is no government subsidy. The benefits are earnings-related and indexed annually to offset the effects of inflation.

The level of retirement pension under the CPP/QPP was set to provide, together with the Old Age Security pension, a replacement ratio of approximately 40% of income up to the national average wage (15% from OAS and 25% from CPP/QPP). It was expected that individuals would make further savings for their retirement, either through personal or group arrangements.

The CPP and QPP are administered by the Minister of National Revenue and the Quebec Minister of Revenue respectively for that part of the plan that relates to coverage and to the collection of contributions, and are the responsibility of the Minister of Human Resources Development and the Quebec Pension Board respectively for the part that relates to benefits.

The Canada and Quebec Pension Plans are very similar in the benefits, contributions and qualifying conditions. This chapter describes the main provisions of the CPP/QPP in force as of January 2002, and notes any significant differences between the two programs.

Phased Retirement and the QPP

Amendments were made to the QPP in 1998 permitting employees in Quebec between the ages of 55 and 70 to reduce their work hours without having their QPP entitlement reduced. In order to participate in a phased-retirement program, an agreement has to be entered into between the employer and the employee, specifying that either part of or all of the employee's reduced salary will be considered to have been paid to the employee for contribution purposes. This enables both the employer and the employee to contribute at the higher earning levels. Additionally, employees who are aged 60 to 65 and who have reduced their work to the extent that at least 20% of their salary is reduced can continue to work part-time and still receive a QPP pension.

Contributions

Contributions to the CPP/QPP are paid on earnings between the "Year's Basic Exemption" (YBE) and the "Year's Maximum Pensionable Earnings" (YMPE). Both the employer and the employee contribute equally. Self-employed persons contribute at the full rate.

The YMPE is linked to the average Canadian wage and is adjusted annually. Beginning in 1975, the amount of the YBE for an employee or a self-employed person changed from 12% of the YMPE to 10% of the YMPE, rounded down to the next $100. Since 1996, the YBE has been $3,500 (it was frozen at this level in 1998), although for the purposes of calculating the Minimum Qualifying Period on disability claims, the YBE continues to increase ($3,900 in 2002).

Until 1986, the total contribution rate was 3.6%. However, as shown in the following table, this rate was progressively increased commencing in 1987. At that time, a new schedule of contribution rates was introduced when it became evident in the respective CPP and QPP Statutory Actuarial Reports that the 3.6% rate was inadequate to meet the long-term benefit obligations of the plans. For the same reasons, a revised higher rate schedule starting in 1992 was introduced. In January 1998, Parliament enacted Bill C-2 and Quebec enacted Bill 149, which amended the CPP and QPP respectively. New CPP/QPP contribution rates were implemented. These new rates were introduced in order to ensure that the plan remained adequately financed and sustainable in the long run, without placing too much financial burden on future generations. The rate increases were based on a six-year schedule that would provide for annual increases in the combined employer-employee contribution rate from 6.0% in 1997 to 9.9% in 2003, and then remain steady thereafter.

CPP/QPP CONTRIBUTION HISTORY FOR SELECTED YEARS						
					Maximum contributions by	
Year	YBE	YMPE	Maximum contributory earnings	Contribution rate	Each of Employer and Employee	Self-Employed Person
	(1)	(2)	(3) = (2) – (1)	(4)	50% × (3) × (4)	(3) × (4)
1967	$ 600	$ 5,000	$ 4,400	3.6%	$ 79.20	$ 158.40
1972	600	5,500	$ 4,900	3.6%	$ 88.20	$ 176.40
1977	900	9,300	$ 8,400	3.6%	$ 151.20	$ 302.40
1982	1,600	16,500	$14,900	3.6%	$ 268.20	$ 536.40
1986	2,500	25,800	$23,300	3.6%	$ 419.40	$ 838.80
1987	2,500	25,900	$23,400	3.8%	$ 444.60	$ 889.20
1988	2,600	26,500	$23,900	4.0%	$ 478.00	$ 956.00
1989	2,700	27,700	$25,000	4.2%	$ 525.00	$1,050.00
1990	2,800	28,900	$26,100	4.4%	$ 574.20	$1,148.40
1991	3,000	30,500	$27,500	4.6%	$ 632.50	$1,265.00
1992	3,200	32,200	$29,000	4.8%	$ 696.00	$1,392.00
1993	3,300	33,400	$30,100	5.0%	$ 752.50	$1,505.00
1994	3,400	34,400	$31,000	5.2%	$ 806.00	$1,612.00
1995	3,400	34,900	$31,500	5.4%	$ 850.50	$1,701.00
1996	3,500	35,400	$31,900	5.6%	$ 893.20	$1,786.40
1997	3,500	35,800	$32,300	6.0%	$ 969.00	$1,938.00
1998	3,500	36,900	$33,400	6.4%	$1,068.80	$2,137.60
1999	3,500	37,400	$33,900	7.0%	$1,186.50	$2,373.00
2000	3,500	37,600	$34,100	7.8%	$1,329.90	$2,659.80
2001	3,500	38,300	$34,800	8.6%	$1,496.40	$2,992.80
2002	3,500	39,100	$35,600	9.4%	$1,673.20	$3,346.40

Contributions are required from attainment of age 18 to the earliest of death, commencement of retirement pension or attainment of age 70.

The contributory period is the above period, less any month for which a disability pension was payable to a contributor, or any month for which a family allowance was payable to a contributor for a child less than seven years of age.

Contributions by self-employed persons for a year are paid directly to the CCRA or Revenue Quebec, as the case may be, by April 30 of the following year, when submitting income tax returns. Employee contributions are deducted from pay and remitted by the employer monthly, together with employer contributions, to the CCRA or Revenue Quebec.

Contributions are charged month by month on all earned income in excess of the YBE until the maximum for the year has been paid. If an employee works for more than one employer in any year, deductions must nevertheless be made by each such employer without regard to the others. The employee may apply for a refund of any over-payments, although the employer may generally not obtain such a refund.

Qualifying Conditions

Retirement Pension

The normal commencement age for a CPP/QPP retirement pension is age 65. A CPP/QPP retirement pension is payable to a person who has contributed to the CPP/QPP for at least one year and has reached the age of 60. However, according to the CPP, a person under age 65 at pension commencement must have "wholly or substantially" ceased working (i.e., having earnings less than the maximum CPP/QPP annual pension ($9,465 in 2002)). Under the QPP, a person under the age of 65 must have either ceased working or have entered into a progressive retirement agreement with his or her employer that reduces the applicant's income by at least 20%. Therefore, the employee under the QPP can continue to work part-time and still receive his or her QPP pension.

If a contributor commences to receive the retirement pension before age 65, the amount of pension will be calculated as if the person were age 65, but reduced by 0.5% for each month between the month in which the pension commences and the month in which the contributor attains age 65. Commencement of retirement pensions may also be deferred to any age between age 65 and 70, and are then increased by 0.5% for each month between the attainment of age 65 and the month of retirement.

Therefore, pensions commencing at age 60 will be 30% less, and at age 70 will be 30% more than the amount calculated on the regular formula for persons at age 65.

Disability Benefits

CPP/QPP disability benefits comprise a pension to the disabled contributor and a pension to any dependent children. These pensions are payable to a contributor who has a severe and prolonged mental or physical disability, such that the contributor is unable to engage in any substantially gainful occupation.

If a person became disabled after December 31, 1997, he or she must have contributed to the Canada Pension Plan in four of the last six years on earnings that are at least 10% of the YMPE to be entitled to these disability pensions under the CPP. Under the QPP, a person must have contributed during: (1) at least two of the last three years or (2) at least five of the last ten years or (3) at least half of the years in his or her contributory period, with a minimum of two years.

Additionally under the QPP, a person aged 60 to 64 (inclusive) can be deemed to be disabled if he or she can no longer regularly pursue the gainful occupation that he or she left because of disability.

Under the CPP/QPP, the disability pension of the disabled contributor is payable as long as the employee is alive and continues to be disabled, or until age 65, when it is replaced by the retirement pension. The retirement pension is calculated based on the YMPE at the time of disablement, indexed to age 65. When payment of this disability pension is approved, the pension is payable monthly, beginning with the fourth month following the month in which the contributor became disabled.

Survivor Benefits

Under the CPP/QPP, survivor benefits are paid to a deceased contributor's estate, surviving spouse or common-law partner and dependent children. There are three different types of benefits: the survivor's pension, the dependent children's benefit and death benefits.

Survivor's Pension

Under the CPP, a survivor — which is defined as a person who was married to or who was the common-law partner of the contributor at the time of the contributor's death — aged 35 or more at the time of the contributor's death, or a survivor regardless of age if the survivor has dependent children or is disabled at the time of the contributor's death, is entitled to receive a CPP survivor's pension.

A surviving spouse (a person who was married to the contributor, was in a civil union with the contributor, or was living with the contributor in a *de facto* union on the day of the death of the contributor) under the QPP, is entitled to a surviving spouse's pension, regardless of age, but the amount of the pension is different for surviving spouses according to the spouse's age, whether or not they have children and whether or not they are disabled.

CPP/QPP survivor benefits are payable if contributions were made for not less than one-third of the total number of calendar years within the contributory period (but not less than three years), or for at least 10 years.

Orphan's Benefit

According to the CPP/QPP, an orphan's benefit is to be paid to each dependent child of a deceased contributor who has made contributions for at least the minimum qualifying period. The deceased contributor must have made contributions for the same minimum qualifying period as for a survivor's pension discussed above.

Death Benefits

A lump-sum death benefit is also payable upon the death of a contributor, under the same eligibility provisions as for the survivor pension.

For contributors who died after December 31, 1997, the CPP death benefit is a lump-sum payment that amounts to six times the amount of the deceased contributor's monthly retirement pension, to a maximum of $2,500. Under the QPP, the death benefit is also a lump-sum payment of $2,500.

Determination and Payment of Benefits

Retirement Pension

The CPP/QPP retirement pension is based on the contributor's past earnings. This involves the calculation of the average earnings up to the YMPE of each year in the period from January 1, 1966 or from age 18, whichever is later, to the date of the claim. The earnings of a contributor are therefore taken into account over the entire contributory period, excluding any "drop-out" months determined as described below.

To compensate for periods of unemployment, low earnings and sickness and disability, the plan allows certain periods to be dropped out or ignored in computing the average earnings. These include:

- Periods while receiving CPP disability benefits;

- Periods while caring for children under the age of seven (QPP/CPP);

- Up to 15% of the contributor's months of lowest earnings prior to age 65, provided that at least 120 months are left in the contributory period (QPP/CPP);

- Months included in a period of indemnity (QPP); and

- Periods after age 65 while contributing to CPP.

A contributor may also substitute a month of earnings after age 65. The months to be dropped out will be those in which the earnings were the smallest, in order to maximize the average earnings and thus the pension.

The CPP/QPP allows for increases in the general level of wages by providing for an adjustment in each year's covered earnings in the computation of average earnings. Before calculating average earnings, the actual contributory earnings in each year are adjusted by the ratio of the average YMPE for the five years ending with the year in which the pension commences to the YMPE for the year in question.

The amount of a retirement pension payable to a contributor aged 65 and over is a basic monthly amount equal to 25% of his or her average monthly pensionable earnings, adjusted to reflect the average of the final five-year maximum pensionable earnings. In 2002 (applicable to a contributor whose earnings during the contributory period were always above the YMPE except in "drop-out" months), the amount is therefore 25% of the average YMPE for 1998, 1999, 2000, 2001 and 2002 ($36,900, $37,400, $37,600, $38,300 and $39,100 respectively), i.e., 25% of $37,860, which amounts to $9,465 a year or $788.75 per month.

The Pension Index is used as a mechanism for determining the increases in the amount of benefits payable from one year to the next. The Pension Index is tied to the Consumer Price Index (CPI), unless the CPI decreases, in which case the Pension Index will remain the same.

Disability Benefits

As noted above, disability benefits consist of a pension for the disabled contributor and an additional pension for any eligible dependent children.

A disabled contributor is entitled to receive a pension that is equal to a flat-rate pension plus an earnings-related component equal to 75% of the contributor's retirement pension. The maximum disability pension in 2002 is $364.49 ($364.46 under the QPP) plus 75% of $788.75, which amounts to $956.05 a month ($956.02 under the QPP).

Pensions for dependent children of disabled contributors are payable at the same amounts as for dependent children of a deceased contributor (see below).

Survivor Pension

The survivor benefits payable by both the CPP and the QPP consist of a pension payable to an eligible spouse or common-law partner, plus a pension to dependent children.

Pension to Eligible Spouse/Survivor

While the survivor is under age 65, the pension is equal to the sum of a flat-rate pension plus an earnings-related component of 37.5% of the contributor's retirement pension. Where the survivor is between the age of 35 and 45 (not disabled and without dependent children) he or she receives reduced benefits. If the survivor is under the age of 35 (not disabled and without dependent children), he or she will not receive any benefits.

The CPP benefits for a survivor under age 65 are shown in the table below:

Age/Status of Survivor At Date of Contributor's Death	Description of Benefit	Maximum Benefit
45 to 64	flat rate ($142.21 per month in 2002) plus 37.5% of contributor's pension	$437.99 per month in 2002
35 to 44	phased reduction based on age (1/120 per month under age 45)	
under 35 (not disabled/without dependent children)	no benefit	
under 45 and disabled or with dependent children	same benefit as for spouse age 45 to 64	

Under the QPP, there are four different flat-rate pensions depending on the surviving spouse's age, disability status and whether or not there are dependent children, as shown in the table below.

Age/Status of Surviving Spouse at Contributor's Date of Death	Flat-Rate Pension in 2002 (per month)	Maximum Pension in 2002 (per month)
55 to 64	$399.59	$695.37
45 to 54 or disabled	$364.46	$660.24
Non-disabled under age 45 with dependent child	$338.40	$634.18
Non-disabled under age 45 without dependent child	$ 93.35	$389.13

Thus, unlike the CPP, the QPP pays a survivor's pension to a non-disabled eligible spouse without dependent children who is under age 35.

An individual may receive both a survivor's pension and a retirement pension as a contributor in his or her own right. Under the CPP, for a survivor who has reached 65 years of age (and whose retirement pension becomes payable after December 31, 1997), the amount of the combined pension will be the retirement pension, plus the lesser of: (1) 60% of the deceased's retirement pension minus the lesser of 40% of that amount and 40% of the survivor's retirement pension before an actuarial adjustment; and (2) the ceiling of the maximum retirement pension in the year of entitlement to the second benefit.

If the survivor is between the ages of 60 and 65, the amount of the combined pension will be the adjusted retirement pension, plus the survivor flat-rate benefit, plus the lesser of: (1) 37.5% of the deceased's retirement pension minus the lesser of 40% of that amount, or 40% of the survivor's retirement pension before actuarial adjustments; and (2) the maximum survivor's retirement pension in the year of entitlement to the second benefit plus the survivor flat rate.

Combined pensions are permitted under the QPP as well. From January 1, 1998, when a surviving spouse is under the age of 65 and becomes entitled to both a retirement pension and a surviving spouse's pension, the monthly amount of the surviving spouse's pension is equal to the sum of:

- The flat-rate benefit for a surviving spouse (a maximum of $399.59 in 2002); and

- An amount equal to the lesser of:

— 37.5% of the amount of the deceased contributor's retirement pension, and

— the difference between the maximum monthly retirement for the year and the amount of the surviving spouse's retirement.

Where a surviving spouse becomes entitled to both a retirement pension and a surviving spouse's pension after reaching 65 years of age, the monthly amount of the surviving spouse's pension is equal to the lesser of:

- The difference between the maximum retirement benefit and the surviving spouse's retirement pension established, and

- The greater of (i) 37.5% of the amount of the contributor's retirement pension and (ii) 60% of the amount of the contributor's retirement pension minus 40% of the amount of the surviving spouse's retirement pension.

Pension to Dependent Children

A survivor's pension is payable to each dependent child of the deceased contributor. Under both the CPP and QPP, this pension is a flat-rate pension, and it stops when the child attains age 18. The amount of the flat-rate pension is significantly different under the CPP ($183.77 per month in 2002) and the QPP ($58.35 per month in 2002). Two other differences exist between the CPP and QPP pensions:

- Under the CPP only, the pension is also payable while the child is between the ages of 18 and 25 and is attending school full-time; and

- Also under the CPP only, an orphan would be eligible for double benefits if both deceased parents were contributors.

Lump-Sum Death Benefits

A lump-sum death benefit is also payable in addition to the survivor pensions described above. Under the CPP, the amount of this lump sum is six times the actual or calculated contributor's retirement pension, to a maximum of $2,500. Under the QPP, the death benefit is a lump-sum payment of $2,500 in respect of a contributor who dies after December 31, 1997

According to the CPP, if there is a will, the executor of the estate must apply for the death benefit within 60 days of the date of death. If there is no will, or the executor did not apply within the 60-day period, payment will be made (1) to the person who paid for the funeral expenses; (2) to the surviving spouse or common-law partner of the deceased; or (3) to the next-of-kin of the deceased, in that order.

According to the QPP, the death benefit will be paid to the person or charity who paid the funeral expenses. An application must be made within 60 days of the contributor's death. If an application is not made within 60 days, it will be payable to the first of the following applicants: (1) the person or charity who paid the funeral expenses; (2) the heirs of the contributor; (3) the surviving spouse of the contributor (if no surviving heirs); (4) the descendants of the contributor (if no surviving heirs or surviving spouse); or (5) the ascendants of the contributor (if no surviving spouse or descendants).

Benefit Amounts

The following table gives a history of the maximum monthly retirement, survivor and disability pensions, and lump-sum death benefits under the CPP/QPP at time of commencement.

CPP/QPP MAXIMUM BENEFIT HISTORY FOR SELECTED YEARS								
Year of Commencement (1)	Retirement Pension	Disability Pension		Survivor's Pension				Lump Sum Death Benefit
				Spouse		Children		
	CPP/QPP	CPP	QPP	CPP[2]	QPP[3]	CPP	QPP	CPP/QPP
1967	10.42	N/A[4]	N/A[4]	N/A[5]	N/A[5]	N/A[5]	N/A[5]	N/A[5]
1972	67.50	111.98	111.98	69.79	69.79	27.60	27.60	550.00
1977	173.61	175.05	245.17	109.94	180.06	44.84	29.00	930.00
1982	307.65	301.42	411.92	186.05	296.55	70.68	29.00	1,650.00
1987	521.52	634.09	634.09	290.36	506.39	94.79	29.00	2,590.00
1992	636.11	783.89	783.89	359.68	631.06	154.70	29.00	3,220.00
1999	751.67	903.55	903.52	414.46	681.47	171.33	54.40	2,500.00
2000	762.92	917.43	917.40	420.80	685.69	174.07	55.27	2,500.00
2001	775.00	935.12	935.09	428.70	690.22	178.42	56.65	2,500.00
2002	788.75	956.05	956.02	437.99	695.37	183.77	58.35	2,500.00

(1) amounts are those payable in January of year; pension is indexed starting on the January 1 following its year of commencement

(2) payable to a spouse aged 45 or more but under 65

(3) payable to a spouse aged 55 or more but under 65

(4) first paid in 1970

(5) first paid in 1968

General Provisions

Indexing of Benefits

Indexation of benefits before retirement is based on a wage index through the indexation of the Year's Maximum Pensionable Earnings (YMPE), whereas after retirement the indexation is based on the Pension Index.

The YMPE, which governs the earnings on which contributions are made and benefits are calculated under the CPP/QPP, is adjusted annually to reflect changes in the Industrial Aggregate Wage Index of weekly wages and salaries in Canada published by Statistics Canada. The YMPE is the previous year's YMPE, multiplied by the ratio of the average wage index during the 12 months ending June 30 of the previous year to the similar average one year earlier (the resulting amount is rounded to the next lower multiple of $100).

Also, pensions in course of payment are adjusted each January 1 by the ratio of the average of the Consumer Price Indices for the 12 months ending with October of the preceding year to the similar average one year earlier. However, under the CPP/QPP, pensions in payment cannot be decreased.

Income Tax

CPP/QPP benefits are taxable income to the beneficiary. Contributions by employers are fully tax deductible, while employees receive a tax credit. For 2001 and subsequent taxation years, the tax credit is 16% of contributions for all employees. Prior to the 2001 taxation year, self-employed individuals were allowed a credit in respect of all their premiums payable under the CPP (which would include both the employer and employee portions of the premiums). Beginning in 2001, a self-employed person can deduct one-half of his or her CPP premiums payable on his or her self-employed earnings, which effectively means that the employer portion of the premiums is deductible from income, while the employee portion is allowed the credit.

Credit Splitting

In the case of a marriage breakdown or where a common-law relationship ends, the contributory earnings are split equally between the two spouses/common-law partners of a given couple in respect of their previous period of cohabitation.

Assignment

A retirement pension in payment may be divided between the two spouses or common-law partners in proportion to the period of cohabitation, provided that both spouses or common-law partners are at least age 60 and have ceased contributing to the CPP/QPP. On the death, divorce, separation (after 12 months), or on request of both spouses or common-law partners, the assignment will come to an end.

Reciprocal Agreements With Other Countries

The federal government and the Quebec government have reciprocal social security agreements with various countries to help people qualify for benefits from either country (i.e., eligible service under the foreign plan may be taken into account to quality for the CPP/QPP benefits). The federal government has entered into approximately 40 agreements and the Quebec government has entered into approximately 25 such agreements.

Integration With CPP/QPP Benefits

Other private or public arrangements may reduce their benefits to take into account the benefits payable from the CPP/QPP. For example, the Guaranteed Income Supplement will be reduced by $1 for each $2 of retirement pension payable under CPP/QPP. Some Workers' Compensation programs take the CPP/QPP disability pension into account.

Many private pension plans may also integrate their employee contribution and benefit level with the CPP/QPP. Integration may be direct (i.e., 2% of final average earnings minus the CPP/QPP benefit), or indirect (i.e., step-rate pension of 1.25% of final average earnings up to the YMPE and 2.0% above). The second method is by far the most popular for benefits.

Similarly, contributions may be integrated directly (i.e., 5% minus CPP/QPP contributions) or indirectly (4.5% up to the YMPE and 6% above).

If the benefits or contributions are in addition to the CPP/QPP benefits or contributions, they are referred to as stacked benefits.

Funding and Future Contributions

The sustainability of the Canada/Quebec Pension Plan has been of considerable concern for both the federal government and the Quebec government. The CPP/QPP were established as pay-as-you-go arrangements, and reserve funds were established to cover two to three years of benefit payout to smooth fluctuations. The *15th Actuarial Report on the CPP* disclosed the unfunded liability of that plan alone at $570 billion. The pay-as-you-go nature of these plans meant that substantial increases in contributions would be required in the future to sustain current benefit levels. The increased contribution needs were due to the maturation of the plans (full retirement benefits have been payable since 1977, when contributions were made for only a portion of employment years), higher than expected disability payments, an ageing population, and slower than expected economic growth since these plans were first implemented.

In 1997, the federal and provincial governments agreed to changes to the CPP to ensure its future sustainability. These changes came into effect in 1998. As a result, the CPP contribution rates have continued to rise and will continue to rise until the year 2003, when the rate will reach 9.9% and remain steady thereafter. The changes also included a new investment policy. One of the most significant aspects of this new policy was the creation of the CPP Investment Board. The objectives of the Board, as set out in section 5 of the *Canada Pension Plan Investment Board Act* are

- To manage funds in the best interests of the contributors and beneficiaries under the CPP; and

- To invest its assets with a view to achieving a maximum rate of return, without undue risk of loss, having regard to the factors that may affect the funding of the CPP and the ability of the CPP to meet its financial obligations.

The CPP Investment Board is a crown corporation that acts at arm's length from the government, and the intent is that this independent board will both diversify and enhance the performance of the CPP assets. As a result, a proportion of the CPP funds are now permitted to be invested beyond government bonds and into other investment vehicles.

In December 1999, the Department of Finance issued a news release regarding the Federal-Provincial Review of the Canada Pension Plan. In the release, the government stated that, according to the actuarial report prepared for the review in December 1998, the CPP was financially sound. It also confirmed that the 9.9 per cent combined employer-employee contribution rate that will be reached in 2003 is expected to be sufficient to sustain the Plan in the face of an ageing population. Former Finance Minister Paul Martin stated: "Current evidence indicates that the changes we put in place two years ago will be sufficient to sustain the CPP. Canadians can rest assured that the CPP will continue to provide the retirement pensions and other CPP benefits that they depend on."

In June 1996, the Quebec government released a working paper, "A Reform of the Quebec Plan", in which it made several proposals to ensure the financial security of the QPP. One of the issues reviewed was the potential contribution rate increases and their effect on the economy and public finances. On December 17, 1997, Bill 149, *An Act to reform the Quebec Pension Plan and to amend various legislative provisions*, received Royal Assent and provided for several significant amendments to the Plan, most of which were to take effect January 1, 1998. As with the CPP, the QPP contributions were scheduled to rise to 9.9% by 2003 and to remain steady after that point. The QPP funds are invested by the *Caisse de dépôt et placement du Quebec* in a combination of government bonds and private-sector assets. The reserve fund had a value of $18.3 billion in 2000.

The 19th Actuarial Report on the CPP concluded that the contribution rates (9.4% in 2002 and 9.9% in 2003 and in subsequent years) are sufficient to pay for future costs and to accumulate assets of $142 billion (4.2 times the annual expenditures) by 2010. It was projected that there would be $1,578 billion in assets (5.9 times the annual expenditures) by 2050.

On June 6, 2002, new legislation was introduced to consolidate the investment management of all CPP assets into the CPP Investment Board, which will occur over a three-year phase-in period. As of March 31, 2002, the Board had investment assets of approximately $14 billion, while the assets being transferred have an approximate value of $40 billion. The Chief Actuary of Canada has estimated that these changes are expected to increase returns on CPP assets by approximately $75 billion over the next 50 years.

ADMINISTRATION AND COMMUNICATION OF PENSION PLANS

Introduction

The success of a retirement savings arrangement does not hinge only on good plan design to meet employee needs; the employer must also deliver and communicate benefits effectively. Efficient operation and effective communication are equally important to ensure that promised benefits are delivered and that employees are satisfied with their retirement savings benefits. For most employees, retirement savings and financial planning involve complicated concepts and goals that are hard to define.

Similar principles apply to both registered and non-registered arrangements. In the case of registered plans, the process is complicated by the considerable regulatory requirements.

The nature of the pension promise is defined by the design of the plan. Once the plan is operational, the design will be revisited periodically and some adjustments may be made to reflect the changing realities: for example, changing profiles of the workforce, legislation, financial considerations, new benefit trends, changes in government programs, and the impact of bargaining agreements. However, once established, the focus shifts to the operation of the plan, responsibility for plan administration, funding and management of pension plan assets. Together, these functions constitute pension plan governance and all are necessary for the sound management of the plan. Historically, this responsibility normally rested with the plan sponsor, generally the employer, acting through its board of directors, committees or designated individuals, or in the case of bargained plans, jointly with the employer and designated representatives of the employees.

For most plans, governance is carried out at a number of levels by the employer. HR staff, often with the assistance of outside advisers, will analyze the ongoing efficiency and effectiveness of:

- The financial operations of the plan (funding, impact on financial statements and investment of pension fund assets);

- The interface with employees in delivery of benefits and record-keeping; and

- Communication to employees.

Senior management may, from time to time, make recommendations for change. Major changes in financial arrangements or administration usually must be ratified by the ultimate owner(s).

No matter what the corporate structure of the enterprise, the effective administrators of a pension plan have, by legislation and common law, serious responsibilities to all beneficiaries of an employer-sponsored pension plan.

Various guidelines and reports have been published on the subject of good governance[1].

The following table summarizes the components and responsibilities for pension plan governance[2]:

---

[1] For example, on May 25, 2001, the Canadian Association of Pension Supervisory Authorities (CAPSA) issued its draft *Pension Governance Guideline and Implementation Tool*, which identifies various principles of good governance. The Guideline outlines 13 principles in relation to good governance, under five main headings; namely, pension plan objectives, governance structure, communication, internal controls, and performance measures and assessment. These Guidelines can be viewed at CAPSA's Web site at **www.capsa-acor.org**. On May 1, 1998, *The Guideline for Governance of Federally Regulated Pension Plans* was issued by The Office of the Superintendent of Financial Institutions (OSFI). It sets out best practices for the governance of federally regulated pension plans. The Guideline's main purpose is to help administrators in their work and to promote prudent and sound governance practices.

[2] Source: *"The Hottest Place in Hell"*, by Gordon M. Hall, Summer 1994 issue of Business Quarterly, The University of Western Ontario.

Pension Plan Governance

	Analyze	Recommend	Decide
Funding	• Merits of different funding methods and amortization periods • Economic assumptions • Asset/liability modelling	• Funding strategy in line with corporate strategy (i.e., cash flow, security of employee benefits)	• Question process and assumptions • Confirm or amend funding policy
Asset Management	• Investment manager performance • Voting of proxies	• Changes in statement of investment policy • Manager searches	• Acceptability of fund performance • Relevance of the statement of investment policy
Administration and Communication	• Range of processes, systems and technologies to administer benefits • Extent and effectiveness of employee communication	• Periodic audits for cost/benefit implications as technology, plan events and legislation evolve	• Confirm or amend systems decisions • Monitor and question employee communication
Focus of the Owners: Board of Directors, Partners, Head Office, etc.	• Legislation, regulations and court cases • Issues monitoring • Public opinion	• Issues to be placed on the board agenda	• Corporate policy on issues such as ethical investing • Confirm or question basic social, financial and ethical assumptions

This chapter deals with the administration of pension plans. Chapter 5 addresses financial management of plans and Chapter 6 covers pension fund investment management.

Pension legislation has assigned some statutory obligations to certain players involved in plan administration. In recent years, there has also been increased litigation on pension matters. The most common litigation issues include surplus ownership, the employer's right to contribution holidays, and issues relating to same-sex spouses. Tighter control on investment management is another area that has attracted considerable attention in recent years.

Recent interpretations of pension legislation together with increased litigation have contributed to redefining the roles of the various parties in the pension arena. A number of them are considered to have fiduciary obligations. Penalties have been applied in cases where there has been a breach of fiduciary obligations.

Pension plans are subject to more than one piece of legislation. First, there is pension standards legislation, which sets out:

- Minimum standards for plan benefits and administrative requirements;
- Minimum funding standards;
- Minimum disclosure requirements;
- Requirements in the case of plan wind-ups;
- Reporting requirements;
- Roles and responsibilities for the supervisory body and for the employer; and
- Remedial actions.

The requirements are very detailed and need to be satisfied for each jurisdiction affecting the pension plan.

The *Income Tax Act* also has jurisdiction over pension plans. It defines acceptable benefits and the applicable limits. It also defines maximum contribution levels that can be made to a plan and deducted by the employer. The *Income Tax Act* also has significant reporting requirements.

Chapters 7 and 8 examine the *Income Tax Act* requirements and pension standards legislation in more detail.

Roles and Responsibilities

Who is involved in the administration of a pension plan? Several partners can be identified. First, there is the plan administrator. Pension standards legislation defines who can be the administrator. Several jurisdictions state that the administrator can be:

- The employer;
- A pension committee generally comprising one or more representatives of the employer, or any person required to make contributions under the plan, and, possibly, members of the plan;
- A pension committee comprising representatives of members of the plan;

- The insurance company guaranteeing the benefits provided under the plan;

- In the case of a multi-employer plan, a board of trustees; or

- A board, agency or commission appointed or established by an Act of the Legislature.

Quebec legislation requires that a pension committee be appointed to administer the plan. It consists of at least three members of whom two must be members of the plan, appointed in accordance with the terms of the plan, and one member who must be independent of both the employer and of the plan members. This pension committee is responsible for all aspects of the plan administration.

According to the federal, British Columbia, Newfoundland and Labrador, and Saskatchewan legislation, if the majority of members in the plan (with a minimum number of 50 members in the plan) requests a pension advisory committee, the employer *must* establish one. In Manitoba the same rule basically applies, except that the minimum number of members is 21 and the rule only applies if the plan is not administered by a body with almost equal member and employer representation. In Ontario, if the administrator is a pension committee and that committee includes at least one member appointed by plan members, there is no right to form an advisory committee. If this is not the case, then the majority of members and former members may establish an advisory committee by majority vote. The legislation in each jurisdiction must be reviewed to determine not only if there is a right to form an advisory committee and what requirements are necessary to establish one, but also to determine the powers of such a committee. As a general rule, the committees are basically powerless and their duties often include monitoring the plan, making recommendations and promoting awareness and understanding of the pension plan.

The administrator is subject to the "prudent person rule" in a number of jurisdictions. This rule requires the administrator to "exercise the care, diligence and skill in the administration and investment of the pension fund that a person of ordinary prudence would exercise in dealing with the property of another person." This prudent person rule has been controversial over the course of recent years, as prudence is somewhat difficult to measure.

Within private-sector corporations, the board of directors generally has final responsibility and accountability for all matters pertaining to the plan. Often a subcommittee of the board is formed to have direct dealings on pension matters — this pension committee would normally be composed not only of board members, but would also include senior management representatives from both human resources and finance. At times, there may even be two such subcommittees involved — one responsible for overseeing the investment area, while the second one dealing with pension policy and benefit matters. The structure will depend on the size of the company and of the pension fund.

There may be a number of external parties involved in the administration of a pension plan. One is the trustee who is responsible for holding the assets of the plan for the benefit of plan members. The trustee must be someone other than the employer.

In the case of a defined benefit plan, there must be an actuary who prepares the actuarial valuations and advises the administrator on the financial position of the plan. Auditors are also involved, as generally, audited statements of the fund holdings must be prepared.

Often, the administrator will appoint one or more investment managers who are responsible for the selection of the investments of the plan. There are strict rules under pension legislation in connection with investments. In addition, investment managers must follow the statement of investment policies and procedures (also referred to as the "statement of investment policies and goals") adopted under the plan. Like the administrator, the investment manager is also subject to the prudent person rule. These issues are examined in Chapter 6.

The regulators are also important players in the administration of a pension plan. They are responsible for interpreting pension legislation and ensuring that the interests of plan members are safeguarded.

Establishing a Plan

As a general rule, an application for registration of a retirement plan must be made with the regulatory authorities by the plan sponsor, or on behalf of the plan sponsor within sixty days after the establishment of the plan. Generally, the descriptive documents that must be filed in support of an application for registration are:

- A prescribed application form;
- A certified copy of the plan document;
- A certified copy of the trust agreement or insurance contract;
- A certified copy of a Board of Directors' resolution adopting the plan;
- A certified copy of a collective agreement (if any);
- A copy of materials provided to employees describing the terms of the plan (i.e., plan booklets);
- A copy of the investment contract (if any);

- Any other documents by virtue of which the plan is established;
- An initial actuarial report and cost certificate (for defined benefit pension plans only); and
- A statement of investment policies and procedures (required in all jurisdictions except Prince Edward Island).

For registered pension plans, there is also a registration fee that must be paid to the appropriate jurisdiction of registration.

In order to receive a tax deduction for employee and employer contributions, the following documents must be submitted to the CCRA for registration:

- A completed CCRA application form (Form T510);
- A certified copy of the plan text;
- An initial actuarial valuation report (for defined benefit pension plans only);
- A certified copy of the funding agreement (typically a trust agreement or insurance contract); and
- A certified copy of any other relevant documentation, such as a by-law or resolution that relates to any of the documents above.

The CCRA also imposes registration and filing obligations on non-registered pension arrangements. For example, a Deferred Profit Sharing Plan (DPSP), which is an arrangement whereby the employer contributes a portion of annual profits from its business, or a related business, to a trustee. The trustee, in turn, holds and invests the contributions for the benefit of employees. These plans offer tax deferral benefits that are similar to RPPs. To obtain these tax advantages, the plan must be registered and the following documents must be submitted to the CCRA for registration:

- Form T2214, with which the trustee and the employer apply for registration of the plan as a DPSP;
- If the employer is a corporation, a certified copy of the resolution of the directors authorizing the application to be made; and
- A certified copy of the trust agreement and plan text (these can be combined in one document) constituting the plan.

Selection of Service Providers

Plan sponsors often require the help of one or more of the following service providers to help set up and maintain their retirement plans:

- Actuaries and Consultants;

- Investment Managers;
- Custodian;
- Administration Service Providers; and
- Communication Specialists.

The role of each of these service providers is discussed below.

Actuaries and Consultants

If the plan sponsor is setting up a defined benefit plan, an actuary is required to complete the initial valuation report and cost certificate. Actuaries and consultants can also assist plan sponsors with:

- Drafting the plan document;
- Board resolutions;
- Review of trust agreements or insurance contracts;
- Preparation of communication material for employees;
- Selection of other suppliers; and
- Regulatory submissions.

Plan sponsors may elect to do some or all of the above tasks themselves, depending on their own internal resources. The actuary/consultant may be hired based on a prior relationship, a recommendation, or through a formal selection process where proposals are solicited from a number of firms, interviews are conducted and a selection is made.

Investment Manager

Investment managers are hired by plan sponsors to manage the plan assets. There are a number of options the plan sponsor should consider when hiring an investment manager. Chapter 6 discusses these issues in detail.

- The plan sponsor may use pooled funds, which tend to have lower fees if the plan assets are not sizable; however, this reduces investment flexibility for the plan sponsor.
- If the plan sponsor elects to use segregated funds, the fees may be higher (depending on the amount of assets in the plan) but the sponsor has more influence in the investment mix of the plan assets.
- Many trust and insurance companies in Canada offer "bundled" services, and are quite capable of providing investment management and custodial services for all types of plans, as well as administration services for most types of defined contribution plans. Such bundled services do not necessarily lower the cost

of the plan. The sponsor may also have problems trying to "unbundle" the services if there is an issue with asset performance or service at a later date.

Custodian

Custodial services are offered by most of the major trust and insurance companies. The custodian is the actual holder of the plan assets and is responsible for those assets. Selection criteria for custodians include reporting capabilities, service, compatibility with the investment manager selected, financial strength, experience and fees.

Administration Service Providers

A plan sponsor may decide to outsource the administration of the plan or administer the arrangements internally. Issues that plan sponsors often consider when outsourcing administration are reporting capabilities, service, experience and costs. (This decision is examined later in this chapter.)

If the plan sponsor wants to outsource the administration duties for a defined contribution plan, they may be performed by the custodian of the plan or may be performed by an independent recordkeeper.

A plan sponsor who chooses to administer a defined benefit plan internally may obtain software from various consulting organizations for this purpose. If they decide to outsource the defined benefit plan administration, there are a number of firms capable of performing the administration. The plan sponsor may have the administration done by the consulting firm that performs the actuarial valuations, or may decide to ask a number of firms to bid on the work. Considerations for the selection of a service provider, and more information on the various functions involved in recordkeeping are provided in a later section of this chapter.

Communication Specialists

Plan sponsors often retain communication specialists to prepare communication materials for plan members. Given the specialized nature of pension benefits, the expertise necessary to adequately communicate pension benefits can be found in employee benefits firms. The range of services vary widely and will be discussed later in this chapter.

The Registration Process

Registered Pension Plans

The following chart illustrates the process of a successful registration from start to finish.

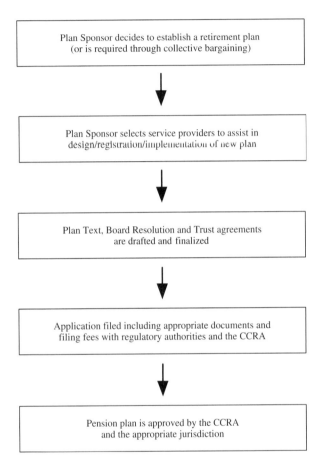

Operation of the Plan

Differences By Type of Arrangement

Registered plans must be registered under pension standards legislation and under the federal *Income Tax Act* in order to qualify as a tax-sheltered arrangement. The actual operation of these registered pension plans is dictated by the various requirements of the regulatory authorities.

Non-registered pension arrangements are not subject to the same rules and regulations as registered plans. Thus, the operation of these plans is much simpler, being driven more by the principles of prudence and good management.

The balance of this section will deal with the operation of registered plans.

Recordkeeping — Issues and Alternatives

Defined Benefit Plans

In every registered pension plan, there is detailed administration work that must be done. This includes keeping records of individual members, sending each member an annual statement, processing retirements, deaths and terminations, answering questions, and filing returns with federal and provincial governments.

Detailed records must be set up and maintained for each plan member, which includes active members, inactive members, pensioners and survivors of deceased members. These records contain important data, such as contributions, service and earnings history, in order to ensure that plan members who become entitled to benefits receive the correct benefit entitlement. They also serve as the source of information for actuarial valuations and various periodic reports required by regulatory authorities for producing annual member statements and for calculating Pension Adjustments (PAs). This data is also necessary for the calculation of pension assets in the case of marriage breakdown proceedings. In addition, these proceedings normally give rise to increased recordkeeping requirements in order to administer pension benefits in accordance with domestic orders.

These recordkeeping functions may be performed in-house or delegated to outside advisers such as the custodian (i.e., a trust or an insurance company), an actuarial consulting company, or a company specializing in third-party pension administration.

The introduction of extensive pension legislation has made pension plan administration extremely complex and an important decision that must be made is who will handle the day-to-day administration of the plan. It should also be noted that this decision should be revisited periodically. It may be appropriate for a plan sponsor to perform the administration of the plan internally for some time and, subsequently, to retain the services of an outside supplier. Conversely, the employer may initially contract out administration until sufficient expertise is available internally to repatriate this function.

Some major factors to be considered when making this decision are as follows:

- *Number of plans and complexity* — are the calculations simple or are they complex?

- *Plan membership and annual turnover* — how many calculations are performed each year?

- *Corporate philosophy* — how much control does the employer want to maintain over the administration of the plan versus outsourcing?

- *Availability and depth of knowledge of existing staff* — will existing staff understand pension administration or will specialists need to be hired?

- *Key person dependency* — what happens in the event of illness or vacation?

- *Internal structure of the company* — will the administration be handled centrally or locally?

- *Internal resources of the company* — will the purchase of computer equipment or the addition of new staff be necessary?

- *Likelihood of future plan restructuring* — will any decisions resulting in significant cost be obsolete in the future as a result of future restructuring?

- *Available budget* — how much money will be set aside to administer the plan?

Defined Contribution Plans

While the alternatives discussed above can be applied to all types of registered pension plans, they are directed primarily at the administration of defined benefit plans.

An employer administering a defined contribution plan may not have as many registration and reporting procedures. However, the plan may offer investment alternatives. If this is the case, the employer needs to ensure that employees can obtain information about the options and their pension investments on an ongoing basis. The administration of defined contribution plans, as a result of increased flexibility in employee investment choice, has become highly sophisticated in the last few years. Consulting firms and insurance companies are offering an "open alliance" arrangement with mutual fund managers, allowing employees to select from a variety of funds that meet their risk requirements and performance criteria. Insurance companies, trust companies and mutual fund companies have quickly become competitive service providers in the administration of defined contribution plans, offering daily valuation of account balances and online voice response.

Benefit Determination and Delivery

A member's benefit entitlement must be calculated within the time limits set by the regulatory authorities, according to the relevant provisions of the pension plan and the applicable legislation.

In all jurisdictions, benefits are calculated on a member's termination of employment, retirement or death and, in some jurisdictions, on marriage breakdown. Benefits are also calculated in the event of termination or partial termination of the pension plan. It is the responsibility of the administrator to provide the member with a written statement outlining the options available to the plan member and to ensure that payment is made in accordance with the elected options.

Financial Reporting

For defined benefit plans, actuarial valuation reports certifying the current service cost, experience gains or deficiencies, unfunded liabilities, solvency deficiencies and amortization payments must be filed at least triennially, but may be filed more frequently. In Ontario, if a plan is not 100% funded on a solvency basis, valuations must be done at least annually.

Investment/custodial reporting and reconciliation must be done at least annually; however, they are often done more frequently. Audited financial statements prepared in accordance with generally accepted accounting principles must be filed annually for plans registered under certain jurisdictions[3] This requirement normally applies to most pension plans; however, under certain conditions, certified statements, as opposed to audited financial statements, may be filed.

Regulatory Reporting

Once a plan is registered with the regulatory authorities, reports must be filed periodically.

Pension Standards Legislation

The timing and nature of reports required by provincial standards legislation vary by jurisdiction.

Annual Information Return (AIR)

An Annual Information Return (AIR) must be filed annually by the administrator of the pension plan in the jurisdiction in which the pension plan is registered. Each jurisdiction has its own prescribed return that must be filed within a specified time frame. A fee, based on membership in the reporting year, must accompany the return. If the information return is filed late, there may be late filing fees.

---

[3] Reference: *CICA Handbook, Section 4100, "Pension Plans"*.

The AIR generally requires the following information:

- Plan membership, by province and sex;
- Number of new employees, retirements, terminations and deaths;
- Total employee required contributions;
- Total employee voluntary contributions;
- Total employer current service contributions;
- Credits or surplus used to reduce employer current service contributions;
- Employer payments to liquidate unfunded liabilities; and
- Employer payments to liquidate experience deficiencies.

In addition, each jurisdiction has its specific requirements.

As part of ongoing initiatives by the CCRA and CAPSA to reduce the administrative requirements on pension plan administrators, a single return has been developed to accommodate the joint filing of the AIR, which meets both the *Income Tax Act* requirements and the requirements under pension standards legislation. As of 2002, the following provinces are participating in the joint filing program: Alberta, British Columbia, Manitoba, New Brunswick, Newfoundland and Labrador, Nova Scotia, Ontario, and Saskatchewan. Quebec, however, has not harmonized its annual return and therefore, for Quebec RPPs, a separate CCRA annual information return must be filed within six months following the end of the fiscal year of the plan.

Amendment Filing Requirements

All pension plan amendments must be filed. The prescribed time limits within which amendments must be filed vary by jurisdiction.

Generally, when an amendment to a plan affects the cost of benefits, creates unfunded liabilities or otherwise affects the solvency of the plan, an actuarial report or a cost certificate must be filed in support of the amendment. The prescribed time limits within which the supporting actuarial reports and cost certificates must be filed vary among the jurisdictions.

CCRA

Once registered status is conferred by the CCRA, registration is ongoing. Certain filings, however, are required. A copy of each amendment to the plan must be filed. The CCRA does not acknowledge or confirm the acceptance of amendments.

T3P

If the pension plan is funded through a trust (or a corporate pension society), the trustee (or society) is required to file a pension plan income tax return, the T3P, annually with the CCRA. The T3P must be filed within 90 days following the end of the taxation year of the trust (or society). All receipts and disbursements of the pension fund during the taxation year must be reported on the T3P. A statement of assets of the fund at year-end with a reconciliation to the previous year-end must be attached to the T3P.

PAs/PARs

The annual PA for each plan member must be reported in a T4 slip to the plan member by the last day of February of the following year. The employer or administrator also sends a copy to the CCRA. A notice of assessment is forwarded by the CCRA to the plan member specifying the maximum deductible RRSP contribution available to the member.

Pension Adjustment Reversals (PARs) are reported on a T10 form and a copy of the form is forwarded to both the plan member and the CCRA. The administrator must file the T10 form no later than 60 days after the end of the calendar quarter in which the member termination occurs. The reported PAR amount will result in an increase in the member's RRSP deduction limit for that year.

Special Events

A pension plan evolves through time — it seldom remains unchanged for long periods of time. Following the introduction of pension and tax reform, and also as a result of the severe recession of the early 1990s, a number of defined benefit plans were either wound up or converted to defined contribution arrangements. There are specific regulatory requirements that must be satisfied before these wind-ups or conversions can become effective. They include the determination of members' entitlements, reporting to regulatory authorities and preparation of a statement of entitlements for affected members. Additional details on legislative requirements can be found in Chapter 8.

Communication of Pension Plans

Effective communication of pension plans and other retirement savings arrangements, based on a firm understanding of personal impact, is critical to helping Canadians plan for the future. Recently, governments, employers, unions, and plan sponsors have been concerned by the low levels of employee awareness of their retirement savings arrangements. Economic pressures on government benefits and workplace turnover have heightened this concern.

Many employers more than meet legislated disclosure requirements. They undertake highly visible, interactive communication and education campaigns. Today, the message for employees, for simple compliance or intensive education, attempts to shift attitudes away from entitlement into shared responsibility, and then toward self-reliance. If employees are to understand the need to save more towards their financial security at retirement, well-designed communication and education programs to provide financial and retirement planning assistance will be imperative. These programs are discussed later in this chapter.

Motivating employees to take greater ownership of their futures presents several challenges. First, workforce diversity creates distinct segments of employees with different communication needs. Differences in age, job expectations, risk tolerance, and business or financial knowledge require targeted strategies. Second, employers converting plans to reflect changing demographics and company philosophies must address inertia, and possible scepticism. Many employees do not appreciate their current plan well enough to make an informed judgment about new plan designs, and they may resent the idea of taking on more responsibility. And third, high priority groups — such as outstanding performers — may be addressed in selective communication.

At the same time, given their fiduciary obligations, employers are increasingly concerned about communicating overly optimistic estimates of what employees can expect to receive from their retirement arrangements. A proper balance must be found to promote the arrangements while providing a realistic assessment of retirement income. With respect to defined contribution arrangements, plan sponsors must provide sufficient education programs to allow employees to make informed decisions on how to invest their account balances. However, employers need to be cautious in distinguishing between information on alternatives and advice or counsel on specific investments if they want to avoid legal liability.

Compliance

Currently, pension standards legislation requires employers or plan sponsors to provide four communication elements:

- A written description of the plan;
- An individual annual statement;
- A statement at termination of membership in a pension plan; and

- Access to information and documentation.

A Written Description of the Plan

All pension standards legislation requires an employer, pension plan sponsor or plan administrator to provide members and eligible employees with an explanation of plan provisions and the member's rights and duties. In federally registered plans, the spouse must receive a copy as well. Most often, members receive simplified summaries of the plan in booklet form. Nevertheless, the plan text prevails; it must be available upon request and all other documentation must align with its terms and conditions. Quebec requires that members of simplified pension plans receive a copy of the actual plan provisions.

Amendments must be described to plan members in writing. The legislated timeframe for making amendments known varies from jurisdiction to jurisdiction.

An Individual Annual Statement

In most jurisdictions, annual statements must be distributed to all active members within six months of the plan's year-end. Statements must also be provided to non-active members in Quebec.

Information reporting varies by jurisdiction, and includes personal data, contribution amounts, service and benefit accruals, as well as retirement dates. Members are provided with a description of benefits available on termination and death, and disclosure of the plan's funded position may also be required.

A Statement at Termination of Membership in a Pension Plan

Active plan members who terminate or retire from employment must receive a statement within 30 to 90 days of the event, depending on the jurisdiction. If a court order or domestic contract requires the division of benefits as a result of marriage breakdown, the spouse or former spouse may be entitled to a copy of the statement. The deferred pension at retirement must be disclosed, as well as any opportunity for early or postponed retirement and its impact on the pension. If the member can transfer funds out of the plan, the transfer value, options and any restrictions related to a solvency deficiency must also be reported.

On the death of a member, in general, the spouse, common-law partner, beneficiary or estate will receive a written statement outlining any outstanding benefits payable from the plan.

Access to Information and Documentation

Once a year, members are allowed to view a variety of plan documents. These may include the plan text, actuarial reports, annual information returns and financial statements of the pension fund. This information can be viewed at the employer's premises or at the provincial regulator's office. In general, the same access is provided to an authorized agent or the spouse of the member in a number of jurisdictions.

Comprehensive Communication Strategies

Many employers and employees benefit from communication programs that go beyond bare minimum statutory requirements. Program design and objectives can be tailored to different circumstances.

Employers' objectives are the starting point for a comprehensive communication strategy. Employers who see retirement savings arrangements as a strategic investment often seek information about employee attitudes and understanding. Focus groups, surveys, and plan implementation committees are commonly used to sense the response to plan philosophy and design, as well as communication themes. For example, research has revealed that younger employees would rather contemplate investments than retirement planning.

The plan design dictates the communication program. For example, except perhaps for investment options and the related risks, defined contribution plans are relatively easy to describe; the critical element is explaining how the plan delivers benefits. On the other hand, defined benefit plans require greater creativity and patience. Employees must be assured, through ongoing communication and education, of the value of the defined benefit as well as the lack of precision in the company's contribution.

Where decisions about optional levels of contribution or investment are required, employees need to understand the cost-benefit equation and any risks involved. The more decisions the employee must make, the greater the need both to provide information and to do whatever is needed for employees to feel assured about how the plan works.

Four phases of employee contact are included in most communication programs:

- *Awareness building* — A personal letter from the employer or plan sponsor sets the stage and adds credibility to a plan change or introduction. Some employers use posters to increase the visibility of their plans. The messages emphasize the reasons for any changes and the benefit to employees.

- *Plan education* — Employee meetings, videos, booklets, and information hot lines or Web sites provide a deeper understanding of plan terms and conditions, comparisons with previous plans, and the impact of future returns. Examples and simple graphics help employees see how their financial future is affected by the plan.

- *Financial planning information* — When employees must make investment decisions as they near retirement or consider levels of contribution, some employers and sponsors provide access to financial planning expertise in seminars, personal counselling, computer modelling programs, information hot lines or Web sites. Employers and consultants generally provide financial information, but do not recommend specific investments. (See later section on "Financial and Retirement Counselling").

- *Ongoing communication* — Beyond compliance, many employers provide comprehensive annual statements tailored to individual employees, publish newsletters, and build employee awareness of investment information. These vehicles consistently reinforce the theme of shared responsibility for planning the future.

In today's corporate environments, interactive technology is playing a greater role in communication planning. The ability to use computers, the Internet, telephones, and other decision-support systems for investment modelling, surveying, and information-sharing, as well as for the administration of enrollments and confirmations, presents more options for reaching employees. These tools create faster and more flexible pathways for communication and reduce administrative handling.

Communication impact is usually measured in terms of employee satisfaction, enrollment or contribution rates, and awareness levels.

Although communication planning must take into account many variables and changing messages, some things stay the same. People are busy and must be convinced that knowing this information is to their benefit. Most respond better to simple concepts than to detailed explanations. Few appreciate percentages, formulas, financial models, or ratios. And, to many employees, guarantees are more attractive than the risk of poor returns or losses. At the end of the day, the key tasks in communicating retirement savings arrangements are creating the urgency for all employees to take notice, and providing the simple explanations and necessary facts that lead to confident decisions.

Financial and Retirement Counselling

Employer pension plans are designed to supplement, not replace, government benefits and personal savings. Often, employees are unaware of the implications of this arrangement. A number of employers now provide financial counselling as both an employee benefit and an effective means of communication about the employer-provided retirement benefits.

Objectives of Programs

Financial and retirement counselling allows employees to prepare for retirement. Many employers also provide financial counselling in the case of special events, such as early retirement windows or downsizing.

Employer-provided financial counselling can be provided for groups or for individuals. A common practice is to run seminars for groups of employees, sometimes followed by individual counselling sessions based on the employee planning undertaken in the seminar workshops. One-on-one financial and retirement counselling can be provided for executives, whose remuneration and tax planning can be complex. Seminars and counselling should be led by experienced professionals.

Employees find it useful to plan for their long-term needs with respect to retirement, estate planning, investment and income security. To do this successfully, they must understand the different components of retirement income — government benefits and individual savings — and how these interact with the employer-sponsored plan. They are made aware of the impact of inflation, and the types of returns and risks associated with different classes of investments. Financial counselling will also cover estate and tax planning. Sessions are usually directed to setting goals for personal and financial objectives (retirement age, income level, etc.) and identifying if there is a need for additional income during retirement.

Special Events

Employers offering early retirement programs may use financial counselling services to ease the transition, educate employees and improve the take-up of the early retirement windows. Counselling will usually cover:

- The package;
- The fit with the employer's pension plan, depending on career position;
- The available government benefits;

- Tax issues — marginal rates and credits, RRSPs, special deductions for retirees; and

- The retirement income options.

Employers who are downsizing may offer special financial counselling for the employees involved. Counselling on downsizing will usually cover:

- The termination payment;

- Termination provisions;

- The fit with the company pension plan;

- Employment insurance;

- Other government programs;

- Transfer of severance and pension entitlements to an RRSP;

- Bridging to the next job; and

- Budget analysis — net worth assessment, income and expenses.

Some employers also provide retirement counselling that covers not only financial preparedness but also life skills such as fitness, activities and adjusting to change.

Executives

High net worth employees — in terms of both their remuneration and their value to the company — can be faced with many complexities in financial and retirement planning: tax planning, the CCRA limit on pensionable earnings, Supplemental Executive Retirement Plans (SERPs), etc. Financial counselling is a strategic service to these individuals, providing a road map that fits all the income pieces together into a coherent plan that will work over time.

Benefit to Employers

Financial and retirement counselling provides a number of benefits to employers.

- *Increased appreciation of the employer's benefits* — Financial counselling is one of the most effective means of communicating the extent and impact of employer benefits.

- *A more self-reliant workforce* — Employees who understand their own responsibilities for their future welfare can plan ahead for themselves.

- *Responsible workforce management* — In the event that circumstances dictate downsizing, either with or without early retirement programs, it is positive for everyone within the company if forward-thinking efforts are made to provide the best transition situation possible.

Legal Implications of Plan Member Communications

Employers are becoming increasingly concerned and increasingly aware of the liabilities that can occur as a result of poor pension plan communication to members. This liability has been further brought to the forefront and exposed by recent court decisions. Clear and accurate information is an absolute necessity and implementing preventative measures will provide the groundwork for avoiding future liability.

While there are a variety of regulatory obligations placed upon employers and administrators to communicate information to employees, the common-law implications must not be overlooked when considering the legal ramifications of employee pension plan communications. Actions have been brought on the basis of breach of contract, negligent misrepresentation and promissory estopple. Disgruntled employees or beneficiaries will always exist, but this only further supports the proposition that employers/administrators need to protect themselves by taking proactive measures.

Negligent Misrepresentation

For employees to succeed in a claim based upon negligent misrepresentation, the following five requirements must be met:

1. There must be a duty of care between the representor and representee based upon a "special relationship";

2. The representation made must be "untrue, inaccurate or misleading";

3. The representor must have acted negligently in making the representation;

4. The representee must have reasonably relied upon the misrepresentation; and

5. The reliance must have been detrimental to the representee, in that damages must have resulted.

After reviewing the list of requirements, one might think that the employer or administrator must actively mislead the employees by actual statements to establish negligent misrepresentation, but this is not so. A failure to disclose pertinent information and available options to employees can also be categorized as negligent misrepresentation.

The case of *Spinks v. Canada* is an example of how an omission, a failure to fully inform the employee, can lead to employer liability on the grounds of negligent misrepresentation. In this case, Mr. Spinks had worked for the Australian Atomic Energy Commission for approximately 20 years prior to emigrating to Canada to take a position with Atomic Energy of Canada Ltd. On his first day of work, he attended a sign-on interview, which was designed to inform new employees about their employment, as well as to provide them with information regarding their pension plan. Mr. Spinks was also provided with a pension administration screening form. In this form, an employee could elect to count previous employment elsewhere as pensionable service under the federal government plan. Mr. Spinks returned the form without having completed the section regarding previous employment. Some years later, he was shocked to learn a colleague who had previously been employed in England had bought back his years of English service. Ultimately, it was held that the duty of the staffing officer was to advise Mr. Spinks competently and to take care in providing that advice, whether or not there was a request for advice. Additionally, although the screening form referred to other forms of employment, it did not refer to employment with foreign governments. This lack of information, which was relied upon by Mr. Spinks, led him to erroneously conclude that he could not buy back his Australian service. This constituted a misleading misrepresentation.

Providing clear and accurate information is an absolute necessity if the employer or administrator wishes to avoid liability. Even relying upon a form prescribed by legislation will not necessarily spare the employer or administrator from resulting liability. In *Deraps v. The Labourer's Pension Fund et al.*, Mrs. Deraps was seeking damages representing the survival benefits she would have otherwise received had she not signed a spousal waiver form in relation to her husband's disability pension. Her husband was stricken with cancer at the time he applied for disability benefits under his union's pension plan. They met with a union pension counsellor who was hired by the union to provide information to members regarding the terms and conditions of their pension plan. Mrs. Deraps stated that she and her husband were not given advice nor much information beyond what was on the forms. She stated that she believed that signing the waiver would mean a reduced survivor pension upon her husband's death — not a complete disentitlement to a pension.

The Ontario Court of Appeal concluded that the union pension counsellor, as agent for the administrator, had been retained to provide information to union members regarding the terms and conditions of the pension plan. As an agent with specialized knowledge, skill and expertise, she had a duty to advise plan members and their spouses about the nature of the options available to them under the plan.

Therefore, her failure to advise Mrs. Deraps and the plan member was "misleading and a misrepresentation". The Court of Appeal stated that the union pension counsellor's following comments were unclear: "If you leave a pension for your wife this is how much you will get. If you don't leave a pension to your wife, this is how much you will get." In its decision, the Court of Appeal stated that as a result of her personal circumstances and the "highly confusing language in the waiver", it was reasonable to conclude that Mrs. Deraps did not understand that she was signing away her entitlement.

It appears as if the *Deraps* case is taking the administrator's duty to a higher level — ensuring that correct information is disseminated is not suffice — administrators must actually ensure that the information is understood by the recipient.

In addition to failing to provide employees with the relevant information required to make informed decisions, the employer or administrator cannot simply rely upon their advice to employees to obtain independent advice in order to avoid liability. In *Allison v. Noranda Inc.*, the employer provided Mr. Allison with a letter informing him of two separation pay options. Under both options, the total amount of severance monies remained the same. One option was a lump-sum option and the other was an instalment option. What the letter and the employer did not explain was the fact that the separation pay option, which Mr. Allison had selected, could significantly affect the amount of pension benefits that he received at age 55. However, the employer did advise Mr. Allison to seek independent advice, which he did.

Upon reaching the age of 55, Mr. Allison applied for his pension benefits and at this point became aware of the consequences of his selection. The New Brunswick Court of Appeal stated that the employer was under a duty to disclose to the employee material information relating to the pension consequences that would occur as a result of his selection of the separation pay options. Such failure constituted a misrepresentation that misled Mr. Allison into believing that his selection would not impact upon his pension benefits. Stating that the employee should receive independent advice does not relieve the employer from its liability, if material facts are not disclosed.

As they say, "honesty is the best policy", and without a doubt, deceptive practices will open the employer or administrator to liability. In *Ford v. Laidlaw*, Laidlaw had made an early retirement offer to its employees. The president of Laidlaw spoke to the trust company, which was the trustee of the employees' benefit plans, to find out how the employees' shares in the retirement plans ("plans") would be valued for pay-out to an employee who accepted an early retirement offer. The trust company provided inaccurate advice to the president. The president in turn reviewed the plan and discovered that the trust company's statements were inaccurate. However despite this knowledge, he conveyed the inaccurate information to the employees. The Court held that Laidlaw's misrepresentation constituted a term of the retirement offer. The employees were therefore entitled to receive from Laidlaw the difference in the amount of the money between what each of them actually received from their retirement plans and what they were told they would receive if they submitted their early notice of retirement.

Contract Interpretation Issues

An employer or administrator who intends to rely upon formal documentation to prevent liability, while stating otherwise through less formal means, cannot anticipate that the terms of the formal documents will always prevail and that the employer or administrator will be shielded from legal liability. The employer/administrator can actually amend the terms of the contract by simply communicating a different version of the formal documentation to employees. It is also important to keep in mind the *contra preferentem* rule, which provides that ambiguous provisions in a written document will be construed against the person who drafted the document.

In *Lawrie v. Deloro*, Deloro was acquiring the employees' company. The surplus in the acquired company's pension plan was owned by the employee plan members. The pension plan was replaced by a new pension plan. Under the terms of the new plan, the surplus was to belong to Deloro. Following the acquisition of the assets of the acquired company, Deloro sent the employees a letter that promised to provide the same pension benefits as before. The Court held that this letter written by Deloro to the employees created a special arrangement between Deloro and the employees, and as a result the employees were entitled to the surplus.

In *Schmidt v. Air Products*, the Supreme Court of Canada dealt with the issue of surplus entitlement. A booklet had been distributed by the company to its employees, which contained a statement that any remaining surplus would be paid to the employees. However, its influence on surplus entitlement was doubtful, since the booklet specifically stated that the plan would be subject to amendment from time to time. The Supreme Court of Canada stated that the statement regarding surplus contained in the booklet could not, in the circumstances of this case, form the basis for an estoppel preventing the company from now claiming the surplus for itself. However, the

Supreme Court left the door open for future cases by making the following statement:

> Documents not normally considered to have legal effect may nonetheless form part of the legal matrix within which the rights of employers and employees participating in a pension plan must be determined. Whether they do so will depend upon the wording of the documents, the circumstances in which they were produced, and the effect which they had on the parties, particularly the employees.

Electronic Communication

A new era is on the horizon: electronic communication in the pension industry. Although many issues surrounding electronic communications will have to be resolved before it becomes a mainstream method, it will, as all things do, become part of the technological revolution that continues to advance. In February 2002, CAPSA released its *Guideline No. 2 — Electronic Communication in the Pension Industry*[4]. In the Guideline, CAPSA states that the benefits of electronic communication are readily identifiable, namely reduced administrative costs, improved service for members and enhanced fiduciary monitoring. As stated in the introduction, the intent of the document is to help administrators and members "apply the provisions of applicable electronic commerce legislation to pension communications required under the pension benefits legislation in each jurisdiction". Furthermore, CAPSA states that the guideline only applies to communications between the administrator and members and is not meant to apply to other forms of pension communication.

As stated in the guideline, where the applicable pension benefits standard legislation requires a written document to be provided to a member or vice versa, such communication can be achieved through electronic means. An electronic document must be accessible by the recipient and capable of being retained so that it can be used for subsequent review.

Most jurisdictions in Canada have introduced e-commerce legislation, which is intended to make the law media neutral. In other words, many documents that previously could only be communicated in paper format will be permitted to be dealt with in electronic form. A common theme running through e-commerce legislation and the CAPSA guideline is that no one should be required to communicate electronically. This is necessary, as some members will not want to communicate electronically and some simply may not be able to communicate electronically.

---

[4] Guideline No. 2 can be viewed at the CAPSA Web site at **www.capsa-acor.org**.

Legislative clarification regarding the status of electronic pension plan communications would resolve some of the current anxiety of administrators, thereby enabling them to forge ahead and to make use of a more efficient communication medium. The Ontario *Electronic Commerce Act, 2000*, for example, specifies what the Act does not apply to, such as wills and codicils, powers of attorney, agreements of purchase and sale, or any documents that create or transfer interests in land, negotiable instruments, and documents that are prescribed regulations. No regulations exist at the time of this writing, so there does remain the possibility that the Ontario government could exclude certain pension documents from application of the Act.

In some situations, documents that are communicated must be signed and this leads to the usage of electronic or digital signatures. According to Ontario's e-commerce legislation, an "electronic signature" is defined as "electronic information that a person creates or adopts in order to sign a document and that is in, attached to or associated with the document". This definition is fairly universal with slight variations from jurisdiction to jurisdiction. According to the CAPSA guideline, an electronic signature must be reliable for the purpose of identifying the plan member and also for the purpose of associating the electronic signature with the relevant document in light of all the circumstances.

As it is still in its infancy, electronic communications in the pension industry will be a topic of discussion in the future. Further clarification is still required from legislators to provide pension administrators with the certainty that they need to move forward into the electronic age.

FINANCIAL MANAGEMENT OF PENSION PLANS

Chapter 4 outlined the three primary components of the operation or governance of retirement savings arrangements:

- Plan administration;

- Financial management; and

- Investment management of pension fund assets.

This chapter deals with financial management issues:

- *Funding policy* — how will the pension promise be secured?

- *Funding methods* — how and in what amounts will funds be accumulated?

- *Financial accounting* — how are pension costs to be measured and recognized in the sponsoring entity's financial statements?

Funding Policy Issues

Funding policy deals with the allocation of assets towards the fulfillment of the pension promise. Sooner or later, assets must be transferred from the employer to the employee to provide the pension. At one extreme, the assets are transferred only as the benefits fall due to the retired employee or his or her survivors. This approach is referred to as "pay-as-you-go". At the other extreme, assets could be transferred immediately, so that the employee takes on the entire responsibility for ensuring that the assets are ultimately used for their intended purpose. Neither of these approaches involves "advance funding" in the way that term is usually used.

In typical usage of the term, "advance funding" of pension benefits involves the creation of a fund held by an outside third party, such as a trust company, a group of individual trustees or an insurance company. This fund receives the employer's contributions (and the employees' contributions, if any), earns investment income, and pays out the benefits promised by the plan as they arise.

Reasons for Funding

With the exception of supplemental arrangements for executives, private-sector pension plans have generally been funded over the last several decades. There are two significant reasons why this has occurred:

- Pension standards legislation in the provincial and federal jurisdictions require advance funding to ensure benefit security; and

- The *Income Tax Act* provides significant tax advantages for advance funding.

Even in the case of plans where these two reasons do not exist, there are nevertheless good reasons to fund a pension plan:

- The accumulated pension fund provides security that the employees will receive the promised benefits, regardless of the employer's fortunes in the future. In the absence of an adequate fund or other security, the employees' pension benefits may just be one of a long list of unsecured debts of the employer.

- Funding provides the employer with an orderly method of managing cash resources, and avoids the situation where contribution requirements rise out of control as the plan matures. It can also help insulate the employer from being hit with a double whammy of high pension payments during a period of economic distress. There is little comfort to employees in an unfunded pension plan when honouring financial commitments helps bring about the collapse of the employer — resulting in both lost jobs and lost pensions.

- Generally accepted accounting principles require the allocation of pension costs over the years that employees perform their services, regardless of when the benefits are ultimately paid. In the absence of advance funding, the recognition of accounting costs will ultimately lead to a large pension liability in the employer's financial statements. In some cases, this could impair the employer's ability to raise additional financing. When the pension promise is funded, the funding contributions offset this build-up of liability.

- Advance funding at an appropriate level can reduce or eliminate transfers of cost between generations of employees, shareholders, taxpayers, or other stakeholders.

Reasons for Not Funding

Where funding is not required by legislation, there may be other reasons not to fund a pension program in advance. In the private sector, the most commonly advanced reason for not funding is that the employer is able to achieve a higher after-tax rate of return by retaining assets within the business than would be possible in an invested fund. In that situation, funding the pension plan would increase its ultimate cost.

In the public sector, other reasons have been advanced for not funding the pension program. In particular, it has been argued that the perpetual nature of governments, combined with their vast ability to tax and to borrow, eliminates any concerns regarding benefit security and cash management. It has been further argued that investment by government of large amounts of money in private capital markets is neither socially desirable nor necessarily financially advantageous, given the opportunity for politically motivated interference in the investment process.

How Much to Fund — Going Concern Versus Wind-Up

The assets needed for a plan to be "fully funded" can be considered from more than one perspective. A plan can be said to be fully funded on a "Wind-up Basis" if the existing assets are sufficient to provide for all benefits that have been accumulated for service to date, determined as if the pension plan were to be discontinued or wound up immediately. On a "Going Concern" basis, the plan is assumed to remain in place indefinitely, and will be considered fully funded if the existing assets plus the normal rate of contributions in the future (which will depend upon the funding method used) will be sufficient to enable all benefits, in respect of future service as well as past service, to be paid as they fall due.

It is quite possible for a pension plan to be fully funded on one of these bases (wind-up or going concern) and have a significant unfunded liability on the other basis. For example, a plan that bases benefits on end-of-career earnings might be able to meet all of its obligations if it were discontinued today, but not have sufficient assets to provide benefits that are based on significantly higher earnings levels expected in the future — at least not without significant increases in future rates of contribution. Conversely, some plans may call for special benefits to be provided in the event of plan discontinuance that would not normally arise in the normal operation of the plan. In these situations, a plan could be fully funded on a going concern basis, but underfunded on a wind-up basis.

How Much to Fund — Risk and Conservatism

Any approach to funding a pension plan involves making assumptions about future events — assumptions that will most likely turn out not to have been entirely accurate. In some cases, the future will turn out to be more favourable than assumed, and in other cases less favourable. Many employers prefer a degree of conservatism in pension funding. That is, they prefer to fund in such a way that the likelihood or risk of favourable outcomes is greater than the risk of unfavourable outcomes.

In some ways, it seems almost obvious that overfunding a pension program is a more favourable outcome for everyone than is underfunding. After all, if the plan is overfunded, the benefits are more secure and the employer can enjoy reduced future costs. On the other hand, if the plan is underfunded, the benefits are less secure, and the employer's future contributions will need to increase.

However, things are not always so simple. In some cases, overfunding may mean that past generations of employees have received lesser benefits than they might have otherwise enjoyed. In other cases, a significant reduction in the employer's contribution rate may result in an inability or unwillingness to return to normal contribution levels when the overfunding condition ends. Finally, the ongoing debate over the appropriate use of actuarial surplus and so-called contribution holidays may ultimately cause employers to view underfunding as a preferred approach from their perspectives.

Regardless of one's perspective on what is favourable or unfavourable, there is often a cost associated with adopting a conservative funding stance (for example, foregone use of cash and investment returns to the company). The need to manage the costs and risks associated with a particular funding approach has led to increasing use of a variety of tools, such as pension forecasting, pension modelling, scenario testing, and asset and liability matching.

Funding Methods

According to the Canadian Institute of Actuaries[1], the funda-mental objectives in advance-funding a pension plan are:

- To accumulate assets systematically to provide security for the benefits provided under the terms of the plan in respect of service that has already been rendered, without further recourse to the assets of the plan sponsor; and

- To allocate contributions among different periods in an orderly and rational manner.

Any particular "orderly and rational manner of allocating contri-butions among different periods" is a funding method. Many funding methods have been developed, modified, redeveloped and used over the years. The terminology used to describe and classify these various funding methods has also undergone significant modification over the years.

Cost Allocation Methods

Cost allocation methods are those that start by determining the total "cost" of the projected benefits to be provided (for both past and future service), and then allocating that cost directly to time periods. Typically, the allocation attempts to make the cost allocated to each future year equal in some sense — in dollar terms perhaps, or as a percentage of pay. This equal cost allocation may be done on an individual-by-individual basis, or only in respect of the plan as a whole. The allocation of cost to past-time periods may be carried out on the same basis as for future periods, or on some entirely different basis.

Funding methods that fall into this family of methods go by names such as "entry age normal", "attained age normal", "aggregate", and "individual level premium". This family of methods has also been called "projected benefit methods" or "level premium methods".

One essential characteristic of this family of methods is that the cost of the plan for the current group of members, expressed in whatever measure is appropriate to the particular method, is designed to remain stable over the future working lifetime of the current group of members — provided, of course, that the various assumptions made in the calculations turn out to accurately reflect future events. As members come and go, however, and as actual experience unfolds, the actual contribution requirements may go up or down over time.

---

[1] *Standard of Practice for Valuation of Pension Plans (1994)* and *Practice-Specific Standards for Pension Plans (2002)*. For information on these Standards view the Canadian Institute of Actuaries Web site at **www.actuaries.ca**.

Benefit Allocation Methods

Benefit allocation methods allocate the projected benefits that are to be provided to specific time periods. The cost associated with a particular time period is then directly determined from the benefit allocated to that period. Benefits may be allocated based upon the way they accrue under the plan provisions, using only historical earnings and service, or they may be projected to retirement (or earlier death or termination) and allocated in proportion to service, salary, or some other relevant quantity.

Funding methods that fall into this family go by names such as "unit credit", "traditional unit credit", "accrued benefit", "projected unit credit", and "projected benefit method pro-rated on services". The benefit allocation family of methods has also been called "accrued benefit methods" or "single premium methods".

One characteristic of the benefit allocation method is that when it is applied to a closed group of plan members, the cost associated with future years tends to increase steadily, and sometimes quite steeply. This increase is mostly due to the ever shortening period of time over which the compounding of interest can occur. It can also be magnified by the benefit allocation methodology, and by the decreased likelihood of termination as employees near retirement. In most plans, however, membership is not closed, and new members are joining continually. As long as the average age of the plan membership is kept reasonably stable by new members joining at younger ages, the contribution rates required can also remain reasonably stable.

All things being equal, benefit allocation methods tend to result in lower levels of funding than do the corresponding cost allocation methods.

Forecast Methods

Unlike the previous two families of funding methods, which assess the funding adequacy of a pension plan at a single point in time based only on the current membership population, forecast methods are designed to assess funding levels over a lengthy period into the future, and typically involve consideration of new entrants. Using forecast methods, one could develop a funding regime that satisfies a broad range of criteria. For example, one might require that the plan be fully funded on a wind-up basis at each year end for the next 30 years, be fully funded on a going concern basis using one of the other methods at the end of that 30-year period, and ensure that benefit payments during the next 30 years can be met from contributions and investment income, without requiring a sale of assets — all while keeping the variation in the employer's contribution rate within some reasonably tight boundary.

According the Canadian Institute of Actuaries' *Practice-Specific Standards for Pension Plans (2002)*, if a plan is a registered pension plan under the *Income Tax Act*, the forecast method should not be used in valuing the plan's liability for funding purposes.

While not directly usable, forecast methods can provide valuable insight into how the funding of the pension plan under one of the more traditional methods is likely to proceed. This can assist the plan sponsor in developing funding policy, or in managing the funding decisions that must be made from valuation to valuation.

Traditionally, these methods have been applied only in the context of large pension plans, due to the cost associated with complex computerized pension models. However, with today's technology, similar techniques can now provide very valuable planning information at more reasonable cost for even the smallest pension plan of all, the Individual Pension Plan or IPP.

Terminal Funding

Under terminal funding, the employer contributes the present value of the benefits promised to each employee as that employee retires or terminates. There are no funds set aside in respect of employees who are still rendering service to the employer. Obviously, the employer's cost will vary widely from year to year, since the retirement pattern is usually irregular — particularly so in a plan with a small membership.

This form of funding was first recognized by the *Income Tax Act* in 1952, and was used in the context of pensions promised under collective bargaining agreements. Under many of those agreements, employees retiring during the term of the agreement were entitled to receive a pension for life, but those retiring after the agreement expired were not legally entitled to anything.

Terminal funding is not acceptable under pension standards legislation, but it often arises in the context of supplementary plans not subject to that legislation. In this context, the lack of benefit security while actively employed may be justifiable or even desirable, if the covered employees are senior executives whose own actions are responsible for the financial viability of the employer. However, in light of the increasing use of supplemental plans for employees below the executive level, questions of benefit security in terminal funding situations arise more frequently. As the *Income Tax Act* limits on pensions affect increasing numbers of employees, it is reasonable to expect increased pressures for funding of supplemental plans.

A variation on the concept of terminal funding is the use of letters of credit to secure supplemental pension promises to executives. In this case, it is the termination of the employer that triggers the funding, rather than the retirement of the employee. As long as the employer is financially viable, and makes the pension payments as they fall due, no funding is in place. As soon as that situation changes, the trustee that holds the letter has the responsibility to call on the letter of credit to fund the balance of the benefits owing to the employee. More information on letters of credit is found in Chapter 9.

Pay-As-You-Go

Pay-as-you-go is not really a funding method at all, since there is no fund accumulated. The employer or plan sponsor simply pays the pension benefits out of current revenue as they fall due — or in the context of a national social security program, the current generation of employees/taxpayers pay for the benefits provided to the current generation of retirees. The advantages and disadvantages of this approach are precisely the reverse of the advantages and disadvantages of funding already discussed.

The pay-as-you-go method is prohibited under the provincial and federal pension standards legislation. However, it is a common method of providing for supplemental executive benefits.

The Canada/Quebec Pension Plan (CPP/QPP), Old Age Security and the Guaranteed Income Supplement are operated on a pay-as-you-go basis.

Actuarial Assumptions and Methods

In order to assess the funding level of the plan, or the pension cost for accounting purposes, it is necessary to make assumptions about a wide variety of possible future events and possible future characteristics of the plan and its members. Often these assumptions are considered in groups, such as:

- *Economic assumptions* — the discount rate or rate of return on investments, the rate of wage and salary increases, and the rate of increases in external indexes affecting benefits such as the consumer price index, the industrial aggregate wage index, the Year's Maximum Pension Earnings (YMPE) under CPP/QPP, the maximum pension limit under the *Income Tax Act*, etc.;

- *Decrement assumptions* — the incidence of early, normal and deferred retirement, the incidence of disability and disability recovery, the incidence of death both before and after retirement or disability, and the incidence of termination of employment;

- *Other demographic assumptions* — family composition, the likelihood of a spousal relationship at termination, death or retirement, the likely age differences between spouses, the number of hours worked by hourly-paid employees, the rates of wage and salary increases due to factors such as seniority, merit and promotion, and the propensity of members to elect from among the various optional forms of benefit delivery; and

- *Other assumptions* — the level of administrative, investment and other expenses, taxes, changes in levels of benefits and contributions under social security programs, future benefit adjustments, and so forth.

The classification of assumptions into these groups is neither unique nor uniformly applied, since many of the assumptions are interrelated, and some contain aspects of more than one group.

Relationships Between Assumptions

Many assumptions are interrelated, particularly the economic assumptions. It is therefore not sufficient to consider each assumption in isolation. The assumptions must also be considered in the aggregate and in relation to each other. For example, investment returns are commonly considered to comprise three components: a basic "risk-free" real rate of return, an inflation component, and a risk premium that reflects the market's demand for additional return to compensate for the acceptance of risk, in whatever form that may be. Similarly, increases in wages and salaries are commonly considered to comprise a number of components: an inflation component, a component reflecting increases in productivity generally, and components reflecting individual increases due to merit, seniority and promotion. Ideally, the inflationary component of these two assumptions, as well as of other assumptions that may be affected by inflation, should be the same.

The effect of a component that is common to several assumptions can be offsetting. For example, assuming a higher level of inflation will typically mean a higher discount rate (reducing pension costs), a higher rate of wage and salary increases (typically increasing pension costs) and a higher rate of post-retirement benefit increases, if applicable (also increasing pension costs).

Often the effect of differing assumptions and the way in which assumptions interrelate depends on the specifics of the plan provisions and the plan membership. For example, the expected future rate of increase in wages and salaries has a very considerable effect on the valuation of a final pay pension plan, but would generally have no effect on the valuation of a typical flat benefit pension plan. In addition, the rate of increase in general wages and salaries can affect the relative impact of the plan's integration with CPP/QPP and also the relative impact of the maximum benefit limits imposed under the *Income Tax Act*.

In order to achieve consistency among the various assumptions, and reasonableness in the aggregate, an actuary may use one or more assumptions that would not be considered reasonable by itself. The important consideration is that the valuation basis as a whole produces reasonable results. Of course, it is often easier to demonstrate overall reasonableness if most of the assumptions are individually reasonable.

Asset Valuation Methods

In the context of an ongoing funded pension plan, the assets and the liabilities of the plan are interrelated, and need to be considered together. It would not, for example, generally be appropriate to measure the liabilities of the pension plan using a discount rate that is significantly higher than the rate of investment return that can reasonably be expected to be achieved in the long term by the assets held in the pension fund.

It is less obvious why or how the value placed on the assets might be affected by the pension plan's liabilities. Surely what you could realize by selling the assets is not related to the pension liabilities. Although the market value of assets, if such a value exists, is not dependent upon the pension liabilities, the market value may not always be the most appropriate value to use in the context of a going concern valuation — particularly if the assets are not expected to be sold. Market value is, after all, just a point-in-time value that is highly sensitive to changes in short-term outlooks.

If the liabilities are being valued using assumptions that ignore or moderate short-term changes in market outlook, then it may be appropriate to use an asset valuation method that moderates or smoothes out short-term market fluctuations to a similar extent. As another example, a pension plan may hold a portfolio of assets — bonds perhaps — that produce cash inflows that are roughly matched to the expected cash outflows needed to pay a certain class of benefits. In that case, it may be most appropriate for those assets to be valued using a discount rate assumption comparable to that used to value the related liabilities. Why should the values be significantly different if the cash flows match?

For going concern funding purposes, the Canadian Institute of Actuaries' *Practice Specific Standards for Pension Plans (2002)*, effective as of December 1, 2002, allows the use of:

- Market value;

- A market value adjusted to moderate volatility;

- Present value of cash flows after the calculation date; or

- A value that assumes a constant rate of return to maturity, in the case of an illiquid asset with a fixed redemption value.

Canadian Institute of Actuaries' Practice-Specific Standards for Pension Plans (2002)

In May 2002, the Canadian Institute of Actuaries approved *Practice-Specific Standards for Pension Plans (2002)*. These standards come into effect on December 1, 2002 and apply to all pension plans except:

- Defined contribution plans;

- Plans whose benefits are guaranteed by a life insurance company; and

- Social security plans, such as the Canada Pension Plan or Quebec Pension Plan or the pension provided by the federal *Old Age Security Act*.

These Standards provide direction with respect to an actuary's advice regarding the "financial position" or "financial condition" of a pension plan. These Standards can be view at the Canadian Institute of Actuaries Web site at **www.actuaries.ca**.

The *Standard of Practice for Valuation of Pension Plans (1994)* will be repealed effective as of December 1, 2002.

Accounting for Pension Costs and Obligations

Background

In early 1986, the Canadian Institute of Chartered Accountants (CICA) issued a revised accounting standard on accounting for pension costs and obligations: *CICA Handbook, Section 3460* (Section 3460). The revision dealt with the accounting for, and disclosure of, pension costs and obligations, and how they are to be reflected in corporate financial statements. In the United States, the equivalent requirements of the Financial Accounting Standards Board (FASB) are Statements 87 and 88 (FAS 87 and 88), which were issued in 1985.

The Section 3460 standards came into existence because it was thought that financial reporting of pension costs and obligations was inadequate. In fact, prior to that time most companies did not even disclose the existence of pension plans in their financial statements.

Rationale

The main objectives of accounting for pension costs are:

- To allocate the cost of the pension plan to the years in which employee services are provided;

- To facilitate comparability in financial statements between periods and between entities; and

- To provide disclosure of the value of plan assets and liabilities.

Prior to the Section 3460 standards, actual contributions required for funding purposes would be the *de facto* pension expense, which was not considered an appropriate basis for accounting. In years when the sponsor took a contribution holiday, pension expense would be nil; in other years, it would be the sum of contributions for current service cost and past service amortizations. The potential for large variations from year to year and between companies in the pension costs, and thus on reported income, was considerable.

In 1994, the Accounting Standards Board (AcSB) established a task force to develop reporting standards that would be harmonized with the U.S. standards and also, wherever possible, would be in line with international standards. In 1999, the AcSB issued *CICA Handbook, Section 3461, "Employee Future Benefits"* (Section 3461).

The new Section 3461 is effective for fiscal years beginning on or after January 1, 2000, and supersedes Section 3460.

The following commentary is drawn from the Section 3461. The remainder of this chapter provides a brief overview of some of the more important issues to be dealt with in accounting for pension costs and obligations. For more detailed information please refer to the *Employee Future Benefits Implementation Guide* and the *Supplement* published by CICA[2].

---

[2] This Guide contains the full text of Section 3461. Visit CICA's Web site at **www.CICA.ca** for more details.

Objectives

As stated in Section 3461, the objective of accounting for the cost of employee future benefits "is to recognize a liability and an expense in the reporting period in which an employee has provided the service that gives rise to the benefits." Benefit plans are regarded as a component of an employee's compensation arrangement. Certain benefit plans require an employer to provide benefits to an employee in future periods for service currently performed by the employee.

Application

Section 3461 accounting standards apply to all retirement plans: formal and informal arrangements, registered or not. Prior to Section 3460, many employers had not recognized pension costs for unfunded, unregistered supplementary plans. Under Section 3460 and its successor 3461, the cost of these arrangements is to be recognized in financial statements. While the requirements deal with both defined benefit and defined contribution plans, defined benefit plans are most affected.

Section 3461 also applies to defined benefit plans that are funded through a life insurance company.

Transition

The transition to the new Section 3461 could be made under either of two methods. The first method is retroactive, so the opening retained earnings for the first year of application are adjusted. The second method is prospective, rather than retroactive. In this case, the retained earnings are not modified, but rather the impact is reflected in future years' expenses through amortization of the transitional obligation or transitional asset. The method selected had to be applied consistently to all employee future benefits provided by the company — both pension and non-pension.

Benefit Plans

A benefit plan is defined as any mutually understood arrangement between an employer and its employees, whereby the employer promises to provide its employees with benefits after active service in exchange for their services. A defined benefit plan is defined as a benefit plan that specifies either the benefits to be received by an employee, or the method of determining those benefits. Any benefit plan that is not a defined contribution plan is a defined benefit plan.

A defined contribution plan is a benefit plan that, rather than specifying the benefits to be received by an employee or the method to determine them, specifies how an employer's contributions to the plan are determined.

Defined Benefit Plans

Terminology

The following are some of the terms used in Section 3461, which will be useful in understanding the accounting concepts discussed below.

- *Actuarial Assumptions* — These are estimates of future events that will impact upon the costs and obligations of the employer in providing benefits (i.e., rates of return on plan assets, administration expenses, disability claim rates, rates of employee turnover, mortality, retirement age, etc.).

- *Actuarial Valuation* — This is an assessment of the financial status of a benefit plan. It includes the valuation of plan assets, if any, and the accrued benefit obligation.

- *Actuarial Present Value* — This is the discounted value of an amount payable, determined as of a specified date by the application of actuarial assumptions.

- *Accrued Benefit Obligation* — This is the actuarial present value of benefits attributed to employee service performed as of a particular date.

- *Current Service Cost* — This is the actuarial present value of benefits attributed to employees' services rendered during the year, reduced to reflect employee contributions.

- *Actuarial Gains and Losses* — These are changes in the value of accrued benefit obligation and plan assets resulting from experience different from that assumed, or changes in actuarial assumptions.

Actuarial Assumptions

The first step in accounting for defined benefit plans is to determine the actuarial assumptions. Section 3461 requires that the actuarial assumptions used for accounting purposes represent a best estimate for each of the assumptions individually, assuming that the plan will continue to be in effect in the absence of evidence to the contrary. Although actuaries will be involved in selecting the actuarial assumptions, the ultimate responsibility for the selection remains with the company's management. Since funding assumptions are made with the objective of assuring benefit security and may include safety margins, whereas accounting assumptions are to reflect best estimates of future events, in general, the assumptions for accounting purposes will differ from those used for funding purposes. In practice, surveys have consistently shown that assumptions used for accounting purposes have been less conservative than those used for funding purposes.

Plan sponsors need to adopt and document a methodology for setting and reviewing the actuarial assumptions that will provide auditors with the confirmations that they require. Management must also keep the assumptions internally consistent, except for the discount rate for which specific guidance is provided. For example, the rate of inflation underlying an assumption about future rates of return on plan assets should be the same as the rate of inflation underlying the assumption regarding future salary levels.

Section 3461 states that actuarial assumptions include (1) demographic assumptions (i.e., mortality, employee turnover rates, disability rates, etc.) and (2) financial assumptions (i.e., discount rate, future salary and benefit levels, the rate of return on plan assets, etc.).

Measurement Date

The accrued benefit obligation and plan assets must be measured as of the date of the employer's year end. However, such measurements may also be made as of a date no more than three months prior to that date, provided the employer adopts this practice consistently from year to year. For example, if the company's year end is December 31st, the measurement date can be no earlier than September 30th of that year.

Discount Rate

Section 3461 states that the objective of "selecting a discount rate is to measure the single amount that, if invested at the measurement date in a portfolio of high-quality debt instruments, would provide the necessary pre-tax cash flows to pay the accrued benefits when due."

There are two rates that can be used to discount expected future benefits:

- Market interest rates at the measurement date on high-quality debt instruments with cash flows matching the timing and amount of the expected payments; or

- The interest rate underlying the amount at which the accrued benefit obligation could be settled.

When available, the rates on high-quality corporate bonds should be used to determine the discount rate. Although Section 3461 does not set out what "high quality debt instruments" are, AA corporate bonds are generally presumed to meet this qualification. Government bond rates should be used if the maturity dates of corporate bonds do not extend far enough into the future to cover the entire period during which benefit payments are anticipated.

Prior to Section 3461, most organizations determined the discount rate based on management's best estimate of the long-term rate of return on its pension fund assets.

Attribution Period

An attribution period is the period of the employee's service to which an obligation for employee future benefits is assigned. The attribution period begins on the employee's date of hire (unless the plan specifies another date after the date of hire) and ends at the full-eligibility date, being the date where the employee has rendered all of the required service to entitle him or her to receive benefits (normally the retirement date).

Components of Pension Expense

The pension expense for defined benefit plans under the CICA consists of several components

- *Current service cost* — This is the actuarial present value of future benefits attributed to employees' service rendered during the year, reduced to reflect employee contributions.

- *Interest cost on the accrued benefit obligation* — This is calculated by applying the discount rate discussed above at the beginning of the reporting period to the accrued benefit obligation. As noted above in the Terminology section, the "accrued benefit obligation" is defined as the actuarial present value as of a certain date attributed to services rendered by employees to that date. One of two actuarial methods can be used in determining the accrued benefit obligation: (1) the accumulated benefit method and (2) the projected benefit method prorated on services. Under the first method, the benefits earned to date are based on the plan formula, the employee's history of pay, service and other factors as of the date of determination. Under the second method, in general, an equal portion of the total estimated future benefit is attributed to each year of service. The portions may differ if the plan defines different amounts of benefits for different years of service. If future salary levels or cost escalation affect the amount of pension benefits to be paid in the future, then the projected benefit method must be used.

On the other hand, where future salary levels or cost escalation do not affect the amount of benefits paid in the future, then the accumulated method should be used.

- *Expected return on plan assets* — The expected return is calculated by applying the expected long-term rate of return to either the fair value or the market-related value of the plan assets. To perform this calculation, it is therefore necessary to determine the value of the plan assets. The fair value is defined in Section 3461 as the amount of consideration that would be agreed upon in an arm's length transaction between knowledgeable parties who are under no obligation to act. The fair value of plan assets is normally market value. A market-related value is an amount "that recognizes changes in the fair value of plan assets in a systematic and rational manner over a period not exceeding five years". Different ways of calculating market-related value may be used for different classes of assets. The example given in Section 3461 is that an entity may use the fair value for bonds and a five-year moving average value for equities. However, it is also important to note that if the market-related value is applied, the basis for calculating the market-related value should be employed consistently from year to year. The ability to use market-related values is intended to allay concerns regarding pension expense volatility, as such volatility could occur due to certain assets being valued at fair value.

The expected long-term rate of return is the anticipated rate of return to be earned over the specified period, until all of the benefits have been paid out of the plan.

- *Amortizations* — Certain items are required to be amortized under Section 3461 such as: (a) past service costs; and (b) actuarial gains or losses.

    (a) *Past Service Costs* — When a plan is first adopted or is subsequently amended, there may be an increase in the accrued benefit obligation occurring as a result of the employee's past service. Such past-service costs should be amortized by assigning an equal amount to each remaining employee service period up to the full eligibility date of each employee who was active at the initiation or amendment date who was not fully eligible for benefits at that date. Section 3461 also permits alternative forms of amortizations, so long as such methods amortize past-service costs more rapidly than the method described above, and that method is used consistently from year to year. If all or almost all of the employees are no longer active (for example, due to retirement or termination), the employer should amortize past-service costs on a straight-line basis over the average remaining life expectancy of the former employees.

If the plan amendment actually reduces the accrued benefit obligation as opposed to increasing it, the reduction will first be applied to offset any existing unamortized past-service costs, and then to reduce any existing unamortized transitional obligation.

(b) *Actuarial Gains and Losses* — As accounting requires various estimates, it is foreseeable that the actual experience will deviate from the assumptions originally made. Actuarial gains and losses are defined in Section 3461 as the changes in value of the accrued benefit obligation and the plan assets that occur as a result of actual experience which is different from that assumed or from changes in the actuarial assumptions. An actuarial gain or loss regarding plan assets is calculated by taking the difference between the actual return on plan assets for the period and the expected return on plan assets for that period. Quite similarly, an actuarial gain or loss on an accrued benefit obligation is calculated by taking the difference between the expected accrued benefit obligation that was actually anticipated at the end of the period and the actual accrued benefit obligation that occurred at that date.

To offset volatility in calculating the pension expense, the "corridor approach" was introduced to provide a counterbalancing mechanism, which enables actuarial gains and losses to be offset over a period of time. This corridor approach basically stipulates that actuarial gains and losses need only be recognized if the *unamortized* gain or loss exceeds *10%* of (i) the accrued benefit obligation at the beginning of the year, and (ii) the fair value or market-related value of plan assets at the beginning of the year. Therefore, amounts that fall within the 10% corridor need not be amortized; whereas, amounts that fall outside of the 10% corridor must be amortized. The minimum amortization for these amounts should be the excess amounts divided by the average remaining service period of active employees expected to receive benefits under the plan. However, when all or almost all of the employees are no longer active, the amortization should be based on the average remaining life expectancy of the former employees.

- *Temporary deviation from the plan* — As the title implies, a temporary deviation is a deviation from the provisions of the plan, which is of a temporary nature. The effect of any temporary deviation from the plan should be recognized immediately.

- *Valuation allowance* — There are several steps required to calculate the valuation allowance. A valuation allowance is the excess of the adjusted benefit assets over the expected future benefit. A change in the valuation allowance should be recognized for the period in which the change occurs. Therefore, the following items must be determined: (a) the adjusted benefit assets; (b) the expected future benefit; and (c) the valuation allowance itself.

  (a) The adjusted benefit assets equal the accrued benefit asset less the amount, if any, by which that the plan's unamortized liabilities (unamortized past-service costs, unamortized actuarial losses and unamortized transitional obligation) exceed any unamortized gains (unamortized actuarial gains and unamortized transitional assets).

  It is therefore necessary to identify the accrued benefit asset component of the adjusted benefit assets definition, an accrued benefit asset occurs when the amount of the employer's contributions to the plan exceeds the accumulated pension expense. The accrued benefit asset may become "impaired" when there is a plan surplus and the employer is not entitled to fully benefit from it. The example given in Section 3461 is that there could be a regulatory moratorium on pension surplus withdrawals or uncertainties as to an employer's entitlement to use the plan surplus. To determine the extent of the impairment, it is necessary to determine the portion of the accrued benefit asset that will not be amortized in future periods' income (i.e., the adjusted benefit asset).

  (b) The expected future benefit is defined in section 3461 as the amount representing the benefit an employer expects to realize from a surplus, which can either be withdrawn from the plan or used to reduce future contributions. The expected future benefit is the sum of (i) the present value of the expected future annual accruals for service for the current number of active employees, less the present value of employee and employer (minimum amount required of employer regardless of surplus) contributions; and (ii) the surplus amount that can be withdrawn from the plan, as permitted under the plan and any applicable laws and regulations,

(c) When the expected future benefit exceeds the adjusted benefit asset, the accrued benefit asset is not impaired, and therefore no valuation allowance is required. If the adjusted benefit asset exceeds the expected future benefit, then a valuation allowance is required.

- *Curtailments and Settlements* — A curtailment is an event that will significantly reduce the expected years of future service for current active employees, or eliminates for a significant number of active employees the right to earn defined benefits for some or all of their future service. Therefore a curtailment could result from such things as a plan termination or a workforce reduction. A settlement occurs when the obligation for accrued benefits is discharged (for example, by an annuity purchase or a lump-sum payment to employees in exchange for their rights to receive benefits). A settlement is to be accounted for generally in the period in which the settlement occurred. A curtailment gain is to be recognized when the event giving rise to the curtailment has occurred, and a curtailment loss is to be recognized when it becomes probable that the curtailment will occur and if the net effects can be reasonably estimated. Special rules apply to partial settlements and partial curtailments.

- *Termination Benefits* — Benefits may be provided to employees by employers upon termination, and such benefits may take various forms such as lump-sum payments, periodic future payments, or both. Most termination benefits are accounted for in accordance with the post-employment benefit rules under Section 3461. However, specific rules are applied to two types of termination benefits: contractual termination benefits and special termination benefits. Contractual termination benefits occur when the existing terms of a benefit plan require benefits to be provided to employees upon the happening of a specified event (such as a plant closure). Special termination benefits are termination benefits that are not contractual termination benefits, and that are only offered for a short period of time (normally not exceeding 12 months) in exchange for an employee's voluntary or involuntary termination of employment.

When contractual termination benefits are offered, the liability and expense must be recognized when it is probable that employees will be entitled to the benefits and the amount can be reasonably estimated. When special termination benefits are offered to employees for voluntary terminations, the liability and expense must be recognized when the employees accept the offer and the amounts can be reasonably estimated. If the terminations are involuntary, the employer should recognize a liability and expense in the period in which certain conditions outlined in Section 3461 are met. The cost of termination benefits will be the amount of any lump-sum payments and the present value of any expected future payments.

Defined Contribution Plans

Section 3461 also sets out the accounting requirements for defined contribution plans. As the requirement to provide benefits to employees under a defined contribution plan is restricted to the requisite plan-specified contributions to be made by the employer, the accounting for defined contribution plans is notably less complex than accounting for defined benefit plans.

Current Service Cost and Interest Cost on Contributions

The current service cost to be recognized for a period under a defined contribution plan is the sum of the employer's contributions required to be made for that period, and the estimated present value of any future employer contributions required to be made that are related to employee services rendered in the current period. The present value of the contributions must be calculated by applying the discount rate using the same method as is used for defined benefit plans. Discounting is not appropriate if the contributions have to be paid within the period or within 12 months thereafter. Interest cost for the period is calculated by applying the discount rate to the present value of the accrued contributions, if any.

Past Service Costs

Contributions required to be made as a result of a plan being initiated or amended should be recognized in a rational and systematic manner over the period during which the employer expects to realize economic benefits from the plan initiation or amendment. This period may be the average remaining service period of active employees expected to receive benefits under the plan. However, depending upon the circumstances, a shorter period may be appropriate. The example given in Section 3461 is that if an employer negotiates its union contracts every three years and usually, at that point, agrees to alter the employees' benefit entitlements, it may in those circumstances be fitting to amortize the resulting past-service costs over three years.

Interest Income on Plan Surplus

When a defined benefit plan is converted to a defined contribution plan, there may actually be surplus that is not attributed to the individual employees' accounts. Interest earned on the surplus can be deducted when determining the expense for the defined contribution plan in that period. Any such plan surplus would be recognized as an accrued benefit asset and would be put through the same impairment assessment as for accrued benefit assets for defined benefit plans.

Disclosures

Section 3461's required disclosures can be broken down into three main categories (1) defined contribution plans, (2) defined benefit plans, and (3) significant accounting policies. The required disclosures enable individuals who review an employer's financial statements to understand the employer's obligation with respect to future employee benefits.

Section 3461 requires separate disclosures for pension plan benefits from other benefits.

Defined Contribution Plans

With respect to a defined contribution plan, an employer should disclose:

- The expense recognized for the period; and

- A description of the nature and effect of each significant change during the period that would affect the comparability of the expenses for the current and prior periods (such as a change in the rate of employer contributions).

Defined Benefit Plans

There are two levels of disclosures for defined benefit plans. Every entity is required to make a specified minimum level of disclosure. Another additional level of disclosure is required for public enterprises, co-operative organizations, deposit-taking institutions and life insurance enterprises. The minimum level of disclosures and additional disclosures is quite extensive. Examples of the minimum levels of disclosure for all entities include:

- The accrued benefit obligation at the end of the period, as determined by the actuarial valuation;

- The fair value of plan assets at the end of the period;

- The resulting plan surplus or deficit at the end of the period; and

- The amount recognized in the balance sheet at the end of the period as an accrued benefit liability or accrued benefit assets, indicating separately the amount of any valuation allowance, etc . . .

Significant Accounting Policies

Disclosure is required for any significant accounting policies that have been adopted in applying Section 3461. Examples of such disclosures include:

- The valuation basis chosen for plan assets for the purpose of calculating the expected return on plan assets;

- The method chosen for recognizing past service costs;

- The method chosen for recognizing actuarial gains and losses;

- The sequence in which a settlement and a curtailment are accounted;

- The use of defined contribution plan accounting by an entity that is part of a multi-employer plan for which the entity has insufficient information to apply defined benefit accounting; and

- The use of defined contribution plan accounting by an entity that is part of a multi-employer plan of a related group of companies.

Impact of CICA Handbook, Section 3461

One of the goals hoped to be achieved by Section 3461 was greater homogeneity of accounting of pension expenses, and thus, the allowance of a more meaningful comparison from year to year and between companies. Unfortunately, while Section 3461 has greatly improved the comparability of pension expense amounts from one organization to another, there is still discretion for organizations to make adjustments up or down. In fact, a recent survey conducted by Morneau Sobeco[3] on economic assumptions used by corporations to establish their pension expense reveals, for example, that the expected return on plan assets varies from about 7% to over 9%. Could this variation be explained only by different investment and asset mix policies?

---

[3] *Survey of Economic Assumptions under CICA section 3461 as of December 31, 2001*. This survey can be found on the Morneau Sobeco Web site at **www.morneausobeco.com**.

PENSION FUND INVESTMENT MANAGEMENT

As outlined in Chapter 4, there are three major components and responsibilities in the operation or governance of pension plans:

- Plan administration;

- Financial management; and

- Investment management of pension fund assets.

This chapter deals with the third component, pension fund investment management.

The financial structure of a pension plan can be captured by this simple equation:

The ultimate costs of the plan will be greatly influenced by the investment returns that are obtained on the fund. For example, an increase of 1% in the fund annual return might make it possible either to reduce the total costs by about 20%[1] or upgrade benefits significantly. If the employees are also contributing to the defined benefit plan, then the employer's cost savings will necessarily be greater than 20%.

Therefore, the soundness of the pension fund investment process is of great importance. Serious shortcomings in the process could not

---

[1] This calculation is based on the assumption that the money remains in the plan for approximately 18 years prior to retirement.

only lead to substantial increases in cost, but could also jeopardize the ability of the fund to deliver the benefits that have been promised.

This chapter will cover the regulatory environment of pension fund investment, the roles of the various parties in pension fund management, and the main elements of the investment management process for pension plans generally. It will also briefly discuss the specific issues related to fund investment for defined contribution arrangements.

Regulatory Environment

Investments of a pension plan must comply with the investment rules under the respective federal or provincial pension standards legislation. The Canada Customs and Revenue Agency (CCRA) also has rules that affect all plans.

The first level of legal constraint is fiduciary requirements of pension investment management. They are similar to those of other pension plan advisers. Persons having a fiduciary relationship to the beneficiaries of a pension fund include any person who has decision-making power with respect to the administration and investment of the fund, and may include:

• The pension committee;

• The trustee or custodian;

• The administrator;

• The investment managers; and

• Other advisors.

The fiduciary relationship can exist whether or not the relevant pension legislation contains an explicit provision to that effect.

The second level of legal constraint is the prudent person rule. It requires a person to exercise the care, diligence and skill in the investment of a pension fund that a person of ordinary prudence would exercise in dealing with the property of another person. It has been expressly adopted in the federal, British Columbia, Manitoba, Ontario, Quebec, Nova Scotia, New Brunswick and Prince Edward Island (to be proclaimed) legislation and may apply in some degree even without express legislative mandate where a fiduciary relationship exists.

The third level of legal constraint is the prudent portfolio rule. As with many other countries, Canada has moved away from the "legal for life" approach (explicitly regulating the quality of investments) to the "prudent portfolio" approach. This approach mainly relates to the overall reasonable level of risk the plan should undertake as a whole, and the appropriate level of diversification of the entire pension fund. Most of the provinces have adopted this approach in some form; however, some are more specific than others, and the provincial pension standards legislation does still contain some specific investment constraints, such as maximum allocations to real estate and resource property investments and maximum allocation to a single stock.

Further progress in relation to the prudent portfolio "cause" has been brought about by the recent passage of Bill 102 in Quebec, *An Act to Amend the Supplemental Pension Plans Act and other Legislative Provisions*. Prior to the amendments, the Quebec Act specified that a pension fund could not invest more than a maximum of 10% of the book value of the plan assets in any one property, group of properties, individuals, etc. This 10% rule was eliminated and replaced by a new "diversified" rule. Section 171.1 of the Act now states "Unless it is reasonable in the circumstances to act otherwise, the pension committee must endeavour to constitute a diversified portfolio so as to minimize the risk of major losses". However, the Quebec Act still prevents more than 10% of the plan's assets from being invested in securities controlled by the employer.

Roles of the Parties in Pension Fund Management

The appropriate investment management of pension fund assets necessitates the integration of two elements:

1. The establishment of a written investment policy statement that will establish guidelines (long-term asset mix target, investment constraints, diversification measures, etc.) for the investment of the pension fund, given the nature of the pension plan obligations, the objectives and risk tolerance of the parties involved, the risk/reward characteristics of asset classes, etc., and

2. The actual selection of securities within the guidelines set out in the investment policy.

The first element is clearly the responsibility of the plan sponsor or pension committee. It is, however, essential that the fund manager understands the investment policy. The manager can also contribute by providing its views on the risk/reward characteristics of the asset classes.

The second element is often delegated to the investment manager. The investment manager then explains its decisions to the plan sponsor or pension committee to allow them to understand the decisions, to ensure the investment manager complies with the policy and then to assess results obtained versus the objectives of the policy.

There are two other parties who may be involved in the management of the pension fund. The first is an investment advisor who helps integrate the plan sponsor's knowledge with investment-related knowledge in order to ensure that the pension fund investment management reflects its objectives and constraints.

The other is the custodian who is the safe keeper of all securities belonging to the pension fund. The pension fund assets are kept in trust by the custodian for the sole benefit of pension plan participants.

Elements of the Investment Management Process

Pension plans are increasingly viewed globally, in an asset/liability context. Therefore, the investment management process starts with the relationships existing between the nature of plan obligations, risk profile of parties involved and fund return objectives.

The investment management process can be illustrated as follows:

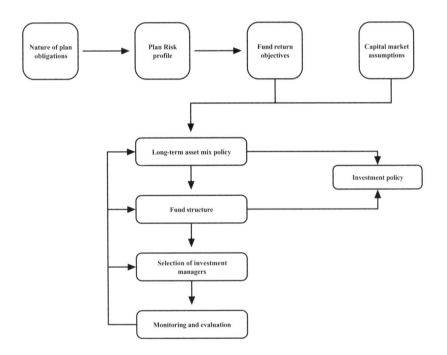

The nature of plan obligations can be defined as a set of specific characteristics, notably: the type of benefits, financial position of the plan, size of the plan relative to the overall company, plan demographics, liquidity requirements, etc. Parties directly involved in the pension plan are the sponsor, the pension committee and the plan members. Their attitude towards risk varies according to the above-noted characteristics, and could be assessed in many different ways, such as volatility of fund returns, volatility of annual contributions, volatility of pension expense, and level of assets versus liabilities.

Combining these factors with the long-term characteristics of financial markets helps to find the appropriate investment policy portfolio and fund structure that will best suit the plan's objectives.

The investment policy is the cornerstone of the investment process and consequently it should be well thought out and documented. Once the investment policy has been completed, investment managers must be selected. The search process should focus on the future; that is, only future performance matters, and past performance may not be predictive of future performance. Quantitative and qualitative criteria such as strength of the organization, decision-making process, and quality and stability of the investment management team should be used to determine a list of potential fund managers.

Once the investment process is in place, it must be monitored. Both the overall fund performance relative to the fund objectives and each manager's performance relative to that manager's specific mandate should be evaluated on a regular basis. The plan sponsor or committee should return to the qualitative and quantitative objectives and constraints set out in the investment policy to assess the success or failure of the investment policy as well as its implementation. At least annually, the plan sponsor or committee should review the policy objectives and guidelines to see if they are still appropriate given the plan's circumstances and any long-term structural changes in the capital markets.

Establishing Investment Policy

The investment policy is the starting point of the investment process, regardless of whether a statement of investment policy is legally required or not. The investment policy statement is a tool to help structure efficient management of the pension fund. A written statement of investment policy must be adopted for all provincial plans, with the exception of Prince Edward Island.

Normally, the investment policy statement will include:

- A description of the nature of the pension plan and its obligations;
- Allocation of responsibilities between the
  — pension committee,
  — management/board of trustees,
  — investment managers,
  — custodian/trustee,
  — consultants, and
  — other parties involved in the investment process;
- Quantitative objectives;
- The long-term asset mix;
- The classes and types of investments in which the plan may invest;
- Quantitative and qualitative constraints; and
- Other issues, such as statements on conflict of interest, lending of securities, delegation of voting rights and valuation of non-market securities.

Description of the Nature of the Pension Plan and Obligations

The description of the pension plan should outline the type of benefits offered, the level of benefit protection from inflation, the liability profile of the plan obligations, the financial position of the plan, the liquidity requirements for the following years, etc. All these characteristics have an impact on the choice of the long-term asset mix in which the fund will be invested.

Quantitative Objectives

When the analysis of plan characteristics is performed, the investment objective that would allow the plan to provide the desired level of benefits at an acceptable cost should be defined.

The quantitative investment objective of the fund should be expressed in straightforward and simple terms. Often, it only refers to the total fund return. It may be for the annual investment return to exceed the annual rate of inflation by a stated percentage (2, 3 or 4%) on average over the long term (10 years, for example).

Long-term Asset Mix

The long-term asset mix of the fund is a critical element that largely determines the performance success of the fund. Studies have found that asset mix policy accounts for a substantial portion of a fund's total return. The optimal portfolio is expected to achieve the stated investment objective with an acceptable level of risk.

Future performance of markets are unknown; assumptions regarding asset class characteristics have to be made in order to determine this optimal portfolio. These assumptions should recognize that a relationship between the level of investment returns and the level of risk taken (the risk-reward trade-off) is to be expected. This means that an asset class with a higher expected return tends to also provide more volatile returns.

Types of Investments In Which the Plan May Invest

The investment policy statement specifies broad asset classes in which the fund invests within the investment policy portfolio, such as fixed-income securities, domestic or foreign equities, real estate, etc. It should also specify the permitted investment categories within each asset class.

The fixed-income security component of total funds may include bonds, coupons and residuals, debentures, notes, mortgage loans, mortgage-backed securities, term deposits, guaranteed investment certificates and insurance contracts. Bonds are debt securities issued by a government or government agency, or by a corporation, with a maturity date and either a fixed or variable coupon rate. Mortgages are loans secured by property and pay a rate of interest periodically.

Equities may include common shares, rights, warrants and securities convertible into common shares. Common stocks represent shares of ownership in a firm, with limited liability. The historical return from this type of investment held over a long period has been higher than that of fixed-income investments such as bonds or short-term securities.

Short-term investments encompass highly liquid debt securities with term to maturity of less than one year. This category includes treasury bills, banker's acceptance and commercial paper.

Real estate investments are possible either directly or through a pooled fund. Some difficulties with this investment are illiquidity, lack of good pricing information and high transaction costs.

Derivatives could be used for hedging the portfolio risk, to replicate a market index or to synthetically change a portfolio's asset mix. Commonly used derivatives include future or forward contracts and options.

Pooled or mutual funds simplify pension fund investment and make self-administration possible for small funds. They may also be used in larger funds for all or part of the assets. A choice of pooled funds is available to the plan sponsor, who can direct the asset mix but need not be concerned with security selection.

Quantitative and Qualitative Constraints

Quantitative constraints limit risk exposure by setting minimum and maximum percentages that can be invested in any one asset category or specific security, thus ensuring reasonable diversification. While some constraints are legally required, others could be imposed by the plan sponsor or pension committee.

The provisions of the federal *Pension Benefits Standard Act* (PBSA) are typical. Under the PBSA, there is no limit on the total holdings of common stock, but a fund may invest only up to 10% of its book value in any one entity, with exceptions (for example, issues guaranteed by a government). A fund is also limited to a maximum of 5% of book value in any one parcel of real estate, a maximum of 15% of book value in resource properties, and a maximum of 25% of book value in the total of real estate, resource properties and mortgage investments. Further, a fund may not hold shares of a corporation that provide more than 30% of the votes necessary to elect the directors.

Currently, under the *Income Tax Act*, the limit on foreign investments is 30% of the book value of the total fund. Investments in excess of this limit incur a 1% per month penalty tax.

Finally, there will generally be constraints on investments in certain classes of securities. For example, the plan sponsor or pension committee may not want to hold bonds with less than an "A" credit rating, or stock in companies that damage the environment.

Once the investment policy has been adopted, it must be implemented and reviewed annually by the plan sponsor or the pension committee to ensure that it still meets the objectives of the plan, which may change over time.

Following the establishment of the investment policy, the plan sponsor or the pension committee will select investment managers who will apply investment strategies in compliance with the investment policy.

Selection of Investment Managers

As discussed earlier in this chapter, the plan sponsor or the pension committee has a fiduciary responsibility to the beneficiaries of the plan. They can delegate the investment management of the pension fund to outside investment managers. However, they are answerable for the care with which they select the investment managers, who play an important role in the implementation of the investment policy.

The plan sponsor or the pension committee also has a responsibility to protect the financial health of the corporation and the pension plan against the potentially damaging impact of insufficient investment returns on pension assets. The plan sponsor or the pension committee should therefore use a thorough process when selecting investment managers. The process should be based on criteria that reflect the investment management approaches they believe offer the highest probability of meeting the objectives of the investment policy.

The plan sponsor or the pension committee should focus on how to obtain acceptable returns in the future. It would be inappropriate to simply use relative measures of historical performance. Numerous studies have shown that there is almost no correlation between historical relative performance and future relative performance delivered by investment managers. Unfortunately, because past performance can be precisely measured and because it offers an easy answer, too much emphasis is often placed on its analysis. Understanding how the manager achieved investment performance provides far greater insight into the manager's potential to generate acceptable future returns than do relative measures of performance

A search process should start with a planning session in which the plan sponsor or the pension committee and investment advisors establish screening criteria based on their objectives concerning manager style, size of firm, etc. These criteria are used to screen the universe of managers and narrow down the number of managers to be considered (i.e., 10 managers) and who will finally be invited to submit a proposal.

Evaluation criteria are also determined during the planning session. They guide the plan sponsor or the pension committee and its investment advisor in selecting the managers. Detailed due diligence is performed to evaluate the candidate managers, and typically a shortlist is selected for interview, after which the successful candidate investment firm is hired. The selected manager will then be given a specific investment mandate that is in accordance with the investment policy.

A thorough selection process for an investment manager should emphasize the analysis of both qualitative (organization, philosophy, investment process, key personnel) and quantitative (performance and portfolio analysis) evaluation criteria. Establishing pertinent evaluation criteria based on the beliefs and investment objectives of pension plan sponsors or pension committees greatly facilitates the selection of the investment manager as well as the ongoing evaluation and monitoring of the manager's investment activities.

Monitoring Investment Performance

Monitoring and evaluating pension fund performance on an ongoing basis are key fiduciary duties. The monitoring process should be based on the criteria used in the manager selection process and the objectives and constraints of the investment policy.

Monitoring investment performance allows plan sponsors or pension committees to appraise the appropriateness of the investment policy and the effectiveness of its implementation. It can help plan sponsors or pension committees to review investment strategies and investment policy constraints in light of the actual performance achieved.

The evaluation process should attempt to increase the future performance of the pension fund at a level of risk acceptable to the pension plan and the plan sponsor.

The performance of the investment manager should also be regularly monitored. Manager performance should have as its goals:

- Ensuring that the manager's activities comply with the investment policy;
- Detecting problems before they can affect the performance;
- Ensuring the manager still meets the selection criteria; and
- Avoiding the unnecessary costly turnover of managers often resulting from only monitoring historical performance quantitatively.

The performance monitoring process should, therefore, combine a quantitative analysis of performance and portfolio attributes with an assessment of qualitative factors that may be key determinants of future performance.

Since there is no correlation between historical relative performance and future relative performance, the evaluation of a fund manager based on a mere analysis of historical returns may be misleading and inappropriate. The comparison of performance numbers of one portfolio with those of other pension funds can only provide general points of reference offering very limited insight, as they do not convey how the manager added value or what level of risk was sustained.

Furthermore, relative performance analysis does not recognize the particular circumstances, objectives and constraints of the fund under analysis.

An effective performance monitoring process usually contains the following steps:

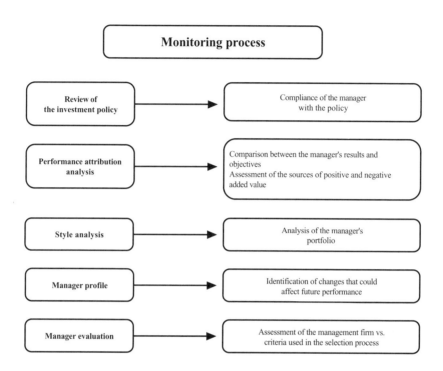

Defined Contribution Arrangements

The issues discussed in this chapter are also applicable to defined contribution arrangements (i.e., defined contribution pension plans, group RRSPs, etc.)

The appropriate management of fund assets is particularly important for these arrangements, since fund returns will have a direct impact on the benefit received by the plan participants. A sound and rigorous investment process is an essential component (some would say the most important) of a defined contribution arrangement.

In defined contribution RPPs, an employer may take responsibility for selecting investments, at least with respect to its contributions. More frequently, however, the employee will make the decisions regarding both his or her contributions (if there are any) and the employer's contributions.

The plan sponsor or pension committee has a very important role to play in:

- Deciding whether the selection of investment options should be made by plan participants or by the plan sponsor/pension committee;

- Deciding what options to offer to plan participants;

- Selecting the administrator, the issuer of guaranteed investment certificates and the investment managers;

- Providing plan members with proper communication/education on investment issues to help them make the best decision given their needs, risk tolerance and objectives; and

- Frequently monitoring the arrangement, the choice of investment options, fund managers and other issues.

Key decisions and guidelines regarding the investment of defined contribution arrangement assets should be clearly documented in an investment policy statement.

Recent Issues and Trends

Capital Accumulation Plans

In recent years, there has been a shift from defined benefit plans to defined contribution arrangements. Some employers cite the fact that both defined benefit and defined contribution RPPs are too regulated and complicated to administer under both federal and provincial legislation, not to mention the *Income Tax Act*. Additionally, plan sponsors have to guarantee the amount of benefit promised in a defined benefit plan, whereas with defined contribution arrangements, there is no obligation other than to contribute the stated amount. The increasing popularity of defined contribution arrangements (registered pension plans, as well as group RRSPs, DPSPs and EPSPs) is leading to increasing concern over the liability and responsibilities of employers.

After the demise of Enron in the United States, many employees began to wonder if the same situation could occur in Canada. The highly questionable actions of Enron executives led to the collapse of the company, and along with it, a significant portion of the employee's 401K retirement plans. According to the plan, employees were able to trade their investments on a daily basis, including any Enron stocks that were purchased with their own contributions. However, the Enron stock that was matched by the company could not be sold until the employee reached the age of 50. At the end of the year 2000, there were 21,000 estimated participants in Enron's 401K plan. Approximately 63% of all 401K stock, worth $1.3 billion, was invested in the company. Little did the employees realize that Enron would soon be facing the largest bankruptcy in American history. Even as late as September 26, 2001, the Chairman and CEO of Enron, Kenneth Lay, through a Web chat with employees, stated that Enron stock, which was then priced at $27/share was an "incredible bargain" and would significantly rise in value over the following years. Making matters worse, employees were barred from trading stock in their 401K plans between October 29 and November 13, 2001, as a result of a "lockout period" due to the switching of plan administrators. During that time, Enron stock had fallen. Shortly thereafter, Enron shares plunged to below $1/share from its peak of $90/share. On December 2, 2001, Enron filed for Chapter 11 bankruptcy protection. Amidst all of the unfolding drama, employees could only helplessly stand by and attempt to digest how their retirement savings and a Fortune 500 company had evaporated before their very eyes.

Could this occur in Canada? As far as defined contribution registered pension plans are concerned, the answer is no. As discussed previously, legislation prevents employees from investing more than 10% in the stock of their employer. However, group RRSPs and DPSPs are not subject to the same regulations as registered pension plans. Although company stock can be quite advantageous to the employee, it should not provide the basis for the employee's retirement funds. Enron is a perfect example of how that situation could play out — a double blow for the employee: no job and no retirement savings.

On April 27, 2001, the Joint Forum of Financial Market Regulators released a paper titled *Proposed Regulation Principles for Capital Accumulation Plans*[2]. As defined in the paper, a Capital Accumulation Plan (CAP) refers to "investment vehicles established by employers for the benefit of their employees that permit those employees to make investment decisions". The paper was designed to address the following issues:

- Employees need to have similar regulatory protection for similar products;

- Employees need to have sufficient information and tools to make investment decisions; and

- Plan sponsors need to have their duties clearly defined.

The Joint Forum outlined the four principles that could form the regulatory model for CAPs. These principles were mainly derived from the current securities, pension and insurance models and the U.S. ERISA (Employee Retirement Income Security Act of 1974) model. The fundamental principles for the proposed regulatory model are:

---

[2] The full text of this paper can be viewed in at the OSFI Web site at **www.fsco.gov.on.ca**.

1. Plan sponsor's obligations with respect to the establishment and maintenance of a CAP:

(a) select, for members, investment options that have a reasonable range of risk and return, each of which is diversified,

(b) prudently select and monitor the investment managers,

(c) permit members to switch between investment options without penalty and by providing them with a reasonable opportunity to do so, and

(d) if no prospectus is provided, ensure that contracts with a third-party provider/investment manager allow the plan sponsor to pursue an action on behalf of members for any misrepresentation regarding the investments;

2. Plan sponsor's duties with regards to providing a minimum level of disclosure for new CAP members and continuous disclosure requirements:

(a) the initial disclosure should include an explanation of the nature of the CAP; the liability of the members and employer for investments; a description of the investment options; instructions on how to make investment choices; information on transfer options, management and investment fee information; details of fund performance, including a discussion of performance against the established benchmarks; default options; a standardized consumer guide; and directions on how to obtain additional investment information,

(b) continuous disclosure should include annual statements summarizing member's account activity, financial statements, fund performance etc.;

3. The plan sponsor should ensure that CAP members may either rely on advice provided by a registered sales representative or advisor, or receive appropriate investment information from a party that owes a fiduciary duty to the members; and

4. The investment products or funds must comply with minimum standards[3].

The proposed principles regarding the plan sponsor's duty to monitor the investment managers and investment funds are somewhat similar to the Safe Harbour Rules under section $404(c)$ of ERISA. However, unlike the U.S. Safe Harbour rules there is no corresponding protection from liability when the specified requirements have been

---

[3] See "A Feather in Your CAP" by Lori Satov, CCH Canadian Limited's *Canadian Employment Benefits and Pension Newsletter*, July 2001, Issue #488.

met. Therefore, if the plan sponsor follows the principles outlined in the Joint Forum's report, they are not explicitly shielded from potential legal actions brought by their employees.

With the passage of Bill 102, *An Act to amend the Supplemental Pension Plans Act*, Quebec is leading the way in the establishment of minimum investment standards for defined contribution registered pension plans. The *Supplemental Pension Plans Act* (SPPA) states that where the plan permits members to make investment decisions, the plan must offer a minimum of three investment options. These options, in turn, must not only be "diversified and involve varying degrees of risk and expected return", but must also allow the "creation of portfolios that are generally well-adapted to the needs of members". It is also interesting to note that no "safe harbour" rules have been provided in the SPPA. Therefore, even if a plan sponsor complies with the minimum investment standards, there are no explicit guarantees that the plan sponsor will be shielded from legal action.

Socially Responsible Investing

Socially responsible investing (SRI) is a recent topic of discussion, one that we will likely hear more about in the future. There is no one uniform definition of SRI. However, socially responsible investing basically refers to a situation whereby certain social, economic or environmental criteria are factored into the investment decision-making process. Socially responsible investing includes three main mechanisms for promoting ethically responsible business practices: (1) screening, (2) shareholder advocacy and (3) community-based investing.

Screening involves using social, economic or environmental criteria in the selection of investments. There are two types of screens: negative and positive. Negative screens exclude companies who fail to meet certain criteria. Therefore, a company involved in activities specified by the investor as undesirable would be excluded from the investment portfolio. For example, typical screening criteria would exclude companies involved in such activities as tobacco, child labour, or the manufacture of alcohol or pornography.

Positive screens include companies who meet certain defined criteria and are thus included in the investment portfolio. For example, a company that is regarded as having exceptional employee relations practices or that supports environmental sustainability would be included in portfolios. On the downside, it is argued that screening may affect the range of industries included in a portfolio. It might be biased towards smaller companies as opposed to larger companies, who will more likely be involved in a wide range of activities, some of which might fail the screening criteria. Such portfolios might therefore simply be unacceptable to certain investors. As a result, many SRI funds use a "best-of-sector" screening approach, which ensures that no industry is completely excluded for investment. In this case the portfolio might have shares in a company that may fail the desired requirements, but that is the least ethically offensive in the industry.

Typical Canadian Screens[4]

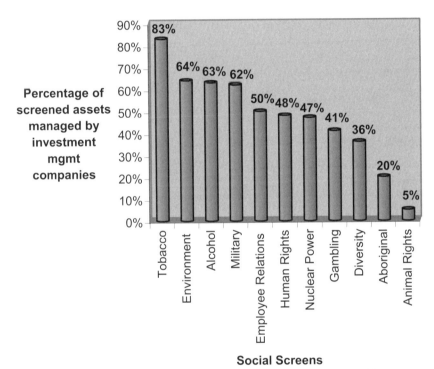

Social Screens
Source: Canadian Social Investment Review 2000

Shareholder advocacy is action taken by shareholders to make the company aware of their social, economic or environmental concerns. This can be accomplished through communications with the company to persuade management to alter its behaviour. It can also be achieved through shareholder proposals and through the selling of shares, if the company refuses to alter its behaviour.

---

[4] The Canadian Social Investment Review 2000 can be viewed at **www.socialinvestment.ca**. Also see "Socially Responsible Investing: Better For Your Soul or Your Bottom Line?", Paul Asmundson and Stephen R. Foerster, *Canadian Investment Review*, Winter 2001, Volume 14, Number 4. The article can be viewed at **www.investment review.com/archives/2001/winter/index.html**.

Community-based investing involves investing in community development or entrepreneurial businesses, often providing loans to those who would find it difficult to obtain funding through normal means.

A source of considerable debate is whether SRI investing is permissible in the pension plan context, which is subject to certain investment constraints (i.e., "prudent person" rule). There is no clear answer. Most regulators suggest that SRI is not in and of itself imprudent, so long as its usage does not compromise the plan sponsor's obligations. The Public Finance Committee of Quebec released a consultation paper in May 2002 entitled *Corporate Social Responsibility and Socially Responsible Investment*[5]. The paper addresses, among other issues, socially responsible investing and pension funds. Questions asked in the paper are:

- Is social investment compatible with protecting the interests of pension fund contributors?

- Should pension funds be required to report their social investments?

It is noted in the consultation paper that in some European countries, pension plan sponsors must reveal their social investment policies in their general investment policy. It is believed that by creating this requirement, contributors will be made aware of the possibility of adopting socially responsible investment principles. The Public Finance Committee of Quebec will be holding hearings in the fall of 2002 regarding corporate social responsibility and socially responsible investment.

Generally in Canada, one notes that in the absence of a precise definition of fiduciary duties, a number of pension fund managers do not believe they have enough freedom to consider social responsibility in their decisions. This is thus an obstacle to increasing corporate social responsibility.

Corporate Social Responsibility and Socially Responsible Investment, Quebec Committee on Public Finance's consultation paper, May 2002.

---

[5] This paper can be viewed in its entirety at **www.assnat.qc.ca/eng/Publications/rapports /concfp1.htm**.

Arguments abound as to whether or not the returns achieved by investing in SRI funds outperform, underperform or perform the same as non-SRI investments. Opponents will argue that SRI investing will necessarily restrict the investment options of the investment manager, and therefore likely cause underperformance. On the other hand, proponents of SRI will argue that because the companies selected will overall be better companies (environmentally friendly, employees treated well, etc.), the socially responsible investments should actually outperform non-SRI investments over the longer term. The results thus far have not been totally conclusive, although at least one Canadian research paper has concluded that on average, those who invest in Canadian SRI mutual funds, at least, are neither losing nor gaining anything with respect to financial returns[6]. The authors concluded "At this relatively early stage, it appears that investing for the soul may not hurt the bottom line, particularly when risk exposure is taken into account"[7].

[6] "Socially Responsible Investing: Better for Your Soul or Your Bottom Line?", Paul Asmundson and Stephen R. Foerster, *Canadian Investment Review*, Winter 2001, Volume 14, Number 4. The article can be viewed at **www.investmentreview.com/archives/2001/winter/index.html**.

[7] *Ibid.*

Chapter 7

REGISTRATION OF PENSION PLANS UNDER THE *INCOME TAX ACT* AND TAXATION OF RETIREMENT SAVINGS

History of Registration of Pension Plans

To obtain preferred tax treatment, a pension plan must be accepted for registration by the Canada Customs and Revenue Agency (CCRA), formerly Revenue Canada. Once registration has been granted, it is usually continued without further review unless the plan is amended. The registration rules are intended to limit the type and extent of benefits that may be paid from a registered pension plan, thereby limiting tax assistance and deferrals.

Contributions to a registered pension plan are deductible up to certain limits, and benefits are fully taxable to employees when paid. Income and capital gains earned by investing the assets of a registered pension plan are not taxable.

From 1972 to 1990, the registration rules for pension plans were not formally included in the *Income Tax Act*, but were described in an Information Circular, the last edition being Information Circular 72–13R8. The Information Circulars are tools for circulating the CCRA's views and administrative policies, and do not constitute laws. It was the practice of pension plan sponsors to conform to the rules set out in the Circular, but as time passed, the government decided that the preferred way to regulate pension plans was to give the rules the force of law by including them in the *Income Tax Act* and Regulations.

On June 27, 1990, the Government of Canada passed Bill C-52, *An Act to Amend the Income Tax Act and Related Acts*. This legislation significantly changed the system for granting tax assistance for retirement savings, but also incorporated into law some of the old, and many new, plan registration rules.

The government's stated objectives in implementing the new regime were:

- To establish a tax framework to encourage increased private retirement savings;

- To eliminate inequities that resulted in some taxpayers being unable to benefit from as much tax assistance as others, depending on the type of their pension and retirement savings plans;

- To enhance the flexibility in the timing of retirement savings; and

- To introduce a system under which dollar limits on contributions and benefits are adjusted for inflation and therefore do not decline in real value. (This objective has been undermined in recent budgets.)

In this chapter, we outline the main provisions of the legislation, the rules for registration of pension plans as well as the taxation of registered pension plans.

Retirement Savings Limits

The legislation is based on the principle that tax assistance should be the same for all individuals with the same incomes, whether they save for retirement through participation in a defined contribution pension plan, a defined benefit pension plan, a Registered Retirement Savings Plan (RRSP), a Deferred Profit Sharing Plan (DPSP), or through a combination of these plans.

The system of retirement saving limits became effective for the 1991 tax year. The following is an outline of the provisions that apply these savings limits to contributors to RRSPs and members of registered pension plans (RPPs) and DPSPs.

Comprehensive Savings Limit

There is a comprehensive savings limit, regardless of whether contributions are made by the individual or an employer, equal to 18% of earned income, subject to a dollar maximum. Tax preferences are not given to retirement savings contributions above these limits.

Pension Adjustments

The system requires that accruals under pension plans in each year be converted to approximate lump-sum values. The approximate lump-sum value, known as a Pension Adjustment (PA), is then compared to the individual's savings limit (referred to in the paragraph above) in order to ascertain whether the plan member has reached his or her annual comprehensive savings limit. To determine in each year the permitted RRSP contribution for an individual who is a member of an RPP or a DPSP, the individual's accrued retirement savings limit for the year is reduced by the individual's previous year's PA.

PAs were first calculated and reported for 1990, affecting 1991 RRSP limits.

In a defined contribution pension plan, the PA is the total of employer and employee contributions in the year. In a DPSP, which has no employee contributions, the PA is equal to the employer contributions on behalf of the employee.

In a defined benefit pension plan, the PA is nine times the approximate amount of annual pension accrued in the year, minus $600. This formula applies regardless of the design of the defined benefit plan, and whether or not the employee is vested. The factor of 9 was chosen as an appropriate average factor to produce the approximate value or cost of a dollar of lifetime pension income under the most generous defined benefit pension plan permitted under the registration rules. The factor, while appropriate for estimating the value of generous plans for employees who participate over their full careers in those plans, is unfortunately applied to value accruals under all defined benefit pension plans, even those less-generous plans, and is applied to employees of all ages. The factor of 9 overvalues the pension accruals in most private-sector defined benefit plans, and particularly overvalues pension accruals for younger employees who most likely will not remain in the same pension plan for their full careers.

The PA is calculated with regard to the individual's "pensionable earnings" in earnings-based defined benefit plans, without projection for future pay increases. Hence, the PA formula does not distinguish between career earnings and final earnings plans, the assumption being that a career earnings plan will probably be updated so as to give much the same result as a final earnings plan.

The 1997 federal budget introduced an adjustment known as a Pension Adjustment Reversal (PAR) to deal with concerns that the factor of 9 used in the defined benefit PA calculation was producing unfair results. The PAR effectively increases the RRSP contribution limit if an employee ceases (after 1996 and before retirement) to be entitled to a benefit under a DPSP or a benefit provision of an RPP.

Prior to 1997 there were special rules that applied when a DPSP or RPP member terminated employment but was not vested. However, beginning in 1997, these special rules have been eliminated as the result of the introduction of PARs. The PA for member of a DPSP or RPP, whose employment is terminated and is not vested is determined in the usual manner.

Taxpayers who do not contribute the maximum allowed for a year to their RRSPs have the right to carry forward indefinitely the unused RRSP contribution room for use in subsequent years.

Employers operating RPPs or DPSPs are required to report the PAs of plan members to the CCRA on a T-4 slip by the end of February each year. These reports are used by the government to calculate the RRSP contribution room for the following year.

Past Service Pension Adjustments

If an employer amends an RPP to increase pensions already earned, a Past Service Pension Adjustment (PSPA) is created. The PSPA is the difference between the sum of PAs actually reported for the earned pensions, and the sum of the PAs that would have been reported for that period had pensions been earned at the upgraded level. PSPAs generally reduce the amount that the employee may contribute to an RRSP, and are applied against unused RRSP contribution room. A PSPA is generally created if the benefit formula in a defined benefit pension plan is increased, or if past service benefits are added for years after 1989. However, a PSPA does not arise if ancillary benefits are improved, such as early retirement subsidies or increased death benefits. PSPAs are not created by upgrading pensions in any way for service before 1990 (although other restrictions apply to upgrades of pre-1990 service.

There are two types of PSPAs:

1. PSPA's requiring certification, and

2. Reportable PSPAs.

Past service upgrades that are applicable to one employee or a small number of employees fall under the first category, and requires certification. Where the past service upgrades affect most of the employees who are members of the plan (and if relatively few of those employees are highly paid) then the PSPA must be reported, but does not need to be certified.

With respect to certification, the administrator must calculate the PSPA for the employees and then report that amount to the CCRA using form T1004. Certification will be granted, an increased past service benefit can be paid to the member and the benefit can be funded by additional contributions, if it is determined that the PSPA does not exceed the sum of $8,000 plus the member's unused RRSP contribution room. A PSPA can cause a negative RRSP contribution room balance of up to $8,000, which reduces the taxpayer's RRSP contribution limit in future years.

If the PSPA for a member exceeds the above amounts (i.e., if the PSPA is more than $8,000 greater than the available contribution room), the member may create PSPA room by withdrawing funds from his or her RRSP in order to bring the amount below the exceeded amount. The employee will be taxed on any such withdrawals.

Past service upgrades granted in respect of service after 1990 may be paid and funded without certification by the Minister if all of the following conditions are met:

- There are at least 10 active members accruing benefits under the provisions being upgraded;

- No more than 25% of the members receiving the upgrade are "specified individuals" (i.e., those who are expected to earn more than 2.5 times of the YMPE in the year of improvement)

- Substantially all active plan members will receive upgraded past service benefits; and

- Disproportionate benefits are not payable to high earners, or to active versus inactive members.

The administrator is still required to report the PSPAs, even if certification is not required. Certification is not required if the above rules are followed, even where the upgrade results in a negative balance of unused RRSP contribution room in excess of $8,000.

Pension Adjustment Reversal (PAR)

The PAR restores RRSP contribution room that was eliminated as a result of pension adjustments. The PAR is the amount that will restore RRSP deduction room to an employee who terminates employment or retires before the normal retirement age, and who receives a termination benefit that is less than the taxpayer's total pension adjustments and past service pension adjustments. If the PAR did not exist, and the employee's benefit was considerably less than the PAs that had been reported, the employee would have suffered in relation to his or her RRSP contribution room; however, with the introduction of the PAR in 1997, this problem was corrected. If the employee's reported PAs exceed the value of the benefits received at termination, the employee will be credited with a PAR. The PAR, in turn, will permit the employee to make additional contributions to an RRSP, which were previously lost due to the reporting of PAs. The intent behind the PAR is to recognize the fact that PAs are often overstated for members of defined benefit pension plans (as a result of the factor of 9 calculation), as well as for employees who terminate employment from a defined contribution pension plan or a DPSP before becoming fully vested.

Contribution Limits to Registered Plans

The current contribution limits are:

- For RRSPs, 18% of earned income in the previous calendar year, subject to the following dollar limits; and

- For defined contribution RPPs, 18% of remuneration in the year, subject to the following dollar limits:

Year	DC RPPs	RRSPs
1996	$ 13,500	$ 13,500
1997	13,500	13,500
1998	13,500	13,500
1999	13,500	13,500
2000	13,500	13,500
2001	13,500	13,500
2002	13,500	13,500
2003	14,500	13,500
2004	15,500	14,500
2005	indexed	15,500
2006		indexed

From 2005 for defined contribution RPPs, and from 2006 for RRSPs, the dollar limits will be increased according to increases in the average wage.

The DPSP dollar limit continues to be set at half of the dollar limit for money purchase pension plans in each year.

Registration Rules and Contribution Limits for Pension Plans

The policy of the federal government to examine pension plans arose during and shortly after World War II. At that time, Canada had a wage freeze and an excess profit tax, but no restrictions on employee benefits. As a result, corporations were tempted to pay large and perhaps unnecessary sums to pension plans, the actual cost to the shareholders being next to nothing.

Over the years, the government became increasingly concerned that pension plans should be *bona fide* as opposed to a device to avoid tax on savings, and that the tax-deductible contributions should not exceed amounts that it considered reasonable in the circumstances. The allowable contributions are described later in this chapter.

A policy of requiring a pension plan to also obtain registration under the provincial or federal pension standards legislation (where there is such legislation applicable to members of the plan) before it is granted registration for tax purposes has been followed.

Regulations to the *Income Tax Act* to prescribe registration rules for pension plans were introduced in December 1989, and apply to all benefits provided under pension plans submitted to the CCRA for registration on or after March 28, 1988, as well as to benefits accruing for service after 1991 under defined benefit pension plans submitted for registration prior to March 28, 1988. However, the guidelines outlined in Information Circular 72–13R8 continue to be applied to benefits accrued for service prior to January 1, 1992 under defined benefit pension plans submitted for registration prior to March 28, 1988. For all defined contribution pension plans, the new rules became law on June 27, 1990, but some rules are retroactive to January 1, 1989.

Failure to adhere to the registration rules at any time after initial registration causes the plan's registered status to become revocable. If the plan's registration is revoked, the arrangement will then be classified as a retirement compensation arrangement from the date it ceases to comply with the rules, and becomes subject to different tax treatment.

The new regulations apply to three categories, as follows:

1. All pension plans;

2. Defined contribution pension plan provisions (DC); or

3. Defined benefit pension plan provisions (DB).

Some of the more important registration rules are described below, but the descriptions are not comprehensive descriptions of all the registration rules. When trying to determine if a particular provision would be permitted, reference should also be made to Chapter 8, which deals with pension standards legislation for all of the jurisdictions.

Rules and Limits Applicable to All Pension Plans

Primary Purpose to Provide Pension Benefits

The primary purpose of a registered pension plan is the provision after retirement of pensions to employees. The pensions must be payable for the employee's lifetime in equal periodic amounts, except where they are adjusted for inflation or reduced after the death of the member or his or her spouse. Additional reasons for varying the amount of pension benefit have recently been added to the Income Tax Regulations.

Pension Commencement Date

Employees are not permitted to participate in RPPs after the end of the year in which they reach age 69, and must start to receive pensions by that date.

Non-Assignability of Rights Under a Pension Plan

All RPPs must include a specific clause prohibiting plan members from assigning or transferring to another, or pledging as security for a debt, their rights under the pension plan. Similarly, plan members cannot surrender or voluntarily forfeit their pension rights. Creditors cannot charge, or apply to seize a member's rights under an RPP in order to satisfy debts owed by the plan member. However, these provisions do not prevent the assignment of benefits pursuant to a court order or settlement agreement upon the breakdown of a marriage or conjugal relationship. It also does not prohibit garnishment of pension benefits for maintenance, nor does it prohibit the distribution of benefits by a deceased plan member's legal representative.

Investments

RPPs must comply with all minimum standards investment regulations of the jurisdictions of registration. As well, the *Income Tax Act* registration rules prohibit RPP assets from being invested in shares or debt instruments of any plan member, any employer who participates in the plan, and generally, any individual connected or related to a plan member or participating employer. The prohibition, however, does not extend to shares or debt obligations of a participating employer where the shares of the corporate employer are listed on a prescribed stock exchange inside or outside of Canada.

An RPP is not permitted to borrow funds, except:

- Where the term of the loan does not exceed 90 days and, if the loan is not used to provide currently payable benefits, none of the RPP's assets are used as security for the loan; or

- Where the borrowed money is used to acquire real property, as long as no RPP asset other than the real property acquired is used as security for the loan.

The *Income Tax Act* limits investments of registered pension fund assets in foreign property to 30% of the pension fund, measured by the original cost of the assets in the fund. Where foreign content in the fund exceeds 30%, a penalty tax is assessed.

Administration

RPPs must be administered pursuant to the provisions of the plan text as registered with the CCRA. Failure to administer in accordance with the registered plan text will place the RPP's registration in a revocable status.

The provisions of an RPP must include the designation of a specific administrator who is responsible for the overall operation and administration of the RPP, and for filing information returns about the RPP to the CCRA . The administrator may be a participating employer, a Canadian resident, or a group of persons, the majority of whom reside in Canada. Non-Canadian administrators are permitted with the permission of the CCRA.

Contributions

An RPP must require the employer to contribute. If employees are required or permitted to contribute, the documents must contain specific information on the amount and nature of contributions. A plan can be designed that neither requires nor permits employee contributions.

Contributions must be made in accordance with the terms of the plan as registered and are subject to the relevant PA limits.

Rules and Limits Applicable to Defined Contribution Pension Plan Provisions

Contributions

Employer contributions must be made in respect of particular employees, and must be allocated to the employees with respect to whom they are made. Unallocated contributions cannot be made.

Employer contributions cannot be made at a time when there is surplus in a defined contribution plan that has not been allocated to employees' accounts, or while there are unallocated pre-1990 forfeited amounts. Amounts forfeited after 1989 by plan members who terminate employment before vesting, and earnings thereon must be reallocated to plan members, used to pay administrative expenses of the plan, used to satisfy the employer's contribution obligations, or refunded to the employer before the end of the year following the year of forfeiture.

All contributions and forfeitures allocated to an employee's credit must be included in the PA of the employee.

Lifetime Pensions

Pensions must be provided by the purchase of annuities from a person licensed or otherwise authorized under the laws of Canada or a province to sell life annuities (generally life insurance companies). While the regulations provide that pensions may also be provided by other means acceptable to the Minister of National Revenue, the Minister has not yet established policies to permit other methods.

Generally, pensions must be payable in equal periodic amounts for the member's lifetime. However, the defined contribution pension plan regulations permit the payment of certain other benefits that are not payable for the duration of the member's life, or that cause the pension to be payable in unequal amounts, in addition to ordinary lifetime pension benefits. For example, pension benefits may be increased as a result of increases in the cost of living, as measured by the Consumer Price Index, or increased at a rate specified in the pension plan terms, where the rate cannot exceed 4% per annum. Temporary bridge benefits may be provided to a member retiring before normal pensionable age, ending no later than the end of the month following the month in which the member reaches age 65, to bridge the time until Old Age Security and Canada Pension Plan benefits start at age 65. These ancillary benefits, payable in addition to the lifetime retirement pension, must be provided by the balance in the member's account. As defined contribution benefits are limited by the contributions and earnings in each member's account, bridging benefits will only be paid out to the extent that the lifetime benefits are actuarially reduced.

Pre-Retirement Death Benefits

In the event that the employee dies before starting to receive the pension, the defined contribution plan must provide a pension to the surviving spouse.

The federal government introduced Bill C-23, the *Modernization of Benefits and Obligations Act,* which received Royal Assent on June 29, 2000. This legislation extends the tax treatment now available to common-law couples to all common-law partners, regardless of gender, as long as they have lived in a conjugal relationship for at least one year or as long as they have lived in a conjugal relationship and have a child in common (the definition is in subsection 248(1) of the *Income Tax Act* under "common-law partner").

The pension can be paid out in any form — other than joint and survivor — that would have been allowed paid to the member. For example, it could be in the form of a pension guaranteed for up to 15 years. Pension payments to the surviving spouse must begin no later than the end of the year when the spouse reaches 69, or, if the spouse has already reached 69 years of age at the time of the member's death, it must begin within one year of such death.

The defined contribution plan may also permit a lump-sum payment to be made to the spouse or to a beneficiary. It cannot be in excess of the amount in the member's account. The spouse, but not a beneficiary who is not a spouse, can transfer the lump-sum benefit to his or her RRSP.

Post-Retirement Death Benefits

A retiring plan member may elect to receive a form of lifetime pension that provides a death benefit to his or her beneficiary. The pension can be guaranteed for up to 15 years from the date the pension commences; if the plan member should die before 15 years of pension payments, the designated beneficiary will receive the remainder of the 15 years of payments. Under this form of guarantee, the retiree may select any individual to receive any benefits that may be payable after the retiree's death. Additionally, if the plan member has a spouse, he or she may elect a form of joint and survivor life annuity, whereby the pension is payable for the retiree's life, and after the retiree's death, the pension will continue in the same or in a lower amount to a surviving spouse.

Minimum pension standards legislation often further restricts the payment options on the death of a member by requiring payment of death benefits to the member's surviving spouse; however, some jurisdictions may permit the spouse to waive his or her entitlement to the survivor pension.

In the case where the retirement benefits have been guaranteed, rather than continuing payments, the commuted value of the remaining payments may be paid in a lump sum to a surviving spouse or a beneficiary. If a lump sum is payable, only the spouse of the member is permitted to transfer the amount to his or her own RRSP.

Rules and Limits Applicable to Defined Benefit Pension Plan Provisions

Eligible Service

Defined benefit pension plan formulas are calculated with reference to the duration of employment. Pensions must be earned relatively evenly over a number of years of service; the registration rules prohibit granting large pensions for only a few years of service. As well, the registration rules permit pension accrual for "eligible service" only.

Eligible service is employment in Canada with an employer who participates in the pension plan, or with a predecessor employer whose business has been acquired by the participating employer. Periods of absence from active employment due to disability qualify as eligible service, regardless of the duration of the disability. Periods of unpaid leave of absence from employment for reasons other than disability qualify as eligible service, subject to an overall lifetime limit on such unpaid leaves of five years, plus up to three additional years for parental leaves.

Service with a former employer can count as eligible service in the current employer's pension plan if the service was included in pensionable service under the former employer's pension plan and the plan member does not retain rights to benefits from that former employer's pension plan.

In certain circumstances, employment outside of Canada can be included as eligible service.

Maximum Benefit Accrual Rate

Where the pension benefit formula under a defined benefit pension plan is based on the member's remuneration, the annual benefit accrual rate cannot exceed 2% of such remuneration.

Post-Retirement Increases to Reflect Cost of Living Increases

After retirement, pensions can be indexed to reflect increases in the cost of living. The most common indexing formulas are based on increases in the Consumer Price Index, or the increases can be set at a certain rate per annum, with such rate not to exceed 4% per annum from the date the pension commences to be paid. Another indexing formula, the "excess earnings" approach, is also permitted. There are certain restrictions that also apply.

Early Retirement Lifetime Pension

An employee may retire and receive a lifetime pension commencing prior to normal retirement age. In this circumstance, the registration rules permit the plan to provide either a benefit that is reduced by virtue of its earlier commencement, or, in certain circumstances, the accrued pension without reduction, subject to restrictions. To receive the accrued pension, without reduction, before normal retirement age, the employee must have satisfied one of the following criteria:

- Attainment of age 60 at pension commencement date;
- 30 years of service; or
- Age plus years of service totalling 80 or more.

For employees in public safety occupations (firefighters, police officers, commercial pilots, corrections officers and air traffic controllers) the criteria are:

- Age 55;
- 25 years of service; or
- Age plus service totalling 75 or more.

If a reduced early retirement pension is provided, the reduction must at least equal 0.25% for each month by which the pension commencement date precedes the earliest date at which an unreduced pension could have been paid. This is quite a generous standard, since many pension plans provide a much greater reduction on early retirement.

Bridge Benefits

Bridge benefits are paid at any time during the period after early pension commencement until the member attains age 65. This allows an income supplement to be paid until the member can collect Old Age

Security benefits and the full unreduced Canada Pension Plan retirement pension.

There is a ceiling on the amount of bridge benefits that may be paid from a defined benefit registered pension plan. The maximum amount of periodic bridge benefit payments is restricted to the sum of the Canada Pension Plan and Old Age Security benefits the member would be able to receive if he or she were age 65 at the date the bridge benefit commences. However, if the plan member has not attained age 60, or has not completed at least 10 years of pensionable service, the maximum bridge benefit is reduced by:

- 0.25% for each month by which the bridge benefit commencement date precedes age 60; and

- If the member has less than 10 years of service, the maximum bridging benefit is also reduced on a prorated basis.

The limit above describes the maximum bridging benefit that a defined benefit plan can provide without affecting the member's lifetime pension. Bridging benefits in excess of that amount are, however, permitted where the portion of the bridging benefit that exceeds the amount determined under this maximum bridging benefit formula is provided in place of a part of the member's lifetime retirement benefit. The member's lifetime benefit reduction will be calculated on an actuarially equivalent basis. However, in total, the bridging benefit cannot exceed 40% of the YMPE for the year when the bridging benefit begins.

Disability Benefits

If an employee is unable to perform the duties of employment as a result of a physical or mental impairment, a defined benefit pension plan may permit the employee to continue accruing pension benefits for the period of disability. The plan may require the disabled employee to continue making the ordinary contributions to the pension plan, or may waive contributions for the period of disability.

An employee who is unable, by reason of physical or mental impairment, to engage in any employment for which he or she is reasonably suited by education or experience, and who can reasonably be expected to remain disabled until death is totally and permanently disabled for the purpose of the registration rules, and may continue to receive pension accruals, as is the case with a disabled employee, or may instead receive an immediate lifetime disability pension. The pension plan may provide the full accrued pension to the totally and permanently disabled employee, unreduced by reason of its early commencement. The normal rules regarding when an unreduced early retirement pension may commence do not apply to a member who is totally and permanently disabled.

The maximum annual lifetime retirement benefit that may be paid to an individual who is totally and permanently disabled is equal to the greater of

(a) the accrued benefits at the time of the disability retirement, without reduction for early retirement, and

(b) the lesser of:

(i) the projected pension that would otherwise have been earned by the employee under the pension plan at age 65, assuming no increase in pay; and

(ii) the Year's Maximum Pensionable Earnings for the year in which disability pension payments start.

The determination of whether an employee is disabled or totally and permanently disabled must be made by the plan administrator, based upon the written report of a medical doctor.

Pre-Retirement Death Benefits

When an employee dies before pension commencement, the plan can provide that a designated beneficiary or spouse receive, in a single lump-sum payment, the value of part or all of the employee's accrued pension (see the discussion regarding the definition of spouse at page 157 under "Pre-Retirement Death Benefits" for defined contribution plans). In the alternative, a lump-sum payment, equal to twice the member's own required contributions to the plan plus interest, may be paid.

Lump-sum payments may be tax-sheltered through transfer to an RRSP or a RRIF, or to another plan only if the beneficiary is the deceased member's spouse. In certain circumstances the Minister of National Revenue's approval will be required to transfer the lump sum to another registered retirement savings vehicle. Where the member was a parent or grandparent and a lump sum is paid out as a result of his or her death to a financially dependent child or grandchild, an offsetting tax deduction is available. This deduction is available if the child or grandchild acquires an annuity for a fixed number of years, not exceeding 18 minus his or her age at the time when the annuity is acquired. The annuity must be purchased in the same year in which the lump sum is included in the child's or grandchild's taxable income, or within 60 days after the end of that year.

In lieu of paying a single lump-sum payment to a beneficiary or surviving spouse, the plan may provide a surviving spouse with an immediate pension equal to up to 66⅔% of the pension accrued to the plan member. The survivor's pension may be paid to the spouse for life, and to eligible dependants for the period during which they remain dependent. A dependant can include a parent, grandparent, brother, sister, or a child or grandchild who was dependent on the member for support at the time of the member's death. The survivor's pension must end once a person no longer qualifies as a dependant. If the survivor's pension is payable to more than one person, the level of survivor's pension can be increased to up to 100% of the pension accrued to the employee at date of death. No more than two-thirds of the accrued pension may be paid to any one particular beneficiary. If the survivor pension is payable to a spouse or former spouse, the lifetime pension can be paid to the spouse in a form that is guaranteed for up to fifteen years.

Post-Retirement Death Benefits

In the case of a member's death following the commencement of pension benefits, a pension plan may provide post-retirement survivor benefits to the spouse and dependants of the deceased member. An employee's pension may be guaranteed for up to 15 years after the date on which the pension commences, if paid in the form of an annuity payable for a single life. Any remaining guaranteed payments after the member's death may continue to be paid to the beneficiary, or may be commuted and paid in a lump sum.

The surviving spouse pension generally cannot exceed 66⅔% of the pension previously payable to the employee, with a maximum guarantee of five years. However, if the employee elects a reduced lifetime pension, the surviving spouse may receive up to 100% of the pension previously payable to the employee or a longer guarantee (up to 15 years).

Survivor benefits to an eligible spouse may continue for the spouse's remaining lifetime, whereas survivor benefits to a dependant may only continue for the eligible survivor period of the dependant. This period ends at the end of the year in which the dependant reaches age 18, or the time at which the dependant ceases to be a full-time student. However, if the dependant is infirm, the payments may continue for as long as the infirmity continues.

Total monthly payments to the spouse and any beneficiary after the survivor pension has begun are not permitted to exceed the total monthly benefits that would be payable to the member if the member were alive. It is also important to note that a plan may provide a guarantee that total payments in respect of a member will not be less than the member's contributions with interest.

Benefits on Termination of Employment

On termination of employment before retirement, a pension plan may provide a deferred pension, or one of the following alternate payments:

- Refund of employee contributions with interest;

- A refund equal to twice employee contributions with interest, if certain conditions are met; or

- A lump-sum payment equal to the value of the pension accrued to the employee at date of termination of employment.

Termination benefits are also subject to pension standards legislation.

Commutation of Pension

Under the *Income Tax Act* regulations, a member may commute all or any portion of his or her pension either before or after the pension has started. However, the right to commute one's pension is also governed by pension standards legislation that restricts the right to commute. The restrictions in those statutes place much greater control over the circumstances under which a pension plan member is able to commute his or her pension.

Plan Participation After Retirement

An employee cannot continue to accrue further defined benefit pension benefits for a period of employment after the employee has started receiving pension payments. However, if the pensioner subsequently is re-employed by his or her previous employer, and wishes to recommence participation in the defined benefit RPP, the member may elect to suspend payment of the pension. In that case, he or she would be permitted to recommence participation in the plan and earn further pension credits. Additionally, the restriction does not apply to accrual of benefits under a defined contribution provision. As a result, after a member commences receiving a defined benefit retirement pension, he or she could begin to accrue benefits under a defined contribution provision.

According to the CCRA, Quebec's recent phased-retirement provisions, which permit an early benefit during the phase-in period prior to retirement, do not contravene the above mentioned rule regarding accruing pensions and receiving payments simultaneously. (For more information on Quebec's phased retirement, refer to Chapter 2.) The CCRA stated that it considers the early benefit as a partial commutation as opposed to a retirement benefit or pension.

Maximum Pension Rules

A defined benefit pension plan is limited in the amount of pension it may provide. At the time of pension commencement, the lifetime pension paid to an employee cannot exceed the lesser of:

- $1,722.22 multiplied by the employee's years of pensionable service; and

- 2% of the employee's highest average indexed compensation, multiplied by the employee's years of pensionable service.

The "highest average indexed compensation" is equal to the average of the best three non-overlapping, 12-month periods of the employee's highest compensation. The 12-month periods are not required to be consecutive. The indexed compensation for a given month is the compensation actually paid in that month, updated to the year of pension commencement to reflect post-1986 increases in the average industrial wage.

There is a different limit with respect to the pension granted after 1989 for years of past service before 1990 in which the employee did not participate in any RPP or deferred profit sharing plan. The benefits payable in respect of those years of past service cannot exceed $1,150 for each year of pre-1990 pensionable service, in recognition of the fact that the employee enjoyed a higher level of RRSP contribution room in those years than individuals who were RPP participants.

Where a pension is received early, the maximum pension limit is not reduced. However, the pension must first be compared to the maximum pension limit (and reduced if necessary) prior to any reduction for early retirement.

The CCRA does allow a pension plan to pay out the lesser of the pension reduced for early retirement and the maximum pension, reduced by 0.25% for each month by which pension commencement precedes the earliest of the following dates:

- The date on which the member would attain age 60;

- The date on which the member would have had 30 years of service; and

- The date on which the member's age plus service would have totalled 80.

For employees in public service occupations, the maximum pension is reduced if pension commencement occurs before the earliest of:

- Age 55;

- 25 years of service; or

- Age plus service totals 75.

Where a defined benefit pension plan provides bridge benefits to persons whose pension commenced before age 65, the combined annual lifetime pension and bridge benefit payable is limited to:

- The defined benefit dollar limit for the year of pension commencement (i.e., $1,722.22, indexed after 2005) multiplied by the employee's pensionable service;

plus

- 25% of the average in the last three Year's Maximum Pensionable Earnings under the Canada Pension Plan, multiplied by pensionable service (maximum 35 years) and divided by 35,

indexed from the year of commencement to the particular year in line with increases in the CPI.

This limit on combined lifetime retirement benefits and bridging benefits only applies to lifetime retirement benefits and bridging benefits for post-1991 pensionable service.

These maximum limits severely restrict the bridging benefits that may be paid to highly compensated members whose lifetime retirement benefits are close to or at the maximum permitted, as well as lower-income members with relatively short periods of service.

Originally it was anticipated that the $1,722.22 limit would be indexed to increases in the average wage after 1995. However, such an increase was twice deferred in two federal budgets, and is now not expected to be indexed to the average wage until 2005. After 2004, the $1,722.22 dollar limit will equal 1/9 of the previous year's defined contribution dollar limit.

Downsizing Programs

An employer who initiates a downsizing program in order to reduce the size of its workforce must apply to the Minister for approval of the downsizing program. If the Minister approves the downsizing program, the employer will be able to offer enriched pension benefits to downsized employees.

The Minister has administratively set criteria for approval of downsizing and early retirement programs. The criteria require that the workforce must be reduced by the greater of 50 employees or 10% of employees in a locality. As well, no more than 35% of the target employees can be in the top earnings quartile for the locality.

If the program is approved, the employer may grant downsized employees, aged 55 or older, extra pensionable service to their normal retirement date, subject to a maximum of 7 such years. As well, early retirement reductions can be waived under a downsizing program if downsizing benefits are paid on or after the earliest of:

- Attainment of age 55;
- Attainment of 25 years of service; and
- Age plus service, equal to 75.

Any additional benefits provided under an approved downsizing program are not subject to the ordinary maximum pension rule, as they are subject to their own rule.

Designated Plans

A defined benefit pension plan is a "designated plan" if it is not maintained pursuant to a collective agreement and if the Pension Adjustments of specified members exceed 50% of all Pension Adjustments earned under the plan in that year. Specified members are:

- Persons who earn over $2\frac{1}{2}$ times the Year's Maximum Pensionable Earnings under the Canada Pension Plan;
- Individuals who own 10% or more of the issued shares of any class of shares of the employer or a related corporation; or
- Individuals who do not otherwise deal at arms length with the employer.

Contributions to a designated plan cannot exceed the amount specified according to the designated plan rules, which apply an artificial cap on employer contributions.

The Minister may exempt a plan with at least 10 active members from designated plan status if the plan operates as a traditional defined benefit plan. A traditional plan is a plan in which:

- The benefit formula does not vary from member to member;

- Members are not involved in the decision-making process regarding the amount of contribution made in respect of the member;

- Members do not have control over the investment of any of the assets; and

- Surplus is not tracked individually for each member.

Employer Contributions to Defined Benefit Plans

Contributions made by an employer to a defined benefit plan are deductible, if based on the recommendation of an actuary certifying that the contributions are required to ensure the assets of the plan are sufficient to fund the benefit promises made under the plan.

Where the funding status of the plan is in a surplus position, there are restrictions placed on further employer contributions. For plans in actuarial surplus, a certain portion of the surplus in a defined benefit plan may be disregarded in determining whether an employer may make eligible contributions. The amount that may be excluded is equal to the lesser of:

- The greater of 10% of the liabilities under the plan, and twice the estimated current service contributions required for the 12-month period following the effective date of the actuarial report; and

- 20% of the actuarial funding liabilities under the plan.

Employee Contributions

Contributions made by an employee to a pension plan for service in the year are fully deductible in determining taxable income, to the extent the contribution was made in accordance with the terms of the plan. A defined benefit registered pension plan may not require employee contributions that exceed the lesser of:

- 9% of the employee's compensation for the year; and

- $1,000 plus 70% of the employee's Pension Adjustment for the year[1].

For a plan that provides a termination or pre-retirement death benefit of twice employee contributions, the figure "70%" is reduced to "50%".

---

[1] Although the offset in the PA calculation was reduced from $1,000 to $600, no similar amendment was made to the contribution formula.

If an employee wishes to make contributions to a defined benefit registered pension plan in order to purchase pension benefits in respect of pre-1990 employment with the employer, the deductibility of such contributions depends on whether in the years of past service the employee was or was not a contributor to any registered pension plan. Where the past-service contribution is made with respect to years of service before 1990 in which the employee was not a contributor to any registered pension plan, the total deductible contribution is limited to $3,500 times the number of years of purchased past service. The deduction for such a past-service contribution can be taken at the rate of $3,500 per calendar year.

Where the past-service contribution was made in respect of years of service prior to 1990 during which the employee contributed to a registered pension plan, the amount paid to purchase pension benefits for such years of past service can be deducted at a rate of $3,500 per year. This deduction is further reduced by all other current and past-service contribution deductions claimed by the employee in the year, so that if the employee makes current or past service required or voluntary contributions in the year totalling $3,500, this deduction is completely eliminated.

Transfer of Assets Between Pension Plans and Registered Retirement Savings Arrangements

Upon separation from employment, especially upon termination of employment, pension benefits are often payable as a commuted value lump sum. To avoid immediate taxation in the employee's hands of the lump-sum payment, the *Income Tax Act* permits transfers of the lump-sum amount, on a tax-deferred basis, between registered retirement savings arrangements. The following types of transfers are recognized:

- A transfer from a money purchase provision of an RPP to a money purchase provision of another RPP, or to an RRSP or RRIF (there is no limit on the amount that can be transferred);

- A transfer from a money purchase provision of an RPP to a defined benefit provision of an RPP (transfer of fund can occur to the extent that it does not exceed the costs of the defined benefits being provided);

- A transfer between defined benefit provisions of RPPs; and

- A transfer from a defined benefit provision of an RPP to a defined contribution provision in another RPP, or to an RRSP or RRIF.

A transfer from a defined benefit plan to an RRSP, RRIF or a defined contribution plan is subject to specified limits in the regulations. The amount that can be transferred is limited through the maximum transfer value factor. With few exceptions, the amount eligible for transfer is equal to the amount of post-age-65 lifetime retirement benefit that is foregone or surrendered, multiplied by the maximum transfer value factor. Certain other transfers are recognized for special situations.

Chapter 8

PENSION STANDARDS LEGISLATION AND CASE LAW AFFECTING PENSION PLANS

This chapter describes the development of pension standards legislation and provides an overview of the principal requirements of the legislation. The chapter also covers significant court decisions affecting pension plans.

History of Pension Standards Legislation

Pension plans are regulated from two perspectives — the control of the terms and operations of the plan, and limits on the tax deferral available. Control of the terms and operations is the primary focus of pension standards legislation. The federal government controls the tax shelter provided for pension plans through the *Income Tax Act*.

The Development of Pension Standards Legislation

The initiation of pension standards legislation was spurred by the phenomenal growth of private pension plans in the 1950s and 1960s, and the concern that employees were losing all of their pension rights when they terminated employment before retirement. A long delay in the vesting of pension rights was the main problem. Vesting is the unconditional right to retain a pension entitlement (or the value thereof). When vesting was available, employees were able to and often did forfeit their pension rights in order to receive refunds of their contributions. As a result of delayed vesting, many employees who had been in several employer-sponsored pension plans received little or nothing from these pension plans upon retirement. A major thrust of pension standards legislation was to preserve pensions on termination of employment prior to retirement so that many workers would benefit, the pressure for public plans would be reduced and the mobility of skilled labour would be improved.

Also, within organized labour, the concept that pensions are deferred pay has prevailed over the idea that they are provided in recognition of long service. The concept of pensions as deferred pay calls for early vesting, if not immediate vesting, at least in theory.

Another reason for action by the provinces in the 1960s was to fill the void left by the breakdown and withdrawal of the federal rules on pension plans. Under Canada's constitution, most pension plans are under provincial, not federal, jurisdiction. Until 1958, the federal authorities in Ottawa were in the unhappy position of trying to do indirectly through the *Income Tax Act* what they were not allowed to do directly. Pressures built up and the federal statement of Principles and Rules Respecting Pension Plans was withdrawn. After a gap of several years the old statement was replaced first by Information Circular 71–4 and then by successive versions of Information Circular 72–13.

In light of these developments, provincial governments stepped in to regulate the terms and operations of employer-sponsored pension plans. Over the 30-year period between 1965 and 1995, pension standards statutes were enacted by most provincial governments, and by the federal government for federally regulated employees. As a result of discussions and negotiations, a large measure of agreement was reached among the authorities having pension legislation and the original statutes and regulations were uniform in their main essentials. Over time, many jurisdictions have amended their pension standards legislation to extend the regulation of pension plans. Many of the original statutes have been substantially revised to further improve the minimum benefit standards. The effective date of these comprehensive changes to the standards is commonly referred to as the reform date. The effective dates (as opposed to the date the legislation was actually enacted) of the first pension standards legislation, and reform dates, are as follows:

Jurisdiction	Effective Date	Reform Date
Alberta	January 1, 1967	January 1, 1987
British Columbia	January 1, 1993	July 15, 1999
Manitoba	July 1, 1976	January 1, 1985
New Brunswick	December 31, 1991	—
Newfoundland and Labrador	January 1, 1985	January 1, 1997
Nova Scotia	January 1, 1977	January 1, 1988
Ontario	January 1, 1965	January 1, 1988
Quebec	January 1, 1966	January 1, 1990
Saskatchewan	January 1, 1969	January 1, 1993
Federal	October 1, 1967	January 1, 1987

Prince Edward Island has passed legislation, but it has not been proclaimed in force.

Some provinces have since adopted a third set of reform-type legislation: Alberta, effective March 1, 2000 and Quebec, effective January 1, 2001. In addition, most provinces continue adjusting their pension legislation on a fairly regular basis.

Pension standards regulation now governs such matters as eligibility for membership, vesting, portability of pensions, death benefits and disclosure of information. Each jurisdiction has enacted its own pension standards legislation to meet the needs of that particular jurisdiction. Today, Canadian pension standards legislation varies from jurisdiction to jurisdiction in almost every respect. These differences have made pension plan administration particularly complicated for pension plans that have members located in various jurisdictions across Canada.

The federal government has also reformed the provisions of the *Income Tax Act* relating to pension plans. Amendments to the *Income Tax Act* concerning assistance for retirement saving became law on June 27, 1990. These amendments replaced, for the most part, the rules under the old Information Circular 72–13. The focus of these more recent rules has been on limiting the amount of funds that can be tax-sheltered by a registered pension plan.

Registration Requirements and Applicable Laws

Pension standards legislation provides two things:

1. A comprehensive set of rules governing the operation of pension plans; and

2. A regulator that has the duty and the remedial authority to enforce compliance with those rules.

No employer is required to set up or maintain a pension plan for its employees, although all employees must, of course, contribute to the Canada or Quebec Pension Plan and the employer must contribute on their behalf. However, if a pension plan is established by an employer and the plan covers employees in a jurisdiction that has pension standards legislation, the plan must be registered and must comply with that legislation. Registration under both the federal *Income Tax Act* and the pension standards legislation is essential if the pension plan is to operate legally and provide a tax shelter.

Pension standards legislation exists for all provinces but one, and applies to employees who work in the province unless the work comes within the application of the federal *Pension Benefits Standards Act* (PBSA). The PBSA applies to employees in any province who are employed in any work, undertaking or business that is within the legislative authority of the federal government. This includes employees of Crown Corporations, banks, railways, airlines, shipping companies, broadcasting and other communications companies, and any undertakings that are declared by Parliament to be for the general advantage of Canada (such as the production of atomic energy), as well as employees in the Yukon, Northwest Territories and Nunavut.

Each government has included in its legislation a provision to allow pension plans to be registered in, and supervised by, the jurisdiction in which the plurality of active members are employed. Thus, the functions, authorities and duties provided to the appointed regulator under each piece of pension standards legislation can be delegated to another regulator. However, the standards of one jurisdiction are not necessarily substituted for the other. A plan operating in more than one jurisdiction must comply with the funding standards of the jurisdiction of registration but is still required to apply the particular benefit standards rules of each jurisdiction for the employees in that jurisdiction. The regulator of the jurisdiction in which the pension plan is registered is expected to enforce all applicable benefit standards, including those of other jurisdictions where the plan has members in more than one jurisdiction.

Regulatory Cooperation Toward Uniformity

The Canadian Association of Pension Supervisory Authorities (CAPSA) was established in 1974. CAPSA is an association of senior government officials who are responsible for the administration of pension standards legislation. Originally, one of CAPSA's prime objectives was to work towards uniformity in the regulatory legislation. However, the political difficulties involved in this process have become evident, and each jurisdiction continues to support whichever policies are most appropriate for that jurisdiction. CAPSA's mandate is now to facilitate an efficient and effective pension regulatory system in Canada. As an organization, it has indicated that it will strive to be a credible leader in the development and harmonization of pension policy and the setting of pension standards.

In 1993, CAPSA issued the first draft of a *Multilateral Agreement Among Canadian Jurisdictions Respecting Pension Plan Regulation and Supervision*. By 1994, the draft Agreement had been revised, and in September 1994, the members of CAPSA agreed to submit the proposed Agreement to their respective governments with the intention of obtaining the necessary legislation for its implementation.

The concept of the Agreement is to permit a pension plan to be governed entirely by the pension legislation of the jurisdiction in which the plan is registered (with some exceptions). Thus, if a plan is registered in Saskatchewan, for example, then only *The Pension Benefits Act* of Saskatchewan would apply, even if some plan members reside in Alberta or Quebec. The exceptions to this general rule would generally fall into two categories. First, transitional rules would preserve the application of some multi-jurisdictional benefit standards for benefits accrued at the coming into force of the Agreement. Second, some provisions, for example the Ontario Pension Benefits Guarantee Fund, for which there is no analogous provision in the other statutes, would apply only to members working in the jurisdiction that enacted the provision. The Agreement also contains rules that are designed to minimize the frequency of change in governing jurisdiction due to changes in plurality of membership.

The CAPSA Agreement is problematic in that it obliges governments to permit the laws of another jurisdiction to protect their residents.

In January 2000, the Association of Canadian Pension Management (ACPM) released *Consultation Materials: Uniform Pension Benefit Standards Act — Changing the Landscape of Pension Legislation in Canada*[1]. ACPM's members are drawn from Canada's major employers, and the actuarial consulting firms, financial institutions, law firms and investment counsellors who provide advice to such employers. Its stated mission is to advocate the growth and health of the retirement income system in Canada.

Regarding the CAPSA Agreement, the ACPM has pointed out in its consultation materials that harmonization of the Agreement with

---

[1] The consultation materials can be viewed at the ACPM's Web site at **www.acpm.com**.

family law, employment and human rights legislation would be difficult, as the agreement itself is not legislation. Additionally interpretation of the Agreement would be challenging for courts and tribunals, for the same reason. Furthermore, the ACPM has stated:

> The most serious criticism . . . is that it constitutes an **acceptance of the lack of uniformity**, rather than **encouraging uniformity**. It does not simplify the legislative system. There is the significant danger that if it should ever be put into effect, governments would consider that sufficient harmonization has been achieved, and it will be another ten years before serious attempts at uniformity will be considered again.

In 1998, the ACPM created a task force to specifically deal with the issue of pension legislation uniformity and to create a draft uniform *Pension Benefit Standards Act*.

The purpose of the draft uniform Act is to:

- Establish minimum standards applicable to pension plans;

- Provide for the enforcement of such standards;

- Encourage the establishment and retention of pension plans and the provision of benefits thereunder;

- Facilitate uniformity of pension benefits standards legislation in Canadian jurisdictions; and

- Facilitate efficient administration of the regulation of pension plans.

The concept is based on the premise that the draft Act would be enacted by each jurisdiction. Pension plans would continue to be registered in the jurisdiction in which there is a plurality of active members. Furthermore, the legislation of the jurisdiction in which the member is employed would be administered by the regulatory authority in each jurisdiction. Since the participating jurisdictions would be specified in regulations, there would be no need for a reciprocal agreement among jurisdictions.

The draft Act states that CAPSA would have an expanded role in creating uniform policies, and in recommending amendments to the legislation to their respective governments.

Minimum Standards

The scope of pension standards legislation in each jurisdiction is similar. However within each area of regulatory control there are differences in the detailed requirements. For example, all pension standards legislation prescribes a minimum period of time after which benefits must become vested, yet even jurisdictions that have undergone pension reform rarely impose exactly the same vesting rule. Some of the key minimum standards are described below. While not exhaustive, the summary describes the prevalent trend and some notable differences.

Eligibility for Membership

An employer is not required to provide a pension plan for its employees. However, when a pension plan does exist, pension standards legislation generally requires that every full-time employee who belongs to the class of employees for whom the plan was established must be allowed to join the plan after two years of employment. It is permissible to require employees to join a plan.

In most jurisdictions, part-time employees who are in the same class as eligible full-time employees and who have earned at least 35% of the Year's Maximum Pensionable Earnings (YMPE), as defined under the *Canada Pension Plan*, for two consecutive years must be allowed to join the pension plan. Alternatively, the employer may set up a separate plan for part-timers if it provides reasonably equivalent benefits.

Manitoba has gone farther than the other governments and compels all eligible full-time employees to join a pension plan, if one exists, except for certain groups that are exempted under the legislation. Part-time employees must join after having earned at least 25% of the YMPE for two years.

Quebec does not make a distinction between full-time and part-time employees. Employees covered by the pension plan must be allowed to join if they have either earned at least 35% of the YMPE or worked 700 hours of employment in the preceding calendar year.

Ontario, Prince Edward Island (to be proclaimed), Saskatchewan and Nova Scotia (effective for Nova Scotia as of January 1, 2003) also extend participation to part-time employees who have completed at least 700 hours of employment in each of two consecutive calendar years.

Vesting and Locking-In

"Vesting" means the right of a plan member who terminates employment to receive a benefit in excess of their own contributions with interest, if any, from the pension plan. "Locking-in" is the requirement that the vested entitlement must provide retirement income. The criteria for vesting are the completion of a specified period of employment or plan membership, and sometimes the attainment of a certain age. These are also the criteria for the locking-in of a member's pension. Jurisdictions that have undergone pension reform now base vesting and locking-in on the period of plan membership or years of employment, regardless of age. The new rule is not made retroactive, in that it does not affect the pension accrued before the reform legislation became operative.

The following table lists the vesting and locking-in minimum requirements in the respective jurisdictions:

Jurisdiction	Vesting and Locking-In Minimum Requirements	Affecting Benefits Earned On and After
Federal	Age 45 and 10 years of continuous service or plan membership	Oct. 1, 1967
	2 years of plan membership	Jan. 1, 1987
Alberta	Age 45 and 10 years of continuous service	Jan. 1, 1967
	5 years of continuous service for benefits accrued after 1986 and prior to 2000, and vesting after 2 years of plan membership for benefits accrued on or after 2000	Jan. 1, 1987
British Columbia	2 years of continuous plan membership. Vesting also applies to all benefits accrued prior to January 1, 1998; however, locking-in applies to post-1992 credits only	Jan. 1, 1998
Manitoba	10 years of continuous service or plan membership for vesting, plus age 45 for locking-in (applies to benefits accrued for service from July 1, 1976 to December 31, 1984)	July 1, 1976
	2 years of continuous service or plan membership for vesting and locking-in (applies to benefits accrued on and after January 1, 1985)	Jan. 1, 1985
New Brunswick	5 years of continuous service benefits accrued before the effective date are vested and locked-in according to the pension plan provisions	Dec. 31, 1991
	5 years of continuous service or 2 years of plan membership beginning on or after January 1, 2001	to be proclaimed
Newfoundland and Labrador	Age 45 and 10 years of continuous service or plan membership	Jan. 1, 1985
	2 years of plan membership	Jan. 1, 1997

Jurisdiction	Vesting and Locking-In Minimum Requirements	Affecting Benefits Earned On and After
Nova Scotia	Age 45 and 10 years of continuous service or plan membership	Jan. 1, 1977
	24 months of plan membership	Jan. 1, 1988
Ontario	Age 45 and 10 years of continuous service or plan membership	Jan. 1, 1965
	24 months of plan membership	Jan. 1, 1987
Prince Edward Island	3 years of plan membership and 5 years of continuous service	To be proclaimed
Quebec	Age 45 and 10 years of continuous service or plan membership	Jan. 1, 1966
	2 years of active plan membership	Jan. 1, 1990
	Immediate full vesting. This includes all benefits accrued prior to January 1, 2001	Jan. 1, 2001
Saskatchewan	1 year of continuous service or plan membership and age plus service or membership is 45 or more	Jan. 1, 1969
	2 years of continuous service	Jan. 1, 1994
	At the earliest of either reaching age 55 or reaching the early retirement date of plan, money can be transferred to unlocked RRIF	April 1, 2002

Several jurisdictions also require 100% vesting at pensionable age or normal retirement date, even if the member has not met the service or membership requirement (Alberta, British Columbia, Manitoba and Saskatchewan). In Quebec, the Quebec *Supplemental Pension Plans Act* (SPPA) now requires immediate full vesting that applies to all benefits, even those that have accrued prior to January 1, 2001.

There are exceptions to the locking-in rule that permit a plan to pay a cash sum in lieu of all or part of the pension entitlement. For most jurisdictions these exceptions are:

- Refund of contributions made before the applicable original pension standards legislation became operative;
- 25% of the value of pre-reform pension;
- The entire value of the pension, where the annual pension is less than 2–10% of the YMPE (all jurisdictions except for

Quebec), or where the commuted value of the pension is less than 4-20% of the YMPE (some jurisdictions)[2];

- The entire value of the pension where the terminating employee's life expectancy is shortened.

Commutation of pension benefits for non-residents is permitted in Alberta, British Columbia, Quebec and under the federal jurisdiction[3].

Effective May 2000 in Ontario, an individual may also be able to access funds in locked-in vehicles in situations involving financial hardship. Qualifying circumstances include such things as the necessity to pay first and last month's rent, to avoid eviction, to pay for medical treatment, to renovate property to accommodate for illness or disability, and low income.

Employees whose employment terminates before meeting the vesting requirement of a contributory pension plan are entitled to a refund of their own contributions with interest. This is not applicable in Quebec, as members vest immediately.

Portability

Portability refers to the ability of a plan member to transfer the commuted value of his or her deferred vested pension to another retirement savings arrangement on termination of employment before retirement age. It is permissible, but not mandatory, for a pension plan to provide portability rights to plan members who have attained retirement age.

Each jurisdiction prescribes the method of calculating commuted values. In most jurisdictions the transfer value basis recommended by the Canadian Institute of Actuaries (CIA) has become the standard method.

The retirement savings arrangements to which a member who is entitled to a deferred pension can typically expect to be able to transfer the value of his or her benefit are:

- Another registered pension plan (RPP), if that other plan permits;

- A locked-in Registered Retirement Saving Plan (locked-in RRSP);

---

[2] In New Brunswick, Bill 30, *An Act to Amend the Pension Benefits Act*, received Royal Assent on June 7, 2002. When proclaimed into effect section 34 of the Act will permit commutation where the *adjusted* commuted value of the pension is less than 40% of the YMPE in the year of termination or when the plan is wound up.

[3] When section 56.1 of the New Brunswick legislation is proclaimed into effect, commutation for non-residents will also be permitted in New Brunswick.

- A Locked-In Retirement Account (LIRA):
- A Life Income Fund (LIF);
- A Locked-In Retirement Income Fund (LRIF);
- A Registered Retirement Income Fund (RRIF);
- An insurance company for purchase of an immediate or deferred life annuity.

The following table summarizes the transfer options that must be provided in each jurisdiction:

Jurisdiction	Transfer Vehicles
Federal	RPP, locked-in RRSP, LIF, or life annuity
Alberta	RPP, LIRA, or, if the plan permits, LIF, LRIF, or life annuity
British Columbia	RPP, locked-in RRSP, life annuity, or LIF (subject to certain conditions)
Manitoba	RPP, locked-in RRSP, LIRA, LIF, LRIF (in defined benefit plan, plan permitting) or life annuity, if specified by plan
New Brunswick	RPP, LIRA, LIF, or life annuity
Newfoundland and Labrador	RPP, LIRA, LIF, LRIF, or life annuity
Nova Scotia	RPP, locked-in RRSP, LIF, or life annuity
Ontario	RPP, LIRA, LIF, LRIF, or life annuity
Prince Edward Island (to be proclaimed)	RPP, prescribed retirement savings arrangement, or life annuity
Quebec	RPP, LIRA, LIF, or life annuity
Saskatchewan	RPP, LIRA, life annuity, or, if plan permits, RRIF

In 2002, Saskatchewan introduced a new portability option giving employees access to their formerly locked-in pension money. This new option, a RRIF, is only locked-in until age 55, and replaces LIFs and LRIFs in Saskatchewan. In New Brunswick, Bill 30, *An Act to Amend the Pension Benefits Act*, received Royal Assent on June 7, 2002. When proclaimed into force, section 40.1 will permit a member, upon termination of employment, to have the administrator of the plan transfer up to 25% of the member's pension to a RRIF.

Certain jurisdictions permit plans to require a compulsory transfer to the vehicles listed above if the commuted value of the pension is less than 10% or 20% of the YMPE: Alberta (20%), British Columbia (20%), New Brunswick (10%), Prince Edward Island (10%) and federal (10%). In certain circumstances, it is possible to force a refund in the province of Quebec as well, for commuted values of less than 20%.

Retirement Age

All jurisdictions require that a pension plan contain rules concerning the earliest date at which a pension is paid without reduction, or the normal retirement age for the plan. In Ontario, Nova Scotia, New Brunswick and Prince Edward Island (to be proclaimed), the normal retirement age cannot be later than one year after age 65 is attained. In Quebec, this age cannot be later than the first of the month following the month in which age 65 is attained, and in Newfoundland and Labrador, it cannot be later than the date the member attains 65. The concept of an earliest unreduced pensionable age or normal retirement date is meaningful for defined benefit plans, whereby the pension payable on the normal retirement date is calculated according to the benefit formula, without reduction for early commencement.

The legislation in Saskatchewan, Ontario, Quebec, New Brunswick, Nova Scotia and Prince Edward Island (to be proclaimed) requires that a plan member whose employment or plan membership ceases within the 10 years before the normal retirement date is entitled to receive an immediate pension. The federal legislation states that early pension entitlement occurs within 10 years of pensionable age, which is the earliest date on which a pension can be received without reduction and without employer consent. Manitoba permits early pension entitlement to be based on reasonable age and service criteria. British Columbia and Newfoundland and Labrador prescribe that the entitlement occurs at age 55. In Alberta, the legislation states that entitlement occurs within 10 years of the pensionable age. All jurisdictions require that if a pension is reduced for early commencement, the reduced pension must be at least actuarially equivalent in value to the pension deferred to normal retirement date.

Quebec and Alberta also have special rules in relation to phased retirement. These rules allow a member to receive an annual lump-sum amount from his or her pension plan to compensate for a reduction in work hours. More information on phased retirement is contained in Chapter 2.

Pension standards legislation sets minimum standards for the treatment of plan members who remain employed beyond the normal retirement date. Generally, a member can delay receipt of pension and continue to earn benefits, subject to any plan rules concerning maximum service or benefit amounts or, as an alternative, commence receiving the pension at normal retirement age even though employment continues.

In Quebec, members may postpone their normal pension if employment continues with the same employer they were employed with at normal retirement date. During the postponement period, members may require payment of all or part of the normal pension, but only to the extent necessary to offset any permanent reduction in remuneration. The amount of the postponed pension not paid is adjusted at the end of the postponement. However, if an agreement is made between the member and the employer, a member may receive all or part of his pension, regardless of the limit (unless otherwise stated in the pension plan). If contributions are paid during the postponement period, the resulting additional amount of pension must be of an equal or greater value than that of the benefits that could be purchased, at the end of the postponement period, with the member's contribution paid during such a period, including accrued interest. An adjustment will be made to ensure that the pension payable at the end of the postponement is actuarially equivalent to the pension had the pension not been postponed.

Death Benefits Before Pension Commencement

Every pension plan must define what benefits, if any, a vested plan member's spouse (as defined by the pension standards legislation), beneficiary or estate will receive if the member dies before pension commencement. These benefits are generally referred to as pre-retirement death benefits.

All jurisdictions now require a pension plan to provide pre-retirement death benefits if a vested plan member dies before pension commencement, either before or after termination of employment. The specifics of the requirements vary considerably. In most jurisdictions 100% or 60% of the commuted value of the post-reform pension earned by the member must be paid to the spouse, or if there is no spouse, to another beneficiary or the member's estate. Some jurisdictions require only a refund of contributions if there is no spouse. An eligible spouse is typically entitled to choose a pension or to take the value of the entitlement in a lump sum. These measures are consistent with the idea that survivors should not be left unprotected, and that vested pensions should not be forfeited.

The following table sets out details of the pre-retirement death benefit requirements in the respective jurisdictions.

Jurisdiction	Pre-Retirement Death Benefit Requirement
Federal	if eligible to retire, 60% of post-1986 vested pension to the spouse
	if not eligible to retire, 100% of the commuted value of post-1986 vested pension to the spouse
Alberta	(a) a refund of pre-1987 contributions with interest plus (b) the greater of (i) 60% of the commuted value of vested pension benefits accrued on and after January 1, 1987 but before January 1, 2000, plus any excess contributions under the 50% rule; and (ii) the member's contributions made on and after January 1, 1987 but before January 1, 2000 with interest plus (c) the commuted value of the pension on and after January 1, 2000.
British Columbia	a refund of pre-1993 contributions with interest plus the greater of (a) 60% of the commuted value of the post-1992 vested pension plus any excess contributions under the 50% rule; and (b) the member's post-1992 contributions with interest
Manitoba	100% of the commuted value of post-1984 vested pension plus excess contributions with interest
New Brunswick	60% of the commuted value of vested pension plus excess contributions with interest or *100% of the commuted value of the vested pension if the member dies on or after the date to be set by proclamation*[4]
Newfoundland and Labrador	100% of commuted value of vested pension benefits that have accrued after 1996
Nova Scotia	60% of the commuted value of the post-1987 vested pension to the spouse; if no spouse, refund of contributions with interest
Ontario	100% of the commuted value of post-1986 vested pension
Prince Edward Island (to be proclaimed)	60% of the commuted value of all vested pension to the spouse; if no spouse, refund of contributions with interest

[4] This provision regarding 100% of the commuted value has not yet, as of the date of this writing, been proclaimed into force.

Jurisdiction	Pre-Retirement Death Benefit Requirement
Quebec	(a) if prior to normal retirement date, a lump-sum benefit equal to or greater than (i) the commuted value of post-1989 vested pension; or (ii) if the member was not entitled to a pension prior to death, the value of the deferred post-reform pension, which the member would have been entitled to had he or she not ceased to be an active member on that day and not died (entitled to excess contributions in either case); (b) if after normal retirement date, the spouse is entitled to a pension equal to at least the greater of (a) above and a 60% joint and survivor pension
Saskatchewan	if eligible to retire, a 60% joint and survivor pension for post-1993 service and a pension equal to the value of pre-1994 contributions with interest
	if not eligible to retire, a pension equal to pre-1994 contributions with interest plus the greater of 100% of the commuted value of post-1993 pension and the value of post-1993 contributions with interest

Death Benefits After Pension Commencement

Every pension plan must specify the form of pension that will be paid to a pensioner. This determines what benefits, if any, the pensioner's spouse, beneficiary or estate will receive when the pensioner dies after pension commencement.

Pension standards legislation does not prescribe forms of pension except:

- To require that the pension must be payable to the pensioner for his or her lifetime; and

- To provide a retiree's eligible spouse (if any) with the right to a survivor pension.

In all jurisdictions, for a member who has an eligible spouse (as defined by pension standards legislation) at the time of pension commencement, the form of pension that must be paid is a joint and survivor pension unless a waiver is signed by the spouse. In all the jurisdictions that require a joint and survivor pension, with the exception of Manitoba, the pension payable to the spouse after the member's death cannot be less than 60% of the pension that the member was receiving. In Manitoba, the pension must not be reduced to less than $2/3$ of the initial amount on the death of either the member or the spouse.

Cost Sharing

Cost sharing is a minimum standard applicable to contributory defined benefit pension plans. It requires the employer to pay for a minimum percentage, being 50% of a member's pension entitlement. This cost sharing requirement is commonly referred to as the "50% rule". All jurisdictions require contributory defined benefit pension plans to provide employer cost sharing. In most jurisdictions, cost sharing became effective when pension standards legislation was reformed.

The 50% rule applies at the time of an employee's death or termination of service. At that time, if the value of the employee's required contributions made after the prescribed date with credited interest is greater than 50% of the commuted value of his or her vested pension earned over the same period, the excess amount of member contributions must be refunded or used to provide additional benefits. In some provinces, the 50% cost-sharing rule is stated to apply to the member's vested pension, while in other provinces, it is stated to apply to the member's vested contributory pension.

In New Brunswick, the 50% minimum limit applies unless the plan specifies a different percentage. Plans subject to the federal *Pension Benefits Standards Act* do not have to apply the 50% rule if the pension plan provides for the annual indexation of deferred pensions (to payment date) at a rate that is at least 75% of the increase in the Consumer Price Index (CPI), less 1%, or an equivalent rate acceptable to the federal authorities.

The following table summarizes the options that must be given to a plan member with respect to excess contributions.

Jurisdiction	Effective Date	Required Options
Federal	January 1, 1987	• increase pension • plan may require locked-in transfer
Alberta	January 1, 1987	• lump-sum refund • transfer to pension plan if that plan permits • transfer to RRSP • if plan provides increase current pension or purchase annuity

Jurisdiction	Effective Date	Required Options
British Columbia	January 1, 1993	• lump-sum refund • transfer to pension plan if that plan permits • transfer to RRSP • transfer to insurance company to purchase annuity • transfer to prescribed RIF • plan may require increased pension
Manitoba	January 1, 1985	• lump-sum refund • increase benefits
New Brunswick	December 31, 1991	• lump-sum refund
Newfoundland and Labrador	January 1, 1997	• lump-sum refund • transfer to pension plan if that plan permits • transfer to retirement savings arrangement • transfer to insurance company to purchase annuity • plan may provide for increased pension
Nova Scotia	January 1, 1988	• lump-sum refund
Ontario	January 1, 1987	• lump-sum refund
Prince Edward Island	(to be proclaimed)	• increase pension
Quebec	January 1, 1990	• increase pension • transfer on locked-in basis as permitted by plan
Saskatchewan	January 1, 1969	• refund • transfer to pension plan if that plan permits • transfer to RRSP • transfer to insurance company to purchase annuity • plan may provide for increased pension

Under the *Income Tax Act*, excess contributions may be transferred to another retirement arrangement on a tax-deferred basis only if the member also elects to transfer the commuted value of his or her deferred pension out of the pension plan. The sum of the commuted value and the excess contributions is subject to the maximum transfer limit under the *Income Tax Act.*

Inflation Protection

Subject to the paragraph set out below respecting Quebec, it is not necessary for any pension plan to provide inflation protection in order to comply with pension standards legislation. However, a federally regulated pension plan must provide either employer cost sharing, or inflation protection for pensions at the rate of 75% of increases in the Consumer Price Index minus 1%.

In Nova Scotia and Ontario, the pension standards legislation contains provisions that appear to mandate inflation protection. However, the legislation in both of these jurisdictions stipulates that the inflation protection is to be provided according to a prescribed formula. Neither province has prescribed the formula for such indexation and so the requirement is treated as having no force or effect.

Effective as of January 1, 2003, the above-mentioned provision regarding inflation protection in the Nova Scotia legislation will be removed from the Act, thereby eliminating the possibility that indexing of pensions will be required in Nova Scotia.

In Quebec, partial indexation is required if the member ceased active membership 10 years or more before the normal retirement age (usually age 55). This only applies to years of service accumulated on or after January 1, 2001 and the indexing only applies to the period between the date the membership ended and the date that is 10 years before the plan's normal retirement age.

Protection of Employee Contributions

Employee-required and voluntary contributions to a pension plan that are received by an employer from the member or deducted directly from the employee's pay are deemed to be held in trust until they are deposited into the pension fund. Each jurisdiction requires the employer to remit employee contributions to the pension fund within certain time frames.

The following table summarizes the permitted delay between receipt of member contributions and remittance to the pension fund for each jurisdiction.

Remittance Deadline	**Jurisdiction**
• Within 30 days after end of the month of receipt or deduction	• Alberta, British Columbia (within this time frame, or according to the terms of any wage assignment or authorization to pay, if earlier), Newfoundland and Labrador, Nova Scotia, Ontario, and Saskatchewan.
• No later than 30 days from the date of receipt or deduction	• Manitoba
• Last day of the month following the month of receipt	• Quebec
• 30 days from the end of the period in which contributions were deducted	• Federal
• 15 days from the end of the month of receipt or deduction	• New Brunswick

Minimum Interest Rate Credited to Employee Contributions

Prior to regulatory controls, employers were able to determine the interest rate (if any) to be credited to employee contributions. All jurisdictions now require that a prescribed minimum rate of interest be credited to employee-required and voluntary contributions.

Generally, the annual rate of interest to be credited to employee contributions made to a defined contribution pension plan is the investment rate of return earned by the pension fund, less administration expenses.

For employee-required contributions made to a defined benefit pension plan, most jurisdictions permit the pension plan to provide a rate based on 5-year personal fixed-term chartered bank deposit rates (CANSIM series B14045) averaged over a period not exceeding 12 months, or the rate of return earned by the pension fund less administration expenses. Manitoba and Saskatchewan permit the CANSIM rate to be rounded down to the next 0.1%.

Defined benefit plans in the federal jurisdiction, and in Alberta, British Columbia, Manitoba, New Brunswick, and Newfoundland and Labrador may also apply either of these two rates to employee voluntary contributions. Nova Scotia, Ontario, Quebec and Saskatchewan require that the pension fund rate of return (less administration expenses) be credited to employee voluntary contributions.

Legislation in many of the jurisdictions requires interest to be credited to employee contributions from the first of the month following the month contributions are required to be deposited into the pension fund. Interest must be credited to a member's date of termination of service. Where contributions are refunded to a member, most jurisdictions require that interest be credited to the month of payment.

Pension Credit Splitting On Marriage Breakdown

In *Clarke v. Clarke*, the Supreme Court of Canada stated that pension benefits are matrimonial assets and subject to division, unless the legislation specifically states otherwise. As such, all provinces treat pension benefits as family property.

Regulations concerning the splitting of pension credits vary considerably in each jurisdiction. There may also be significant variations in the rights of the spouses depending on whether they were married or were common-law partners.

Also, the different jurisdictions have different options regarding when the non-member spouse will receive his or her portion of the benefit. At times, there will be an immediate payment, while at other times the benefit will not be paid until a triggering event occurs, such as termination or retirement.

All of the jurisdictions permit separating spouses to offset the value of pension benefits against other matrimonial assets, as opposed to dividing the actual pension benefits.

The following table summarizes some of the main characteristics of pension splitting rules as they apply to spouses and the jurisdictions in which they apply. The following are general guidelines. Each jurisdiction must be reviewed for specific exceptions.

RULE	JURISDICTION
Division is mandatory	Manitoba
Calculations are prescribed to determine the commuted value of the pension to be divided	Alberta, British Columbia[5], Manitoba, Nova Scotia, New Brunswick, Quebec, Saskatchewan and Federal
Benefit Accrual Period	
Date of commencement of common-law relationship or marriage to date of relationship termination or marriage breakdown, subject to order or agreement	Alberta, Manitoba, New Brunswick, Newfoundland and Labrador, Ontario and Prince Edward Island (to be proclaimed)
Date of relationship commencement/ marriage to specified date and specified date is:	
● Date set by court order	Nova Scotia and Saskatchewan
● Entitlement date set out by court or by parties	British Columbia[6]

---

[5] The *Family Relations Act* governs credit splitting in British Columbia.

[6] Also worthy of note is *M.J.S. v. L.S.*, a decision of the British Columbia Supreme Court that held that the date of marriage is not necessarily the commencement date for valuing a pension for division. In this case the Court selected a date earlier than the date of marriage, where the parties were cohabiting with an expectation of marriage.

RULE	JURISDICTION
● Date of institution of action or, if stated in order, date of marriage breakdown or termination of relationship	Quebec
Date of plan membership to date of assignment of benefit, unless otherwise specified in court order or agreement	Federal

Earliest date that pension is payable to member's spouse

Payment to the member's spouse is delayed until the member's employment terminates or the member reaches normal retirement age, whichever is earlier	Ontario and Prince Edward Island (to be proclaimed)
Payment to member's spouse can be made immediately	Alberta, British Columbia (defined contribution only), Newfoundland and Labrador (if court order must wait until all appeals heard or time for appeal expired) and Nova Scotia (defined contribution only)
Payment to member's spouse can be made at date of agreement or court order	Manitoba, New Brunswick and Saskatchewan
Payment can be made at the earlier of termination or eligibility for early retirement	British Columbia (defined benefit)
Payment can be made at the earlier of termination or pension commencement	Nova Scotia (defined benefit)
Payment can be made upon written request, pursuant to court order or agreement	Federal and Quebec

Spouse's Options Regarding Benefits

The spouse's portion of the pension entitlement must be transferred to locked-in arrangement if the funds are locked-in. If pension is of a small amount or not vested, cash payment may be made	Alberta, British Columbia, Manitoba (no cash payments), New Brunswick, Newfoundland and Labrador (no cash payments if not vested), Nova Scotia (defined benefit can only be transferred at retirement/termination if plan permits, otherwise spouse will receive own pension at retirement of member), Ontario, Prince Edward Island (not yet proclaimed and no cash payments), Quebec (if plan permits, separate pension at spouse's request), Saskatchewan (no cash payments), and Federal

RULE	**JURISDICTION**
Maximum amount payable to member's spouse	

Maximum amount of pension payable to member's spouse

● 50%	Alberta, British Columbia, Manitoba, New Brunswick, Newfoundland and Labrador, Nova Scotia, Ontario, Prince Edward Island (to be proclaimed) Quebec and Saskatchewan
● 100%	Federal

Evolution of Marriage-Like Relationships and the Definition of Spouse

One area of the law that has evolved and continues to evolve is in relation to the extension of rights and obligations to persons who are living with same-sex partners. The registration of same-sex unions has become a reality in Canada, first in Nova Scotia and then in Quebec. In Nova Scotia, same-sex couples and unmarried opposite-sex couples can file domestic-partner declarations with the province to create legally-recognized "domestic partnerships". As a result, domestic partners are entitled to enjoy all of the same rights as married spouses under pension benefits legislation.

In Quebec, a new "marriage-like" state has been created — the civil union. The legislation defines a civil union as "a commitment between two persons eighteen years of age or over who express their free and enlightened consent to live together and to uphold the rights and obligations that derive from that status". Individuals in a civil union must be unmarried and cannot be parties to another civil union, nor may the parties be siblings, ascendants or descendants. The union must be formally solemnized by an officiant who is legally authorized to solemnize marriages in Quebec.

However, there is also a movement to look beyond the scope of opposite-sex/same-sex conjugal relationships. According to a recent Law Commission of Canada Report, *Beyond Conjugality*[7], it is suggested that these rights and obligations be expanded to an even broader group. Although the Law Commission report supports same-sex marriages, it also states that governments focus too much on conjugal relationships, while ignoring non-conjugal relationships of importance, such as adult children living with parents and caregivers living with those to whom they provide care. According to the report, the Law Commission recommends that Parliament and the provincial/territorial legislatures pass laws that would allow adults to register

---

[7] This report can be viewed at **www.lcc.gc.ca**.

their relationships. This registration would not be restricted to conjugal relationships, and it would provide for a set of commitments, including caring arrangements, consent to treatment dispositions, and support and sharing in property.

The following table sets out the definition of spouse, common-law partners and same-sex partners as provided in the various minimum standards legislation.

Jurisdiction	Definition of Spouse/Common-law Partners
Federal	A "spouse" of an individual is defined as a person who is married to the individual and includes a void marriage. A "common-law partner" is a person who is cohabiting with another individual in a conjugal relationship, having so cohabited for a period of at least one year. "Same-sex partner" is included in the definition of common-law partner.
Alberta	A "spouse" is (a) a person who is married to the member and has not been living separate and apart from the member for three or more consecutive years; or (b) if not married, a person of the opposite sex who cohabited with the member for three years. No definition of "same-sex partner" has been included in the Act; however, it is understood that plans *may* provide spousal benefits to same-sex partners. The plan text must still adopt and maintain the definition and priority of a "spouse" as written in the Act.
British Columbia	A "spouse" means (a) a person who is married to the member, and who, if living separate and apart from the member, has not lived separate and apart from that other person for the two-year period or longer than the two-year period immediately preceding the relevant time, or (b) if paragraph (a) does not apply, a person who has been living and cohabiting with the member in a marriage-like relationship (including same sex) for a period of at least two years immediately preceding the relevant time. "Same-sex partner" is included under the definition of spouse.
Manitoba	A "spouse" of an individual is a person who is married to the individual. A "common-law partner" of a member or former member means a person who, not being married to the member or former member, cohabited with him or her in a conjugal relationship (a) for a period of at least three years, if either of them is married, or (b) for a period of at least one year, if neither of them is married. "Same-sex partner" is included in the definition of common-law partner.

Jurisdiction	Definition of Spouse/Common-law Partners
New Brunswick	A "spouse" means either of a man and a woman who (a) are married to each other, (b) are married to each other by a marriage that is voidable (c) have gone through a marriage in good faith that is void and have cohabited within the preceding year, or (d) not being married to each other, have cohabited (i) continuously for a period of not less than 3 years in a conjugal relationship in which one person has been substantially dependent upon the other for support, or (ii) in a relationship of some permanence where there is a child born of whom they are the natural parents, and have cohabited within the preceding year. Same-sex spouses are not permitted.
Newfoundland and Labrador	A "spouse" means (except in relation to the splitting of credits upon marital breakdown, in which case "spouse" must meet the definition set out in the *Family Law Act*) a person who (a) is married to the member or former member, (b) is married to the member or former member by a marriage that is voidable or (c) has gone through a marriage in good faith that is void and is cohabiting or has cohabited with the member or former member within the preceding year. A "cohabiting partner", (a) in relation to a member or former member who has a spouse, means a person who is not the spouse of the member or former member and who has cohabited continuously with the member or former member in a conjugal relationship for not less than three years, or (b) in relation to a member or former member who does not have a spouse, means a person who has cohabited continuously with the member or former member in a conjugal relationship for not less than one year. "Same-sex partner" is included in the definition of cohabiting partner.
Nova Scotia	A "spouse" means either of a man and woman who (a) are married to each other, (b) are married to each other by a marriage that is voidable, or (c) have gone through a marriage in good faith, that is void and are cohabiting or, if they have ceased to cohabit, have cohabited within the 12-month period immediately preceding the date of entitlement. A "common-law partner" of an individual means another individual who has cohabited with the individual in a conjugal relationship for a period of at least two years, neither of them being a spouse. "Same-sex partner" is included in the definition of common-law partner.

Jurisdiction	Definition of Spouse/Common-law Partners
Ontario	A "spouse" means either of a man and woman who, (a) are married to each other, or (b) are not married to each other and are living together in a conjugal relationship, (i) continuously for a period of not less than three years, or (ii) in a relationship of some permanence, if they are the natural or adoptive parents of a child, both as defined in the *Family Law Act.* A "same-sex partner" means either of two persons of the same sex who are living together in a conjugal relationship, (a) continuously for a period of not less than three years, or (b) in a relationship of some permanence, if they are the natural or adoptive parents of a child, both as defined in the *Family Law Act.*
Prince Edward Island (to be proclaimed)	A "spouse" means either of a man and woman who (a) are married to each other, (b) are married to each other by a marriage that is voidable or (c) have gone through a form of marriage that is void and are cohabiting or, if they have ceased to cohabit, have cohabited within the 12-month period immediately preceding the date of entitlement, or (d) have cohabited for three years and are cohabiting at the relevant time. Same-sex spouses not permitted.
Quebec	A "spouse" of a member is a person who (a) is married to or in a civil union with the member or (b) has been living in a conjugal relationship (opposite- or same-sex) with the member who is not married and is not in a civil union for a period of not less than three years or for a period of not less than one year if (i) they have at least one child, (ii) they have adopted jointly at least one child, or (iii) one of them has adopted at least one child who is the child of the other. "Same-sex spouse" is included in the definition of spouse.
Saskatchewan	A "spouse" means (a) a person who is married to a member or former member, or (b) if a member or former member is not married, a person with whom the member or former member is cohabiting as a spouse at the relevant time and who has been cohabiting continuously with the member or former member as his or her spouse for at least one year prior to the relevant time. "Same-sex spouse" is included in the definition of spouse.

Gender Discrimination

Legislation in all jurisdictions other than Alberta, Newfoundland and Labrador, and Quebec prohibits the use of different eligibility rules for plan membership, different employee contribution rates and different pension benefits based on the gender of an employee. In most jurisdictions that impose these unisex standards, the requirements apply to pension benefits earned after the effective date of pension reform.

Financial Issues

Pension standards legislation focuses on the funding and financial operations of pension plans, as well as on benefit standards. While Chapter 5 deals with the financial management of pension plans, the focus of the following section of this chapter is to provide an overview of the impact of pension standards legislation on the financial operations of a pension plan. The concepts discussed here, such as solvency liabilities, are in many jurisdictions defined with considerable precision and there is significant variation from jurisdiction to jurisdiction.

Funding Requirements — Defined Benefit Plans

Ongoing and Solvency

When an employer establishes a defined benefit pension plan, it assumes an obligation to fund the plan in accordance with applicable pension standards legislation. That legislation requires that a pension plan must be pre-funded or be in the process of becoming fully pre-funded. The reason for the pre-funding requirement is to provide security for the benefits the employer has promised to the members and that have accrued to their credit. In contrast, the thrust of the *Income Tax Act* provisions governing an employer's contributions to a pension plan is to ensure that there is adequate actuarial justification for the contributions, with a view to ensuring that the employer does not overfund.

Pension standards legislation requires that a plan be valued at least every three years. An actuarial valuation involves the comparison of the value of the assets in the plan fund to the value of the benefits the plan is expected to pay. Valuations to determine funding requirements are required on two very different bases — an ongoing basis, and a solvency basis. An ongoing valuation focuses on the ability of the plan to meet its obligations, assuming that it continues to operate. For example, in a final average earnings plan, the valuation on an ongoing basis views the plan as if members will continue to accrue benefits and receive pay increases, in accordance with the plan terms and assumptions used in the valuation respectively. The ongoing valuation attempts to show whether the funding of the plan is on course, just as a personal review of income and expenses would show if an individual is on course to meet his or her financial targets.

A solvency valuation focuses on the ability of the plan to meet its obligations if it is terminated as at the review date. At first glance, it may seem more likely that a plan will be fully funded on a solvency basis simply because members cease to accrue benefits. However, the plan terms or pension standards legislation may result in the plan having additional liabilities on termination that it does not have if it continues on an ongoing basis. The solvency of a plan is determined as the aggregate of the market value of the plan assets and the present value of future special payments, over the liabilities of the plan where the liabilities are determined on a plan termination basis, including additional benefits that may become payable as a result of plan termination. If liabilities exceed assets, the plan has a solvency deficiency, and if assets exceed liabilities, the plan has a solvency excess.

Contributions

There are two basic types of payments that must be made by an employer to a pension plan — current service cost (sometimes referred to as normal cost) and special payments. The current service cost is the employer's obligation to contribute to the plan in respect of benefits expected to accrue to members in each year of the valuation period. Special payments are required if actuarial liabilities exceed the value of pension fund assets. "Special payments" is a catch-all term encompassing payments that must be made to fund the plan as a result of certain triggering events, such as an amendment that increases accrued benefits, a change in actuarial methods or assumptions, or plan experience (i.e., investment returns or mortality rate) that is less or more favourable than anticipated. Generally, when special payments are required, the employer is not required to fully fund the amount of the special payments immediately. Instead, the special payments may be amortized over a period of five to 15 years, as set out in the applicable pension standards legislation. Payments made to fund a solvency deficiency are included in the special payments.

When the assets of a plan exceed its liabilities, the plan is said to have surplus assets. It is normal actuarial practice to take the surplus into account when determining whether or not an employer must make contributions in order to properly fund a plan. A "contribution holiday" occurs when the sponsoring employer decides not to make new contributions to the pension plan, because an actuary has determined that the plan is more than fully funded, having assets in excess of its liabilities. All pension standards legislation now permits the employer to take a contribution holiday, if the plan permits, for as long as the actuary determines that the plan will remain fully funded without further contributions.

Recently in Quebec, new rules have been added to the legislation. These rules allow employers to take contribution holidays under the Act, and if certain requirements are met, they are afforded protection from claims of Quebec members that the contribution holidays were improperly taken. The legal protection only applies to contribution holidays taken after the later of December 31, 2000 and the date the employer has complied with the legislated requirements. For the most part, the provisions are not mandatory. Employers can either apply the new provisions or continue on as before. Compliance, however, creates protection for the employer.

Regardless of the new provisions, an employer is permitted to take contribution holidays if permitted by the plan or by an agreement. From January 1, 2001, an employer's right to use surplus to take contribution holidays can be confirmed by amending the plan and by obtaining all of the required consents to the proposal. If there is a dispute regarding consent, the matter will be referred to binding arbitration.

Under the *Income Tax Act*, contributions are not permitted if surplus exceeds set limits.

Insufficient Assets — Defined Benefit Plans

The prospect of a plan winding up with insufficient assets to meet its liabilities is dealt with in pension standards legislation in a number of ways. Typically, the legislation requires the employer to continue to fund the plan. Where that is not possible, there are provisions for the orderly reduction of benefits.

Ontario is unique in Canada, as it maintains a fund, the Pension Benefits Guarantee Fund (PBGF), to pay pensions when a pension fund is unable to do so. The PBGF guarantees specified benefits in respect of service in Ontario in a pension plan registered under the Ontario legislation or a designated province, where the plan is wound up in whole or in part, and the Superintendent of Financial Services is of the opinion that the funding requirements prescribed by the legislation cannot be satisfied. Ideally, the PBGF is reimbursed by the employer who continues to have an obligation to fund the benefits. In practice, payments are made from the PBGF where the employer is bankrupt or insolvent. The PBGF has no application to a plan that has been established for less than three years, benefits that have been granted within the preceding three years, multi-employer plans, benefits under a defined benefit plan where the employer's contributions are set by collective agreement, and pension plans excluded in the regulations.

Payments under the PBGF are specified in the regulations under the Ontario legislation. In general, these payments are 100% of the benefits guaranteed by the PBGF, plus a proportion of other benefits included in calculating the Ontario wind-up liability. The PBGF pays for benefits only up to $1,000 per month per member.

The PBGF is intended to be self-financing via contributions from sponsors of defined benefit plans. The plan sponsor must pay an assessment rate each year. The assessment rates are generally equal to the least of

- $100 multiplied by the number of Ontario plan members;

- The sum of $1 for each Ontario plan member plus a certain percentage of the PBGF Assessment base (PBGF liabilities minus (solvency assets $\times$ PBGF liabilities) / total solvency liabilities); and

- $4 million.

In determining the funded position of a plan, special rules used to apply to a plan sponsor that maintained one or more pension plans with assets in excess of $500,000,000. Effective June 28, 2002, the Regulations under the Ontario Pension Benefits Act have been amended to prevent any additional employers from electing to have their pension plans qualify for special treatment.

Investment Rules

For the sponsor of a pension plan, investments are obviously an important consideration, as it is not desirable from the employer's perspective to consistently make large, unexpected contributions to a plan to compensate for poor investment performance. Both pension standards regulators and the tax authorities have an interest in pension fund investment. Pension standards legislation is concerned with ensuring that a plan is sufficiently funded to meet its obligations, both on an ongoing basis and in the event the plan is terminated. It follows that pension standards legislation is concerned with ensuring that pension funds are invested appropriately, as determined under the applicable statute. The CCRA, through the *Income Tax Act*, is also interested in the appropriateness of pension fund investments. As contributions to a pension fund are tax deductible, the tax authorities do not want pension funds losing large amounts of capital.

Income Tax Act

The *Income Tax Act* prohibits investment in shares (unless they are shares listed on a prescribed stock exchange) or other obligations of an employer who participates in the plan, and anyone who participates in the plan or is connected or does not deal at arm's length with the plan sponsor. Finally, the *Income Tax Act* restricts investment in foreign property to 30% of the book value of the pension fund. In the event a pension plan exceeds this limit, the excess is subject to a penalty tax of 1% per month.

Pension Standards Legislation

Under pension standards legislation, the concept of prudence has two aspects, one of which is the prudent portfolio. A given investment is analyzed from the perspective of how it affects the risk and return of the portfolio taken as a whole. This differs from the traditional "legal for life" approach, in which the risk and return characteristics of the particular investment are analyzed in isolation from the rest of the portfolio. The legal for life approach was followed under the federal PBSA prior to July 1, 1993. There has been a distinct move away from legal for life investment in Canada and other countries (most notably England and the United States). Most of the provinces have adopted the prudent portfolio approach in some form; some more specific than others. Prior to recent reforms, the Quebec SPPA specified that a pension fund could not invest more than a maximum of 10% of the book value of the plan assets in any one property or individual. This 10% rule was basically eliminated and replaced by a new "diversified" rule, and thus Quebec has taken the furthest step forward towards true "prudent portfolio" investment. Section 171.1 of the SPPA now states "Unless it is reasonable in the circumstances to act otherwise, the pension committee must endeavour to constitute a diversified portfolio so as to minimize the risk of major losses."

The other aspect of prudence is the prudent person. The plan administrator and its agents are required to exercise the care, diligence and skill in the investment of the pension fund that a person of ordinary prudence would exercise in dealing with the property of another person. This is a very high standard of conduct, and is higher even than the standard normally imposed on trustees. In addition, the relevant persons must exercise all relevant knowledge that they possess or ought to possess by reason of their business. This requirement is explicit in the federal jurisdiction, Manitoba, Ontario, Quebec, New Brunswick, Nova Scotia and Prince Edward Island (to be proclaimed).

Since prudence requires that the portfolio as a whole be analyzed, it is necessary to have a statement of investment policies and procedures for the pension fund. All jurisdictions require that a written investment policy be adopted by the plan administrator or the pension committee. The required contents of this statement are discussed in Chapter 6.

Special Situations

Successor Employers

Most pension standards legislation addresses the pension rights of employees who are affected by the sale of their employer's business. The legislation preserves entitlement to the benefits accrued to the date of sale or merger.

Where a business or part of a business is sold, the affected employees either lose their jobs or become employed by the purchaser of the business. In many jurisdictions, the pension legislation provides that where the purchasing employer does not provide a pension plan for the transferred employees to join, the vendor's pension plan is deemed to be terminated or partially terminated, and the plan termination rules will govern. However, where the purchaser does have a pension plan that is provided to some or all of the transferring employees (a successor plan), the legislation provides different rules.

Generally, where a vendor who contributes to a pension plan sells, assigns or otherwise disposes of all or a portion of its business or business assets, a member of the pension plan who continues employment with the purchaser continues to be entitled to those benefits accrued under the vendor's plan prior to the effective date of the sale. Alternatively, the purchaser and vendor can agree that the purchaser will assume liability for the pension benefits earned prior to the sale in the vendor's plan. In that case assets from the vendor's plan are transferred to the successor plan.

Where the purchaser provides a successor plan, the employment of employees who continue with the purchaser is deemed by most pension standards legislation not to be terminated. Therefore, regardless of whether or not the purchaser assumes liability for the pension benefits accrued under the vendor's plan, the "service" of an employee will include service with both the vendor and purchaser in both the vendor's and purchaser's pension plans when determining:

1. The vesting of benefits;

2. Eligibility for ancillary benefits that depend on length of service or plan membership;

3. The locking-in of benefits; and

4. Eligibility for membership in the purchaser's pension plan.

The successor pension plan is not required by pension legislation to recognize past service with the vendor for the purposes of benefit accruals. The purchaser's plan simply commences the accrual of pension benefits by the transferred employees from the date of sale forward, as it would for any new employee. In order to ensure that service with the purchaser is taken into account for vesting and other purposes in the vendor's plan, the benefits in the vendor's plan are typically not paid out until eventual termination of employment with the purchaser.

The consent of the regulatory authority in the province in which the vendor's plan is registered is required before any assets are transferred from the vendor's plan to the successor plan. Typically something like the Ontario standard of review will apply, so that consent will not be granted unless the benefits of affected members are protected.

Under the *Income Tax Act*, the transfer of assets to cover liabilities that may be assumed by a purchaser is governed by the rules set out in section 147.3.

Merger

The merger of two or more pension plans is a subject that is sparsely addressed, if at all, in pension legislation. The Quebec legislation, however, does contain rules specific to plan mergers that grant the regulatory authority the power to approve a merger on conditions it may prescribe. In addition, the legislation requires that either the merging plans have provisions dealing with the treatment of surplus on plan termination that are of identical effect, or the terms of the absorbing plan are more advantageous for the members and beneficiaries. Alternatively, if the provisions do not have identical effects and the terms of the absorbing plan are not more advantageous, the plan merger can still be approved if, after receiving the prescribed notice, fewer than 30% of the affected members object to the merger. Under the Alberta regulations, a "plan transfer" is defined to occur where a specific and identifiable class or group of members of a plan become members of another plan that is an active plan due to the disposal of all or part of the employer's business, undertaking assets, the merger of an employer, the merger of plans or the division of a plan.

Among the other jurisdictions, the regulatory control over the merger process is derived from the regulator's general authority to consent to or deny approval for the transfer of assets from one plan to another. For example, the Ontario legislation provides that where assets are transferred from one plan to another, the consent of the Superintendent is required. That consent cannot be given unless the pension benefits and other benefits of the members of the transferring plan are protected.

Generally speaking, the regulators' policies surrounding the approval process require that valuations be prepared to report on the financial status of the merging plans, and that benefits earned prior to the merger are preserved or otherwise protected.

Under the *Income Tax Act*, an asset transfer due to the merger of pension plans is governed by the transfer rules contained in section 147.3. Advance approval is not required. However, a new valuation report for the continuing plan will be necessary.

Termination of a Pension Plan

The terms "terminate" and "wind-up" are often used interchangeably. However, their technical meaning is distinct. The termination of a pension plan results in members ceasing to accrue further pension benefits. The wind-up process involves the disposition of the pension fund assets, including the settlement of pension benefits for the members, former members and other persons, such as beneficiaries who have entitlements under the plan.

The termination and winding-up of a pension plan is a complex process subject to a myriad of legislative requirements. The wind-up of a defined benefit pension plan involving the ownership and distribution of any surplus assets can be an especially complex and lengthy process.

A pension plan is not considered to be fully wound up until the employer, plan sponsor or Superintendent-appointed administrator has satisfied all of the legislative requirements, received approval from the applicable regulatory authority and has arranged for the disposition of all of the pension fund assets, including the settlement of pension benefits to plan members.

In many cases, the termination of a pension plan is the result of a voluntary decision made by the employer or plan sponsor to discontinue the plan. The decision is often the result of a business event, such as a sale, merger or corporate reorganization, where a number of employees cease to be employed, although an employer can terminate a plan where members' employment continues. Pension plans and funding agreements generally include provisions that provide the employer with the authority to voluntarily terminate the pension plan, in whole or in part, at any time. Pension plans established through a collective bargaining agreement will be subject to the legal obligations applicable under those circumstances.

A pension plan can be partially terminated. The partial termination of a pension plan involves the settlement of pension benefits for a specific group of plan members. Partial pension plan terminations are normally the result of the sale or discontinuance of a part of the employer's business operations or a significant reduction in plan membership resulting from employee terminations and lay-offs. All jurisdictions (except Quebec and Prince Edward Island (to be proclaimed)) require that plan members who are affected by the partial termination of a pension plan be given the same rights that they would have under a full termination of the plan. Alberta and British Columbia, however, clarify that this provision does not entitle members affected by a partial termination to share in any distribution of the surplus on the partial termination, and New Brunswick indicates that surplus may be distributed to plan members unless the plan provides for payment of surplus to the employer. In Quebec, as a result of changes to the legislation, an employer is no longer able to partially terminate a pension plan, effective as of January 1, 2001.

The pension regulators in each of the jurisdictions have a discretionary power to declare or order the full or partial termination of a pension plan if certain circumstances exist. The main grounds for a regulatory authority to order a full or partial termination of a pension plan include the discontinuance of all or part of an employer's business operations, bankruptcy of the employer, the discontinuance or suspension of employer contributions, failure to satisfy prescribed solvency tests, or non-compliance with applicable pension standards legislation. If there is no pension plan administrator, or the administrator fails to act on an order to fully or partially terminate a pension plan, most jurisdictions permit the regulatory authority to appoint an administrator or trustee to manage the plan termination and wind-up.

When a partial or full plan termination occurs, affected plan members gain certain special rights by virtue of the pension standards legislation. Most jurisdictions generally require that members be fully vested in their pension benefits accrued to the termination date, regardless of the vesting provisions provided under the pension plan. The majority of jurisdictions also explicitly provide for transfer rights with respect of the commuted value of their pension upon termination of the pension plan.

The legislation in some jurisdictions includes provisions relating to early retirement in the context of a plan termination. Legislation in Nova Scotia and Ontario also requires that certain members be given "grow in" rights[8]. Eligible members are those whose age plus years of employment equal 55 or more. They are entitled to receive the following:

---

[8] Effective as of January 1, 2003, multi-employer pension plans are exempt from the "grow in" requirements under the Nova Scotia legislation

- An immediate pension in accordance with the terms of the pension plan, if eligible under the plan;

- A pension in accordance with the terms of the plan to begin at the earlier of:

— the plan's normal retirement date, or

— the date the member would have been entitled to an actuarially unreduced pension if the plan had not wound up and if membership had continued;

- An actuarially reduced pension in the amount payable under the plan and commencing on the date the member would have been entitled to a reduced pension, if the member's membership had continued to that date.

These "grow in" rights are significant for pension plans that provide generous early retirement benefits, such as an unreduced pension at a specified age prior to normal retirement age. Eligible members also grow into bridge benefits, if they have at least 10 years of employment or plan membership at the date of the plan termination.

The 50% rule is a standard applicable to contributory defined benefit pension plans. It requires that the employer pay for a minimum percentage of a member's pension entitlement and it applies when the plan is terminated. The Alberta, British Columbia, Newfoundland and Labrador, and Saskatchewan legislation stipulates that upon the termination of a pension plan, where the member's contributions with interest exceed 50% of the pension's commuted value, the member shall have the option of having the excess:

- Returned;

- Transferred to another pension plan (if the other plan permits);

- Transferred to an RRSP;

- Transferred to an insurance company to purchase a deferred pension; or

- If and to the extent that the plan so provides, used to increase the amount of the pension.

This rule is applicable in New Brunswick as well, except that in that province, the plan may set a percentage different than 50%.

Although the legislation in Manitoba, Nova Scotia, Ontario and Quebec does not specifically refer to the 50% rule in the pension plan termination context, the legislation does refer to a 50% rule in a general context and it can therefore be presumed to apply when a pension plan is terminated.

Pension standards legislation in all jurisdictions contains specific provisions setting out the wind-up procedures that must be followed by the plan administrator. The following is a brief summary of the major requirements in effect in most jurisdictions:

- A written notice of the proposal to terminate the pension plan must be provided to all affected plan members and the pension authority. Other interested parties, such as a trade union that represents affected members and any advisory committee are also entitled to notice.

- The written notice must include information concerning the name and registration number of the pension plan, the proposed termination date, notification that each member will be provided with an individual statement that sets out his or her pension entitlements and settlement options, and where a plan provides contributory benefits, notice of the member's right to make contributions in respect of the period of notice of termination of employment.

- As soon as notice has been given, the payment of benefits to affected members is prohibited until the regulatory authority has approved the plan wind-up report. All jurisdictions permit pensions already in payment to continue, and also permit refunds of member contributions to be made, as exceptions to this asset freeze.

- The wind-up report must be filed with the regulatory authority within a certain time frame following the termination date of the pension plan. The report must be prepared by an actuary. The report must include information on the benefits to be provided to members, former members and other persons who have pension entitlements, the assets and liabilities of the plan, and the methods of allocating and distributing the pension plan assets.

- Members must be provided with a written statement that sets out information concerning their pension benefit entitlements and settlement options.

Where a pension plan is terminated, all jurisdictions require the employer to contribute to the fund the amount owing but not yet paid, or the amount required to fund the plan on a solvency basis. Ontario is the only jurisdiction that operates a Pension Benefits Guarantee Fund, which is designed to provide benefits to members until the employer has funded the benefit. A more detailed description of the Ontario Pension Benefits Guarantee Fund is found under the heading "Financial Issues" in this chapter. Most pension standards legislation also contains specific rules governing the reduction of benefits on a plan termination, where there are insufficient assets to secure all benefits and no prospect of full funding.

Where a defined benefit pension plan is fully terminated, there may be surplus assets in the pension fund. When a plan is fully terminated, surplus represents the value of excess pension fund assets not needed to pay or settle all benefits. For partial plan terminations, pension standards legislation requires that the surplus attributable to the part of the plan being terminated be identified in the wind-up valuation report.

All pension standards legislation, with the exception of Quebec, provides that members affected by a partial plan termination have the same benefits and rights that they would have if the plan were fully terminated. It is for this purpose that the identification of surplus attributable to the part of the plan being terminated is relevant. The legislation in both Alberta and British Columbia states that a member affected by a partial termination is not entitled to share in any surplus assets on partial termination; however, the plan may provide for such an entitlement. As previously indicated, the legislation in the province of New Brunswick indicates that surplus may be distributed to plan members unless the plan provides for payment of surplus to the employer. In Quebec, the legislation no longer recognizes partial terminations and therefore, surplus distribution on such an occurrence is not an issue.

The full termination of a pension plan that is in a surplus position will require the assessment of surplus rights in order for the assets to be fully distributed. It is always possible for the employer to pay surplus to members, either as benefit improvements (subject to maximums imposed by the *Income Tax Act*) or as cash payments, provided that the plan contains provisions that specify how this will be done (or is amended to so provide). If the employer wishes to withdraw the surplus, the consent of the regulatory authority is required. Generally this consent cannot be given unless the employer is entitled to withdraw the surplus according to the plan terms. Although the legislation typically states this requirement, in most cases the regulatory authority does not have the ability to make a binding determination of entitlement. An employer may have to obtain a court ruling on the entitlement in order to proceed. Many jurisdictions impose further requirements, such as notice to all members of the proposed withdrawal. In New Brunswick, notice need only be given to the trade union and each member of the advisory committee. Ontario regulations contain a temporary rule (frequently extended and currently set to expire at the end of 2002) that two-thirds of the plan members must agree to the withdrawal. In Nova Scotia, effective January 1, 2003, even if it is not provided for in the plan, an employer will be able to withdraw surplus upon termination if the employer has received at least ⅔ consent from (a) members of the pension plan (b) former members, and (c) other persons within a prescribed class. In Quebec, the allocation of any surplus assets from a terminated pension plan is subject to (a) an agreement to be made between the employer, the members and the beneficiaries of the plan (where no more than 30% of the members and beneficiaries oppose the agreement in writing); or (b) where the plan is established pursuant to a collective agreement, an arbitration award or an order that renders such an agreement compulsory.

A surplus withdrawal by an employer on partial plan termination is governed by the rules for surplus withdrawal from an ongoing plan, which are generally more prohibitive than those rules that apply on full plan termination. This is consistent with the purpose of the legislation to ensure the continued financial health of a pension plan, and with the fact that surplus exists only notionally in a plan that has continuing liabilities. In Quebec, an employer may not withdraw surplus from an ongoing plan.

Surplus

Some pension standards legislation defines surplus. With minor differences, surplus is essentially the excess of the value of plan assets over the liabilities of the plan. Additional discussion of surplus is found under the heading "Financial Issues" in this chapter.

Most pension standards legislation[9] requires a plan text to contain provisions that specify how surplus is to be dealt with in the plan while it is a going concern, and on plan termination. Some legislation further provides that if the plan is silent, the plan will be deemed to provide that the employer is not entitled to withdraw surplus from the plan.

For purposes of the plan as a going concern, all pension standards legislation permits contribution holidays, provided that the provisions of the plan do not prohibit this practice. On the other hand, strict controls are imposed on any withdrawal of surplus by the employer

---

[9] In July 2001, the Ontario Government introduced a Consultation Paper entitled *Surplus Distribution from Defined Benefit Plans*, which, if adopted, would substantially alter the treatment of surplus. Key proposals relate to the treatment of surplus in the event of (a) full plan wind-up, (b) partial plan wind-up (c) ongoing plans and (d) contribution holidays. The paper can be viewed at **www.gov.on.ca/FIN**.

from an ongoing plan. Regulatory approval of the withdrawal is required, and that approval cannot be granted unless the employer has established an entitlement to withdraw the surplus. An employer who wishes to withdraw surplus from an ongoing plan faces significant procedural requirements, such as an extensive notification and disclosure process for all plan members. Often the consent of plan members is required by the legislation. Pension standards legislation typically restricts the amount of surplus that can be withdrawn, in order to ensure that a sufficient amount remains in the plan to preserve the fully funded status of the plan.

Pension standards legislation does not impose any restrictions on the amount of surplus that may accumulate in a pension plan. This is consistent with the underlying purposes of pension standards legislation to ensure that a pension plan is adequately funded. However, investment income earned by a pension fund is not taxed. As a means of controlling tax revenue foregone arising as a result of not taxing the investment income, the *Income Tax Act* prohibits the accumulation of surplus beyond a specified level. An employer cannot contribute to a pension plan if the plan has surplus greater than:

- 20% of the plan's actuarial liabilities; or
- If less, the greater of:
  — two times the estimated current service contributions that would be required to be made by the employer and employees for the 12 months following the effective date of the actuarial valuation on which the actuary's recommendation for contributions is based; and
  — 10% of liabilities.

Although the pension standards regulators would undoubtedly prefer that the *Income Tax Act* not impose a cap on the surplus in a plan, pension standards legislation does not conflict with the provisions of the *Income Tax Act*.

Case Law

Given the potential financial significance of pension issues for employers and for plan members, it is inevitable that the courts are asked to resolve some questions of entitlement. In all jurisdictions that have pension standards legislation in force, a regulatory authority is charged with the responsibility for interpreting the statute and regulation and for making decisions that affect employers and plan members. An appeal of such decisions to a court is normally available. The following discussion is an overview of the major decisions made by Canadian courts on pension matters.

Surplus

The nature of legislative provisions dealing with surplus is discussed under the heading "Special Situations" in this chapter. Despite the fact that there are ordinarily legislative provisions that deal with matters pertaining to pension plan surplus, there is no legislation that specifically overrides explicit plan provisions respecting the ability of a sponsoring employer to take a contribution holiday or to recapture surplus on plan termination. Therefore, there has been considerable activity in the courts on the subject of whether or not plan provisions prohibit or permit contribution holidays, or provide surplus rights to the employer or to plan members on plan termination.

Contribution Holidays

There was uncertainty in Canada's common law jurisdictions regarding contribution holidays until the Supreme Court of Canada decision in *Schmidt v. Air Products*. In that case, the Supreme Court of Canada indicated that contribution holidays are permitted if provided for explicitly or implicitly by plan provisions, and that such a right is not dependent on who is entitled to the surplus in the event of plan termination. The court stated quite clearly that a contribution holiday is not a derogation of members' rights to surplus on plan termination, where that right exists. It could also be considered to follow from the principles applied in the decision, that in the absence of a restrictive amending clause or contractual obligations of the employer prohibiting the amendment, an amendment that changes the nature of the employer's contribution obligation from a fixed obligation to one that can fluctuate depending on the funded status of the plan, is valid.

Prior to the Supreme Court providing a definitive answer on this issue, the courts were arriving at different results, not only because of the particularities of the plan provisions being considered, but also from disagreement about what principles of law should be applied. Some courts considered the use of surplus for a contribution holiday to be the same as a withdrawal of surplus by the employer, while others took the approach that was eventually confirmed by the Supreme Court. It should be noted that the *Air Products* case has settled the issue in this way only for Canada's common law jurisdictions (i.e., all except Quebec).

In the wake of *Air Products*, however, the results in each case can differ depending on the court's interpretation of the contribution provisions of the pension plan. In *Hockin v. Bank of British Columbia*, the Court of Appeal for British Columbia accepted the *Air Products* holdings, but decided the employer was not entitled to take contribution holidays because the plan did not permit it. The court also found that the provisions of the federal *Pension Benefits Standards Act* prior to 1987 did not permit it. (All pension standards legislation now permits contribution holidays if the plan provisions permit.) In *Maurer v. McMaster University*, the Ontario Court of Appeal also followed the reasoning set out in *Air Products* and held that plan language stating that the employer's contribution obligation is determined by the actuary, based on the sufficiency of the fund, permits the employer to take contribution holidays if the fund is in surplus.

In Quebec, the courts have determined the contribution holiday issue quite differently under the civil law. The leading case in Quebec is *Châteauneuf v. TSCO of Canada Ltd (Singer)*. In that case, the Quebec Court of Appeal ruled that in the absence of language specifically pertaining to contribution holidays, contribution holidays are not permitted. Also, based on civil law principles, the Court of Appeal departed from the Supreme Court of Canada ruling in *Air Products* and commented that if employees own the surplus in case of plan termination, the use of surplus by the employer to meet its contribution requirement is a misappropriation of funds.

Entitlement to Surplus on Plan Termination

There has also been uncertainty concerning the issue of surplus entitlement on plan termination. The uncertainty existed because pension plans had not received much judicial attention until significant surpluses arose in the 1980s, and because many pension plans established in the preceding decades were silent or ambiguous with respect to the disposition of surplus on plan termination. Employers had an expectation, even where the documentation was silent, that they were entitled to surplus in accordance with the principle that the plan fund had been established only to ensure that the promised benefits would be paid. Faced with silent or ambiguous plan documentation, the courts disagreed about whether a pension plan should be treated as a contract or as a trust, even where the plan's funding documents clearly fell into one or the other category. Even within trust law or contract law, various principles could be applied. Neither body of law by itself adequately addressed the fact that a pension plan consists of a bundle of rights typically created unilaterally by an employer, concerning an ever-changing group of beneficiaries, and applying over a long period of time, and neither could bridge the gap between the employer's expectation of entitlement versus the apparent effect of the plan documentation. Complicating the matter was the fact that in many cases, the plan members had developed their own expectations, also in many cases inconsistent with the plan documents or the employer's understanding of their rights. The result was considerable variance in surplus entitlement determinations, depending on particular facts in each case and on the legal analysis preferred by the court.

The *Air Products* decision settled much of the uncertainty for common law jurisdictions, particularly with respect to the application of trust principles to pension plans whose funds are established pursuant to a trust. The Supreme Court confirmed the principle that the settlor of a trust cannot revoke the trust unless the power to do so is expressly reserved in the original terms of the trust, and clarified that a general power of amendment is not sufficient to give the employer the power to revoke the trust. Therefore, if a pension trust fund is established that has the effect of giving the beneficiaries an interest in surplus funds, the employer cannot later unilaterally amend the trust to take that interest away, unless the plan clearly allows such an amendment to be made. One of the two pension plans in question was subject to a trust and did not contain language allowing the employer to revoke the trust.

The *Air Products* decision also establishes that if a pension plan is not subject to a trust, then the surplus entitlement can be determined in accordance with principles of contract. The Court dealt with a plan that was subject to a contract. That plan stated from its inception that surplus on termination would revert to the employer. It also included wording that no amendment could divert part of the pension fund to purposes other than for the exclusive benefit of the members. The Court was of the view that this language applied only to the benefits defined in the plan. This, combined with the surplus reversion provision, resulted in the employer owning the surplus in that part of the plan. In matters of contract, considerable uncertainty still exists because a myriad of considerations will apply, including the terms of the plan documentation as they are amended from time to time and relevant communications between the employer and the plan members.

The law in Quebec has developed quite differently. In *Le Syndicat national des Salariés des outils Simonds c. Eljer Manufacturing Canada Inc.*, the pension plan was analyzed as a contract by the Quebec Court of Appeal. The plan provided that surplus on wind-up would be paid to members and that the employer could amend the plan, provided the amendment did not adversely affect the inherent or acquired rights of the members. The court held that surplus entitlement was an "inherent right", and therefore the plan could not be amended to provide surplus reversion to the employer. In *Châteauneuf c. TSCO of Canada Ltd.* (Singer), the pension plan was characterized as a "stipulation pour autrui" by the Quebec Court of Appeal. The effect of such a characterization is that surplus rights cannot be altered without the consent of the members. The court held invalid an amendment providing surplus reversion to the employer, since the employer did not obtain member consent. It should be added that though this case was decided before the enactment of rules governing the establishment and operation of trusts for pension purposes in the *Civil Code of Quebec*, the result would also have been favourable to the plan members under the new civil law of trusts.

Surplus on Partial Plan Wind-ups

In *Monsanto v. Superintendent of Financial Services (Ontario)* the Regulator refused to accept a partial wind-up report due to the employer's failure to distribute the surplus to terminated members. This decision has created considerable concern among plan sponsors, who oppose the idea of distributing surplus on partial plan terminations, while labour groups, on the other hand, have applauded the decision. In *Monsanto*, 146 active members of the Plan were terminated due to a reorganization involving a plant closure. Monsanto offered the affected members a benefits package, which included cash severance and pension improvements for their more senior members. Amendments were filed with the pension regulator to provide enhanced benefits. Only 45 of the affected 146 members were eligible for the enhanced benefits. Following the initial registration of the amendments, Monsanto submitted its partial wind-up report. At that time, there was an actuarial surplus. The Superintendent of Financial Services refused to accept the report, mainly because of the failure to distribute the surplus. Monsanto then appealed to the Financial Services Tribunal. The majority of the Tribunal agreed with Monsanto that the Ontario *Pensions Benefit Act* did not oblige Monsanto to distribute the surplus upon partial wind-up. Subsection 70(6) of the Act, which deals with partial wind-up of a pension plan, reads as follows:

> On the partial wind up of a pension plan, members, former members and other persons entitled to benefits under the pension plan shall have rights and benefits that are not less than the rights and benefits they would have on a full wind up of the pension plan on the effective date of the partial wind up.

Additionally, the majority stated that Monsanto had a legitimate expectation that its report would not be refused. It concluded that Monsanto "had relied, directly or indirectly, to its detriment on the relevant practice of the pension regulator in structuring the partial wind up and in providing the benefit enhancements, which reliance was reflected in the partial wind up report." The minority decision of the Tribunal, written by Louis Erlichman, stated that it would have upheld the Superintendent's refusal to accept Monsanto's partial wind-up report. Among various other reason's, Erlichman stated that there was no reason to exclude surplus right's from the rights referred to in subsection 70(6) of the Act. Regarding the "legitimate expectations" argument, Erlichman stated that the members' rights cannot be ignored simply because of the lack of clarity in the Superintendent's and the Pension Commission's (now FSCO) prior statements. The Tribunal's decision was appealed to the Ontario Divisional Court and the issue on appeal was confined to the surplus distribution issue and the legitimate expectation issue.

The Divisional Court set aside the order of the Financial Services Tribunal dated April 14, 2000 and directed the Superintendent of Financial Services to carry out the proposal to refuse the partial wind-up report submitted by Monsanto. On both of the issues on appeal, surplus distribution and legitimate expectation, the Court agreed with and adopted the reasons of the Minority Tribunal decision. However, the Court also stated that the language in subsection 70(6) was not clear and that the Legislature ought to rectify this at the earliest reasonable opportunity. With respect to the legitimate expectation issue, in addition to reasons given by the minority, it was the Court's opinion that the doctrine of legitimate expectation can give rise to procedural rights, at most, and cannot justify any disregard for the requirements of the law.

The *Monsanto* decision was appealed to the Ontario Court of Appeal. The case was argued in front of the Court of Appeal at the end of April 2002. No decision had yet been released at the time of writing of this material.

Pension Plan Governance

R. v. Blair is an Ontario case dealing with pension plan governance and the role and responsibilities of plan administrators (the Enfield case). At the trial division level, the members of the pension committee appointed by the plan sponsor to administer the plan were convicted for having failed to properly supervise the internal investment manager of the pension fund. The manager invested a large proportion of the fund assets in securities of the plan sponsor, in violation of the limits prescribed under the *Pension Benefits Act* of Ontario. The trial judge found that though the plan text named the individual corporate plan sponsor as administrator, the committee was the *de facto* administrator of the plan and, therefore, personal liability attached to its members for not ensuring that appropriate systems for pension plan and pension fund administration were in place and operating adequately. The judge further stated that a plan administrator cannot delegate, to an external trustee, the responsibility of monitoring the daily activities of the investment manager with respect to complying with regulatory restrictions on pension investments.

The Court of Appeal overturned this decision and exonerated the members of the pension committee. The court held that the *Pension Benefits Act* of Ontario permits the appointment of only one administrator, and that it would be impossible to have a "legal administrator" and a separate "*de facto* administrator" with each having liability as "administrator" under the Act. The corporate plan sponsor named in the pension plan was the administrator, and the committee was simply the agent of the administrator to which some functions had been delegated. Based on the facts of the case, the court concluded that the investment manager was not an agent of the committee, but an agent of the plan sponsor. Therefore, the committee members did not have the responsibility for assessing the investment manager's qualifications and activities. The court also stated clearly that it was appropriate for an agent to subdelegate the investment monitoring function to a professional pension fund trustee. The court implied that there might in fact have been a breach of duty by the plan sponsor, as administrator, in the supervision of the investment manager. However, charges were not laid against the corporation.

Marriage Breakdown

The division of pension benefits upon relationship breakdown is another complex area of pension law. Adding to the complexity is the fact that this area is regulated by provincial matrimonial property legislation as well as by pension legislation. As with many pension matters, the rules pertaining to pension splitting are not always consistent across jurisdictions. Some legislation states that the splitting of pension benefits can occur either as of the date of marital breakdown or as of the date of the member's termination or retirement. Further, rules regarding when the non-member spouse is entitled to receive his or her share of the pension benefits also vary — payment may be made immediately, or only on the occurrence of a specified event, such as the member's retirement or termination, or at any of these times.

Family law also varies from province to province. At this time, there is no jurisdictional synchronization regarding who is a spouse in relation to pension splitting on "marriage" breakdown. For example, Alberta, New Brunswick and Prince Edward Island do not recognize common-law partners in matrimonial property legislation. As a result, pension division is not available for common-law partners (same sex or opposite sex) in these provinces. While Ontario and Newfoundland and Labrador also do not recognize common-law partners in matrimonial property legislation, members and their common-law partners in these provinces have the option of including pensions within their separation or cohabitation agreements. British Columbia and Manitoba members may elect to have the marital breakdown provisions apply to their common-law partners.

In Nova Scotia, Quebec and Saskatchewan, however, the law has changed to accommodate same-sex and opposite-sex common-law partners. In Nova Scotia, same-sex couples and unmarried opposite-sex couples can file domestic-partner declarations with the province to create legally-recognized "domestic partnerships". As a result, domestic partners are entitled to enjoy all of the same rights as married spouses under the Nova Scotia *Matrimonial Property Act*.

Quebec Bill 84, *An Act instituting civil unions and establishing new rules of filiation*, was assented to on June 8, 2002. The legislation defines a civil union as "a commitment between two persons eighteen years of age or over who express their free and enlightened consent to live together and to uphold the rights and obligations that derive from that status". Individuals in a civil union must be unmarried and cannot be parties to another civil union, nor may the parties be siblings, ascendants or descendants. A civil union is dissolved by a notarized joint declaration, by a court judgment or by the death of either spouse. If a civil union dissolves, partners will have the same rights and obligations with respect to assets as they would in a divorce.

The legislation regarding the division of pension benefits has not always provided sufficient guidelines to enable the resolution of such disputes with as little conflict as possible. As with all matters that lack legislative clarity, it is often left to the courts to provide some form of guidance. Recently the Supreme Court of Canada has attempted to provide some clarification with respect to "double-dipping".

In *Boston v. Boston*, the Supreme Court of Canada considered the "double-dipping"/"double recovery" issue. Double-dipping arises where, after retirement, the pension converts from a capital asset into an income asset, resulting in "double recovery" if spousal support is paid out of income earned on pension assets that were already considered in the equalization. In *Boston*, the husband and his wife had been married for 36 years and she had remained at home to raise their seven children, while the husband pursued his career in education and financially supported the family. The parties had consented to a judgment dividing their assets. The husband received approximately $385,000, of which $333,329 was the value of his teacher's pension. His wife received the matrimonial home, and some other assets, which totaled approximately $370,000. Additionally, the husband agreed to pay spousal support in the amount of $3,200 monthly, indexed to the cost of living. At the time of judgment, the husband was earning $115,476 as a Director of Education, while the wife had no employment income.

Subsequently, the husband retired and began receiving pension income of $8,000 per month, of which $5,300 was derived from pension assets retained on equalization, $2,300 was derived from pension assets acquired after equalization, and the balance was a CPP benefit. His net assets totalled $7,000, while the wife's assets had grown to more than $493,000. The husband brought an application to reduce the amount of spousal support, claiming that his retirement on a reduced income and the "systematic depletion" of his pension amounted to a material change in circumstances. The motions judge concurred and reduced the amount of monthly support to $950, unindexed. The Ontario Court of Appeal acknowledged that there was a material change in circumstances, but nonetheless raised the amount to $2,000 per month, indexed. The husband appealed to the Supreme Court of Canada.

The Supreme Court of Canada allowed the appeal and restored the $950 per month award, but did permit indexing for inflation. The Supreme Court concluded that it is *generally* unfair to permit double recovery.

If post-retirement spousal support is paid out of income from pension assets that were not subject to equalization, then the double recovery dilemma will be effectively circumvented. In this case, the motions judge rightfully concluded that the quantum of support should be based on the portion of the husband's pension that was acquired after the equalization date. The wife did not suffer economic hardship from the avoidance of double recovery.

Despite the Supreme Court's ruling against double recovery in this case, the Court also clearly stated that double recovery cannot always be avoided. In certain situations, a pension that has been equalized can also be used later to provide support when the pension is in pay. Double recovery may be permitted where:

- The member has the financial means to pay support;

- The non-member spouse has made a reasonable effort to use the equalized assets in an income-producing way, and yet despite this, economic hardship continues; and

- Spousal support orders are based on need as opposed to compensation.

Prior to the *Boston* decision, the Supreme Court of Canada considered another contentious issue: the determination of the appropriate pension valuation method upon marital breakdown. Pension valuation involves determining the present value of an income stream that will be received in the future, based upon certain presumed factors. This amount will then be divided between the spouses. Valuation of many matrimonial assets is relatively simple as compared to pension assets, as frequently certain factors in pension valuations must be based on assumptions rather than absolutes.

In *Best v. Best*, the parties had a relatively short marriage of 12 years and during their relationship, the husband worked as a school principal, and continued to work as such at the time of trial. His pension plan was a defined benefit plan, which provided that the benefit was equal to two per cent of the average of the husband's five highest annual salaries, multiplied by the total number of years of service prior to retirement.

In the calculation of the parties' net family property, a dispute arose over the value to be assigned to the pension at the date of marriage. The husband favoured the *pro rata* method, while the wife favoured the value-added method. The amount attributable to the period of the marriage was smaller under the *pro rata* method. At trial, the Court valued the pension using the "termination value-added" method, therefore ruling in favour of the wife. The judge also ordered that the husband could satisfy the equalization payment over 10 years. The Ontario Court of Appeal upheld the trial decision. The husband appealed to the Supreme Court of Canada.

Speaking for the majority, Justice Major concluded that, absent special circumstances, a *pro rata* method of pension valuation best achieves the purpose of the *Family Law Act*; that is, the equitable division of assets between spouses. The *pro rata* method calculates the pension benefit accrued during the marriage by first calculating the present value of the pension benefit accrued on the date of separation. Second, the pension's value on the date of marriage is determined by multiplying the first value by the ratio of the number of years of pensionable service prior to the marriage, divided by the total pensionable service up to the date of separation. The amount attributable to the period of marriage is the difference between the value on the date of marriage and the value on the date of separation. The value-added approach is calculated by subtracting the pension's value at the date of marriage from the value of the pension at the date of separation.

Each successive year of pensionable service is of increasingly greater value, if the value-added method is used. It apportions more value to the later years of pension holding than to earlier years. As a result, where there is significant pensionable service prior to the marriage, this method may result in a disproportionate share being attributed to the marriage. In the *Best* case, the value-added method apportioned 88% of the value of the appellant's 32 years of pensionable service to the 12-year marriage, whereas with the *pro rata* method, all pensionable service years are treated equally — the pension increases in value at a constant rate over time. In this particular case, 37% of the pension's value was attributable to the period of marriage.

The Court also noted that the *pro rata* method will not always be preferable. However, as a general rule, the *pro rata* method will be favored due to the nature of a defined benefit plan. Justice Major commented that legislative changes were required to provide guidance on pension valuation. In fact, some jurisdictions in Canada do endorse some form of *pro rata* approach to pension valuation. The lack of direction in other jurisdictions requires parties to select an agreed-upon valuation method. This is certainly not an easy task, as was illustrated in the *Best* case. The results can vary significantly, depending upon the valuation method selected.

SUPPLEMENTARY PENSION ARRANGEMENTS

Where an employer provides a registered pension plan to employees, the level of benefits that can be provided from that plan is limited by the registration rules of the *Income Tax Act*. A supplementary arrangement is needed if the pension income that the employer wishes to provide is in excess of that limit.

Supplementary pension arrangements are commonly known as Supplementary Executive Retirement Plans (SERPs) or Supplementary Retirement Plans (SRPs). They are also called top-up or top hat plans. SERPs may take a variety of designs and may be formal or informal, funded or unfunded. They are growing in frequency and coverage.

This chapter looks at:

- The emergence of supplementary arrangements;

- The design of these plans;

- Funding issues and approaches; and

- Documentation.

Emergence of Supplementary Arrangements

Income Tax Act Limit for Registered Pension Plans

Supplementary arrangements have emerged following the inclusion in the *Income Tax Act* of a limit on the retirement income payable from a registered pension plan (RPP). In 1976, this limit was set at $1,715 per year of pensionable service, to a maximum of 35 years. This produces an annual pension of $60,025 after 35 years of service. This limit affected employees earning more than $85,750 in a plan providing an accrual rate of 2%, and an income replacement of up to 70% could be achieved. In 1976 the affected earnings level was approximately six times the average industrial wage, and therefore supplementary arrangements were needed only for executives. This limit remained unchanged from 1976 to 1990. By 1990, earnings of $85,750 were approximately 2½ times the average wage, and the limit had begun to affect employees below the executive level.

The limit was slightly revised in 1990 to $1,722.22 per year of pensionable service, and was originally scheduled to be indexed to the average wage beginning in 1995. In addition, the 35-year limit on pensionable service was eliminated for service after 1989 (1991 for plans in place on March 27, 1988). The indexing was intended to stop the erosion of the limit. However, in successive budgets since 1990, the federal government has repeatedly postponed indexation of the limit — first to 1996 and then to 1999 and most recently with the 1996 budget, to 2005. As a result, the erosion of the limit and the expansion of its application continues.

The table below shows the amount of pensionable earnings above which individuals are affected by the limit for different benefit rates under the pension plan.

For plans providing a benefit rate per year of service of:	The limit is affecting employees earning more than
2.0%	$ 86,111
1.5%	$114,815
1.0%	$172,222

The provision of supplementary pension arrangements was once a concern only for executive employees. The trend since the late 1980s has been for more employers to put supplementary arrangements in place, and to expand the membership of existing arrangements to include all employees affected by the maximum. In Morneau Sobeco's 2001 survey of Executive Retirement Arrangements, 32.3% of the plans providing supplementary pension benefits were open to all employees affected by the maximum pension limits under the *Income Tax Act*. Of the balance, 40.3% of the plans were for executives designated by the Board, and 27.4% were based on job category.

Competitive Compensation

Supplementary arrangements are not only used for topping up the benefits that would otherwise be paid from a registered plan if not for the maximum, they are also often used to attract and retain executive employees. A supplementary arrangement, being unencumbered by registration requirements, is a flexible tool that can provide generous pensions on bases that differ from those normally used in a registered pension plan. Hence, for executives hired at mid-career for whom the regular plan can provide only a relatively small benefit, the supplementary arrangement can be designed to compensate for short service. For example, a supplementary arrangement could provide pension income based on an accrual rate of 4% of earnings or 200% of service, or simply promise an income replacement of 70% of final pay.

Where the market for talented executives is competitive, a supplementary arrangement can be an important element of the total compensation package.

Prevalence of Supplementary Arrangements

The size of the company and the nature of the industry have been major determinants in the prevalence of supplementary arrangements. For example, all of Canada's large banks offer supplementary arrangements to their executives. Banks are typical of stable, long-term-oriented enterprises that develop talent over many years and want to retain it.

With the continued delay in the indexation of the maximum pension limit for registered pension plans, there will likely be a continuation of the trend in which supplementary arrangements are increasingly offered to more employees below executive ranks, in smaller companies, and in new industries.

SEC Disclosure

The Ontario Securities Exchange Commission requires publicly owned companies to disclose the compensation of their top five highest paid executives. This disclosure includes pensions.

Design Issues

When designing supplementary arrangements, there are a number of concerns and questions that must be addressed in order to deliver supplementary benefits that will meet the objectives of the employer in an efficient manner. These are discussed in the following pages.

Eligibility

The first question to be addressed is who should be eligible to participate in the supplementary arrangement.

Most commonly, supplementary arrangements are designed to meet the needs of highly compensated employees whose registered pensions are limited by the registration rules of the *Income Tax Act*. Supplementary arrangements can be grouped into two categories in relation to the eligibility criteria.

"Top-Up" Plans

In top-up plans, enrollment is automatic as soon as any employee's registered plan entitlement is restricted by the maximum. It is the most straightforward kind of supplementary arrangement.

Selected Enrollment Arrangements

The criteria to determine who participates in selected enrollment plans vary widely: Chief Executive Officer only, automatically for selected officers, at board discretion for selected officers, all employees above a certain position or all employees above a certain salary.

Benefit Formula

The vast majority (approximately 85–90%) of supplementary arrangements are of the defined benefit type. However, where the base plan is a defined contribution plan, the supplementary arrangement is more often also a defined contribution with real or notional contributions.

Top up plans generally provide for benefits in excess of those payable from the registered pension plan to produce a total benefit from both sources that would equal the benefit that would have been available from the registered pension plan if the *Income Tax Act* maximum had not existed.

In selected enrollment arrangements, provisions may be very similar to those of the registered pension plan covering the named executives, but in many instances, they are structured to meet special criteria for employees in senior positions. For example:

- To provide an attractive retirement income for executives hired in mid-career or to make up for pension credits forfeited as a result of leaving prior employment; and

- To help retain key executives as they approach retirement age.

These special provisions may include:

- An accrual rate higher than 2%;

- Additional service credits;

- Pensions as a flat percentage of final average earnings (i.e., 60%), irrespective of service; or

- Coordination with long-term incentives (although this approach is quite uncommon).

Covered earnings are usually tightly related to the corresponding registered pension plan provision, especially for top-up plans. Earnings used under the supplementary arrangement may either include or exclude cash bonuses. When they are included, most of the time actual bonuses are used, but sometimes target bonuses, or a fraction of them, are selected.

Some plans have a maximum on covered earnings or on credited service. A fairly common provision for selected enrollment arrangements using a benefit rate in excess of 2% is to specify a maximum benefit as a percentage of covered earnings (i.e., 60%).

Covered service is generally the same as for the registered pension plan. However, some plans may only recognize service since the inception of the supplementary plan, or may recognize service with a previous employer.

Ancillary Benefits

One consideration when designing a supplementary arrangement is to ensure that the combination of benefits provided by the registered pension plan and the supplementary arrangement achieves the desired objective at an acceptable cost. For example, one way to control costs and increase tax effectiveness is to maximize the ancillary benefits under the registered pension plan and provide reduced ancillary benefits under the supplementary arrangement.

The rules and benefits for early retirement are often based on the same conditions as in the registered pension plan. However, in many cases, generous supplementary arrangement provisions are accompanied by stringent vesting or early retirement provisions in order to retain executives. For example, it is not uncommon to provide no benefits under the supplementary arrangement if the employee terminates employment before becoming eligible to retire. In some circumstances, early retirement subsidies are subject to retirement with company consent. Also, it is not unusual to see variation in benefits according to whether termination of employment is voluntary or involuntary.

Indexing is another example where benefits under the supplementary arrangements and the registered pension plan may be coordinated. Many supplementary arrangements provide for the same indexation pattern as the registered pension plan (discretionary or automatic). However, to optimize tax effectiveness and benefit security, some supplementary arrangements provide that the total benefit is not indexed, or only partially indexed, but that the registered plan portion is fully indexed so that the supplementary arrangement portion of the total obligation reduces over time.

In the case of death prior to retirement, most plans provide for a spousal pension or for the payment of the commuted value. Some plans have a service condition and others provide that the benefit is only payable if death occurs after an age condition, such as age 55. Finally, some plans provide for no benefit at all. Should the employee die after retirement, plans typically provide a joint and survivor pension or a life pension with a guaranteed period as the normal form of payment.

Contributions

Almost all supplementary arrangements are non-contributory. For those plans that are contributory, most supplementary arrangements use the same contribution formulas as those contained in the underlying registered pension plan.

Other Provisions

There are other provisions that may appear in some supplementary arrangements. These include non-compete provisions where the provision of benefits is conditional on the executive not engaging in certain activities considered to compete with his or her former employer. There may also be a provision to cover the continuity of benefits or enhancement of benefits under the supplementary plan in the event of a change in control or ownership of the organization.

Retiring Allowances

A supplementary arrangement is often designed to utilize the tax advantages available under the *Income Tax Act* with respect to retiring allowances.

Under the *Income Tax Act*, a retiring allowance is an amount received upon or after retirement from an office or employment, in recognition of long service or in respect of loss of office or employment. A retiring allowance is usually paid as a single sum, but it can also be paid out in a limited series of installments. Retiring allowances are often paid in addition to the registered pension plan benefits to encourage an employee to retire. In the absence of a pension plan, they are also used to reward long-service employees.

Although a retiring allowance must be included as taxable income in the year received, tax may be avoided if the retiring allowance is transferred to a registered pension plan or to a Registered Retirement Savings Plan (RRSP), subject to certain limits. For 1996 and subsequent taxation years, the amount that can be transferred to a registered pension plan or RRSP is limited to:

1. $2,000 times the number of years before 1996 during which the employee was employed by the employer or a related employer; plus

2. an additional $1,500 for each of these years of service, prior to 1989, in respect of which employer contributions to a registered pension plan or a deferred profit sharing plan had not vested in the employee.

Because of the limits, retiring allowances are used mostly as severance payments to terminated employees, or as "sweeteners" to induce employees to accept an early retirement offer. However, it also makes sense to take advantage of the tax relief upon planned retirement. Supplemental arrangements are often used to provide retiring allowance payments.

Funding

The tax relief that makes funding registered pension plans attractive is not available when assets are set aside to fund the benefits promised under a supplementary arrangement. Therefore, historically, few supplementary arrangements have been funded. Where supplementary arrangements are not funded, the pension benefits are paid as they fall due out of the company's current revenues (pay-as-you-go basis).

There are as many reasons to fund supplementary pensions as there are not to fund them. Supplementary pensions that are not funded can be a source of concern to corporate directors who may be worried that they will be held responsible for unfulfilled promises made to employees if there are deficiencies in compliance or communication. At the same time, the lack of funding can be a source of concern to employees who expect to receive supplementary pensions. There is a risk that the fortunes of the employer will deteriorate, rendering the employer unable to pay.

On the other hand, some companies feel that funding executive pensions is inappropriate; "if the ship goes down, those on the bridge are expected to go with it". Depending on the reasons why the supplementary arrangement was put in place, a corporation might consider the supplementary pension to be part of incentives for active employees rather than as a provision for the employee's retirement security in the future. Despite this rationale, it is nevertheless difficult to dismiss the concern of the retired employee to have a secure income that does not depend on the future success of the company.

Funding is only one way to provide security. In certain companies, the prospect of corporate failure during the remaining lifetime of its retiring employees is not a concern, and pay-as-you-go arrangements are felt to be secure. In other situations and for many reasons, security is an issue, and can be achieved in whole or in part, depending on the means.

As a result of new accounting rules, which came into effect as of January 1, 2000, it was thought that once employers were accounting for the costs of these supplementary arrangements on an accrual basis, they might be more inclined to fund them. This has not necessarily been the case. Additionally, according to Watson Wyatt's 2000 SERP survey, 23% of defined benefit supplementary arrangements are not accounted for on an accrual basis, despite accounting requirements to do so.

Methods for Securing Benefits

Security against default of payment may be obtained, or at least enhanced, in various ways. A brief description of possible approaches follows. It should be noted that the most common are the funded Retirement Compensation Arrangement (RCA) followed by an RCA that holds a letter of credit.

Funded RCAs

Under the *Income Tax Act*, where assets are transferred by an employer to another person (typically a trustee), or are held in trust by the employer to secure supplementary pension benefits, the arrangement is treated as an RCA. The contributions to an RCA and the investment income earned by RCA assets attract a 50% refundable tax.

It should be noted that there are 14 specific arrangements that are excepted from the definition of an RCA, and these excluded arrangements include registered pension plans, salary deferral arrangements and plans that are dealt with under other provisions of the Act, such as a deferred profit sharing plan, an employee profit sharing plan, a registered retirement savings plan, an employee trust and certain health, disability, unemployment benefit plans and certain foreign-service plans for non-residents. There is also an exception for plans established for the purpose of deferring the salary of a professional athlete. Life insurance premiums and insurance policies are also excluded. However, there are instances where a life insurance policy can be deemed to be an RCA. Additionally, certain "prescribed plans or arrangements" under the Income Tax Regulations will not be considered an RCA.

Employer contributions to an RCA are deductible under the *Income Tax Act*. Employee contributions made to an RCA are deductible subject to certain conditions. Distributions from the RCA fund are taxable income in the hands of the employee on receipt. However, 50% of the contributions and the realized investment earnings of the fund must be remitted to the CCRA as a refundable tax. On the other hand, this 50% tax is refunded, without interest, at the rate of 50% of all disbursements made by the fund. The net effect is that only half the monies contributed to an RCA generate investment returns.

The main advantage of funding through an RCA is that it provides security to the participating employee, since the assets in the RCA will typically be separate from company assets, and are therefore protected from the employer's creditors.

The cost related to funding through an RCA is greater than for a registered pension plan, because it does not benefit from the same advantageous tax treatment.

Letter of Credit RCA

The most common mechanism to provide security for a supplementary pension arrangement is a letter of credit. Although the letter of credit is not an immediate source of funding itself, it can provide a form of security against circumstances such as bankruptcy and change of control.

A letter of credit is an irrevocable promise by a financial institution, usually a bank, to pay a specified amount if certain conditions unfold (such as the failure to pay a pension). The letter of credit strategy defers the actual funding of the non-registered benefit until such time as the company does not meet its obligation to pay the benefit or to provide a replacement letter of credit. At that time, upon request of the appointed trustees, the lending institution advances the face amount of the letter of credit to fund the benefit, and thereby becomes a creditor of the employer.

The premium paid to the bank for the letter of credit in the amount needed to secure the unfunded accrued pension promise is analogous to an insurance premium for coverage that will facilitate payment of these benefits. It is a recurring expenditure. Normally, the term of a letter of credit is one year. For purposes of securing a long-term obligation such as pension income, successive letters of credit are put in place, each of which will become payable for the benefit of the retiree(s) if the company fails to provide the next letter of credit.

Letter of credit rate-setting is dependent upon the institution's assessment of the employer's credit-worthiness, and will be influenced by a number of factors, including risk assessment, usage of overall credit by the employer, terms of the promissory note from the employer to the institution in the event that the letter of credit is called, terms of the letter of credit, and the nature of the banking relationship. The annual charge for a letter of credit is typically in the range of ½% to 1½% of the face amount.

Generally, the employer will establish an RCA and will contribute twice the fee charged by the financial institution issuing the letter of credit and ½ of the contributions will be paid to the Receiver General. This contribution will be done on an annual basis as letters of credits are put in place. The RCA will use the contributions to purchase the letter of credit from the financial institution Seeing as there is no property held in the RCA, other than the letter of credit, there are no earnings inside the RCA subject to the refundable 50% tax.

The benefits would be paid out to the employee on a pay-as-you-go basis, and the letter of credit would only be called upon where the employer failed to make the payments or some other specified event occurred which would trigger the letter of credit.

Life Insurance Policies

As a result of special deeming rules under the *Income Tax Act*, when an employer acquires an interest in a life insurance policy with the intent to use that policy to fund retirement benefits, the RCA rules will apply. These special deeming rules can be summarized as follows[1]:

(a) the employer who purchased the policy is deemed to be the custodian of an RCA;

(b) the policy is deemed to be the property of the RCA;

(c) twice the amount of any premium paid in respect of the policy is deemed to be a contribution to an RCA and will be subject to the 50% refundable tax;

---

[1] These rules also apply to annuities.

(d) a repayment of a policy loan is also considered to be a contribution to an RCA; and

(e) any payments received pursuant to the policy, including policy loans will be treated as distributions from an RCA and will trigger the 50% refund.

Accordingly, the person who holds the interest in the policy will be liable to pay refundable tax equal to the amount of any policy premiums and repayments of policy loans.

Since the proceeds of the insurance policy are the unencumbered property of the company, the executive may have no security should the company encounter financial difficulties or a take-over bid.

An exempt life insurance policy held by an RCA to fund retirement benefits can provide advantageous tax treatment. The income earned under an exempt life insurance policy is not subject to the 50% RCA refundable tax. Thus, this can be a more cost-effective way to fund supplementary pension benefits than other securities such as GICs and bonds. However, these savings must be measured against the additional cost of insurance, the need for additional life insurance coverage, and the lack of true security against corporate financial failure.

Any payments from the life insurance policy would cause the refundable tax to be paid out to the employer, who is the custodian. Refunds from the RCA to the employer will be included in the employer's income. As for the employee, there will be no tax consequences until the employee actually receives the benefit, at which time he or she will be taxed. Additionally, any death benefits paid out to beneficiaries are considered taxable.

However, the above situation must be distinguished from the situation whereby the RCA trust purchases a life insurance policy (or annuity contract) on the life of the employee to fund retirement benefits. In such a situation, the employer would have funded the RCA previously and paid the refundable tax at that point. Therefore, the insurance premiums paid by the custodian of the RCA would not have been subject to the 50% refundable tax. As mentioned above, if the insurance policy is an exempt policy, any income earned will not be subject to the 50% refundable tax on income earned in an RCA trust. The death benefits paid out of an insurance policy to the RCA are exempt; however, any such proceeds paid out to the employee or a beneficiary will be taxable income to either the employee or the beneficiary.

Secular Trusts

A secular trust is an arrangement whereby the employer pays to the employee additional salary on the condition that the employee will in turn establish a trust to hold the additional amounts. The employee is the beneficiary of the trust. To ensure that the funds are used to provide retirement income, the employee agrees that the trust will contain terms that constrain the timing and amount of income the employee can withdraw from the trust. The capital used to establish the secular trust is taxable income to the employee. As a result, a gross-up may be required to offset the taxes paid. The employee pays tax on the income of the trust; thus, such trusts do not defer tax. The employer can normally obtain a deduction for the additional salary paid. A secular trust can be particularly tax-effective if the top marginal tax rate is less than the 50% rate applicable to RCAs.

Terminal Funding

Under this approach, the employer pays the present value of the employee's pension in a lump sum or by installments over a short period of time, at the time the employee retires. Terminal funding has the disadvantage that the employer's outlay may be substantial in certain circumstances. It will also vary widely from year to year, because the retirement pattern is usually irregular.

Paying a lump sum at retirement rather than periodic payments may be an acceptable compromise in many cases from a security perspective for the employee, but the lump sum amount is fully taxable to the employee in the year of receipt. From the employee's perspective, the lump-sum value of the supplementary arrangements entitlement should be calculated using the employee's after-tax expected rate of return.

However, many employers believe that where a lump-sum option exists, any additional tax liability should be the responsibility of the executive and they would require the lump sum to be determined using the employee's pre-tax expected rate of return. Plan documents need to be clear on the basis to be used when lump-sum payments are available.

Where it is the intention to provide the employee with a given amount of after-tax income each year, assumptions as to the employee's future marginal tax rate can be made and a prescribed annuity contract can be purchased from a life insurance company to provide the desired level of income. The employer would provide a bonus to the employee, who would then use the after-tax proceeds to purchase the annuity.

Cost of Funding

As noted in Chapter 5, determination of the cost of unfunded supplementary arrangements and, in particular, the choice of an appropriate discount rate assumption, involves a multi-faceted set of considerations. The additional cost of advance funding of the supplementary arrangement involves quantifying the return forfeited, if any, as a result of investing capital in a segregated trust versus investing in the business entity. To the extent that funds are borrowed to fund the obligations accruing under the supplementary arrangement in advance, the additional cost can be represented by the following formula:

$$\boxed{\text{(after-tax cost of borrowing) - (RCA after-tax rate of return)}}$$

$$\times$$

$$\boxed{\text{RCA fund average value}}$$

Whether or not the supplementary arrangement is funded, employers are required to account for its costs and to disclose its related obligations in their financial statements. Chapter 5 discusses these financial management issues related to supplementary arrangements.

Documentation

The documentation of the supplementary pension promise is important and should not be neglected. The wording of the plan text or individual agreements is very important to the security of the promise, and is also crucial at the employee termination or retirement date, especially in the context of a difficult separation. If the documentation of a supplementary arrangement is restricted to a board of directors' resolution or to a letter signifying intent, the lack of details concerning benefit delivery or the contractual underpinnings of the commitment can cause significant problems years after the supplementary arrangement is established.

A more formal policy can be in the form of a contract between the employee and the company, or a plan text accompanied with a designation letter to the employee.

Plan sponsors should be aware that the documentation will also have an impact on the ease (or lack of it) of plan administration and communication to the members of the plan.

Chapter 10

OTHER RETIREMENT INCOME, SAVINGS AND DEFERRED COMPENSATION ARRANGEMENTS

Over the last two decades, the pension legal environment in Canada has grown in complexity — there has been an important reform of the pension standards legislation as well as of the *Income Tax Act*. As a result, some employers, especially smaller ones, have chosen to terminate their defined benefit pension plans in favor of defined contribution arrangements, including group Registered Retirement Savings Plans (group RRSPs) and Deferred Profit Sharing Plans (DPSPs). Also, many employers have viewed a defined contribution arrangement as a vehicle to help them control future costs and support a new element of corporate culture — the shift of responsibility to employees.

This chapter provides an overview of retirement income arrangements other than pension plans, as well as other savings programs that can generate additional retirement income, even though this may not be their main purpose.

Registered Retirement Savings Plans

The legislation creating Registered Retirement Savings Plans (RRSPs) was enacted in 1957 and was designed to encourage individuals to save for their retirement on a tax-sheltered basis. Assets under RRSPs have grown rapidly, particularly since the 1991 changes to the *Income Tax Act* that increased contribution limits, and now constitute a significant proportion of total Canadian retirement savings.

These plans are of particular value to the self-employed, who have no other opportunity to accumulate retirement savings on a tax-preferred basis, but they may also be used by employees, whether or not they are members of pension or profit sharing plans.

An RRSP is a contract between an individual and an authorized insurer, trustee or corporation. Contributions made by a taxpayer out of earned income are deductible for taxation purposes, within the contribution limits described in Chapter 7. Taxpayers may also elect to contribute to their spouses' RRSPs within the prescribed limits; however, certain restrictions apply on withdrawals of money from a spousal RRSP. The investment earnings on the assets of RRSPs are tax-sheltered; however, withdrawals from the plans are taxable unless they are "excluded withdrawals" pursuant to the Home Buyers Plan or the Lifelong Learning Plan[1].

Initially, the funds from an RRSP had to be used to purchase a life annuity from an insurance company. Such annuities may be based upon the life of the taxpayer alone, or on the lifetime of the taxpayer and the taxpayer's spouse. This type of annuity may have a guaranteed term, but the guaranteed term must not exceed 90 minus the age of the annuitant, or when the annuitant's spouse is younger and the annuitant elects, 90 minus the age of the annuitant's spouse. Amendments to the *Income Tax Act* effective in 1978 allowed two retirement income options in addition to the life annuity:

- The Registered Retirement Income Fund (RRIF) was introduced in order to allow the individual more control over the investment of the fund after the RRSP matures and more flexibility in the timing of withdrawals from the fund.

- The other option is an annuity certain (a fixed-term annuity) for the term of years equal to 90 minus the age of the annuitant when the annuity commences, or if the annuitant so elects, 90 minus the age of the annuitant's spouse where the spouse is younger than the annuitant.

Therefore there are three options: a RRIF, a life annuity or a fixed-term annuity.

---

[1] The Home Buyers Plan allows individuals to withdraw up to $20,000 from RRSPs tax-free to purchase a first home. They are allowed a period of up to 15 years to repay the withdrawn funds. Under the Lifelong Learning Plan (LLP), an individual is allowed to withdraw funds from his or her RRSP on a tax-free basis for the purpose of financing full-time studies of the individual or the individual's spouse or common-law partner. The aggregate withdrawal is limited to $20,000. The amounts withdrawn under the LLP must be repaid to the RRSP over a period not exceeding 10 years, beginning with the earlier of the second year after the last year that the student was enrolled in full-time studies and fifth year after the first year in which an LLP withdrawal was made.

The RRSP may be matured or annuitized at any time, except that the annuitant payments must commence or the funds must be transferred to a RRIF prior to the end of the year in which the taxpayer's 69th birthday is reached (71st birthday before 1996).

Pension standards legislation generally allows the value of the pension benefits from a registered pension plan of a terminating employee to be transferred into an RRSP. However, if the pension benefits are locked-in, the transfer must be made, depending upon the applicable pension standards legislation, to either a locked-in RRSP, a Locked-In Retirement Account (LIRA), a Life Income Fund (LIF), Locked-in Retirement Income Fund (LRIF), or a RRIF (only applicable in Saskatchewan)[2].

Locked-in RRSPs provide the individual with investment control and are similar to regular RRSPs. However, they differ from regular RRSPs in that a locked-in RRSP, as the name implies, is locked in until retirement age and the money must be used to provide retirement income. Subsequent to the advent of the locked-in RRSP, the LIRA was introduced and is essentially identical to a locked-in RRSP. A LIF is very similar to a RRIF, except that maximum and minimum annual withdrawals are prescribed by the applicable pension standards legislation and that a life annuity must be purchased with the balance of the fund at an age not exceeding 80. An LRIF is also basically identical to a LIF, except the employee never has to buy an annuity.

In 2002, Saskatchewan introduced a new portability option giving employees access to their formerly locked-in pension money. This new option, a RRIF, is only locked-in until age 55 and replaces LIFs and LRIFs in Saskatchewan.

Where a written separation agreement or a competent tribunal so directs, a taxpayer may generally transfer funds from the RRSP to an RRSP under which the taxpayer's spouse or former spouse is the annuitant. However, some provinces still prohibit this type of transfer in the case of locked-in benefits from employment pension plans.

Group RRSPs

Group RRSPs have gained in popularity in recent years as an alternative to pension plans. This trend follows a more general trend toward more defined contribution arrangements. Some employers have chosen a group RRSP as opposed to a defined contribution pen-

---

[2] In New Brunswick, Bill 30, *An Act to Amend the Pension Benefits Act*, received Royal Assent on June 7, 2002. When proclaimed into force, section 40.1 will permit a member, upon termination of employment, to have the administrator of the plan transfer up to 25% of the member's pension to a RRIF.

sion plan, a primary reason being that group RRSPs are not subject to pension standards legislation. More particularly, there is

- No plan text to be registered with a governmental supervisory authority;

- No locking-in;

- More flexibility to vary employer contributions among plan members;

- More flexibility in establishing eligibility conditions;

- No restriction on beneficiary designation;

- No mandatory joint and survivor pension when there is a spouse;

- No pension committee required (as required for Quebec registered pension plans);

- No plan members annual meeting required (also as required for Quebec pension plans); and

- Opportunity for the employee to arrange income splitting through spousal RRSPs.

On the other hand, there are some employer costs in operating a group RRSP as compared to a defined contribution pension plan, since "employer contributions" to RRSPs are considered salary to the employee for income tax and other purposes. These costs include:

- Immediate vesting of "employer contributions"; and

- Contributions to government plans on "employer contributions":

— Canada/Quebec Pension Plan (employer and employees);

— Employment Insurance (employer and employees);

— Provincial health care plans in some jurisdictions (employer); and

— Worker's Compensation (employer).

However, it also important to note, that if the employee's remuneration is greater than the maximum assessable earnings for payroll taxes, an increase in the employee's compensation to finance the Group RRSPs will not create an increase in the amount of payroll tax deducted.

Under the *Income Tax Act*, group RRSPs are merely a collection of individual RRSPs.

Group RRSPs also provide some advantages to the employees as opposed to individual RRSPs, even if the employer does not contribute. Advantages include:

- Saving for retirement through payroll deductions is very convenient, and the tax deductibility of the contribution is possible when withholding taxes;

- Employees can benefit from the advantages of the greater purchasing power of a group through:

— reduced administration and fund management costs, which may be paid or partially paid by the employer;

— access to a wide variety of investment funds (GICs, short-term deposit funds, equity funds, fixed-income funds, balanced funds, foreign equities funds, etc.).

Some of the very features in a group RRSP that offer flexibility make it difficult for employers to use this arrangement as a human resources management tool. Employer contributions to the group RRSP are immediately vested to the employee. It is difficult to ensure that the funds will eventually be used for retirement purposes rather than for any other personal purposes. It may be possible when such a plan is established to include non-withdrawal clauses in the arrangement. Otherwise, there is no legal basis on which to prevent withdrawals. To discourage contribution withdrawals, some employers suspend matching contributions for a period of one to five years in the event withdrawals are made during employment.

Group RRSPs are often used on a stand-alone basis, but they are also often found as a supplement to a non-contributory defined benefit pension plan or to a DPSP. A DPSP is used in these cases to receive employer contributions, as they are not considered as salary subject to payroll taxes. Other conditions governing DPSPs are described later in this chapter.

Fiduciary Responsibility for Group RRSPs

Even though a group RRSP is not subject to pension standards legislation, the employer establishing it may face some fiduciary or near fiduciary responsibility. It is usually the employer who selects the administrator and fund manager(s) who will act within the parameters set by the employer.

In such circumstances, the employer has a responsibility to make the selection with prudence and diligence. After the initial selection, the employer also has a responsibility to monitor and evaluate the fund manager's performance on an ongoing basis. These functions are crucial under a group RRSP, since the benefits to the participants are directly related to the performance of the fund manager and the investment selections. Chapter 6 discusses these issues in further detail.

Taxation of RRSPs

Contributions

Contributions to an RRSP are tax deductible within limits. Prior to 1991, self-employed persons and individuals who were not in an RPP or DPSP were permitted a higher maximum contribution than those who participated in such a plan. Today, the deductibility of RRSP contributions is governed by a retirement savings system based on the principle that tax assistance should be the same for all individuals with the same income, regardless of the arrangement in which they participate.

> *Post-1990 calculation of an individual's RRSP contribution limit*
>
> Contribution Limit = A + B + C - D
>
> A = Taxpayer's unused contribution room at the end of the preceding taxation year
>
> B = (lesser of 18% of "earned income" or "RRSP dollar limit" being $13,500 in 2002) - PA for preceding year
>
> C = Taxpayer's PAR for the year
>
> D = Taxpayer's net PSPA for the year.

See Chapter 7 for definitions of PAs, PARs and PSPAs.

What constitutes "earned income" is set out in the *Income Tax Act* and includes such things as employment income, business income, royalties, rental income, alimony or maintenance payments, payments received under a supplementary unemployment benefit plan, and research grants.

A taxpayer's "RRSP dollar limit" is defined in the *Income Tax Act* as being, for years other than 1996, the money purchase limit for the immediately preceding calendar year and for 1996, $13,500. Based on the "money purchase limits" the RRSP dollar limits are as follows

- For 1996 to 2003, $13,500;

- For 2004, $14,500; and

- For 2005, $15,500.

After 2005, the RRSP dollar limit is suppose to be increased based on the growth in the average industrial wage.

Investment Income

Investment income earned in an RRSP is not taxable until paid out, at which time the entire amount of any withdrawal is taxable as ordinary income. Lump sums payable from a spousal plan are added to the contributor's income if the withdrawal is made within three years of a contribution; otherwise they are taxed as income of the spouse. If an individual borrows money to finance an RRSP contribution, the interest payable on the loan taken is not tax deductible.

Assets may be transferred from one RRSP to another, or to a RRIF or RPP, without attracting tax at the time of transfer. Similarly, there is no tax on lump-sum transfers to an RRSP from an RPP or DPSP. Retiring allowances may be transferred to an RRSP, tax-free, subject to specified maximum amounts described in Chapter 9.

RRSP Investments

RRSPs may be invested in a combination of securities, including Canadian and foreign common stocks, fixed-income securities and mortgages chosen by the annuitant, provided that they are qualified investments for RRSPs under the *Income Tax Act*. RRSPs cannot invest more than 30% of the total assets (based on book value) in foreign securities.

Generally, RRSPs are invested in a combination of fixed income and equity investments. In making the investment decision, the individual will consider the type and amount of his or her other savings and investments, the economic outlook and the time remaining until retirement. Individuals may choose to invest RRSPs in a deferred annuity contract with an insurance company, in the pooled funds of a trust company or in a mutual fund. Guaranteed investment certificates are the most popular. However, in recent years, pooled funds and mutual funds have gained in popularity, giving a choice of investment in equities, bonds, mortgages or a combination thereof. Alternatively, a self-administered RRSP can be established under an agreement with a corporate trustee or other authorized corporation, which permits the annuitant to select the investments.

Registered Retirement Income Funds

This alternative to annuity purchase as a form of settlement under an RRSP was introduced in 1978. An annuitant may elect to have the RRSP assets transferred into a RRIF before the RRSP reaches maturity; however, RRSP funds that are locked in by virtue of pension legislation are not eligible for transfer to a RRIF. This, however, has recently changed in Saskatchewan, as discussed above. The annuitant may elect to receive any amount up to the total balance in the fund, but must make a minimum annual withdrawal. The minimum annual withdrawal follows a table of factors varying according to the attained age prescribed in the *Income Tax Act*.

Under normal conditions, if only the minimum payments are made, the payments will initially be less than the investment return, although they will rise from year to year. Hence the amount of the RRIF assets can be expected to rise for several years and then start to decrease; in consequence the fund can provide a substantial estate if death occurs before age 90.

A RRIF will tend to appeal to those who have maintained an individually managed RRSP until retirement. It enables such taxpayers to continue to control their investments during retirement.

A taxpayer must transfer his or her RRSP into a RRIF or retirement annuity (or some combination of both) by the end of the year he or she turns 69 years of age. A taxpayer does not have to withdraw any amount in the year the RRIF is established. However, commencing in the following year, a minimum amount must be withdrawn.

The "minimum amount" is nil for the year in which the annuitant enters into the fund. For each subsequent year, the minimum amount is computed by multiplying the fair market value of the property held in connection with the fund at the beginning of the year by a prescribed factor. The prescribed factors are listed in the following table.

Age	Minimum Withdrawal %
69	4.76
70	5.00
71	7.38
72	7.48
73	7.59
74	7.71
75	7.85
76	7.99
77	8.15
78	8.33
79	8.53
80	8.75
81	8.99
82	9.27
83	9.58
84	9.93
85	10.33
86	10.79
87	11.33
88	11.96
89	12.71
90	13.62
91	14.73
92	16.12
93	17.92
94 or older	20.00

If an annuitant has a RRIF when he or she is under the age of 69, the minimum payout is determined by the formula $1/(90 - Y)$ where Y equals one's age at the beginning of that year.

Example

John is 70 years of age at the beginning of the year and he has $375,000 in his RRIF. John must withdraw 5% of this amount. Therefore, he must withdraw at least $18,750 from his plan. This amount will be added to John's taxable income and will qualify for the pension income tax credit.

Profit Sharing Plans

Profit sharing plans can be defined as plans whereby amounts paid to or for the benefit of the employees are calculated by reference to the employer's profits. Profit sharing plans are designed to reward good performance and to instill a sense of partnership between the employer and each participating employee. It is anticipated that the plan will lead to increased productivity and increased profits. The intention is to establish a common interest for employees, management and shareholders.

A profit sharing plan frequently improves labour relations, with the result that absenteeism and labour turnover are reduced. These benefits are obtained without management's having to incur a fixed financial commitment.

Profit sharing plans can be established to provide immediate or deferred benefits.

Cash Profit Sharing

The immediate distribution or cash profit sharing plan is the simplest to establish and administer. As long as the regular wage or salary is reasonable and competitive, a cash profit sharing plan will be readily acceptable to employees and will provide the desired incentive. Such arrangements may also be used in lieu of part of regular compensation where employers and employees partner in attempt to turn company operations around.

A profit sharing bonus tends to be used immediately to raise the current standard of living. For this reason, they are not usually intended as a retirement income vehicle.

The amounts received by the employees as cash payments, whether on an annual or more frequent basis, are taxed as ordinary income in the year received. The company can deduct them from its taxable income as though they were wages.

Profit Sharing With Deferred Benefits

Under the deferred payment type of profit sharing plan, the profit shares of the employees are generally set aside in a fund instead of being paid out in cash. A separate account is maintained for each employee and credited with interest until such time as the share is paid out, usually on the employee's death, retirement, permanent disability, or termination of employment.

A profit sharing plan that is intended to provide retirement income for employees has certain disadvantages in addition to the limitations imposed by the *Income Tax Act*. The plan is indefinite as to the ultimate amount of retirement income that the employees will receive, depending as it does on future profits, the investment yield of the trust and the price at which annuities may be purchased.

Profit sharing plans with deferred benefits may be divided into three main types determined largely by which provisions of the *Income Tax Act* apply. These are:

- Profit Sharing Pension Plans;
- Deferred Profit Sharing Plans; and
- Employees Profit Sharing Plans.

Registered Profit Sharing Pension Plans

Profit sharing pension plans are registered pension plans subject to the *Income Tax Act* and pension standards legislation. As discussed in Chapter 1, they constitute a type of money purchase pension plan, distinguished merely by the fact that the company contributions are related to profits. A minimum contribution from the employer of at least 1% of the remuneration of participating employees must be paid in any year regardless of profits. As with other RPPs, employees may not withdraw cash from the plan while in service or a lump sum upon retirement.

Employee contributions are tax deductible and employees are not taxed on employer contributions or investment earnings placed to their credit. The interest income of the trust fund is free of tax, but all benefits are taxable when paid out. The maximums on tax deductible contributions are the same as for other money purchase pension plans.

Deferred Profit Sharing Plans

A Deferred Profit Sharing Plan (DPSP) is an arrangement whereby the employer contributes to the plan and the employer's contributions are calculated by "reference to the employer's profits" (or profits from a related corporation) or "out of profits" from the employer's business. These contributions are paid to a trustee who holds and invests the contributions for employees. The trustee under a DPSP is usually a Canadian trust company, which will charge fees to the employer for the administration of the plan. Contributions made by "reference to profits" are expressed as a percentage of profits for the year (i.e., 5% of profits per year). The employer can base these contributions on its own profits for the year or on the combined profits for it and a related corporation. As a result, if there are no profits in the year, no contributions will be made. Alternatively, if contributions are computed "out of profits", they can be expressed through various means and they can be defined either as profits for the year or undistributed profits for the year and any previous years. The contribution calculation may be based on a formula such as a fixed dollar amount per employee or a percentage of the employee's salary.

Deferred profit sharing plans are frequently used as a retirement income vehicle on a stand alone or supplementary basis. One of the major differences between DPSPs and RPPs is that lump-sum distributions from DPSPs are allowed upon retirement. Some people consider this flexibility to be an important advantage of DPSPs. Further, DPSPs are not subject to the detailed minimum pension standards legislation. Registered pension plans, however, offer higher tax-deductible contribution limits and, therefore, a greater degree of tax deferral. This is especially the case where RPPs can allow for past service contributions; that is, contributions for previous years' service.

Prior to 1991, a DPSP also permitted voluntary or mandatory employee contributions, which were not tax deductible. However, any earnings on such contributions accumulated on a tax-deferred basis in the plan. For 1991 and thereafter, employee contributions are not permitted.

Tax deductible employer contributions to a DPSP (when added to any reallocated forfeitures) cannot exceed a maximum contribution per employee that is limited to the lesser of:

- One-half of the money purchase pension plan limit for the year (this is $6,750 until 2003), and

- 18% of the compensation for the year.

The following table outlines the maximum dollar limit for DPSP contributions:

Year	Maximum DPSP Contribution
1991	$6,250
1992	$6,250
1993	$6,750
1994	$7,250
1995	$7,750
1996–2002	$6,750
2003	$7,250
2004	$7,750
2005	indexed in accordance with the growth in the average industrial wage

Forfeited amounts under the plan must either be paid to the employer or be reallocated to the beneficiaries under the plan on or before the end of the calendar year immediately following the calendar year in which the amount is forfeited.

As noted in Chapter 7, the overall contribution limits apply to the total of employer and employee contributions to defined contribution RPPs, RRSPs and DPSPs. Thus, the maximum employer contribution to a DPSP may be reduced as a result of contributions to other registered arrangements. The converse is also true.

The employer contribution is deductible to the extent it is paid in accordance with the plan as registered, and it must be made in the taxation year or within 120 days after the end of the taxation year.

Benefits received by employees or their beneficiaries are subject to income tax, except for the return of their own contributions. (Before 1991, non-deductible employee contributions were permitted, to a maximum of $5,500 a year). All amounts vested in the employee (or his or her beneficiary or estate upon death) must become payable no later than 90 days after the earliest of the following times:

- The end of the year in which the beneficiary turns 69 years of age; and

- 90 days after the earliest of the following dates:

— the date of the employee's death,

— the date he or she ceases to be employed by the employer, and

— the date of winding-up of the plan.

There are also a number of options available with respect to the form of such payments. The payment may be received as a lump sum. However, if the plan permits, all or part of the amount payable can be paid in installments. These installments must be paid at least annually, but can be paid more frequently for up to 10 years from the date on which the amount becomes payable. Additionally, if the employee so chooses, an annuity can be purchased and the annuity payments must begin on or before the employee's 69th birthday. If the employee does select an annuity, the amount used to purchase the annuity will not be immediately included in income. Instead, the annuity payments will be included in income as they are received.

Allocations to a member's account must vest immediately if the member has completed 24 months of DPSP membership.

To qualify for registration, a DPSP must satisfy several other registration requirements, including the following:

- All payments into the trust and the investment returns must be allocated to plan members each year;

- Employees may not borrow from the fund, nor surrender nor assign their interests;

- The trustees must be resident in Canada;

- The trustees must inform all new beneficiaries of their rights;

- The plan must provide that all income received, capital gains made and capital losses sustained by the trust be allocated to the beneficiaries within 90 days after the end of the trust, unless previously allocated.

There is also a tax penalty unless the DPSP fund is invested in Qualified Investments as defined in section 204(*e*) of the *Income Tax Act*. The investment limitations are broadly comparable to those contained in provincial pension legislation, although there is no 10% limit on the investment in one security. Hence, the plan may invest heavily in the employer's own common stock, although not in the employer's notes or bonds.

The tax on acquisition of non-qualified investments is equal to 100% of the cost of the non-qualified investment. On sale of a non-qualified investment, a tax refund equal to the lesser of the tax paid or the proceeds of sale is available. In addition, if foreign investments exceed 30% of the trust fund at book value, the excess over 30% is taxed at 1% per month.

In order to prevent the abuse of DPSPs by an employer who might arrange for large amounts of forfeitures to be transferred into the accounts of a few chosen employees, the CCRA has prohibited significant shareholders and their family members from participating in the plans. A special tax applies when the DPSP transfers property to a taxpayer at less than fair market value or acquires property from a taxpayer at greater than fair market value.

In addition to the specific requirements of the *Income Tax Act*, DPSPs must comply with the rules in Information Circular 77–1R4.

The absence of a mandatory relationship between profits and contributions results in a DPSP being more of a savings plan than a profit sharing plan.

Employees Profit Sharing Plans

Employees Profit Sharing Plans (EPSPs) are governed by section 144 of the *Income Tax Act* and tend to operate either as profit sharing bonus plans or long-term savings or thrift plans. Employee access to their account varies widely from plan to plan, ranging from virtually immediate vesting to vesting deferred until death, termination of employment or retirement. Cash withdrawals by employees in service are allowed.

Typically, the funds are invested in shares of the employer, as these plans have the advantage of not being subject to investment restrictions. Moreover, there is no limit on the amount of deductible employer contributions.

The employer's contributions to the plan must be computed by reference to the employer's profits from its business, or by reference to its profits and the profits from the business of a corporation not dealing at arm's length with the employer. A plan that provides for the employer to make contributions "out of profits" will satisfy the EPSP requirements. If the contributions are made by reference to profits, the minimum employer contribution rate is 1% of current year's profits. If it is made out of profits, the minimum is expressed as 1% of the employee's salary or $100 per member, if it is expressed as a fixed-dollar amount.

The disadvantage of these plans is that the employee members must pay tax on all amounts allocated to their individual accounts each year, excluding their own contributions, which come from after-tax income. All income of the trust must be allocated to individual members either absolutely or contingently, and this income includes the company's profit sharing payment to the plan, the investment income from trust property and realized capital gains or losses, in addition to the employee's own contributions. Realized capital gains of the trust fund must be allocated to members and are taxed as capital gains of the members. When dividends from taxable Canadian corporations are included, however, the benefit of the dividend tax credit is passed on to the members. It should be noted that interest income is deemed to be employment income.

The allocation is usually in proportion.to the employee's earnings or length of service or such other equitable formula as may be adopted.

Since all input is taxed, payments out of the plan when actually received (usually in a lump sum) will not be included in the employees' taxable incomes.

Serious inequities are possible under EPSPs, because the employee who is taxed on amounts contingently allocated to him or her may never receive those amounts due to his or her failure to qualify for benefits under the plan's rules. Amounts allocated to an employee, but forfeited on termination of service without full vesting will normally be reallocated to other employees and subject to tax in their hands. Relief is provided by the *Income Tax Act*, in that any employee who ceases to be a beneficiary under an EPSP is allowed to deduct an amount equal to the amount on which he or she paid tax but cannot receive, less certain adjustments.

Communication to Employees

Communication is particularly important to the success of a profit sharing plan. Management must show that it believes in the principle of profit sharing. It must encourage employees to participate with management in a spirit of mutual trust and confidence. The announcement and explanation of the plan to employees should clearly set out the principles and philosophy of profit sharing. The plan features must be clearly defined so that all employees understand precisely the purpose of the plan, what they will receive and what is expected of them.

The communication of the plan must be pursued on a regular and continuing basis to keep employees enthusiastic and aware of their interest in the success of the corporate enterprise. Many employers believe that there should be employee representation on whatever body is established to administer the plan.

Other Savings Plans and Deferred Compensation Arrangements

Savings Plans

A variety of plans have been developed to encourage employees to save and to own investments. Savings can be available for short-term needs, including exceptional expenditures or reduced income or, if not needed for an emergency, to supplement retirement income.

Savings plans may be classified according to whether the employees have an immediate entitlement to the company's contributions, or whether entitlement depends on a vesting qualification. In the latter case, the savings plan may suffer from unfavourable tax treatment, especially if it is taxed under section 144 of the *Income Tax Act* as an EPSP described earlier in this chapter. In savings plans with immediate vesting, the company's allocations are ordinary income of the employee and as such are taxable. The investment income and capital gain or loss in the employee's savings account are taxed like the returns from any other investments the employee may have.

Savings plans may offer a variety of investments. Some companies encourage their employees to hold stock in the company and become shareholders in its success. In some savings plans, employees acquire unissued stock of the company and in others the company's stock is bought in the market. The plan may also make other investment available — frequently the employer will make a number of the trustee's investment funds available.

Savings plans, often called Thrift Plans, are similar to simple money purchase pension plans in the sense that contributions by an employee and by the employer are credited to an individual account, together with accumulated interest.

In a typical savings plan, the company may pay 50 cents into the savings fund for every dollar put into the fund by the employees. The employees are allowed to contribute up to a certain maximum amount. The employer's contributions vest completely in the employee in the case of death, total disability, or retirement. In the case of termination of employment, vesting may take place after a fixed term of years or on a graduated basis, depending on the employee's years of service. If the employee leaves without full vesting, the employer contributions on his or her behalf are forfeited and reallocated among remaining members.

Some savings plans provide for automatic payment out of the fund of both employer and employee contributions plus investment earnings after a fixed term of years. In nearly all savings plans, cash withdrawals are permitted at any time, up to the amount that has vested in the employee's account. Where forfeitures are reallocated, many employees elect to leave their money in the fund as long as possible so as to obtain the most benefit of such forfeitures. Distribution is made to the employee in the event of retirement or termination of employment and to the estate in the event of death.

As noted above, the tax treatment of unregistered savings plans is not particularly favourable. Many of the plans in existence are extensions of United States designs, adopted by Canadian subsidiaries of US companies although the tax rules are different in the two countries. To improve the tax situation, some companies have registered their plans as DPSPs or have established group RRSPs.

Salary Deferral Arrangements

A Salary Deferral Arrangement (SDA) is defined in the *Income Tax Act* as any arrangement, whether funded or not, one of the main purposes of which is the deferral of receipt of remuneration that would otherwise have been paid to an employee for services rendered in the year or in a preceding year.

Under the income tax rules, the amount of deferred salary or wages under an SDA is included in the employee's income in the year it is earned, not the year it is received. Any interest or other additional amount accrued in the year to which the employee is legally entitled under the terms of the plan is also taxable to the employee as it is earned. Amounts the employer is legally obligated to pay to the employee are tax deductible in the same year they are taxable to the employee.

The SDA rules essentially apply to current remuneration; that is, to salary, wages or bonuses that the employee would have received for services rendered in the year but under the arrangement are paid in a subsequent year. However, there are two special exceptions to the SDA rules — one for bonus plans where employees receive their bonuses within three years after the end of the year for which the bonus is payable, and one for sabbatical leave plans. Amounts for which payment is deferred under these plans are included in the employee's income in the year it is received.

Additionally, the *Income Tax Act* also specifically excludes the following as SDAs:

- A registered pension plan;

- A disability or income maintenance insurance plan under a policy with an insurance corporation;

- A deferred profit sharing plan;

- An employees profit sharing plan;

- An employee trust;

- A group sickness or accident insurance plan;

- A supplementary unemployment benefit plan;

- A vacation pay trust;

- A plan or arrangement, the sole purpose of which is to provide education or training for employees of an employer to improve their work or work-related skills and abilities; and

- A plan or arrangement established for the purpose of deferring the salary or wages of a professional athlete for the services of the athlete as such with a team that participates in a league having regularly scheduled games.

Prior to the introduction of the Salary Deferral Arrangement rules, an Employee Benefit Plan was sometimes used to defer salary. An Employee Benefit Plan is a trust to which an employer can contribute for the benefit of employees, but which does not provide any immediate tax shelter. Non-taxable and tax-exempt employers, unconcerned by the lack of an immediate tax deduction for company contributions to the Employee Benefit Plan, used the plan as a salary deferral vehicle for their employees. The use of Employee Benefit Plans in this way has effectively been eliminated by the Salary Deferral Arrangement rules.

Stock Purchase Plans

Stock purchase plans are designed to encourage a group of employees to save and invest in their company's stock. Participation is often open to the majority of employees, but can be tailor-made for executives only. The savings feature of these plans is promoted by the convenience of payroll deductions.

Participation in stock purchase plans is voluntary. A maximum is placed on the number of shares a member may buy or, more often, on the amount of money that may be applied to share purchase each month. The maximum is often related to the employee's earnings. The administrator purchases the appropriate number of shares for the account of each participating employee, usually at the current market price of the company stock.

If the subscription price of the shares is less than the fair market value of the shares, the employee must pay tax on the difference. It is deemed to be a benefit by virtue of employment and is therefore taxed in the same manner as the employee's salary. The amount of the taxable benefit is added to the adjusted cost base of the shares. Once the shares have been purchased, the dividends are taxable and realized appreciation or depreciation will be treated for tax purposes in the same way as other capital gains or losses.

Some companies grant low-interest or interest-free loans to employees so that they may buy shares under the stock purchase plan. The *Income Tax Act* provides that if the loan is interest-free, or bears interest at a rate below a prescribed rate, the difference will be a taxable benefit. However, this taxable benefit can be offset in the case of a share purchase loan, since the employee can deduct the imputed interest expense on money borrowed for investment purposes

Stock Option Plans

Companies grant stock options for three main reasons:

- As incentives for employees to increase the company's profitability and thus raise the price of its shares;

- As a method to retain key employees by creating an opportunity cost if they were to leave employment (assuming the proper vesting conditions, i.e., the right to exercise the optioned shares at, say, 20% per year); and

- As a method of compensating employees that is more tax-effective than straight salary increases.

Because stock options provide employees with some of the satisfaction derived from ownership of the company (the opportunity of capital gains, dividends and voting rights), they are often established to attract the talent needed by the company, hold experienced staff or serve as production incentives for senior or middle management.

Under a stock option plan, eligible employees are given options to buy specified amounts of the capital stock of a company (or an affiliated company) at a price fixed on the day the option is granted. The employee is usually given a period of up to 10 years during which the option may be exercised. The option price is often the market price of the stock on the day the option is granted, but may be lower.

The employee obviously gains if, during the period before he or she exercises the option, the company's stock increases in value.

The terms of the stock option plan will define the number of shares to be optioned, the class of employees eligible, the last date for exercising the options, the option price and other details. The board of directors or a committee appointed by the board will award the options to individual employees.

Specific approval of the company's shareholders may be required to implement a stock option plan. The board of directors may have the right, under the company's articles of incorporation, to sell or option unissued capital stock without such approval. However, since the exercise of stock options results in a dilution of shareholders' equity, prior approval of the shareholders is often necessary. Applicable securities legislation and stock exchange requirements must also be considered.

Tax Considerations

According to the *Income Tax Act*, when shares are acquired under a stock option agreement (in other words, the option is exercised), the amount of the employment benefit will be the fair market price less the option price. Recent tax developments have "softened" this provision to provide employees, in certain circumstances, with some tax deferral and tax reduction opportunities previously not available to employees of publicly traded corporations.

To assist corporations in retaining and attracting employees, and to make the tax treatment of stock options more competitive with the United States, the 2000 federal budget proposed to allow employees to defer the income inclusion from exercising employee stock options for publicly listed shares until the actual disposition of shares. The new rules are now in effect and the deferral is only available with respect to shares acquired after February 27, 2000, irrespective of when the options were granted. The tax deferral is limited to the benefits from $100,000 of options that vest in a year, based on the fair market value of the underlying shares at the time of grant. There are certain restrictions regarding who is an eligible employee (i.e., deals at arms length with employer and does not own more than 10% of company shares) and what is an eligible option (certain shares traded on a prescribed Canadian or Foreign stock exchange, the exercise price is not less than the fair market value of the share at the time the option is granted).

The taxable benefit may be deferred until the earliest of the following occurs:

- The year the employee disposes of the share;

- The year the employee dies; or

- The year in which the employee becomes a non-resident.

It should also be noted that the deferral is not automatic and the employee must actually file an election with the employer. In turn, the deferred amount must be reported on the employee's T4 slip in the year the shares were acquired.

Example

Susan is an executive for Company "X", which offers a stock option plan to its executives. The exercise price is $20, which is the fair market value of the share in 1998, the year in which the option was granted. In 2001, Susan decides to exercise her option and acquire a share in the company. In 2001, the fair market value of the share is $200. Since Susan is an eligible employee and the share is an eligible option, Susan files an election with her employer to defer the employment benefit. The deferred benefit of $180 ($200 - $20) is reported on Susan's T4 slip. The stock has continued to increase in value and in 2005, Susan decides to sell her share for $280. For Susan's 2005 tax return, she will have to include her $180 benefit as employment income and will also have to include her capital gain of $80 ($280 - $200).

In addition to tax deferral provisions discussed above, there are also provisions that enhance the reduction of the taxable benefit owing. Subject to certain conditions, a deduction of 50% (after October 17, 2000) of the taxable benefit may be granted. The effect of this deduction is to tax the benefit at capital gains rates. Examples of the applicable conditions include the fact that the option price must not be less than the fair market value of the share at the time the agreement was made; the share must be a prescribed share; and the employee must deal at arm's length with the employer.

Also, if the stock under the plan is in a "Canadian controlled private corporation" as defined in the *Income Tax Act* (i.e., a private corporation that is not controlled by non-residents or by one or more Canadian public corporations), the employee's entire tax liability will be deferred until the ultimate disposition of the shares. Subject to certain conditions, a deduction of 50% of the taxable benefit will be granted, provided the shares have been held for two years or the requirements set out above have been satisfied.

Phantom Stock and Performance Share Plans

These are bonus or incentive plans where the amount of the bonus is determined by reference to the value of the company's stock. Under a phantom stock plan, the account of each participant is credited with a specific number of notional shares, although no share transaction actually takes place. The account may also be credited with amounts equivalent to the dividends paid and the capital appreciation on the notional holding of company stock. The value of the member's account is either paid out in cash currently or accumulated until death, termination or retirement. Typically, a phantom stock plan is used when the issuance of shares is undesirable or not possible or when shares cannot be issued for control purposes.

A performance share plan is the same, except that the calculation of the amount allocated to the participant is based upon some combination of the company's earnings, the growth of its stock price and the participant's individual performance.

The main advantage of a phantom stock plan is that the executive has no downside risk. Moreover, the company can take a tax deduction when the benefit is actually paid and the company does not incur a large expense at the commencement of the plan.

The disadvantage of such a plan is that the executive does not obtain capital gains treatment, nor can the executive take advantage of fluctuations in the market by trading the "stock". The disadvantage to the company is that if the stock increases in value quickly, the benefit can be very expensive, since it will be paid in cash rather than being absorbed by the market.

A phantom stock plan is similar to a stock option plan except that the value of the phantom shares are paid after a specified time and not at the executive's discretion when shares are vested.

Like a stock option plan, a phantom stock plan provides access to participate in increases in the value of the shares of the corporation.

PART II
EMPLOYEE BENEFITS

OVERVIEW OF EMPLOYEE BENEFITS

Background

For most employees, employee benefits are a valued component of the compensation provided by employers to employees. In the context of this *Handbook*, employee benefits include a wide range of survivor protection, disability income protection, and medical and dental coverages.

Employee benefits evolved largely to supplement the basic protection offered by various government programs. At one time, there was little concern with the possibility that government benefits might be reduced or eliminated. Recent fiscal realities have raised doubts as to the long-term sustainability of our many social programs in their present forms.

A combination of internal and external factors contributed to the shape of benefit plans as they exist today, and continues to define the structure of benefit plans that employers will provide to employees in the future. Internal factors include individual corporate philosophy and business objectives. External factors are driven by economic cycles and changes to government policy. The dynamic nature of the benefit environment increases the complexity of benefit plan management for the human resources professional and the financial officer.

During the growth years after World War II, federal and provincial governments gradually introduced basic levels of protection, including medical care, occupational disability, employment insurance and other social security benefits. At the same time, employers were willing to add new benefits to attract employees. A parallel trend was visible in the United States.

In the recession years, particularly during periods of wage freeze, benefits were added or expanded in place of wage increases. Benefits came to be viewed as separate from cash compensation and were generally perceived to be of lower economic value.

Present Situation

Diminished funding for government-sponsored benefits places increasing pressure on the employer and the individual to assume the additional financial responsibility to maintain the standards of access and protection to which Canadians have become accustomed. In addition, a number of factors are contributing to the increasing cost of delivering benefits, such as our ageing workforce and new advances in medical treatment. On the other hand, business priorities and competition limit the total financial liability that can be assumed by the employer-sponsored plan.

Managing a benefit plan requires an ongoing assessment of the ability of the government to sustain current coverage levels, and a realistic evaluation of the objectives of the benefit plan. Many employee benefit programs were designed in the 1960s and 1970s during the expansionary phase of social security benefits. As such, most medical and disability plans were inadvertently designed to assume any benefits deleted or reduced by the government programs. Covered medical services and benefits tend to be defined in terms linked to the social security plan and may be difficult for the employer to control. In sharp contrast, dental plans in Canada were designed without a government-sponsored core. The explicit list of covered dental services and procedures is more directly controlled by the employer.

Benefits as Compensation

While the majority of employers view benefits as a supplement to cash compensation, some employers are beginning to formally recognize benefits as an integral component of the compensation structure. The concept of total compensation is driven by the tax-effectiveness of employee benefits, the social value of protection against unexpected financial catastrophes, the ability of employees to meet individual needs and the business objectives of the enterprise.

Benefit Plan Objectives

Benefit plan objectives vary by organization, and sometimes by business unit within the same organization. Basic themes include cost-effectiveness, competitiveness and meeting employee needs. Throughout the 1990s and up to the current time, business priorities have been harsh and may conflict with the benefit plan objectives. Common business priorities include survival, meeting global competition, and a need to tie all business investments, including benefits, into the overall corporate strategy.

Benefit philosophies cannot easily be borrowed from other organizations where business objectives may differ. Even when a Canadian subsidiary adopts the philosophy of the parent company, significant customization is necessary to reflect the Canadian social and business environment.

The workforce has changed and continues to change, with increasing diversity in the ages, family status, career objectives and cultural composition of the employee base. The benefit program of the 1970s has undergone rapid change in the 1990s and continues to evolve in the new millennium. Employers across Canada are redesigning benefit programs to achieve their current objectives and to be more adaptable to the ongoing changes expected in the next decades.

Benefit Plan Reviews

Benefit plans should be reviewed periodically against the unique needs of the organization and its employees. Employers need to consider the diversity of needs and values within the current employee group, and the market pressures that influence future employees in their choice of employers. There are numerous surveys available to compare benefit plans by general population or by industry sector, providing a benchmark against the competition. However, measurement against competition ignores the need to link benefits into the corporate agenda.

A benefit review is an opportunity to make any necessary adjustments to keep pace with changes in government benefits, taxation, the economy, the workforce, benefit cost trends, competitive practice and the emergence of new benefits.

The general approach to a benefit review begins with identification and relative prioritization of the objectives, including the budget. An inventory of the current plans, their cost, and their history creates a baseline where the benefit plans are today.

On an overall basis, by carefully reviewing each benefit, it is possible to systematically assess whether the benefit is meeting its target, and to isolate aspects of each benefit that should be restructured. To the extent that meeting employee needs is one of the objectives, it may be necessary to look more closely at employee needs and to segment the workforce by their needs and priorities.

Summary

The complexity of financial, administrative and legal arrangements for group benefits has increased as employers develop an array of funding vehicles to creatively manage the risk in a tax-effective manner. The challenges are highlighted as governments and the courts change the rules under which plans may operate.

Part II of this *Handbook* provides an overview of each major benefit category and addresses the variations and trends within each benefit. From a strategic perspective, it summarizes the administrative and financial considerations necessary for human resources professionals and financial officers.

Chapter 12

PROVINCIAL HOSPITAL AND MEDICAL INSURANCE PLANS

Canadians receive basic hospital and medical care through a system of provincial government plans. The federal government is an unequal partner in today's health care system, as the role of coordination becomes increasingly difficult, and as federal funding becomes increasingly scarce. This chapter deals primarily with the mechanics and historical context of government involvement in health care. Fiscal realities of increasing cost and decreasing funds are forcing governments, both provincial and federal, to make difficult decisions. The pace of change in the area of government health care is anticipated to increase significantly given these present challenges.

Legislation

Health care falls under provincial jurisdiction. However, in the late 1970s, the federal government became concerned that some of the basic conditions and standards governing provincial health plans were being seriously eroded. On the grounds that access to health care should not depend on the wealth of the patient, the federal government strongly objected to user fees charged by hospitals and extra billing by doctors that were allowed by some provinces.

The federal *Canada Health Act* became effective on April 1, 1984, replacing both the *Hospital Insurance and Diagnostic Services Act* (July 1, 1958) and the *Medical Care Act* (July 1, 1968). In the *Canada Health Act*, the federal government gave itself the power to impose financial penalties on provinces that do not allow reasonable access to essential health services without financial or other barriers. In the 1990s, the provinces faced cuts in federal transfer payments. Provinces have responded by scaling down their health care programs, which in turn shifts costs to employer health plans and to individuals. The provincial health care programs most likely to be trimmed are those that will not compromise federal funding under the *Canada Health Act*.

Canada Health Act Criteria

The *Canada Health Act* sets out the criteria and conditions that a provincial health program must meet to be eligible for unreduced federal funding. The conditions for federal assistance, as established in the *Canada Health Act*, are:

1. *Public Administration:* The program must be administered on a non-profit basis by a public authority, appointed by and accountable to the provincial government.

2. *Comprehensiveness:* The program must cover all necessary hospital and medical services. An extensive list of medically necessary services includes standard ward accommodation, physician expenses, services of other health care practitioners while confined to hospital, surgical-dental services rendered in hospital, and many associated supplies and services. Provinces are encouraged to include additional extended health care services, although the provision of extended health care services has no impact on qualifying for unreduced federal funding.

3. *Universality:* All eligible residents must be covered for insured health services.

4. *Portability:* Coverage must be portable from one province to another. The waiting period for new residents must not exceed three months. Insured health services must be available to Canadians temporarily out of their own province. In such cases, payment for services within Canada is generally made by the home province at the "host" province payment levels. Payment for services out-of-Canada is usually made at the home province payment levels.

5. *Accessibility:* Insured services must be provided on uniform terms and conditions for all residents. Reasonable access to insured services must not be precluded or impeded, either directly or indirectly, by charges or other mechanisms. Reasonable compensation must be made to physicians and dentists, and adequate payments made to hospitals, in respect of insured health services. Financial impediments, such as

deductibles, for essential medical services are viewed as a breach of the criteria at the federal level and the funding reduction can be equal to the value of the deductible.

Scope of Coverage

Hospital Services

All provincial plans cover all necessary costs of a hospitalization up to ward level rates. Necessary nursing care, drugs and antibiotics administered in hospital, operating room and anaesthetic facilities, laboratory and diagnostic services, radiotherapy and physiotherapy facilities, and out-patient services for emergencies are all insured services that are considered medically necessary. There is no limit on the length of stay in the hospital, other than that the stay must be medically necessary for active treatment.

Only some jurisdictions cover ambulance fees, occupational speech and therapy, psychiatric care, renal dialysis and rehabilitation services. Provincial health plans do not cover elective services such as private duty nursing, semi-private or private room accommodation, cosmetic surgery or drugs to be taken home from the hospital.

Prior to the *Canada Health Act*, many provinces allowed "user fees" to be charged by hospitals for standard ward accommodation and out-patient services. User fees were abolished under the *Canada Health Act*. The Act allows provinces to charge a user fee if the hospitalization is for chronic care (in the opinion of the attending physician) and the individual is more or less permanently resident in the hospital. For chronic or extended care hospital stays, approximately half of the jurisdictions levy a user fee.

Medical Services

All provincial plans cover fees for medically required physician services. Most jurisdictional plans include coverage for medically required surgical services and the administration of anaesthetics. X-ray, diagnostic and laboratory tests considered necessary by the attending physician are also covered services. Certain oral surgical procedures are covered when performed in a hospital.

A number of jurisdictions provide limited coverage for other health care practitioners such as optometrists, physiotherapists, chiropractors, osteopaths, and podiatrists.

To comply with the *Canada Health Act*, physicians participating in the provincial health plan cannot charge the patient anything above what the physician receives from the provincial plan. Extra billing by participating physicians is not allowed. In some provinces, a physician may choose not to participate in the provincial plan, in which case, the patient pays the physician as billed, and the patient submits a claim to the provincial plan for consideration. However, most provinces limit any reimbursement to their applicable provincial or territorial fee schedule, and Quebec will not reimburse any services by a physician who is a non-participating physician.

Supplementary Benefits

Many provinces have expanded their health plan coverage beyond hospital care and medical services. Common benefit enhancements include dental care for children, annual eye examinations, and coverage for prescription drugs for residents over age 65 or for residents in receipt of social assistance. Most provinces have recently had to cut back, apply user fees or eliminate these supplementary benefits because of financial considerations.

Basic dental services for children (up to varying ages) are presently still covered by the provincial health plans in Newfoundland and Labrador, Prince Edward Island and Quebec. Alberta also provides coverage for certain children in low-income families and pays a portion of basic services for seniors. There is also a program in Ontario that provides children who have urgent treatment needs and whose families have no dental insurance and would have difficulty paying for dental treatment. This program is restricted to children in Grade 8 and under. British Columbia has established a Healthy Kids program that extends basic dental services to children age 18 and under in low- and moderate-income families who are not already covered by federal or employer-sponsored insurance plans. Nova Scotia has removed (May 2002) basic dental services for children under age 10, should they have coverage under an employer-sponsored insurance plan.

Drug coverage benefits vary from jurisdiction to jurisdiction. Each jurisdiction has a list of drugs that is covered under its respective program. Increasingly, the provincial plans are looking to fees, co-payments and deductibles to curtail the increasing cost without compromising the level of access to basic necessities. For example, in British Columbia, residents under the age of 65 have an annual deductible of $1,000 per family. Until the out-of-pocket annual maximum of $2,000 is paid, the plan pays 70% of the drug cost, and thereafter 100%. Prescription drug coverage for seniors and those receiving some form of social assistance is provided for by the majority of jurisdictions.

In Quebec, effective January 1, 1997 (effective August 1, 1996 for seniors and social assistance recipients), the Quebec government introduced a new universal drug plan through the Régie d'assurance-maladie du Quebec (RAMQ). This program was an original concept in Canada, as it stipulated that all Quebec residents must either be covered by the plan or by a private group insurance program.

Supplementary health and dental expenses, if not covered by provincial plans, are insurable under private plans.

Most jurisdictions cover some form of vision care (usually an annual eye exam) for children and seniors.

Out-of-Province Benefits

For out-of-province medical services, all jurisdictions, except for Quebec, have a reciprocal fee arrangement. Under this arrangement each jurisdiction agrees to pay for the medical services provided in the other jurisdiction. The jurisdiction that provided the service will automatically bill the medical plan of the jurisdiction in which the person who received medical services resides. As a general rule, non-residents who receive services in Quebec must pay the service provider and then seek reimbursement from their own medical plan.

Most plans cover emergency hospital and medical costs arising outside Canada, but only up to the amount that would have been paid if the service had been performed in the province of residence, or up to a pre-set limit per day. Subject to prior approval of the province, some non-emergency services provided outside Canada may be covered. It is necessary to demonstrate that the service is medically necessary, and that an acceptable equivalent is not available within the province. Out-of-Canada hospital and medical charges, if not covered by the provincial plans, are insurable under private plans.

Financing

Federal

The federal and provincial governments once shared the cost of health care on an approximately equal basis. In recent years, however, the federal portion of the health care bill has fallen to below half. Notwithstanding its decreasing share of the budget, the federal government can still impose financial penalties on any province failing to meet any of the conditions specified in the *Canada Health Act*. The Canada Health and Social Transfer (CHST), implemented in 1995, is a federal transfer to provinces and territories, providing them with cash payments and tax transfers in support of health care, post-secondary education, social assistance and social services. The problem with such block transfers is that it is difficult to determine how the money being transferred is being spent. This leads to the continual arguments between the provinces and the federal government as to who is actually paying how much of the health care bill.

The federal government also finances health care programs for certain groups of individuals who fall outside the jurisdiction of the provincial plans, including the Armed Forces, the Royal Canadian Mounted Police and the various programs for native Canadians.

Provincial

Provincial hospital and medical plans that meet the criteria of the *Canada Health Act* are financed in part from the federal government through transfer payments.

Each province and territory has established a method of financing the balance of the cost not covered by federal funding. Only two provinces, British Columbia and Alberta, require direct cost-sharing by residents. The monthly premiums at May 2002 are:

	Single	Family of two	Family of three or more
British Columbia	$54	$96	$108
Alberta	$44	$88	$88

For Alberta residents 65 years of age and older, the premiums vary based on income. In 1995, Nova Scotia introduced a voluntary prescription drug program for seniors with annual premiums of $215 (in 2002) per individual.

Other provinces levy a payroll tax on employers. The rates of payroll tax payable by employers in 2002:

Province	Cost
Ontario..............................	1.95% of payroll
Quebec...............................	4.26% of payroll
Newfoundland and Labrador	2.0% of payroll
Manitoba............................	2.15% of payroll

There are various adjustments to these payroll taxes, including the size or annual revenue of the employer. For example, in Ontario, the payroll tax rate of 1.95% only applies to employers with $400,001 or more in gross annual payroll. Employers with $400,000 or less in payroll pay zero.

New Brunswick, Nova Scotia, Prince Edward Island, Saskatchewan, Yukon, Northwest Territories and Nunavut all raise funds for health care through general revenue.

Additional provincial funding has been generated through the taxation of group insurance plans, including most self-insured plans. Group benefit plan premiums attract retail sales tax of 8% in Ontario and 9% in Quebec (7.5% for self-insured plans subject to GST).

Taxation

The *Income Tax Act* does not permit the deduction of premium payments to a provincial health services plan from individual taxpayer income (20% tax credit on an individual's contributions to the Quebec Health Services Fund). Further, if the employer pays any portion of the provincial health premium on behalf of an individual, the contribution is taxable as income to the individual.

For 1988 and subsequent taxation years, an individual may claim a non-refundable and non-transferable tax credit for medical expenses. The amount of the medical expense tax credit is equal to 16 per cent of the qualifying medical expenses, paid within any 12-month period ending in the taxation year, in excess of the lesser of $1,737 (for the 2002 tax year) and 3 per cent of net income for the year.

Most employer health and dental plans are constructed and administered in accordance with the definition of a private health services plan. Except in Quebec, employer contributions to a private health services plan do not give rise to taxable benefits for income tax purposes.

WORKERS' COMPENSATION

Background

The beginning of the twentieth century was a period of increasing industrialization. At the same time, the incidence of workplace accidents outpaced the ability of the legal system to provide fair and equitable recourse for injured employees. Both employer and labour groups were putting increasing pressure on the government to address the situation.

In 1910, Mr. Justice Meredith was appointed by the Premier of Ontario to head a Royal Commission to study Workers' Compensation schemes currently being developed or implemented in other countries. Meredith completed his study in 1913. The Ontario Workers' Compensation Board (the Board) and the Ontario *Workers' Compensation Act* (the Act) came into force on January 1, 1915. The other provinces had implemented their own Acts and Regulations by 1950, joined by the Yukon and Northwest Territories by 1977.

The operating principle behind a Workers' Compensation system is no-fault insurance. An injured employee is guaranteed benefits for injury, disease or death "arising out of and in the course of employment", in exchange for which the employee forfeits the right to sue the employer for negligence.

Compensation to which an employee is entitled under the Acts replaces the right of legal action against the employer for damages or injuries sustained in the course of employment. With some exceptions, this extends to potential legal action against any other covered employer or employee.

The employee is entitled to prompt medical and rehabilitation treatment and reasonable compensation for lost earnings. An employee may have a choice of taking action against other third parties for negligence or of claiming Workers' Compensation benefits. If the employee claims Workers' Compensation benefits, the right to sue the responsible party is acquired by the Board.

An objective appeal mechanism is integral to the Workers' Compensation system. Appeals may be initiated by the employer or by the employee.

Over time, the scope of benefits and services provided under Workers' Compensation has expanded well beyond compensation for lost earnings and medical treatment for workplace accidents. A wide range of health care, disability benefits, rehabilitation services and survivor benefits are paid through the Workers' Compensation Boards (WCB).

Eligibility

Workers' Compensation coverage is generally mandatory for all employees in industrial occupations. In some provinces, domestic employees, casual employees, employees in certain service industries, and employees in the "knowledge" industries, such as finance and insurance, are exempt from mandatory coverage. Employee groups exempt from mandatory coverage may be covered for Workers' Compensation on application by the employer.

Sole proprietors and executive officers are not subject to mandatory coverage, but may elect to be covered as employees. Voluntary coverage from a private insurer may be preferable for executives and proprietors to provide benefits commensurate with earnings.

Assessment Basis

The Workers' Compensation system is funded solely by assessments paid by covered employers to the Board. Contributions from employees are not permitted. Assessments are based on either individual liability or collective liability.

Individual liability is the assessment basis used for government or public agencies, Crown corporations and large public transportation organizations (i.e., shipping, airlines, railways). Each employer is self-insured, or individually liable for accident and sickness costs as they occur. The annual assessments that are paid to the Boards reflect the actual costs of accident and sickness occurrences, plus the Board's administration expenses in adjudicating the claims. Generally, the costs are assessed on a pay-as-you-go basis. In some jurisdictions, deposits are required to cover the capitalized value of costs.

The vast majority of industries in Canada are assessed on the basis of collective liability. Employers are divided into industry classes or rate groups according to similar business activity and inherent accident and hazard risks. Each class or rate group is responsible for the cost of its own claims. Each year, the rate group is assessed a rate, as a percentage of payroll, which must be sufficient to cover the cost of:

- Expected current and future benefit costs of new claims;

- Administration expenses, cost of accident prevention programs/agencies and other statutory obligations; and

- All or some portion of funding deficiencies of previous years.

The employers' assessments vary within a province and across provinces. For example, in Ontario, using the figures for 2002, the assessment rate was $0.17 per $100 of annual covered payroll (accounting offices), while the assessment rate was $16.43 per $100 of annual covered payroll (sandblasting). The average rate of assessment in Ontario for 2002 is $2.13 per $100 of annual covered payroll for all covered industries combined.

The assessment rate is applied to the annual payroll of the covered employees, up to an assessable earnings maximum. The maximum varies significantly by jurisdiction, and changes every calendar year in most jurisdictions. For example, the maximum assessable earnings for 2002 in Quebec were $52,500, while in Yukon and Prince Edward Island, they were $65,100 and $39,300, respectively.

Jurisdiction	Maximum Assessable Earnings	Average Assessment Rate
Alberta	$58,000	$1.68
British Columbia	$59,600	$1.91
Manitoba	$54,590	$1.49 up to June 30; $1.56 effective July 1
New Brunswick	$47,600	$1.90
Newfoundland and Labrador	$45,500	$3.24
Nova Scotia	$41,100	$2.54
Ontario	$64,600	$2.13
Prince Edward Island	$39,300	$2.29
Quebec	$52,500	$1.85
Saskatchewan	$48,000	$1.75
Yukon	$65,100	$1.25
NWT	$63,350	$1.18
Nunavut	$63,350	$1.18

Accountability

To manage the cost of workplace accidents, and to encourage employers to participate in accident prevention and early return to work initiatives, eleven out of the thirteen Workers' Compensation jurisdictions offer an experience rating for employers subject to collective liability. All jurisdictions, except the Northwest Territories and Nunavut, have some type of experience rating program. There are two equally common types of experience rating methods that serve to link assessment and actual experience for an employer:

1. *Prospective*–The average industry assessment rate is adjusted for an employer by applying discounts or surcharges to the rate for the current year, based on the experience of the employer in the past years.

2. *Retrospective*–Assessments are adjusted after the year has passed, by providing refunds or surcharges based on the actual experience of the employer for the year (or years).

Most provinces have elected one type of experience rating method. British Columbia, Manitoba, Nova Scotia, Prince Edward Island and Newfoundland and Labrador use only the prospective method. Saskatchewan only uses the retrospective method, while Alberta, New Brunswick, Ontario and Quebec use both prospective and retrospective experience rating methods.

Benefits

Workers' Compensation benefits can be discussed in five broad categories:

- Health Care;

- Short-Term Disability (STD);

- Long-Term Disability (LTD);

- Rehabilitation; and

- Survivor.

Money that is paid to the employee to compensate for financial loss goes beyond income replacement to include health care, rehabilitation services and survivor benefits. Short- and long-term disability benefits are expressed as a percentage of wages, up to an annual compensable maximum. In all of the jurisdictions, the annual compensable maximum is equal to the assessable earnings maximum on which assessments are based.

Health Care

All medical expenses incurred as a result of an industrial accident or disease are paid by the Workers' Compensation system. Covered medical expenses include hospital charges and physician and surgeon fees normally covered by the provincial health care schemes, as well as the cost of drugs and ancillary services usually covered by private medical insurance plans. Transportation costs for treatment, clothing allowances and long-term care allowances are also covered under the system.

Short-Term Disability

Short-term disability benefits are payable to the disabled employee until the employee has recovered and is capable of returning to the pre-accident occupation or, having gone through a rehabilitation program, is estimated capable of earning at the same level as prior to the accident. The percentage of earnings used to calculate the benefit amounts vary from jurisdiction to jurisdiction; however, in general, it usually ranges from 75% of gross earnings to 90% of net earnings.

A disabled employee who cannot return to work, or who is incapable of replacing pre-accident earnings becomes eligible for long-term disability benefits.

Long-Term Disability

A severe injury may cause the employee to be disabled beyond the short-term disability period. Prior to implementing wage-loss systems, compensation for a permanent impairment fell under two different categories of benefits: (i) permanent partial disability and (ii) permanent total disability.

Where the employee, as a result of the industrial accident or disease, was unlikely to ever work again, that employee was entitled to a permanent total disability benefit. In this case, the employee was generally paid a monthly benefit. The percentage used to calculate the benefit was the same as for a weekly temporary total benefit up to a maximum, payable in a lump sum or on a monthly basis. The maximum varied from jurisdiction to jurisdiction. The benefit was paid until the employee reached age 65, at which point an annuity or pension was received.

In situations where as a result of the injury or disease, the employee was permanently unable to perform his or her regular job functions but could perform some type of employment or participate in a rehabilitation program, he or she was entitled to a permanent partial disability benefit. In general, a monthly benefit was payable based on a portion of average earnings. Normally, the amount of the benefit was determined with some reference to the nature and extent of the injury or disease.

During the 1980's and 1990's, several Canadian jurisdictions changed their permanent disability award systems to allow for a "dual award system". This dual award system is both a monthly benefit based on an earnings loss system (usually calculated as a percentage, such as 90% of net income), which is paid out until age 65, and a lump-sum payment awarded for the non-economic impacts of the permanent impairment. The following is an example of how non-economic loss is calculated in Ontario. According to the legislation, the benefit is calculated by taking a base amount ($51,844.99 in 2002), plus an amount ($1,152.51 in 2002) for each year of age the worker is under 45 years of age and minus an amount for each year the worker is over age 45 ($1,152.51 in 2002). After the base amount is adjusted for age and inflation, it is multiplied by the percentage of the worker's permanent impairment. For example Worker A is 50 years old and has a 40% impairment. Worker A would thus receive a benefit of $23,043.02 (($51,844.99 - $5,762.55) x 40%).

As disability benefits vary from province to province, it is important to review the specific details for each jurisdiction. The Association of Workers' Compensation Boards of Canada publishes an annual summary of benefits information entitled *Workers' Compensation Benefit Comparison*[1]. Additionally, in the majority of jurisdictions, the various Workers' Compensation Boards have Web sites that explain in basic terms the types of awards provided to injured or diseased workers.

---

[1] To review a summary of publications published by the AWCBC, visit their Web site at **www.awcbc.org**.

Long-term disability benefits under Workers' Compensation are adjusted for cost-of-living increases. In most jurisdictions, the payments are indexed annually.

Rehabilitation

To facilitate a return to work, the injured employee may participate in a medical or vocational rehabilitation program funded by the Workers' Compensation Board. A variety of rehabilitation programs exist, and determination of what programs are available to the employee must be based on a jurisdiction-by-jurisdiction basis. Examples of some services provided include counselling, job search assistance, ergonomic modifications, tuition, homemaker assistance and on-the-job training. Some jurisdictions also provide relocation assistance, self-employment and legal services.

Survivor Benefits

In the event that an employee dies as a result of an injury or industrial disease incurred in the course of employment, the surviving spouse and children will receive an income-replacement benefit from the Board. Most jurisdictions reduce the benefit amount if a CPP/QPP survivor's pension is also being paid out. All jurisdictions pay an additional lump-sum benefit for burial expenses, and a certain amount for transportation of the employee's body.

Other than the lump-sum amounts that may be paid, the benefits for the spouse are usually based on a fixed percentage of the net pre-injury earnings. The amounts paid may also be dependent upon the spouse's age, the number and ages of the dependent children, and whether or not the spouse is an invalid.

Previously, the spousal benefits generally ceased upon remarriage, and the spouse was paid a lump sum upon remarriage; however, this is no longer the case.

The benefits for dependent children generally terminate at age 18 but may be extended if the child is disabled or attending school.

Taxation

The tax situation regarding employees' compensation may be summarized as follows:

- The employer contribution is a tax-deductible operating expense;

- The employer contribution is not a taxable benefit for employees; and

- Payments to injured employees are not subject to tax.

EMPLOYMENT INSURANCE

History and Objectives

The *Unemployment Insurance Act* was first introduced in Canada as an amendment to the *British North America Act* in 1940 and exclusive jurisdiction in matters pertaining to employment insurance was conferred on the federal government. This contrasts with welfare assistance, which is a provincial responsibility, and with the situation in the United States, where both employment insurance and social welfare are essentially handled by the various states.

Employment insurance provides individuals with temporary income replacement as a result of employment interruptions due to work shortages, sickness, non-occupational accidents, maternity leave, parental leave and adoption leave. It also promotes "active" re-employment assistance to help unemployed workers to find and create jobs.

Governing Legislation

Through the passage of Bill C-12, the *Unemployment Insurance Act* was replaced by the *Employment Insurance Act*, which received Royal Assent on June 20, 1996. The major changes to the Act were phased in between 1997 and 2001. Because of the significant changes that were being implemented, measures were put in place during those years to monitor and assess their impact and to make any necessary adjustment.

Changes to the Act in 1996 were intended to bring together, in a single statute, all provisions for income support and employment assistance for eligible unemployed persons in a manner that better accommodated the variety of work arrangements in today's labour market. The Act provides self-employment assistance to help claimants start their own enterprises and job creation programs. All prior references to "unemployment insurance" (UI) were replaced by employment insurance (EI).

In 1993, the Department of Human Resources Development Canada (HRDC) was created and this department is responsible for the administration of the *Employment Insurance Act*. The existing Canada Employment and Immigration Commission was then replaced by the Canada Employment Insurance Commission (CEIC), which became part of HRDC.

Eligibility

Under the 1971 Act, UI covered all employees working in Canada for the same employer for at least 15 hours a week, or earning at least 20% of the maximum insurable earnings. A person involved in work-sharing, a job creation project, or training may have been eligible for benefits, but only if the minimum hours requirement was satisfied. Employment by a provincial or foreign government was excluded. A provincial government, however, has the right to waive the exception and agree to have its employees insured.

The *Employment Insurance Act* is intended to more closely link earnings and benefits, to reduce the penalties for accepting lesser hours or wages when steady work is not available and to create a more level playing field for the growing numbers of Canadians operating outside of traditional full-time employment. Individuals working less than 15 hours per week are no longer excluded. All hours worked during the qualification period will count towards the minimum eligibility criteria, which will be 420 hours in areas where unemployment is above 13% and 700 hours where unemployment is less than 6%. The qualifying period is the shorter of (a) the 52-week period immediately before the start date of a claim, or (b) the period since the start of a previous claim, if that claim had started during the 52-week period. The qualifying period may be extended to 104 weeks under certain circumstances. Exemption of provincial and foreign government employment remains unchanged. New entrants and those re-entering the work force after two years will be required to work 910 hours (approximately six months) within the reference period to be eligible for benefits.

Prior to October 1, 2000, parents who had been out of the work force raising a family for a year or more were penalized, as they fell into the re-entrant category. After re-entering the work force, parents were required to have 910 hours of insurable employment to qualify for regular EI benefits, no matter where they lived. Effective as of October 1, 2000, however, re-entrant parents who had received at least one week of maternity or parental benefits in the 208 weeks before the 52 weeks prior to their qualifying period require the same number of hours as other workers to qualify for regular benefits. Such a claimant now needs to meet the minimum number of hours based on the regional rate of unemployment like any regular claimant.

The following table outlines the number of hours work required to qualify.

Insurable Hours Required	
Regional Unemployment Rate	**Hours of Work Needed to Qualify for Benefits**
6.0% and under	700
6.1% to 7.0%	665
7.1% to 8.0%	630
8.1% to 9.0%	595
9.1% to 10.0%	560
10.1% to 11.0%	525
11.1% to 12.0%	490
12.1% to 13.0%	455
13.1% and over *people are working*	420 AB

Maximum Insurable Earnings

The maximum insurable earning (MIE) — the maximum amount on which EI premiums are paid — is $39,000 in 2002. The current MIE limit of $39,000[1] will not be increased until the average industrial wage catches up to that level. After that, it will reflect the average industrial wage.

Contributions

The EI program is financed from employee and employer contributions, with certain special programs and benefits funded by the federal government. The employer contribution rate is 1.4 times the employee's rate. The rates are set each year.

Contribution rates are expressed per $100 of weekly insurable earnings, subject to Maximum Insurable Earnings. In 2002, rates were lowered to $2.20 for employees and $3.08 for employers. Therefore,

---

[1] The MIE has been at this level since 1996.

based on the 2002 premium rate and the 2002 maximum insurable earnings, the 2002 annual maximum contributions are as follows:

- Employee contributions — $858

- Employer contributions — $1,201

Employers with an approved wage loss replacement plan qualify for a rate reduction.

Under the *Employment Insurance Act*, employers and employees base contributions on all insurable earnings, up to the MIE. Employees earning less than $2,000 are entitled to a refund of contributions. No refund is provided for employers in respect of employees earning less than $2,000.

Scope of Coverage

Regular benefits are payable to individuals unemployed due to loss of work, through no fault of the claimant. Special benefits are also paid to individuals who are not working because of sickness, pregnancy, or parental leave to care for a newborn or adopted child. An eligible employee who becomes legitimately unable to work for any of these specified reasons may claim EI benefits.

However, there are specified exceptions to claim entitlement. The claimant who refuses or fails to apply for suitable employment, or fails to take a training course designated by the CEIC, without good cause, will not receive EI benefits. Individuals who leave jobs voluntarily without just cause, or who lose jobs due to misconduct, do not qualify for EI benefits. Benefits are similarly not paid if an employee is out of work because of a strike or lockout by a bargaining unit of which the employee is a member.

Where there are voluntary separations by individuals that result in someone else being able to remain in employment, the disqualification to receive benefits for voluntarily leaving one's job will not apply. In order for the exemption to apply, the claimant has to have voluntarily quit his or her job under a work force reduction plan and as a result someone else's job is preserved. The work force reduction plan must be initiated and documented by the employer, must contain the option to quit and must have as its objective a permanent reduction in the overall number of workers.

Amount of Benefit

The basic benefit rate is 55% of the individual's average insured earnings up to a maximum amount. For 2002, the maximum weekly insurable earnings are $750, and therefore the maximum weekly benefit is $413 (55% of $750). The benefit rate is based on the claimant's average insured earnings in the most recent 26 weeks worked. The insured earnings are determined by dividing the claimant's total earnings in the last 26 weeks by the greater of

- The number of weeks worked in the last 26-week period; or
- The minimum divisor number (see chart below).

The result from this calculation is then multiplied by 55% to determine the claimant's weekly benefit.

Regional rate of unemployment	Divisor
6% and under	22
6.1% to 7%	21
7.1% to 8%	20
8.1% to 9%	19
9.1% to 10%	18
10.1% to 11%	17
11.1% to 12%	16
12.1% to 13%	15
13.1% and over	14

EXAMPLE:

David Nate worked 22 weeks in the last 26 weeks and earned a total of $9,500. He lived in a region where the unemployment rate was 10.5% (therefore the divisor is 17)

Step 1:

Calculate average weekly earnings

$9,500/22 = $431.82

(number of weeks worked used as opposed to minimum divisor as number of weeks worked is greater)

Step 2:

Calculate weekly benefit

$431.82 × 55% = $237.50 ✓

If certain conditions are met, claimants are entitled to exclude "small weeks" — in which the claimant earned $150 or less — in calculating their weekly benefit rate.

Intensity Rule

Claimants who made extensive use of the EI system were affected by a new Intensity Rule for the period between July 1, 1996 and October 1, 2000. The Intensity Rule was put in place to discourage repeated use of EI by reducing the benefit rate of frequent EI claimants. After the first 20 weeks a claimant received EI benefits within a five-year period, the claimant's regular EI benefit rate was reduced by 1% to a maximum of 5%. Any weeks of benefits collected between July 1, 1996 and October 1, 2000 were subject to the Intensity Rule and were taken into account when determining the benefit rate of an individual's future claims.

The rule, however, proved to be ineffective and had the unintended effect of being simply punitive, especially as it affected regions of the country where workers rely on seasonal work.

Therefore, as of October 1, 2000, the Intensity Rule was eliminated and all claimants returned to receiving at least 55% of their maximum insurable earnings.

Family Supplement

The Family Supplement provides additional benefits to low-income families with children (income below $25,921). A claimant does not have to apply for this supplement; it is automatically added to his or her EI payment. Only individuals who receive the Canada Child Tax Benefits, a program administered by the CCRA, will be entitled to benefits. The Family supplement has increased in phases from a maximum benefit rate of 65% in 1997 to a maximum benefit rate as high as 80% in 2000 and thereafter. However, it is important to note that the maximum benefit that a claimant can receive will not exceed the current maximum weekly benefit of $413.

Duration of Benefit

The period for which benefits are payable to an individual reflects the number of hours of insurable employment during the reference period and the rate of unemployment in the region in which the individual resides. The maximum benefit payment period for regular benefits in 2002 is 45 weeks. For special benefits, the maximum number of weeks of benefits for a "major attachment" claimant[2] depends on the claim cause as follows:

- 15 weeks for maternity;
- 35 weeks for parental, including adoption; and
- 15 weeks for sickness.

For natural or adoptive parents, the period during which maternity and, since April 21, 2002, parental benefits may be claimed may be extended by the number of weeks during which the child is hospitalized. However, the maximum number of weeks of benefits remains the same. For example, parental benefits may normally be claimed during the period of 52 weeks following the date of birth or the date on which the adopted child is placed with the parent. But for a parental benefit period beginning on or after April 21, 2002, the 52-week period may be

---

[2] A major attachment claimant is defined as a claimant who has been employed in insurable employment for 600 hours or more in the qualifying period.

extended by the number of weeks during which the child is hospitalized, to a maximum of 104 weeks.

More than one type of special benefit (maternity, parental or sickness) may be claimed within one benefit period, up to a maximum of 50 weeks. However, if a claimant is receiving benefits for all three types of special benefits during a benefit period that has not ended before March 3, 2002, or that begins on or after that date, the claimant could receive up to a maximum of 65 weeks of combined benefits, rather than the normal combined maximum of 50 weeks. To be eligible for the increased number of weeks, the following conditions must be met during the claimant's benefit period:

- Claimant has not been paid regular benefits;
- Claimant has been paid sickness, maternity and parental benefits; and
- Claimant has been paid less than the maximum of 15 weeks of sickness benefits or less than 35 weeks of parental benefits.

In addition, claimants are able to receive special benefits in combination with regular benefits, so long as the total does not exceed 50 weeks.

Waiting Period

The benefit period begins on the later of the Sunday of the week in which the lost time claim occurs, or the Sunday of the week in which the claim is submitted. A waiting period for the first two weeks of the benefit period applies before EI benefits are payable.

Working While Receiving EI

Except for periods during which they are receiving maternity or sickness benefits, individuals are able to earn up to $50 per week, or 25% of the benefit, whichever is higher, without reducing the EI benefit. This allows claimants with low incomes more opportunity to engage in temporary work without affecting their EI benefits. Earnings for work performed during the waiting period will continue to be deducted from EI benefit payments.

Premium Reduction Program

An employer plan is deemed to be the "first payer" and EI is deemed to be the "second payer" of disability benefits. Any payment received from a short-term disability plan reduces the EI benefit paid for the same week. As a result, the cost to the EI fund is reduced if the employer operates a short-term disability plan for employees.

In recognition, employer EI premiums are reduced if a short-term disability plan is approved by and registered with HRDC. Weekly indemnity plans and Cumulative Paid Sick Leave Plans are short-term disability plans that can qualify for an EI premium reduction. The amount of the reduction depends on the type of plan. At least $^{5}/_{12}$ of the premium reduction must be returned, directly or indirectly, to the employees. Such sharing can be achieved through the following examples of acceptable arrangements:

- A written mutual agreement on how the savings will be returned to the employees;

- A cash rebate equal to $^{5}/_{12}$ of the savings divided amongst the employees, which is treated as employment income subject to source deductions (i.e., EI, CPP/QPP);

- Providing new or increased benefits, including upgrading existing benefits, or providing more holidays or time off work.

After initial approval of the plan for EI premium reduction, the employer must renew their entitlement to the reduction by completing an annual renewal application.

For each calendar year, the rates of premium reduction are determined based on four categories of qualified plans, with a different rates for each category. These rates can be viewed on HRDC's Web site[3].

To qualify for EI premium reduction, a short-term disability plan must provide disability benefits that are at least equal to the EI benefits in terms of benefit amount, duration and contract provisions. The employer must have a formal written commitment to provide disability benefits after service of no more than three months of continuous employment.

Minimum requirements to qualify for EI premium reduction include:

- Disability benefits that are at least equal to the EI sickness benefits (i.e., 55% of insurable earnings);

- Payment of benefits starting on or before the 15th day of disability;

- In the case of weekly indemnity plans, payment of benefits for at least 15 weeks for each disability occurrence;

- Payment of benefits with no reduction for EI benefits received during the same period; and

- In the case of weekly indemnity plans, reinstatement of full disability coverage after a disability within one month of return to work for future disabilities not related to the initial disability cause, and within three months of return to work for a recurrence of the initial disability cause.

---

[3] HRDC's Web site pertaining to employment insurance can be viewed at **www.hrdc.gc.ca/ei**.

Income Tax on Employment Insurance

- EI premiums paid by the employer are a tax-deductible expense to the employer and do not give rise to taxable income for the employee.

- Premiums paid by the employee give rise to a tax credit, which reduces the amount of income tax. The tax credit is 16% of EI premiums for federal tax purposes.

- EI benefits are taxable income to the recipient.

- The benefit repayment (the "clawback") was introduced in 1979. The intent of the clawback is to discourage individuals with higher annual incomes from repeatedly collecting benefits. Effective for the year 2000 and forward, the following rules apply regarding the repayment of EI benefits for individuals whose income exceeds a certain amount:

— all first-time claimants (defined as those who were paid regular benefits for less than one week in the 10 taxation years before the current taxation year) are exempted from benefit repayment since they are not, by definition, repeat claimants;

— all those who receive special benefits (maternity, parental and sickness) will no longer have to repay any of those benefits; parents who stay at home with their newborn/newly adopted children or workers who are too sick to work are not penalized;

— if the claimant' net income exceeds $48,750, he or she will be required to repay 30% of the lesser of (a) the claimant's net income in excess of $48,750 or (b) the total regular benefits paid in the taxation year.

Chapter 15

HOSPITAL, MEDICAL, DRUG, DENTAL AND VISION CARE PLANS

There is a wide range of expenses that could be covered by a private health plan. Eligible expenses may include any combination of the following: supplementary hospital, drugs, private-duty nursing, paramedical services, medical supplies and services, ambulance services, out-of-province emergency hospital and medical expenses, hearing aids, vision care and dental expenses. There are also limitless plan design variations, such as eligibility, contribution requirements, deductibles, reimbursement percentages and maximum benefits. Today, an employer can design a health plan to reflect the influence of location, industry, demographics of covered employees, and union involvement, as well as benefit objectives and budget.

For the most part, private health plans were established to wrap around the coverage provided through government sponsored health programs. All provincial and territorial governments have enacted legislation that covers residents for standard ward accommodation in hospital and for basic medical expenses. The provincial plans vary in the additional benefits provided and in how the benefits are funded.

In relation to provincial medical programs, private health plans operate as second payer. Medical expenses must first be submitted through the provincial or territorial plan for reimbursement. Consideration for payment under a private health plan is given to medically necessary expenses not paid by the provincial plan, and in accordance with the provisions of the employer plan. Overall direction in terms of who, and what, should be covered by the provincial plans is provided by the federal government through the *Canada Health Act* and by each of the provinces. The *Income Tax Act* defines, in very broad terms, who and what may be covered by private health plans on a tax-favoured basis. Provincial employment standards legislation and human rights codes may also impact the provision of benefits to employees.

Private health plans were originally based on the concept that protection was needed by employees in the event of catastrophic illnesses or accidents that could result in large medical bills. Routine medical and dental expenses were thought to be affordable for most employees and could be budgeted along with other living expenses. Today, private health plans cover many routine expenses. The evolution of employer health plans was primarily driven by the desire to provide employees with enhanced and tax-effective compensation. Employee surveys usually confirm that health benefits are a highly valued component of an overall benefit package.

Managing the cost of Extended Health and Dental plans is of increasing concern to many employers. Additional costs are absorbed by private health plans as a result of reduced coverage in provincial plans. Cost increases are also being driven by factors such as higher utilization and more costly medical services and supplies. Employers are challenged to establish a balance between cost management and the quality of care. Many employers are starting to limit the impact of cost shifting through plan design changes or contractual revisions.

Features and Terminology

Many terms are used interchangeably to describe private health plans. Common terminology includes Extended Health, Supplementary Health and Major Medical. Most employer health plans are comprehensive and include coverage for a full range of medical expenses. Separate plans for Prescription Drug, Hospital, and Vision Care are becoming less common, with these expenses being incorporated under the Extended Health plan. Dental programs have historically been, and continue to be, separate from Extended Health plans.

Coverage under Extended Health and Dental plans generally includes employees and their eligible dependants. The definition of an employee generally means active, full-time employees. However, many employers also include part-time employees in the definition.

Dependants generally include legally married or common-law spouses together with dependent children under the age of 18. The age limit for dependent children is often increased to age 25 for full-time students, and waived for children who are severely physically or mentally disadvantaged. More benefit plans now include coverage for same-sex partners. Failing to provide such coverage places the employer at risk of a human rights legislation violation claim.

The cost of Extended Health and Dental plans may be shared with employees in a variety of ways. The most direct method is to have the employee pay a portion of the monthly plan premiums through payroll deduction. However, employees can also pay for a portion of the plan cost through a deductible or a coinsurance provision.

With a deductible, the employee is required to pay the first fixed dollar amount of incurred expenses out-of-pocket before the plan will consider the remaining expenses for reimbursement. For example, a $100 per person calendar year deductible requires that individual to pay the first $100 of eligible expenses incurred during the year before the Extended Health or Dental plan reimburses any additional expenses. Deductibles can be expressed as a flat dollar amount per calendar year or as a flat dollar amount per claim (for example, $2 per prescription). The deductible may also vary depending on whether the employee has single, couple or family coverage.

A coinsurance provision defines that a percentage of an eligible expense will be paid by the plan, and the remaining percentage will be paid by the claimant. If, for example, the coinsurance factor is 80%, the plan will pay for 80% of eligible expenses with the claimant paying the remaining 20%.

Hospital Plans

Provincial medical plans in Canada pay for hospital accommodation limited to ward level, unless semi-private or private accommodation is deemed essential for medical reasons. Supplemental hospital plans were designed to insure the additional cost of semi-private or private hospital accommodation.

Medically necessary services paid for by a provincial medical plan include physician services, nursing care, in-hospital lab tests, drugs administered in-hospital, out-patient emergency services, operating rooms, surgical equipment, and supplies.

Although the number of private health plans that cover unlimited private accommodation is decreasing, many still cover the full cost of semi-private for an unlimited period of hospital confinement. The hospital benefit can be provided as a separate benefit or as part of the

Extended Health Plan. In either case, the hospital benefit can be subject to, or exempt from, any deductible and coinsurance provisions applicable to other medical expenses.

Most insurance companies make payments directly to the hospital, eliminating advance payment by the individual other than for incidental costs not covered by the plan, such as telephone service. In most cases, the claimant assigns payment to the hospital and the hospital submits the claim to the insurance company. The patient seldom sees the bill from the hospital.

The average length of stay in hospital has decreased over time but the average *per diem* rates charged by hospitals have increased dramatically. The net result is an overall cost increase associated with providing hospital coverage under a private health plan.

In an effort to manage the cost of hospital benefits, employers have implemented a number of plan design changes. Some have introduced coinsurance up to a fixed amount per year. Others have applied fixed *per diem* rates or have set upper limits on the number of days covered per illness. No doubt additional variations will emerge as employers and the health care system strive to attain a sustainable balance.

Drug Plans

Upward pressure on drug plan costs comes from a variety of sources, including the introduction of more expensive drugs and the shift towards early release from hospital. Employers, faced with spiraling costs and the realization that roughly 75% (when no vision care is provided) of private health care costs are drug-related, are forced to rethink what, and how, they provide for drug coverage.

Coverage of drugs under private health plans varies considerably. The differences have an impact on the definition of drugs eligible under the plan, the reimbursement basis and the data collection methodology. The following discussion applies whether drug coverage is structured as a separate benefit or as part of the Extended Health Care plan.

The most prevalent definition of eligible drugs is a "prescription drug" plan that covers only those drugs that legally require a prescription. Non-prescription life sustaining drugs, such as insulin for diabetes, are generally also covered.

By comparison, a "prescribed" plan is much more liberal, and covers any drugs dispensed by a pharmacist and prescribed by a physician, whether or not a prescription is legally required. This includes medicines that are otherwise available over-the-counter, without payment of a dispensing fee. Currently, most drugs claimed under private health plans are processed on a reimbursement, or pay-direct basis. The individual pays the pharmacist in full at the time the prescription is filled and files a claim with the insurance company for reimbursement. The insurance company adjudicates the relevant information at the time the claim is processed. Along with the reimbursement cheque, the employee receives an explanation of benefits statement that indicates whether the medication was eligible, and whether deductible and coinsurance were applicable.

At the other end of the spectrum from a paper-based reimbursement basis, pay-direct reimbursement combines paperless data processing with online real-time claim adjudication. Under a pay-direct reimbursement basis, the individual presents a pay-direct drug card at the time the prescription is filled. The claim is adjudicated for price and eligibility through electronic transmission, directly between the insurance company (or most often by a Third Party Administrator) and the pharmacist. The pharmacist is able to advise the employee immediately whether the medication is eligible, and what amount the plan will pay. The individual only pays the pharmacist any required plan deductible or coinsurance.

The convenience of a pay-direct card generally results in a first year cost increase associated with increased utilization. However, the cost-control opportunities of pay-direct, real-time electronic adjudication relative to manual adjudication may outweigh the cost increase over time. While clearly not a panacea, a well executed pay-direct reimbursement system can augment the more sophisticated plan features available to manage drug costs.

Managing Drug Plan Costs

There are a number of measures employers can take to control and manage prescription drug costs, particularly in conjunction with a drug card. Such measures include the following.

Generic Substitution

Generic drugs contain the same active ingredients and strength as brand-name drugs that are no longer protected by patent. The difference is usually a lower cost (as much as 60% savings can be achieved through generic drug utilization). Most provinces, including Ontario, have mandated generic substitution unless expressly prohibited by the physician. A pay-direct basis allows for uniform application of generic substitution provisions of the plan and monitors the cost of non-compliance, whether approved or inadvertent.

Lowest Cost Alternatives

Instead of limiting the medications available under the plan, this feature limits reimbursement. Payment is based on the price of the lowest-cost drug that contains the same active ingredients and the same strength. This may also apply to the coverage of many new medications on the market, such as time-release capsules, that represent a more convenient form of an existing medication.

Therapeutic Substitutions

This feature involves the substitution of a less expensive drug within the same therapeutic classification but with different active ingredients than the prescribed drug. The general intent is to move the patient through a medically accepted protocol of treatment for the condition, generally moving from least to most expensive medication in sequence.

Lifestyle Drugs

Some employers choose to limit certain drugs on the basis that usage is related to lifestyle, and as such not considered medically necessary under the plan. Examples include smoking cessation, sexual dysfunction, fertility drugs, and oral contraceptives.

Formularies

A formulary covers a specific list of eligible drugs. Some formularies mirror the provincial drug programs available to seniors and those on social assistance. In this case, as the provincial plans delist drugs, the drug plan would also remove these drugs as an eligible expense. Other formularies may be based on the provincial plan plus selected drugs, or, less often, a specific list of drugs tailored to an employee population. A viable formulary is not static and requires regular review of new medication to evaluate comparative efficacy and cost relative to the current list of eligible drugs.

Utilization Review

Most drug claims adjudicators have developed tools to analyze the drug usage profiles of the group, at least on an annual retrospective basis. A pay-direct basis makes it possible to review the appropriateness of the medication before it is dispensed. Some pharmacies have initiated a service that monitors interactions and compliance for prescriptions filled at one or several locations. Utilization review is one of the most rapidly evolving areas of benefit claim management.

Health Care Spending Accounts

A Health Care Spending Account (HCSA) is an individual employee account that involves the allocation of a fixed dollar amount by the employer to a pre-tax fund (subject to provincial taxes in Quebec). The account allows for maximum flexibility with the dollars so designated, since individual choice is made at the level of service. Therefore, the employee has a certain amount of money to spend and there are no restrictions on the drugs selected.

Positive Dependant Enrollment and Coordination of Benefits

Capturing dependant information and applying the information at point of sale can ensure that reimbursement is limited only to eligible dependants. If the electronic file also includes information on the benefit plan of the spouse/common-law partner, the coordination of benefits provision can be administered online with the result that the employee receives appropriate maximum reimbursement from both benefit plans.

Mail Order Pharmacy

An alternative delivery system, mail order companies claim to achieve savings through lower fixed professional fees, aggressive generic substitution and dispensing larger quantities on maintenance drugs. Actual savings will depend on the drug-use profile of the group and the level of employee satisfaction with the mail order provider. Claims can be handled on a reimbursement basis, or with electronic adjudication.

Preferred Provider Networks (PPNs)

Preferred Provider Networks (PPNs) represent effective application of economic principles. A pharmacy, or group of pharmacies, agrees to certain pricing and quality control standards in servicing the employees of an employer or group of employers. The advantage to the pharmacy is higher volume. The advantage to the employer is lower overall cost and more attention to outcome management. The incentive for the employee is a function of plan design and convenience.

Three-Tier Co-Payments

Under a three-tier co-payment program, the employee can choose either a generic, brand name or lifestyle drug/high cost drug, each with a different co-payment amount. For example, for the first tier of co-pays, which would be for the generic drugs, the amount paid by the employee could be $15, the second-tier could be set at $25, and for the third-tier, which would be for drugs that would ordinarily not be covered, the co-payments could be about $40. The three-tier co-payment system is very new in Canada.

Pharmacy Benefit Manager (PBM)

Pharmacy benefit managers claim to offer all the services of pay-direct, real-time adjudicators with additional features, including sophisticated mechanisms to evaluate and assess individual health management beyond medication therapies.

Prior to any major change in plan design or delivery system, it is prudent to conduct a review of drug utilization. The audit covers the drug plan's detailed history and evaluates how the employee population, or individual participants, may be affected by altering the plan design. A thorough review allows the employer to establish a cost baseline for the status quo, and to understand the implications of the changes under consideration.

Extended Health Care Plans

Extended Health Care plans were initially intended to protect employees and dependants against health care costs associated with catastrophic illnesses. Prior to the introduction of provincial medical plans, costs related to prevention and treatment were the responsibility of each individual. Since provincial medical plans provide for basic health care needs, Extended Health Care plans have been designed to supplement the provincial plans and provide reimbursement of expenses for services not covered by these plans.

Extended Health Care plans vary in structure. The most common structure is to have all eligible medical expenses covered under one benefit plan, subject to either an annual deductible or coinsurance, or both.

As health care costs have increased dramatically, there has been a movement towards higher deductibles and lower coinsurance. While many plans still have relatively low deductibles, some plans are designed to cover more catastrophic events, leaving the individual responsible for routine expenses. For example, the deductible may be $250 per person per year or more, with 80% coinsurance over the deductible. In most cases, the coinsurance reverts to 100% after the individual has out-of-pocket expenses of some fixed dollar amount per year. The objective of this design is to promote partnering with individuals through cost-sharing, and still provide financial safeguards for the employee against an unexpected large expense.

Covered eligible expenses under Extended Health Care plans are not uniform, although there is a great deal of similarity among plans. As noted earlier, hospital and prescription drug benefits may be included under the Extended Health Care plan. Typically, Extended Health Care plans cover the following expenses:

- Private duty nursing;

- Medical supplies and appliances;

- Hospital accommodations (beyond ward access);

- Ambulance services;

- Out-of-country/out-of-province emergency health expenses and travel assistance services;

- Medical technicians and other practitioners, such as chiropractors, speech therapists, and physiotherapists;

- Vision care;

- Hearing aids; and

- Accidental dental.

Rising Costs of Extended Health Care Plans

The cost of Extended Health Care plans continue to escalate and some of the main cost drivers behind these increases are:

- *Health care inflation*–The cost of medical services and supplies is increasing at a rate well in excess of the general rate of inflation. Increasing costs of prescription drugs and semi-private/private hospital expenses are some of the main contributors.

- *Changing demographics*–The working and general population is ageing. On average, older people take more prescriptions and claim for medications that are generally more expensive. In addition, people are living longer as a result of modern medical therapies. A combination of these factors results in higher plan utilization that impacts ongoing plan costs.

- *Government cost-shifting*–With reductions in federal transfer payments, provincial government plans are reducing and/or eliminating coverage. The impact of this is to transfer health care responsibilities and costs to private Extended Health Care plans.

Other factors contributing to rising costs include legislation, taxation, innovation and technology, and an increase in provider expenses.

In response to these cost pressures, plans are being modified to incorporate cost-containment measures. High-risk expenses are being identified, and where necessary, reduced or eliminated. The objective is to balance the comprehensive protection of the plan against the need for affordable benefits.

As health care costs continue to rise, placing demands on private health care plans, innovative cost-containment measures will emerge to help manage and control the ongoing impact of cost pressures on Extended Health Care plans.

Vision Care

Most provincial plans cover the costs of professional fees for eye examinations and testing for certain residents. Due to reductions in federal transfer payments and health-cost pressures, most provincial plans have limited coverage to children and seniors only. All of the provinces cover medically necessary eye exams. Reimbursement for eye examinations can be provided under a private health plan if not covered under a provincial medical plan.

Since eyeglasses and contact lenses are not covered under provincial medical plans for the working population, coverage can be provided as a benefit under an Extended Health Care plan or as a separate plan. Most extended health care and vision care plans do not provide reimbursement for laser eye surgery.

Typically, vision care provides a maximum reimbursement of $100 to $250 in any 24-month period. For contact lenses required to bring an individual's visual acuity to a medically acceptable level, a higher maximum is usually provided. The objective is to provide corrective eye-wear, not to provide a fashion statement. Even so, some vision deficits require corrective lenses substantially more expensive than the benefit provided under the Extended Health Care plan.

Vision care benefits tend to be expressed as 100% coinsurance up to a fixed dollar maximum. The fixed dollar limit tends to be less than the cost of an average pair of adult glasses, and offers the plan some protection against inflation.

To stretch the value of the benefit dollar, some insurance companies participate in a preferred provider network of vision care retailers. These retailers typically allow discounts of 10% to 20% to their preferred customers. This feature is provided as part of a vision care plan at no extra cost, and serves to reduce the amount that the employee would otherwise pay out-of-pocket above the plan maximum.

Dental Plans

Dental plans were first introduced in the late 1960s. The majority of employee benefit programs now include dental coverage, which represents approximately 25% of employers' total health costs.

Many of the earliest dental plans were introduced as a result of collective bargaining. Unlike medical plans, dental plans evolved in the absence of any fundamental coverage provided by the provinces. From the earliest days, dental plans in Canada explicitly detailed which procedures were covered, and how much was payable for each procedure.

The dental association of each province (except Quebec and Alberta) selects from the procedure codes that it wishes to include in the suggested fee guide. The procedure codes are prepared by the Canadian Dental Association, which represents Canadian dentists on national issues. Procedure codes are five-digit numbers. The first digits reflect the category of service and specific types of procedures within the category of service. The latter digits identify the tooth or the surface on which the service was performed. In 1997, the Alberta Dental association stated that it would no longer be providing a dental fee guide.

Dental benefit plans can be broadly categorized into three major areas of coverage that relate to the type of service, the general frequency and the financial severity of the service.

1. *Basic services*–diagnostic (i.e., exams, x-rays), preventive (i.e., tooth sealants), restorative (i.e., fillings), endodontics (i.e., root canals), periodontics (i.e., gum surgery), and oral surgical (i.e., extractions).

2. *Major services*–crowns, removable prosthodontics (i.e., partial and complete dentures) and fixed prosthodontics (i.e., bridges).

3. *Orthodontics*–braces to correct misaligned teeth.

Generally, employers introducing dental benefits will limit the plan to basic services, and may require a minimum service period for eligibility. In smaller plans, coverage may be limited to natural teeth that are present at the time the adult individual becomes eligible under the plan.

Typically, dental plans provide the highest coinsurance for basic services. Coinsurance is generally set at a lower percentage for major services orthodontics. Annual dollar limits usually apply to basic and major services on a per person basis. Orthodontic service limits are expressed as a flat-dollar amount per lifetime. Any deductible is expressed as a flat-dollar amount per covered person or per family per calendar year.

Adjudication of eligible expenses under dental plans is typically limited to the maximum suggested fee specified for general practitioners in the current Dental Fee Guide of the employee's province of residence. Some dental plans use a fee guide from a prior year (lagged fee guide).

When significant expenses are anticipated (i.e., greater than $300), dentists can file a statement of proposed services and fees, known as a pre-treatment review. The pre-treatment review determines what portion of the total expense will be reimbursed by the plan, thus avoiding misunderstandings or misgivings before the work is done.

Where there is a choice of dental services that an individual may receive, some plans will limit payment to the least costly, professionally acceptable alternative. For example, there may be a choice of replacing missing teeth with a bridge or with a less costly partial denture. If the plan features an Alternate Benefit Clause, the employee may still receive a more costly treatment but would have to pay for the additional cost out-of-pocket.

Until recent cost increases caused employers to consider cost management strategies, the trend had been towards increasing coinsurance and benefit maximums and lowering deductibles. More recently, employers have had to look hard at the cost drivers in the dental plans.

The most dramatic recent increases in dental claims have been in the area of recall examinations and the staggering increase in periodontal services. Not surprisingly, some employers have responded by reducing the frequency of recall examination coverage for adults from 6 to 9 or 12 months, and lowering periodontal coinsurance or placing limits on the units of periodontal service covered per person per year.

The standard dental claim form includes a section which, if signed by the employee, assigns the expense reimbursement directly to the dentist. Assignment of benefits reduces the employee's initial cash outlay, but the employee is still financially responsible for any portion not reimbursed by the plan. The percentage of assigned claims varies significantly in different regions of the country. Some employers do not permit assignment of benefits out of concern that assignment leads to higher costs because the employee will have no incentive to verify services and fees stated on the claim form. Although several insurance companies have attempted to prove or disprove this conjecture, results have been inconclusive.

Electronic data interchange (EDI) is the electronic transmission of claim data from the point of service — in this case the dental office — to the claim payer. The transmission alerts the dentist to verify coverage under the plan while the patient waits for confirmation of the amount paid under the benefit plan. Completing a paper claim form is not required when using EDI. The volume of dental claims submitted electronically is increasing as more dentists computerize and more insurance companies update their computer systems or outsource to claim specialists capable of adjudicating claims online and in real time.

An effective dental plan design encourages appropriate cost effective dental services based on need and risk factors of the plan participant. Review of historic claim patterns allows the employer to evaluate plan design alternatives against the benefit plan objectives.

Some cost-containment alternatives include capitation plans, preferred provider networks and dental health maintenance organization. These alternatives provide employers with the opportunities to reduce costs and still provide the dental benefits desired by employees.

Income Tax on Health Plans

The following is an overview of the current income tax treatment of employer-sponsored private health services plans, including Hospital, Medical, Drug, Dental and Vision Care Plans:

- If the plan is contributory, the premiums paid by the employee are not directly deductible from income for tax purposes. However, the employee contribution may be included in the calculation of the individual's medical expense tax credit (subsection 118.2(2)(*q*) of the *Income Tax Act*).

- Employer contributions can be charged as an operating expense of the employer for tax purposes.

- Employer contributions to a private health services plan are not added to employee income for tax purposes, with one exception. In Quebec, effective May 21, 1993, employer contributions (as defined in the provincial regulations) are included as a taxable benefit for the purposes of calculating provincial income tax payable. The amount of the taxable benefit may be included in the calculation of the individual medical expense tax credit.

- It had been Revenue Canada's (now the CCRA) position that a private health services plan could not provide benefits for a same-sex couple. That position has been reversed, effective September 9, 1996.

- If an employer pays, in whole or in part, the employee contribution under any provincial hospital or medical plan, the payment is deemed to be taxable income in the hands of the employee.

- For 1988 and subsequent taxation years, an individual may claim a non-refundable and non-transferable tax credit for medical expenses. The amount of the medical expense tax credit is equal to 16 per cent of the qualifying medical expenses, paid within any 12-month period ending in the taxation year, in excess of the lesser of $1,737 (for the 2002 tax year) and three per cent of net income for the year.

Medical expenses that have been reimbursed or are eligible for reimbursement are not eligible expenses for tax purposes. Similarly, premiums paid to provincial medical or hospitalization insurance plans are not eligible expenses.

DISABILITY INCOME PLANS

Background

Most employers provide employees with some level of disability income replacement coverage in the event of absence from work due to illness or accident, whether or not the cause is related to work. The range of contingencies addressed by disability income plans begins with occasional absences, through to short-term and on to serious disabilities that result in long-term absences from work.

The sources of disability income benefits may be broadly classified into the following major categories. The first two are addressed in this chapter.

- Short-Term Disability Plans (STD);

- Long-Term Disability Plans (LTD);

- Government plans providing disability benefits, including Employment Insurance (EI), Canada and Quebec Pension Plans (CPP/QPP), Workers' Compensation (WC), and provincial Automobile Insurance Plans; and

- Private plans providing some form of disability income, including pension plans, group life insurance plans, individual life insurance plans, individual disability plans and automobile insurance plans.

Short-Term Disability Plans (STD)

Sick Leave Plans

Sick leave is a term used interchangeably with salary continuance to describe short-term income replacement plans. Sick leave plans are generally self-insured, as well as adjudicated and administered by the employer. Benefits are normally paid directly from payroll, and as such, are subject to all the normal taxes and payroll deductions. Taxes and payroll deductions typically include income and payroll taxes, union dues, pension and insurance contributions, CPP/QPP contributions and EI premiums. Employer contributions for CPP/QPP, EI and WC, and any provincial health taxes on payroll also generally apply. Benefits paid through a Health and Welfare Trust will not be subject to all of the same payroll taxes and contributions. Contributions made to the Trust will however attract premium tax and sales tax in some provinces.

A sick leave plan can be either formal or informal. Under an informal plan, there is no set policy regarding the payment of sick leave benefits. There has been a decrease in such plans, most likely as a result of employers' fear of claims of discrimination. Under a formal plan, the payment is usually the full amount of the employee's salary, minus the normal deductions. The employee's length of service can be associated with the length of time he or she will receive such payments. Under a sick leave bank, the employer must decide the number of days of sick leave granted, whether the sick leave can accumulate, and whether sick leave credits are earned gradually during periods of active work or allocated at the beginning of a reference period. For example, the plan might credit 20 sick days at the beginning of each year, with unused sick leave days carried forward for use in future years. In general, most sick leave banks pay 100% of salary. A common concern with sick leave banks is that some employees who become genuinely disabled will not have sufficient sick leave days accumulated to carry them through to the commencement of long-term disability benefits.

Under some sick leave banks, employers "buy back" excess sick leave days by paying out a cash bonus at the end of the year. The buy back is a percentage of value of the days that would have been lost if the employee had been absent. Buy backs and other awards and incentives for good work attendance are mechanisms employers can use to decrease employee absenteeism.

For fiscal years beginning on or after January 1, 2000, the accounting method used by Canadian companies to calculate the annual expense for post-employment benefits and compensated absences has changed. Prior to that date, these benefits were accounted for on a pay-as-you-go basis by many companies. Now, according to *CICA Handbook, Section 3461, "Employee Future Benefits"* (Section 3461), post-employment benefits and compensated absences should be accounted for in the reporting period in which the employee has rendered service, rather than in the future, after the employee begins to receive benefits. Irrespective of whether or not a plan is formal or informal, Section 3461 might apply, and such plans may therefore be subject to the accounting rules under Section 3461.

Whether or not sick leave banks will be subject to these accounting requirements depends upon whether or not the benefits "vest" or "accumulate". If the benefit vests or accumulates, Section 3461 will apply. Basically, vesting occurs if after a specific or determinable date, the employee's entitlement to the benefit is no longer dependent upon the employee being employed by the employer. If, for example, the unused sick leave credits are vested, with employees receiving all or part of their unused sick leave in a lump sum when they retire or terminate employment, these benefits will have to be accounted for on an accrual basis. A benefit accumulates if the employee can carry forward to one or more periods after the period in which it was earned, even though there may be a limit with respect to the amount that can be carried forward. In general, any benefits that vary with the amount of additional service performed by the employee are benefits that accumulate. If, for example, the employer buys back sick leave days, Section 3461 would not apply, as the benefit is not carried forward into the next period.

Other non-accounting issues arise with respect to a vested sick leave plan. For example, it may encourage employees to develop a sense of entitlement such that the benefit has been earned and can be used for discretionary absences, including those unrelated to illness or injury. Additionally, an employee may accrue sick leave at a low rate of pay (in the early years of employment) but have it paid out at a relatively high rate of pay (during the later years of employment), compounding the unfunded liability associated with vested sick leave plans.

As employers began to realize the potential liability that can accumulate, especially with accumulating plans, there was and has been an increased interest in eliminating sick leave banks. The introduction of Section 3461 has only added fuel to the fire.

Short-Term Disability Plans

Weekly indemnity and short-term disability (STD) are terms used to describe an income replacement plan that may be self-insured or insured, and in which claims are generally adjudicated by a third party. The most obvious distinction between sick leave plans and short-term disability plans is the involvement of an insurance company or other third party in claims adjudication.

Self-insured plans often use the services of an outside provider to perform specific services such as adjudicating and paying claims. The employer may retain some administrative responsibilities, or may sub-contract the administration to the third party. Where the provider is an insurance company, the arrangement is described as an Administrative Services Only (ASO) arrangement to indicate that the employer remains fully responsible for the financial risk.

Self-insured STD plans are typically funded through the payroll system. Benefits paid to disabled employees through payroll are subject to CPP/QPP, EI and WC contributions in addition to income tax deduction and payroll taxes. A third party arrangement can be structured to establish an arm's length relationship for claims adjudication. Benefits paid under an arm's length arrangement would not be subject to payroll tax or CPP/QPP, EI and WC contributions, but would be subject to income tax for the recipient; premium tax and sales tax will apply to such arrangements in some provinces.

Benefits are generally expressed as a percentage of pay, and may vary by length of service. For example, the STD benefit may be a lower percentage of earnings for employees in their first year of service. Benefits are usually paid from the first day, for a maximum duration such as 15 or 26 weeks. The benefit duration is chosen to dovetail with the commencement of long-term disability benefits.

Short-term disability plans may provide a percentage of pay ranging between 55% and 70% of gross weekly earnings.

Short-term disability amounts may be integrated with other disability benefits to ensure that employee income during a period of disability does not exceed income while actively working. Other disability benefits include CPP/QPP, WC, automobile insurance or any other disability benefit that may be payable to the employee. EI benefits are not offset against weekly indemnity benefits, as the employer plan is first payer; however, in carve-out plans, STD payments may be suspended while the employee is eligible to receive EI benefits.

Benefits typically begin on the first day of absence if the disability is caused by a non-work related accident or if the employee is hospitalized, and on the 8th day (shorter and longer waiting periods sometimes also occur) for absence related to illness. The waiting period for illness is intended to discourage casual absences. The maximum benefit period is usually in the range of 15 to 26 weeks, but in very rare cases may be as high as 104 weeks.

Benefits received by the employee are taxable income, unless the premiums have been entirely paid by the employee deduction. CPP/QPP and EI contributions, and other employer and employee payroll taxes are not applicable if the weekly indemnity plan is insured or administered by a third party at arm's length from the employer, but such arrangements would attract premium taxes and sales taxes in some provinces.

Supplemental Unemployment Benefits (SUB) Plans

The Supplemental Unemployment Benefits (SUB) plan, as the name implies, tops up or supplements the EI disability benefits. SUB plans are a form of self-insured income replacement that can be structured to pay benefits during periods of unemployment due to temporary stoppage of work, training, illness, injury, quarantine, or periods while receiving maternity or parental benefits. SUBs are different, in that unlike other forms of employment income or disability benefits received by the employee, they will not reduce the amount of EI benefits payable.

Benefits under EI are payable for up to 15 weeks in the event of maternity leave and 35 weeks for parental leave. EI benefits are often lower than the disability income benefits provided by the employer. Two well-known court decisions, *Brooks v Canada Safeway* and *Parcels v. The Alberta Hospital Association*, stipulated that disability coverage should be maintained during a period of maternity leave, and that all pregnancies have some period of disability related to delivery. SUB plans are commonly used to "top up" the EI benefit to make total disability benefits equivalent to the employer plan.

As distinct from other SUB plan applications, SUB plan registration for maternity or parental supplements is not required. It is necessary to formally document the program in order to ensure eligibility of SUB Plan status under EI benefits. SUB plans for sickness, quarantine and lay-off still require annual registration with Human Resources Development Canada.

Maternity and parental SUB plans can supplement up to 100% of earnings. All other SUB plans can supplement up to 95% of earnings.

Income received from a SUB plan is included for purposes of calculating any applicable EI clawback. Some SUB plans expressly state that the plan will compensate the individual for the effect of the clawback. Other SUB plans expressly state that the plan is not responsible for any income clawed back.

Long-Term Disability Plans (LTD)

Long-Term Disability (LTD) payments commence after a qualifying disability period that typically coincides with the end of the Sick Leave, STD or a Weekly Indemnity plan. Because of the financial impact associated with long-term liabilities and potentially significant monthly benefits, LTD benefits tend to be insured. The employer is responsible for making certain that the insurance contract fully reflects the benefit provisions communicated to employees.

LTD plans are designed to reflect continuous disability. Many insurance contracts allow for short periods of active employment during the qualifying disability period, to avoid a negative incentive for employers and employees to attempt partial or early return to work. LTD benefits are expressed as a percentage of pay, ranging from 50% to 70% of gross income.

LTD benefits are integrated with other sources of disability income such as Workers' Compensation, CPP/QPP and other employer and government sources. The objective of integrating disability income from other sources is to limit the disability income received from all sources to a reasonable percentage of pre-disability earnings, thus providing adequate income while maintaining an incentive for the employee to return to work. Methods of integration range from a direct offset, or reduction in the amount of LTD benefit payable for every dollar paid under government sponsored benefits programs, to an offset only after disability income from all sources exceeds a fixed percentage of the pre-disability earnings of the employee.

LTD payments generally continue for as long as the employee remains disabled, as defined in the contract, but generally not past the age of 65. Criteria for disability are carefully defined in the plan and benefits are paid only when an employee meets the "Definition of Disability" test, as defined in the plan contract.

It is in the best interest of all parties to have the LTD plan provide financial encouragement for the employee to try to return to work. Typically, the incentive would be a rehabilitation benefit that would allow the employee to earn an income and still receive LTD benefits. The LTD plan may offset only 50% of the income earned under an approved rehabilitation program, or it may not reduce the LTD benefit until the individual's total income reaches 100% of earnings prior to disability. Some LTD plans support rehabilitation during the short-term disability period by not extending the qualifying period for LTD for the period during which the individual was engaged in approved rehabilitation employment.

Benefits are not taxable on receipt if the entire premium was paid by the employee from after-tax dollars. Employer contributions are not taxable, but render the benefit taxable on receipt. The relative merits of taxable and non-taxable LTD plans for a particular group depend on a number of factors, including the income levels of the employees in the group.

Design Issues

When designing a disability income plan, several fundamental issues must be taken into account. These issues are discussed below.

Definition of Disability

The definition of disability establishes the criteria that will be applied to determine whether a compensable disability exists, and therefore whether benefits will be paid. Usually, the definition is segmented into two phases, an "own occupation" phase and an "any occupation" phase.

The own occupation phase is most often the short-term disability period, plus the first two years of the LTD claim. The any occupation phase follows until the maximum LTD benefit period is reached. Claimants are considered disabled if the illness or injury prevents the employee from performing the essential duties of either their own or any occupation during the corresponding phases of the definition.

Evaluation of disability can be made more objective by quantifying the test. For example, the employee might be considered disabled if unable to perform at least 60% of normal duties during the own occupation phase. During the any occupation phase, the employee may be considered disabled if he or she is unable to perform a job that paid at least 60% of his or her pre-disability earnings. The percentage can be changed to make the criteria less or more stringent, and there are differences among insurance companies. Education, training, age and experience would be taken into consideration, particularly in the adjudication of the any occupation definition of disability.

Pre-Existing Conditions Limitation

Some insurers limit their liability by restricting coverage for medical conditions that existed before the employee became insured. For example, the pre-existing condition clause may state that if an employee was receiving medical treatment for a condition that existed during the three-month period immediately prior to being covered, disability benefits would not be payable for that specific condition until the employee had been covered under the program and working for 12 months, or until after a 90-day period, during which the employee received no medical care for the pre-existing condition. Disability coverage in respect of unrelated causes would not be affected. Restrictions are more common in small groups or in industries with a high turnover rate.

Exclusions

Most STD and LTD plans specify circumstances under which no disability benefits will be paid to the employee. Examples of some standard exclusions include:

- Disabilities arising from an attempted suicide, or self-inflicted injuries;

- Injuries incurred as a result of war;

- Disabilities incurred as a result of the commission of a criminal offence;

- Benefits will not be paid if the employee is in prison; and

- Any period in which the employee is not under the care of a licensed physician.

Replacement Ratios

Taking income from all sources into account, an LTD replacement ratio in the range of 80% to 85% of pre-disability income balances the employee objective of income security against the employer objective of a reasonable benefit with some room for financial motivation to return to work. For short-term disability plans, a higher replacement rate may be acceptable to the employer.

EI Premium Reduction

Employers whose Sick Leave, Weekly Indemnity or STD plans match or exceed EI disability benefits are eligible for EI premium reduction. Five-twelfths of this reduction must be shared, directly or indirectly, with the employees covered under the plan. The employer may provide a cash rebate (which is taxable income), new employee benefits, or increased existing benefits.

The employer must complete an initial application form, along with supporting documentation, to Human Resources Development Canada (HRDC). If the application is approved, the employer is advised of the reduced rate to which it is entitled. The amount of the reduction will be set out in cents per one hundred dollars of insured earnings. The premium rate is specified as a multiple of the employee premium rate. HRDC then sends out a "Conditional Authorization to a Reduced Employment Insurance Premium" notice each December, informing the employer of the reduced rate that it may apply in the following year. During the first half of the following year the employer is sent a renewal application, which must be completed and returned to HRDC.

The Management of Disability Claim Issues

The management of disability claims is becoming increasingly complex. Relative to other employee benefits, the non-financial needs and service expectations of the claimant have considerable impact on the outcome of disability income claims.

Measuring the Cost of Absences

Disability Income plans represent a substantial financial liability for the employer. According to Watson Wyatt's 2000 Canadian Staying@Work Survey, short-term absences amounted to 4.2% of total payroll costs and long-term disability costs had increased by 8% from 1997 to 2000. Judging from the results of this survey, employers must take whatever steps possible to control these increasing costs.

An employer has limited control over many of the factors influencing cost; however, cost is influenced by the disability claims adjudication process. Early intervention, progressive return to work policies, and support of rehabilitation programs have reduced disability costs for a number of employers.

In support of early intervention:
- Every LTD claim originates as an STD claim;
- Early intervention means early in the disability, not early in the LTD claim;
- The likelihood of return to work from disability is less than 50% after 6 months of absence.

In addition to the disability benefits paid to the disabled employee, there are other costs associated with an employee's absence from work. The employer generally assumes the cost of continuing life insurance, health and pension benefits. Measuring the cost of absence also takes into account the cost of replacement workers or overtime costs for existing workers, and the physical and emotional strain on co-workers and supervisors who must absorb the extra work. Prevention and active management of disability claims have helped employers control the costs associated with employee absence.

Managing Disability Income Plans

Attendance management programs focus primarily on handling occasional absences (i.e., those lasting only one or two days or no more than a week). Employers have developed many different programs to improve attendance. The range of programs includes disciplinary action for inappropriate behaviour, providing no income during casual absence, and incentives for perfect attendance. An increasingly large number is also putting in place programs to accommodate work and family responsibilities. The most effective attendance management for an organization will depend on a number of factors, including the levels of absence, the industry and the corporate culture.

After a period of absence of approximately one week, the focus moves from absence management to disability management. In the past, employers and insurers generally thought of two distinct categories of disability benefits: short-term and long-term. This distinction led to an awkward transition of the claim from the short-term plan to the long-term plan. Although administration and claims documentation may be different for short-term and long-term plans, the focus today is to manage all disability claims with the intent of getting the employee back to work as soon as possible, even if in a reduced capacity.

The focus on early intervention and early return to work applies equally to both non-occupational and occupational disabilities. The likelihood of successful return to full-time employment reduces with each day that the person remains absent from work.

Claims management reduces the cost of disability plans, the number of claims initially approved, or their duration through the use of contractual limitations or stringent adjudication guidelines. Claims management remains important for cost control, but the impact of human rights legislation and changing societal philosophies and values requires a shift beyond managing the claim to managing the disability.

Managing disabilities results in the lowering of the cost of disability insurance and disabled employees receiving much-needed additional assistance. The emphasis shifts from a focus on lost abilities to identifying residual capacities.

Disability management programs operate during both the short- and long-term phases of disability. Features of a disability management program include early intervention, case management, rehabilitation and support by the employer.

Prevention

Employers should also consider taking preventative steps to effectively decrease the number of disability claims. Such steps include creating workplace wellness programs and Employee Assistance Programs (EAPs). Workplace wellness can be viewed as having two key elements: Organizational wellness and Employee wellness. Organizational wellness involves managing business functions and employee well-being in a manner that allows the organization to be more resistant to environmental pressure. Employee wellness involves managing both psychological and physical issues in response to environmental stress, including one's work environment. EAPs offer a confidential and professional consulting service to help employees and their families identify and resolve a wide range of personal difficulties and work-related problems. Their primary focus is to provide assessment and referral services, as well short-term counselling to employees and their families. EAPs have evolved to become proactive in their approach and are increasingly looked upon as a means to promote well-being, good health and problem prevention.

Early Intervention

Early intervention is, simply, timely and pro-active disability management. In early intervention, the employee is contacted shortly after the onset of a medical absence (usually within 5 days) to determine whether he or she is a candidate for a return to work, or whether various interventions are needed to promote the return to work.

Case Management

Action plans are of little value unless implementation and accountability are assigned to an individual or a team. In most insurance companies, a case manager is assigned to coordinate the activities of the plan and work in liaison with all caregivers, the claimant, the employer, and any other stakeholders. The case manager may be the adjudicator, the rehabilitation consultant or someone specifically designated by the insurance company. The case managers are able to intervene and to assist in the employee's re-integration into the workplace before problems are too big to be resolved.

Rehabilitation

There are two distinct types of rehabilitation: medical rehabilitation and vocation rehabilitation. Medical rehabilitation deals with medical recovery and the restoration of function. Medical professionals, including doctors, nurses, physiotherapists and others control this process. Vocational rehabilitation deals with the re-establishment of employment at the prior job, or through retraining. Vocational rehabilitation is conducted by specialists in this field. The case manager generally coordinates all these functions.

Support of the Employee

All parties gain when an individual returns to full or partial function after a disability. The employer often needs to make accommodations to facilitate early return to work. Light or modified duties, special equipment or modifications to the work site may be necessary. The cost and inconvenience of the accommodation are usually outweighed by the value of returning the employee to work. This duty to accommodate the employee, which has been confirmed by the Courts, extends to the point of undue hardship on the employer, a notion still not well-defined.

Challenges of New and Emerging Illnesses

New and emerging illnesses present tremendous medical and vocational rehabilitation challenges to employers, insurers, and health care practitioners. While the number of new disability claims each year is relatively stable, the proportion of new claims related to stress and mental and nervous disorders is increasing each year. At the same time, there has been a sharp rise in the number of disability claims attributed to new diagnoses such as fibromyalgia, multiple chemical sensitivity, environmental diseases, repetitive strain injury, and chronic fatigue syndrome.

Successful recovery from physical and mental disabilities requires a multi-disciplinary approach, addressing the emotional and psychological needs of the claimant, as well as the medical condition and symptoms. The chances of success are increased with a supportive employer and suitable workplace accommodations available during the recovery phase.

Role of Health Care Providers and Insurance Carriers in Adjudication

The physician was traditionally expected to provide answers that would satisfy the competing interests of the patient, the employer and the insurer. More recently, it is being recognized that responsibility for adjudication of disability benefits rests with the insurer, not the physician. The trend is not to ask the physician whether the employee is "disabled." The physician is being asked to identify restrictions and limitations, and provide objective findings that describe the condition. The insurer uses factual information from the physician to draw a conclusion on the presence and degree of disability and impairment.

There is growing recognition of the need for a multi-disciplinary model of health care in treating most mental and physical impairments. Employers and insurers are beginning to involve other health care practitioners in the assessment and treatment of disabling conditions.

Burden of Proof

Under an income replacement plan, the burden of proof is on the claimant to provide evidence of disability in order to receive payment. The adjudicator requires objective and medical support to evaluate whether the requirements for disability are met under the terms of the contract. For example, where the plan requires inability to perform the essential duties of the job, and a slight change in duties would keep the employee at work, the employee would not be considered disabled.

After a disability is admitted as a claim, the burden of proof effectively shifts to the insurer. It is relatively difficult to show cause for benefit termination once payments have commenced. Most insurers are relatively stringent in their initial adjudication.

The ability to defend an objective decision made by a professionally qualified claim examiner leads many employers to retain third-party services for disability claim management.

Subrogation

The purpose of subrogation (the substitution of one party for another as creditor) is to make certain that the right party pays and that a claimant does not get paid twice for the same loss. Subrogation is a right that exists under common law. Most disability plans include an explicit subrogation clause in the policy wording. Under civil law in Quebec, subrogation is not an automatic contractual right. An explicit contract provision must detail how and when subrogation terms will be applied.

Accounting — STD/LTD

Short- and long-term disability plans are also encompassed in the accounting standards provided for under Section 3461, which came into effect in 2000. Where the post-employment benefits and compensated absences do not vest or accumulate, the cost is recognized when a situation occurs that requires the employer to provide a benefit. As a result, if the STD or LTD benefits are not related to service, then the cost is recognized when the employee becomes entitled to receive the STD/LTD benefit. Most STD and LTD plans are not service-related. If, however, in the rare circumstance that the STD/LTD benefits were service-related, the liability would be accounted for on an accrual basis. It is important to note that if the risk of liability has been transferred to an insurance company, the liability would be limited to any outstanding premiums at that time.

Tax Issues

The tax treatment of various disability benefits is somewhat complex. The following are a few general rules associated with disability plans:

- Employer-paid contributions or premiums to disability plans are deductible business expenses for the employer.

- Employee-paid contributions or premiums to disability plans are not eligible income tax deductions or credits in the year they are paid; cumulative contributions can be deducted from taxable disability benefits received.

- Employer-paid contributions or premiums to disability plans are not taxable benefits to employees.

- Disability benefits received by a disabled employee are generally taxable income. The main exceptions to this are Workers' Compensation and employer-sponsored disability plans that are fully funded by employee contributions. Interpretation Bulletin IT-428 states that the onus is on the employer to clearly establish that the plan is an "Employee Pay-All Plan". As a result, to avoid the possibility of benefits being taxed, the plan should be documented at the time it is established as an employee-paid plan.

- Where a plan is providing taxable benefits to disabled employees and operating at arm's length from the employer, the income is not subject to CPP/QPP or EI deductions. Where the plan is not operating at arm's length, then the income is subject to CPP/QPP and EI deduction.

- Where the plan is a shared contribution plan between the employer and employee, the benefits paid out are taxable to the extent that they exceed the cumulative premiums paid by the employee.

GROUP LIFE AND ACCIDENT INSURANCE

Background

Life insurance was one of the earliest employee benefits and remains the most common group benefit in Canada. Although there are different types of group life, by far the most common type is group term life, which is one-year term insurance, renewable each year but not having a guaranteed renewal rate. It represents pure life insurance coverage only, and includes no element of investment or savings. It provides a lump-sum death benefit payable to the employee's designated beneficiary in the event of the employee's death from any cause while insured.

A paramount feature of group life contracts is that health evidence for coverage is kept to a minimum. Contracts are generally issued with an overall maximum on the amount of insurance per life insured, and a lower non-medical maximum per covered person. All eligible employees in the group can be insured up to the non-medical maximum, without submitting any health evidence. Amounts in excess of the non-medical maximum must be approved by the insurance company based on the medical evidence submitted by each employee. In the case of very small groups of 10 employees or less, all amounts of coverage may be subject to evidence of good health.

In group term life insurance, the insurance company agrees to insure each employee for one year only, at a rate per $1,000 of coverage based on the ages of all employees at the time of the contract. The contract is renewable each year, subject to the right of the insurance company to adjust the rates based on the employees' ages. The rate per employee increases each year as the employee becomes older, but the cost to the employer remains the same, provided that the average age and distribution of insurance for the group do not change, and that there is no adjustment required on account of mortality and morbidity experience[1]. In general, the average rate tends to remain remarkably stable over the years as young employees continually enter the group to replace retiring employees and to offset the gradual ageing of the other remaining employees.

The renewal rates for a small group are generally not affected by the group's mortality and morbidity experience, as this experience is "pooled" by the insurance company with other groups of similar size. It is the insurance company's mortality and morbidity experience of its total pool of small group life insurance contracts that will affect the overall rating of its small group life insurance contracts. In the case of a large group, however, the renewal rates are affected less by the insurance company's overall experience than by that of the actual group itself. In large groups, the employer's cost is often determined entirely by the mortality and morbidity experience of the group.

Group insurance premiums are typically lower than individual premiums because the marketing and administrative costs for each individual are lower.

Governing Guidelines

There is no specific legislation governing group life insurance in Canada. The Canadian Life and Health Insurance Association (CLHIA) has drafted guidelines with respect to group insurance, replacing guidelines previously issued by the Association of the Provincial Superintendents of Insurance. The CLHIA guidelines provide minimum standards of practice for life insurance companies with respect to:

- Provision and contents of plan descriptions made available to employees;
- The life insurance conversion privilege;

---

[1] The mortality and morbidity experience refers to the mortality and morbidity that actually occurs to a group of insured employees of a given insurance company, in contrast to expected mortality and morbidity.

- **Mortality** — The number of deaths in a group of people, usually expressed as deaths per thousand. The age and sex of the insured are normally part of the mortality element.

- **Morbidity** — The incidence and severity of sicknesses and accidents in a well-defined class or classes or persons.

- Continuation of coverage when the life contract terminates; and

- Assumption of risk in a change of carrier situation.

By and large, group benefit insurers in Canada comply with these guidelines.

The Canadian Constitution, the *Charter of Rights and Freedoms* and associated federal and provincial human rights legislation prohibit discrimination on enumerated grounds. The significance of the human rights legislation to benefit plans is that the criteria for coverage eligibility must be common for all employees in a class. Group life plans cannot discriminate in terms of eligibility requirements or amount of coverage provided on the basis of a variety of personal characteristics, including age, sex, sexual orientation or marital status. Premiums, however, may be structured to reflect actuarially supportable risk characteristics.

The major impact of various employment standards legislation on group life insurance is to provide benefit continuation during the statutory termination notice period and to ensure information on conversion privileges is made available to the employee.

Death Benefits Under Government Plans

The Canada and Quebec Pension Plans (CPP/QPP) provide death and survivor benefits. The lump-sum death benefit is a modest amount (maximum in 2002 is $2,500) that is intended to cover immediate cash needs. A survivor benefit is an ongoing benefit payable to a spouse or common-law partner (which includes same-sex partners) and dependent children who meet the requirements specified under the CPP/QPP.

Workers' Compensation plans also provide an immediate lump-sum death benefit to defray immediate costs resulting from the employee's death, and ongoing pensions to the survivor and dependent children. Benefit amounts vary by province and territory.

Structure of Group Plans

Schedule of Insurance

The level of insurance provided under an employer-sponsored group insurance plan reflects affordability, competitive pressures, the level of paternalism and, where applicable, the outcome of collective bargaining.

The amount of employer-paid life insurance takes into account all other sources of employer-sponsored death benefits. Such benefits may be payable under registered pension plans, profit-sharing plans, survivor income, optional life insurance and other plans. The schedule of benefits for a class of employees defines the amount of life insurance payable. Benefits negotiated through the collective bargaining process tend to be expressed as flat or uniform amounts for all members of the bargaining unit. For salaried employees and hourly employees who are not members of a union, group life insurance benefits are usually expressed as a multiple of annual earnings.

The amount of life insurance protection provided by the employer can be nominal or very substantial. The trend is to supplement the amount of basic mandatory life insurance with employee-paid optional life insurance. Additional basic coverage is sometimes provided in the event of a death while travelling on the business of the employer.

The insurance company will review the proposed schedule of insurance for the group to make certain that the coverage amounts do not exceed its risk limits, and that the distribution of coverage amounts are reasonable. Although the insurance company has an interest in maximizing the insurance amounts, there may be a concern with the viability of a plan that provides low benefit amounts to the majority of employees and extremely high benefit amounts to a small group of executives.

Employees can choose the amount of optional life insurance based on personal circumstances, including the income required by the family, personal debt, investments and other sources of income. The maximum amount of optional life insurance available is negotiated between the employer and the insurance company. Medical evidence of good health will generally be required.

Eligibility and Participation

It is not necessary to offer group life insurance to all employees of an employer, but the group eligible for coverage must be well-defined. For example, if certain part-time employees are eligible for insurance, eligibility can be based on the number of hours worked per week. Written communication should specify the minimum service requirements, and any other conditions for eligibility.

Group life plans that are fully employer-paid generally have 100% participation by all eligible employees. Where employee contributions are required, insurers generally require participation by at least 75% of the eligible group to avoid adverse selection (i.e., enrollment weighted to those employees most at risk). If participation is less than 75%, coverage is usually subject to the approval of medical evidence of insurability. However, lower participation may be allowed for certain large groups without medical evidence requirements.

Benefit Provisions

Waiver of Premium

A waiver of premium provision is commonly included in group life insurance contracts. Under a waiver of premium provision, if an employee becomes disabled before age 65, the insurance company continues the life coverage during the period of total disability with no further premium payment. If the policy with the insurer is terminated, the insurance coverage with the original insurer remains in force for the disabled employee. There are differences among insurance contracts with respect to the criteria for total disability.

Employers may choose not to insure the waiver of premium provision. Under policies with no premium waiver provision, the ongoing premium rate may be slightly lower. However, premium payments must be continued during periods of disability in order to maintain the life insurance coverage in force. If the plan is transferred to another insurer, arrangements must be made with the new insurer regarding the assumption of the disabled risk and the amount of premium necessary to continue coverage.

Instalment Disability

Under an instalment disability provision, an employee who becomes totally and permanently disabled receives the amount of life insurance paid in monthly instalments, until the total amount is paid out. The instalment disability benefit attempts to use the group life insurance to pay long-term disability benefits in addition to death benefits.

The monthly payments are usually equal to the amount of life insurance divided by 60, which assumes benefits are payable for a maximum of five years. The monthly payments are usually adjusted to reflect interest credits during the payment period. The payments are not related to the financial needs of the disabled employee.

The definition of disability is usually restrictive. Few disabled employees qualify for instalment disability benefits.

If an employee dies before the end of the payment period, the death benefit is reduced by any instalment benefits paid to the employee. The instalment disability benefit compromises the primary purpose of group life coverage.

With the increasing provision of long-term disability income benefits over the past twenty years, the instalment disability benefit has
become relatively uncommon. It can be found in some older contracts
subject to collective bargaining, particularly in the absence of
long-term disability benefits. The insurance community has also developed more flexible alternatives for advancing death benefit proceeds
to provide financial assistance to the terminally ill.

Living Benefits

Payment of life insurance proceeds to terminally ill individuals
was a concept introduced in the late 1980s to provide necessary
income for the employee. Terminal payments are made in the case
where medical prognosis indicates death is imminent for the insured
individual. The advance payment is typically limited to one-half of the
policy (usually up to a maximum of a $50,000). Most insurers require
the written consent of the beneficiary.

The payment is administratively treated as a loan and interest is
charged. Principal and total interest are deducted from the remaining
death benefit before payment is made to the beneficiary.

Although this option is generally available, it has not been widely
used. This could be partially as a result of the requirement to obtain
the beneficiary's consent (which will inevitably lead to the beneficiary
receiving less funds) and the fact that the living benefits option is not
broadly advertised.

Conversion Privilege

CLHIA guidelines require group life contracts to provide
employees under 65 with an opportunity to convert group life insurance within 31 days of termination for any reason. Conversion allows
the employee to purchase an individual insurance policy from the
insurance company at standard individual rates without any medical
evidence of insurability. Death within 31 days of termination of group
life coverage is treated as if the individual had exercised the conversion privilege. The employer is responsible for advising the terminated
employee of the conversion features.

The employee may convert all or part of the amount for which the
employee was insured under the group life contract. A maximum of
$200,000 is allowed under the guidelines, but a higher limit may be
negotiated with the insurance company. The employee usually has the
choice of a one-year term contract, a term to age 65 contract or a
contract of permanent life insurance. An employee selecting a

one-year term contract may convert it during the first year to a term to age 65 or a permanent life insurance contract.

The conversion privilege was designed to protect employees in poor health who would otherwise be unable to purchase insurance at a reasonable price, if at all. Employees in good health have the option of purchasing a variety of individual insurance plans at more competitive prices.

Variations on Group Life Plans

Accidental Death and Dismemberment

Accidental Death and Dismemberment (AD&D) coverage pays a benefit if an employee dies or suffers a traumatic injury as the result of an accident. Dismemberment usually includes loss of sight of an eye, loss of hearing, loss of use of limbs, or permanent paralysis. The payment generally depends on the severity of the injury. Additional benefits, such as rehabilitation and repatriation of the deceased, are not uncommon.

AD&D policies usually exclude payment of benefits in the event of death as the result of war, riot or other hostilities, self-inflicted injury, commission of a crime, air travel while acting as a pilot, and other conditions.

AD&D coverage is relatively inexpensive and is frequently offered in a principal sum amount equal to group life insurance. At present, AD&D benefits most commonly provide 24-hour coverage, which includes accidents occurring either at or away from the workplace. Some, however, only cover non-workplace accidents for employees who are covered by workers' compensation.

Basic AD&D plans are usually employer-paid. Many employers offer AD&D on an optional, fully employee-paid basis. Optional programs can be designed to allow employees to purchase AD&D coverage for the employee and the family in amounts that reflect the additional income perceived necessary in the event of accidental death.

Optional Group Life

Optional life plans allow employees to supplement basic group life insurance based on individual need. Coverage can be offered in multiples of salary or multiples of any flat dollar unit, with a maximum amount of coverage dictated by the insurance company. Premiums are usually paid by the employee, through payroll deduction.

Optional life insurance usually requires medical evidence of insurability. For larger groups, coverage may be offered on a guaranteed issue basis during the initial enrollment and at the time employees first become eligible.

Most optional life rates are age-related or based on five-year age bands. Increasingly, rates reflect not only age, but also gender and smoker/non-smoker status. Rates based on age encourage higher participation as younger employees are not subsidizing older employees, and similarly, non-smokers are not subsidizing smokers.

Optional life insurance provides employees with the advantage of lower administration fees, lower commissions and the convenience of payroll deduction. For most employees, optional life premiums are competitive with an individual policy. However, for some employees, an individual insurance policy may be less expensive.

Group Universal Life

Group universal life differs from term insurance in that it includes an investment component. Insurance and administration expenses are reported separately from interest-earning cash values, so that employees can select the most appropriate combination of insurance protection and cash accumulation to meet individual needs. Within specific guidelines, investment earnings accumulate on a tax-free basis and are only taxed on withdrawal.

Although group universal life insurance has existed since the 1980's, it is not widely utilized and term insurance remains the more common-form of group insurance.

Group Ordinary Life Insurance

Whole life insurance is occasionally issued on a group basis. Most whole life policies provide for level premiums, which are based on the employee's age at employment and not his or her age at retirement/termination. With level premiums, annual premiums remain unchanged each year, and are payable for the life of the contract.

In regular group term life insurance, the contributions of the employee (if any) are not refunded on termination of employment. Although this is entirely justifiable because the employee has in fact received protection under the coverage for which he or she contributed, there has always been a criticism of this form of insurance; employees receive no benefit in terms of a refund of contributions. With group ordinary life, the policy will normally have built up a cash value, which the employee can potentially access upon termination.

The downside of group ordinary life insurance is that, in relation to the coverage provided, it is much more costly than term life insurance and has had only limited success in Canada. In order to counter the notion of equity with regard to employee contributions, many employers have simply made their plans non-contributory.

Dependant Life Insurance

Some employers provide nominal amounts of dependant life coverage as part of the basic benefit package. It is more common to offer dependant life insurance on an optional basis, with the employee paying for the chosen level of coverage.

The coverage amounts are generally expressed as a nominal flat amount, such as $5,000 for a spouse/partner[2] and $2,000 for a dependent child. However, the amounts can vary depending upon the schedule selected by the employer.

Dependant life is usually not available to retirees. Coverage for the spouse/partner may include a conversion privilege on the employee's death or termination of employment.

There is usually a waiver of premium provision to continue the dependant life insurance without further premium payment in the event that the employee is admitted as a disability claimant under the group life insurance plan.

Premium rates for basic dependant life are expressed as a flat monthly rate per family unit, irrespective of the actual ages of the insured dependants.

Survivor Income Benefit

Survivor income benefits describe a particular form of employee life insurance under which the proceeds are paid as an annuity to the surviving family/beneficiary. The annuity is commonly a percentage of salary for the spouse (which may include same-sex or opposite-sex common-law partners) and an additional benefit for each child. No survivor income benefit would be paid on the death of an employee with no spouse and no dependent children. Benefits may or may not be integrated with survivor benefits payable under the CPP/QPP.

Payments to the spouse are normally for life, while those for children generally cease at a fixed age, such as 21, or 25 (26 in Quebec) if at school. Annuitizing the death benefit provides a steady flow of income and eliminates much of the investment and budgeting responsibility for the spouse.

---

[2] See Chapter 22 for a more in-depth discussion of domestic partner benefits.

The premise of survivor income benefits is to relate death benefits more closely to the needs of surviving dependants by providing a steady flow of income to replace the salary of the employee. Survivor income benefits are inconsistent with the move to a less paternalistic approach to group benefits. In addition, ongoing administration of the annuity benefit and the taxable benefit calculation create more complexities than a lump-sum benefit payment.

Some employers are now stating that the benefits can be paid to a designated beneficiary, which can include a common-law spouse or same-sex partner, or they simply state that the definition of spouse includes common-law and same-sex partners. Different employers specify different prerequisites for establishing that an individual will be considered a common-law or same-sex partner entitled to receive the benefit. For example, the insurer may require proof of cohabitation for a period of at least one year.

Tax Issues

- An employer may deduct premiums paid to a group life insurance policy, for income tax purposes, in the same way as wages or other operating expenses. The same applies to premiums for survivor income, dependant life, and accidental death and dismemberment insurance.

- Employees may not deduct their own contributions to a group life, survivor income, dependant life or accidental death and dismemberment plan from their incomes for tax purposes.

- Life insurance premiums are subject to premium tax and, in the provinces of Ontario and Quebec, to retail sales tax. Premium tax varies by province and territory (in 2002, the insured rate ranged from 2% to 4%).

- An employee is taxed on employer contributions for employee and dependant group life insurance, including any related premium and retail sales tax. Premiums for AD&D are not taxable to the employee, except in Quebec.

- Death benefits paid to beneficiaries under group life, dependant life or accidental death and dismemberment policies are not taxable as income. Any interest paid by the insurer is taxable to the beneficiary.

- An employer may make direct payments of death benefits to the spouse or common-law partner of a deceased employee in recognition of his or her service. Under the *Income Tax Act*, the first $10,000 of such death benefits are received tax-free. A beneficiary other than the surviving spouse or common-law partner is also eligible to receive a tax-free death benefit, to the extent that the $10,000 amount is not fully utilized by the surviving spouse/common-law partner. The definition of death benefit was amended in 2001 and subsequent taxation years to refer to a surviving spouse or common-law partner. This has the effect of recognizing same-sex common-law partners. As a transitional rule, persons who would have qualified as common-law partners in either 1998, 1999 or 2000 are allowed to make a retroactive joint election to be treated as common-law partners for those years.

POST-RETIREMENT BENEFITS

Background

In addition to pensions, many Canadian employers provide other post-retirement benefits to retired employees. These benefits can include life insurance, health and dental benefits.

Employers provide retiree benefits for a number of reasons:

- *Paternalism* — The employer may accept an obligation to take care of, or to reward long-service employees.

- *Extension of active employee benefits* — Retiree benefits may be considered a natural extension of the active employee benefits.

- *Competitiveness* — Retiree benefits may help employers to attract and retain employees, particularly mature employees whose skill sets may be irreplaceable.

- *Negotiation* — Retiree benefits are often part of a union-negotiated package.

Post-retirement benefits were once considered a low-cost ancillary benefit because there were few retirees, and provincial health plans covered most health care expenses. Post-retirement medical plans have risen in cost, however, subject to pressures similar to health plans for active employees. In addition, provincial health plan coverage of prescription drugs for seniors has been dramatically reduced, transferring additional expenses to the post-retirement medical plan or to the retiree.

Additionally, for fiscal years beginning on or after January 1, 2000, the accounting method used by Canadian employers (private sector) for post-retirement benefits changed. Prior to that date, these benefits were calculated on a pay-as-you-go basis. According to *CICA Handbook, Section 3461, "Employee Future Benefits"* (Section 3461), "post-retirement benefits must be accounted for on an accrual basis". Therefore, they must be accounted for not in the future, when the employee retires and receives the benefit, but in the period the employee provided the service. This new accounting requirement was an enlightening process for some employers who suddenly became aware of how expensive post-retirement benefits were and the impact on their financial statements of providing these benefits.

Similar accounting methods for public-sector employers will come into effect in 2004.

Issues

The issues facing Canadian employers on post-retirement benefits can be summarized as follows:

- The number of retirees is growing. Life expectancy continues to increase and employees are retiring earlier. For many Canadians, the years spent in retirement will exceed the years spent in active employment.

- Benefit cost inflation has historically outpaced general wage and price inflation. Contributing factors include higher utilization, advancements in technology and new, more effective drugs and other services introduced to the market at substantially higher prices.

- Reductions in government-sponsored benefits have increased the cost of health care benefits for employers and individuals, particularly the cost of post-retirement benefits. Some cutbacks are immediately recognizable, such as requirements for retiree premiums or deductibles. Others are more subtle, such as reduction of the list of drugs covered by provincial plans, or restriction to certain services, such as ambulance services or physiotherapy. Unless employer medical plans are worded carefully, the liability for benefits removed from provincial health plans may automatically be covered by the employer plan.

- Differences between provincial health plan coverage for active employees are not immaterial for a national employer. The challenge is magnified for the employer to develop a sustainable and equitable approach to post-retirement benefits for retirees across Canada. For example, in Ontario, Manitoba, Newfoundland and Labrador, and Quebec, a payroll tax is levied on employers. The national employer needs a strategy that covers all contingencies, as government programs continue to change.

- As a rule, an individual's use of medical benefits increases with age, particularly in retirement years. Accordingly, as the retiree population ages, utilization of medical benefits also increases.

- Accounting changes, as a result of Section 3461 (effective for fiscal years beginning on or after January 1, 2000) have brought focus on the costs and liabilities associated with providing post-retirement benefits.

As a result of these issues, many employers are reviewing the very nature of the retiree promise and the corresponding financial obligations.

Types of Post-Retirement Benefits

Life Insurance

Employer-paid life insurance is the most prevalent post-retirement benefit. Retiree life insurance is typically in one of the following forms:

- A flat amount (i.e., $5,000 or $10,000) intended to cover burial costs; or

- An amount related to earnings at retirement, which may or may not reduce in the following years.

The life insurance benefit is not generally integrated with other death benefits under the company pension plan, or the Canada/Quebec Pension Plans. The term of the coverage is typically for the life of the retiree. Some plans only provide coverage for early retirees to age 65. Dependant life insurance benefits usually cease at retirement.

There are several funding alternatives for retiree life insurance benefits. The simplest and most common funding method is to purchase one-year renewable term insurance, usually in conjunction with one-year renewable term insurance for the active employee benefit plan. In some cases, the active and retiree benefit experience is combined into one policy, and a blended rate is charged. Alternatively, the retiree and active rates can be separate, reflecting the experience and demographics of each group.

Another funding method for post-retirement benefits is for the employer to self-insure the benefits. Under current tax regulations, life insurance can be self-insured up to $10,000 of coverage. Because death benefits in excess of $10,000 are considered as taxable income to the recipient if not paid through insurance, life insurance above this amount tends to be insured. Health and dental benefits may be insured or self-insured.

A third funding method is to pre-fund the cost of retiree benefits. The retiree life insurance can be purchased from an insurance company on a single premium, paid-up basis.

Health Insurance

Retiree medical coverage is another common benefit provided to retirees. The retiree health plan usually mirrors the active employee medical plan, possibly with lower internal limits and a lower lifetime maximum. Most employers do not require retiree contributions, although this is becoming more common.

Health benefits are particularly valuable to the retiree living on a fixed income. Claims for prescription drugs, hospital services and private-duty nursing care increase dramatically with age. Ancillary benefits, such as out-of-country coverage and payment of any provincial medical premiums, are also meaningful to the retiree. Unfortunately, the evidence indicates that even though funding for government health care programs continues to decline, fewer employers are actually providing post-retirement health care benefits for future retirees. According to the Watson Wyatt 2001 COMPARISON™ Canada Study, only 31 per cent of the organizations surveyed offered retiree health care coverage, as compared to 50 per cent of organization surveyed in 1996.

The employer's promise to pay health care benefits is not generally pre-funded, and most benefits are paid on a pay-as-you-go basis. There is no financial or tax incentive, at present, for employers seeking to pre-fund the post-retirement health care liability. Tax-sheltered vehicles, such as those that have encouraged the growth of pension plan funds, do not exist. Until such vehicles are available, pre-funding retiree benefits represents a significant challenge, and is an area where product development can be expected.

Dental Care

Not as common as retiree life or medical insurance, dental care is sometimes provided to retirees. The plan design would tend to mirror the benefits provided to active employees, possibly with lower annual benefit amounts and usually without orthodontia.

Other Post-retirement Benefits

Some companies provide products or services to their retirees at no cost to the retiree, or at a discount. Examples include reduced transportation fares and discounts on merchandise.

Retiree Post-Retirement Benefit Cost Containment Strategies

Mechanisms for reducing the costs of post-retirement benefits have become particularly important since Section 3461 came into effect. Employers have turned to a variety of cost-containment measures, which enable them to continue providing benefits to their retirees. Such strategies include:

- Establishing or increasing existing employee eligibility requirements. For example, post-retirement benefits could be limited to those employees who have completed a minimum number of years of service with the employer;

- Increased cost sharing through higher deductibles and coinsurance;

- Re-pricing retiree plan contributions to ensure that retirees pay their true premium share (i.e., 50%, 100%) with no subsidization from the active employees' plan experience;

- Providing employees with lump-sum payments in exchange for the elimination or reduction of post-retirement benefits;

- Substituting benefits by exchanging post-retirement benefits for other benefits. For example, the employer could specify that it would provide contributions to group RRSPs in exchange for the elimination of post-retirement benefits;

- Converting from a defined benefit plan to a defined contribution plan;

- To manage and control prescription drugs costs, the employer could enter into arrangements that can provide medications at discounted rates. There are a variety of options, such as preferred provider networks, pharmacy benefit managers, mail order pharmacies and drug formularies; and

- Negotiating a conversion option, whereby the retirees can convert their group policy to an individual policy without providing evidence of insurability and at preferred rates.

Changing the Terms of Post-Retirement Plans — Legal Issues

Employee benefits play an important role in the compensation package and post-retirement benefits are of particular importance to retirees, who are in a much more vulnerable position. As a result of increasing costs incurred by employers in relation to employee benefits, more employers are attempting to contain such costs. Cost-containment measures may include significant changes, such as completely overhauling the plan, or it may involve rather minor changes, such as increasing deductibles or coinsurance. What employers need to be aware of are the potential legal ramifications of altering or terminating employee benefit plans.

If an employer alters or terminates a plan, they will open themselves to the possibility that the employees will claim that the employer breached a fundamental term of the employment contract, thereby allowing them to sue for constructive dismissal. The following discussion will mainly refer to non-unionized environments, as union retirees are governed by collective agreements and labour statutes. Whether employee benefits are fundamental terms of the contract must be determined in each individual case. The primary question that must be asked is "How important is the benefit in relation to the employee's overall compensation?" Another factor to consider: "Was the change as a result of a corporate agenda of economic restraint?" Case law has established that in this situation, the benefit reduction would not be considered a fundamental breach. Additionally, "Was the employee given reasonable notice?" must be asked. Reasonable notice is determined on a case-by-case basis, and will consider such factors as the employee's age, occupation and length of service.

The employer will encounter greater legal difficulties in attempting to reduce or terminate employee benefits that are being paid out to retirees as compared to active employees. The crystallization of the post-retirement retiree benefit promise is not as clear cut as for pensions, and is only now emerging through case law. There have been numerous cases in the United States, but relatively few in Canada to date that have dealt with this issue.

With respect to retiree benefits in the unionized context, it is important to note the 1993 decision of *Dayco (Canada) Limited v. The National Automobile Aerospace and Agriculture Implement*

Workers Union of Canada. In that case, the Supreme Court of Canada held that retiree benefits are capable of vesting at the time of retirement, and therefore could be grieved after the expiry of a collective agreement. The case involved an attempt to terminate post-retirement medical benefits for retirees already in receipt of the benefits. In the Ontario court decision of *Emery v. Royal Oak Mines*, the employee had been dismissed from his position. Subsequently, the benefits to which he was entitled at the time of his termination were reduced. The Court held that the employee was entitled to post-retirement benefits at the time of his dismissal, because at that time, there was no notice of the benefit reduction when the parties' obligations were set.

When an employer in a non-unionized environment wishes to implement cost-containment measures and to protect itself from employee claims, it should consider the following:

- The employer should expressly reserve the right to either terminate or amend its plan without notice. The employer can do this through various forms of communication, such as in the employment contract or benefit booklets.

- The employer should have employees sign an acknowledgment form that stipulates that the employee is aware of the employer's right to either terminate or amend the benefits plan.

- The employer should give reasonable notice of any significant change to its plan, thereby giving employees the opportunity to mitigate their losses[1].

Effect of Flexible Benefits on Post-Retirement Coverage

Traditionally, post-retirement plans have resembled plans designed for the actively employed individual. As such, their design does not consider either the issues of a senior or the benefits available to seniors from the public programs. Additionally, as the senior population increases and their associated health care costs increase as well, the employer is becoming increasingly concerned with the costs of such programs.

A post-retirement benefit plan must satisfy the needs of an individual over many years. Retirement can be as early as age 55, and coverage can extend to death. The differences in coverage requirements over this age span can be addressed by the provision of a flex

---

[1] Source: *Legal Issues in Changing the Terms of Employee Benefit Plans*, by Marsha Reid CCH Canadian Limited's CANADIAN EMPLOYMENT BENEFITS & PENSION GUIDE NEWSLETTER, July 19, 1999 Issue #464.

plan with different options designed to address the needs of the individual at different times in life.

Taxation

- For income tax purposes, an employer may deduct premiums or contributions to post-retirement life, medical or dental plans for current retirees in the same way as wages or other operating expenses.

- All provinces charge premium tax on all group insurance premiums, and in some jurisdictions (namely Ontario, Quebec and Newfoundland and Labrador), contributions to self-insured health and dental plans are subject to the premium tax. Insurance premiums are also subject to sales tax in Ontario and Quebec. Premium tax varies by province and by territory (in 2002, it ranges from 2% to 4%).

- A retiree is taxed on employer contributions for post-retirement life insurance, including any related premium and sales tax. Paid-up life insurance premiums are taxable to the retiree in the year of purchase, except in Quebec, where the premium is amortized over the expected lifetime of the retiree.

- Except in Quebec, the retiree is not taxed on the employer's contribution to the medical or dental plan. In Quebec, effective May 21, 1993, employer contributions (as defined in the provincial regulations) are included as a taxable benefit for the purposes of calculating provincial income tax payable. The amount of the taxable benefit may be included in the calculation of the individual medical expense tax credit.

Accounting

Historically, accounting for post-retirement benefits was handled on a pay-as-you-go basis. The expenses were reflected in the financial statements as the benefit was paid to retirees. In essence, companies had obligations that were not reflected on the balance sheet. Accounting standards have changed in the United States and in Canada.

In December 1990, the accounting profession in the United States adopted Financial Accounting Standard 106 (FAS 106) requiring companies to recognize:

- The cost of retiree benefits over the working lifetimes of the employees; and

- An accrued liability for the future costs of retiree benefits for active members and current retirees.

The accrual accounting method of accounting for the post-retirement benefits reflects the benefit value over the active working career of the employee. It is similar to the methodology for expense and liability recognition under pension plans.

Canadian subsidiaries of American companies and Canadian companies listed on U.S. stock exchanges were required to comply with FAS 106 for fiscal years beginning after December 15, 1994. All Canadian companies subject to Canadian Institute of Chartered Accountants (CICA) accounting standards were affected when the CICA introduced a comparable accounting standard. For fiscal years beginning on or after January 1, 2000, the accounting method used by Canadian employers for post-retirement benefits changed. According to Section 3461, post-retirement benefits must be accounted for on an accrual basis. Similar accounting methods for public-sector employees will come into effect in 2004.

Chapter 19

ADMINISTRATION AND
COMMUNICATION
OF EMPLOYEE BENEFITS

Administration

Background

Accurate and efficient administration is fundamental to the successful operation of an employee benefit plan. Although administration is not directly visible to the employee, it drives the employee records, which, in turn, run premium and claims payment processes.

Employers can select from a wide range of administrative arrangements, each with a different level of resource involvement and costs for the employer. The most appropriate administration arrangement will depend on the corporate culture, the internal resources of the employer, the technology available, the number of divisions, and level of decentralization. Regardless of the administrative arrangement chosen by the employer, tasks and responsibilities need to be clearly defined, and confidentiality of employee records remains paramount.

There are several reasons why there has been a growing trend towards outsourcing the administration of group benefits. First of all, to be competitive, many employers are focusing on their core businesses and expertise. This may lead to strategic alliances or the outsourcing of some generic functions. In the case of pensions and benefits, employers will often outsource some functions of administration and communication, while retaining control of the strategic components that are most important to the individual employee/employer relationships. Another reason for outsourcing is the growing complexity of administration and increased exposure to litigation.

Employers will not want, or cannot afford, to retain sufficient expertise in-house. Additionally, the increasing cost of investments in technology to administer benefits means that more employers will not be able to justify the investment for in-house use only.

An employer has the option of outsourcing either to its insurer or to a third party administrator. A third party administrator (TPA) is an organization that specializes in benefit administration. The use of TPAs has been growing in Canada, due to the fact that they not only provide expertise in benefit administration, but also because they have invested in the required technology.

Privacy Issues

The federal *Personal Information Protection and Electronic Documents Act* came into force on January 1, 2001. Any organization covered by the Act must obtain the consent of an individual before they collect, use or disclose the personal information of that individual. The Act is being phased in over a three-year period. Beginning January 1, 2001, it applies to federal works, undertakings and businesses (i.e., banks, airlines, telecommunication companies), and the personal information that is collected, used or disclosed by these organizations about their employees. On January 1, 2002, the Act applies to personal health information that is collected, used or disclosed by organizations covered in the first phase. Finally, on January 1, 2004, the Act will apply to all organizations regarding the collection, use and disclosure of personal information in the course of "commercial activity" within a province, unless the province has adopted "substantially similar" privacy legislation.

Personal information, as defined in the Act, includes information, both factual and subjective, about an individual. It includes information such as age, ID numbers, income, blood type, evaluations and disciplinary actions, credit records, and medical records. Personal information does not, however, include such things as a person's name, title or business address. Personal health information is described as an individual's mental or physical health information, and that includes information regarding health services provided, and tests and examinations.

For those involved in benefit administration, the most important provision in the Act is the requirement to obtain an individual's consent before collecting, using or disclosing information. The intent behind this provision is to ensure that the information is only used for the purpose for which it was collected. If an organization is going to use it for another purpose, consent must be obtained again. An employee cannot be reprimanded for refusing to provide consent. For employers and insurers, concerns remain due to the fact that some issues are not expressly addressed in the Act: What type of consent is required? Written or oral consent? Expressed or deemed consent? Will a general consent signed by an employee be acceptable?

Another provision in the Act specifies that information must be appropriately safeguarded. Employees should be assured that their information will be protected by specific security measures, including measures such as locked cabinets, computer passwords or encryption. It is also essential that those who work with this information understand their obligations under the Act, to ensure that employees' personal information is properly secured.

Maintaining Employee Data Records

Much of the employee data necessary for benefit purposes can be gathered during the enrolment process. The employee provides basic information at the time of enrolment, including his or her full name, gender and date of birth. The employer adds the date of hire, salary or insurable earnings and an identification number. The identification number assigned by the employer may be the same as the Social Insurance Number (SIN), in which case an authorization to use the SIN should be part of the enrolment form. The federal *Income Tax Act* specifically states that an employer is not to communicate an individual's Social Insurance Number without the individual's written consent, other than in connection with requirements under the *Income Tax Act* itself.

In Quebec, specific authorization is necessary to permit the employer to use personal information for the administration of the plan. For further information regarding consent and other privacy issues in Canada, see the discussion under *Privacy Issues*.

For medical and dental benefits, the employee will need to indicate whether coverage is required for the employee alone, or for their dependants, as well.

Additional benefit enrolment forms typically include the beneficiary designation for life insurance benefits, and any evidence of insurability required.

Having gathered all of the necessary information, the benefit administrator will either enter the information in the administration system, or relay the information to the insurance company or TPA. Changes in employee data are inevitable, and may range from a change in the dependant information, to a change in the status of the employee for benefit coverage. The employer remains responsible for maintaining accurate records and for protecting the confidentiality of personal information of the employee.

Premium Billing

Premiums, or, in the case of self-insured plans, deposit rates, are based on employee data. The exact data vary by benefit. For life insurance, premiums are based on the insured volumes. Disability premiums are based on either the monthly benefit or the monthly insured payroll. Health and dental premiums are typically based on the number of employees covered, and by single and family status.

The monthly billing can be prepared by the insurance company, a third party administrator, or by the employer.

In the case of the insurance company or TPA preparing the billing statement, the employer notifies the insurance company of any changes in employee data since the prior billing period. The employer may produce the billing statement itself using an internal administration system that keeps track of the employee data. The administration system may be developed by the employer or purchased from a vendor.

Administering Employee Contributions

Most benefit administration systems are designed to automatically calculate any employee contributions required, provided the system has current data and current rates.

The interface between the benefit administration system and the payroll system may be electronic, or may require human intervention to transfer the information each pay period. In some cases, the employer relies on the payroll system to calculate and administer deductions, and maintains a separate administration system for benefit records.

Alternative procedures may be necessary to administer employee contributions for employees not on the active payroll system. Post-dated cheques or electronic fund transfers can be arranged for employee contributions during unpaid leave, maternity leave, retirement or for employees in receipt of disability benefits.

In Quebec, employee contributions for medical and dental plans can be included in the tax credit for medical expenses, and should be recorded separately from other employee contributions.

Claim Payment

When an employee submits a claim, the claim must be adjudicated to determine whether the claimed item is covered, and the amount of reimbursement to be paid. The objective is to pay the claim as fairly and as promptly as possible. The claim administration function may be performed by the insurance company, by the employer or by a TPA. Most medical and dental claims are handled by an outside source, such as an insurance company or TPA. Such claims are rarely handled by the employer. Insurance company/TPA validation of an employee's eligibility streamlines the process and provides the employee with a greater sense of confidentiality. The trend towards insurance company/TPA validation is reinforced by the growing use of electronic data interchange in adjudicating claims at point of purchase.

Management Reports

The insurance company/TPA should be able to produce financial and claims management reports as required for each benefit. Interpretation of the information provided by the insurance company/TPA may require supplementary data from the benefit administration system. For example, an increase in paid claims may be entirely expected in a period of growth, but alarming during a period of stability or reduction.

Benefits that are self-insured and self-administered rely solely on internal systems to develop the analytical tools essential to govern the plan. It may be necessary to integrate data from several sources, including the benefit administration and payroll systems.

The benefit administration system stores information on the employee population, which can in turn be compared to the claimant demographics for plan review and pricing. Demographic profiling is particularly important in terms of pricing for flexible benefits.

Lastly, it may be necessary to audit the accuracy of the insurance company/TPA records. Reconciliation can be conducted by comparing data files, or by performing an audit on the premises of the insurance company/TPA.

Administration In A Union Environment

At minimum, administration of benefits in a union environment requires the ability both to segregate the employees by coverage classification and to administer more than one distinct set of plan rules. Often, there are several collective bargaining units that may negotiate benefits and wages at different times.

Negotiated benefit changes may be retroactive, placing additional stress on the administration system. Many benefit administration systems have not automated the ability to implement plan-wide retroactive changes, and require adjustment at the individual record level.

Benefit Administration Systems

As employers develop benefit plans that respond to diversity and changing needs, the ability to provide effective communication and administrative solutions becomes critical to the success of the plan design. Human resource and benefit administration systems can be bought, adapted or created internally, depending on the employer's needs and resources. The resources and budget required to create a full human resource system are beyond the means of most employers.

An administration system purchased by an employer for in-house use should take into account the corporate methodologies in terms of technology, architecture and supported solutions. The ability to maintain the system with internal resources allows the employer to keep the system responsive to a changing environment. In addition, the employer may be able to add or build additional modules that are not dependent upon outside proprietary databases.

Benefit administration can be addressed as a separate stand-alone system or as a module of a complete human resource administration system. Administration packages are available with a wide range of features and functions.

Full-service software providers deliver a significant degree of custom design, performed in partnership between the vendor and the employer. The product is ready to be installed when delivered to the employer. By contrast, tool-kit or shelf-ware applications are developed by the vendor, with the employer assuming all responsibility for the costs of customization, construction of interfaces, testing and ongoing maintenance. Some vendors in both categories will provide additional support using their technical personnel on a fee-for-service or contract basis.

Implementing benefit guidelines on a consistent and timely basis has always been a challenge to human resource professionals and benefit administrators. Rules-based or table-driven applications use the administration system itself to manage policy guidelines, reducing the incidence of *ad hoc* changes required. For example, eligibility rules can include a screening process to ensure that only eligible employees participate in selected benefits or options. Rules-based applications can also initiate benefit changes automatically upon certain life events, including a change in marital status or a change in employee status.

Administration packages vary in the level of flexibility, compatibility and ease of implementation. The more rigid systems essentially force the employer to adapt to a rigid set of pre-defined codes. A more versatile system allows the employer to define the codes to match their own.

To be able to manage retroactive adjustments, the administration system must accommodate not only all changes predating the current deduction period, but also the discrete periods in which these changes were in effect. Employee premiums and taxable benefits at both federal and provincial levels can be addressed within a well-designed benefit administration system to avoid the need for manual calculation. The need to administer multiple concurrent changes will depend on the plan design, but will definitely increase with the number of employees in the group and the frequency of changes allowed under the plan.

A flexible benefit environment will affect the enrolment process and the maintenance of employee data. In addition to the information noted above, the employer will need to record the benefit options chosen by the employees. There are typically credits or contributions that need to be calculated to reflect not only the benefit option chosen, but also the date of entry into the plan.

In a flexible benefit plan, the employee may have discretion over the allocation of credits. Some benefit elections will have no taxable benefit implications. Others will give rise to a taxable benefit just as if the employer had contributed directly to the premiums. The order in which credits are applied is an essential consideration of the administration system and the taxable benefit calculation.

In-house administration systems are not the only solutions for employers. As technology continues to progress, many employers find themselves continuously updating their software. This can be costly for the employer in terms of money expended for the upgrades and employee hours spent ensuring proper implementation of the software. As a solution, a few employers have turned to Application Service Providers (ASPs). An ASP is a third party that manages and distributes software-based services. Basically, ASPs provide another method of software delivery. Rather than purchasing and upgrading software, the employer accesses the ASP software via the Internet. Ongoing support from the ASP is available.

Another recent development in benefits administration is the trend toward self-service Web sites for employees. Not only can employees obtain information about their benefits via the Internet, but they can also enroll in flexible benefits plans and print off forms and information that they require. Although some employers question the practicality of using the Internet due to lack of employee access and computer literacy, statistics show that Internet usage is increasing. To increase employee access to the Internet, employers can provide kiosks at the work site.

Also of great advantage to employees are benefit modelling tools, as they make the educational and administrative stages of the system more streamlined. Using a flexible benefits modelling tool, the employee would be able to consider the different options available and the costs and taxable benefits at different levels of coverage.

Another advantage of online enrolment is the ability to ensure that the employee completes all of the necessary information. When the employee fails to enter the required information, or the information is incorrect, the employee will be notified of the error and will be unable to proceed until the necessary information is provided. In the paper-based environment, the errors are not detected until they are processed, causing administrative delays. Another advantage of self-service Web sites is the ability to provide access for employees 24 hours a day. Employees can access the site in the evenings, on weekends, or at whatever time is convenient for them.

Not only can information regarding the company's benefits be addressed online, but information and links can be provided as a useful source of reference material. For example, "B" is an employee of company "X". B has an elderly parent who requires assistance. B logs onto the company Web site for information and finds an "Eldercare" link on the site. B then finds information regarding company programs (i.e., flextime, telecommuting, financial assistance). Additionally B finds a list of books related to that topic, as well as different contacts and links to useful resources regarding eldercare (government information, support groups, eldercare providers, etc.).

From the employer's perspective, self-service benefits can save costs, promote increased efficiency and accuracy, and eliminate paperwork. Employers do have some legitimate concerns, however. Security is probably the most pressing concern for employers and employees when dealing with confidential information over the Internet. To address this, it is necessary that the site be encrypted. Each employee will need a secure personal identification number and a password. If appropriate steps are taken, security concerns should be allayed.

Communication

Background

A benefit plan represents a substantial commitment for the employer and an increasingly significant portion of the compensation package for employees. To maximize their return on this investment, most employers recognize the need to effectively communicate the benefit plan to employees. Poor communication can create misunderstanding and may contribute to higher administration costs.

Employee communication is especially important in a flexible benefit environment, where employees are asked to make decisions concerning their benefits, based on the information presented to them. Employers surveyed about their flexible benefit plans overwhelmingly respond that the communications strategy was the one aspect of the implementation that they would improve, given the opportunity and the clarity of hindsight.

Preparing a communication strategy includes setting the objectives, defining the target audience, developing a framework of the subjects to cover and selecting the best media. The timetable must allow for each step of the process to be well-executed, including production and delivery.

Benefit communication is most effective when it reflects the values and objectives of the organization. It is generally appropriate to link the benefit communication strategy to the theme of the human resources strategy or to the business strategy of the organization.

Setting the Objectives

Three objectives are common to most benefit communication strategies:

- *Awareness* — making sure employees are fully aware of *what* is offered to them;

- *Understanding* — making sure employees understand *how* the plans work; and

- *Application* — making sure that employees put the plan to use *when* they need it.

Specific communication objectives may include education on certain aspects of benefits, wellness promotion, or development of a sense of partnership. Meeting the objectives should increase employee appreciation of the benefits offered.

Defining the Target Audience

A communication strategy depends in part on the people being addressed. The target audience can be defined in terms of number, location, language, age group, level of reading comprehension and education. It may also be helpful to get a sense of how employees perceive the organization and the benefit plans. It is essential that written communication be simple, clear and in non-technical terms. To be enforceable, the explanation of any limitations or exclusions must be explicit and precise.

Developing the Framework

The communication strategy will be shaped by the subject matter and the key message. In a changing environment, dialogue with employees may be necessary to ensure that they have a broader understanding of some benefit issues. Basic communication on the benefit plan typically goes beyond plan design information to address a range of employee questions, which may include:

- Basic insurance principles, explaining why there are deductibles, maximums and limitations;

- Administrative procedures, including how to submit claims and how to get more information;

- The cost of benefits, which may address what portion of the compensation package is allocated to provide benefits, what the link is between claims and cost, and whether the cost is changing year to year;

- The benefits available under government plans, and changes to government benefits as they are introduced;

- Taxation of benefits and contributions, and an explanation of what is taxable and what is not; and

- Health care issues, reinforcing why prevention is important, why health care costs are increasing, and how employees can be wiser health care consumers.

Selecting the Media

Benefit specialists have a broad range of communication media available to them. Studies show that human understanding and retention of new topics increases with the use of a combination of media. The choice of media should reflect the characteristics of the audience, the message being communicated and the structure of the organization. Production and distribution requirements may also influence the choice of media. Other factors may include the communication culture of the organization, the environment, budget constraints and the need for frequent updating. Examples of approaches that are used when introducing employee choice or making plan design changes include:

- Direct Contact: focus groups, general employee meetings, individual employee meetings and information hot lines (using toll-free numbers);

- Print: newsletters, posters, booklets, workbooks, question and answer (Q & A) sheets and faxes; and

- Electronic: software programs, CD-ROMs, Web-based technology, video, voicemail, interactive voice response systems and kiosks.

The traditional and still widely used medium is the paper-based booklet that employees can read for general knowledge of their coverage. Before incurring medical or dental expenses, employees may refer to the booklet to determine whether products or services are covered under the benefit plan or option.

As a supplement to the booklet, it may be necessary to plan ongoing, periodic communication to reinforce messages, to communicate changes or even to educate employees on emerging benefit issues. Periodic communication may include personal statements, benefit newsletters and electronic or traditional bulletin boards.

Face-to-face communication remains one of the most effective means of delivering a message and engaging employees in open dialogue. Surveys indicate that employees prefer to receive information on benefits in small group meetings, where they can direct questions to specialists. Employee meetings provide an opportunity to gather feedback on what employees understand and appreciate in their benefit package.

Effective communication does not need to be expensive, particularly if the communication is linked to a message of benefit austerity. Simple, well-written communication, combined with an open forum discussion, may often be as effective as full-colour booklets or sophisticated videos. Badly written and poorly presented communication may diminish employee perception of the value and quality of the benefits, and may undermine the intended message.

Benefit communication is adapting to a paperless environment. The use of technology offers a wide range of innovative and effective communication tools. Depending on the nature of the organization and its workforce, using the telephone and the computer as communication media may be economical and well-received. The telephone can serve as a link to reference material. Interactive voice response systems and personalized electronic enrolment models have powerful applications. Through a local network or the Internet, the computer can augment or replace traditional printed material by allowing employees to access a hypertext electronic version of the booklet, or by using electronic mail for questions and record updates. CD-ROMs are another medium for providing information to employees. They are fairly inexpensive, and can store a great deal of information. Where computers are not readily accessible to employees, the employer can set up kiosks at the work site that enable the employer to provide employees with PC/Web access.

Planning and Execution

Preparing benefit communication requires time and dedicated resources. After the messages are defined and the media chosen, the planning begins. A typical communication plan would include the following elements:

- Research and writing;
- Review by specialists and rewriting;
- Translation, when necessary;
- Testing the material with employees;
- Production; and
- Distribution.

Evaluating the Efforts

As employee need for information grows, and as the organization itself changes, the communication strategy has to be periodically evaluated. It may be useful to ask employees to evaluate what is successful in terms of content and delivery. This can be done through a survey, or through focus groups or informal discussions, depending on time and budget constraints.

Chapter 20

FINANCIAL MANAGEMENT OF EMPLOYEE BENEFIT PLANS

Background

This chapter addresses the financial aspects of benefit plan stewardship, and the many alternatives available to employers.

In a typical group insurance contract, the insurance company agrees to insure specific group benefits that are payable to the individuals eligible under the plan. The employer agrees to pay the premiums to maintain the contract in good standing for the year, and to provide the insurance company with necessary records to administer the benefit. In the case of a self-insured benefit, the insurance company would provide Administrative Services Only (ASO) and the employer would contractually accept the financial liability for all claim payments and administration charges.

Financing Employee Group Benefit Plans

Renewal Process

Group insurance policies and related agreements are generally written on a one-year renewable basis. The annual cycle lends itself to a review of all aspects of the relationship between the insurance company and the employer at least once a year.

As part of the annual renewal process, the insurance company has the right to adjust its premium rates, expenses and reserves for the upcoming year. Conversely, the employer has the right to renew the contract or to seek alternatives in the marketplace. Cost continues to be a key factor in the evaluation of the relationship. The definition of cost will depend on whether the employer has purchased pure insurance (pooled) or whether the employer shares in the risk either through retention (refund) accounting or through self-insurance.

Premium defines the gross cost of the benefit. The premium is calculated at the beginning of the year by the insurance company. The premium calculation may take into account prior claims experience, demographics, risk distribution, occupations within the group, geographic location and plan design. In this context, claim experience would include the insurer's reserve and administrative expenses, as well as projected inflation and anticipated utilization. Unless the employer is participating in some form of retention accounting, or the benefit is self-insured, the premium represents the cost of providing the benefit. Negotiating the lowest sustainable cost is generally in the best interest of the employer and the employees.

Net cost is gross cost less any experience refunds the employer is entitled to receive. The net cost is calculated as the paid claims, plus the insurance company administration expenses, reserves and any interest adjustments. The definition of net cost applies to retention accounting and to self-insured benefits that are administered by the insurance company on an ASO basis.

Underwriting Considerations

Employers select from a continuum of risk arrangements or underwriting options that allocate the risk between the insurance company and the employer. Risk is defined as the potential for loss or gain resulting from the variance between premiums (projected cost) and actual cost.

At one extreme, benefits are underwritten on a fully pooled basis, with the insurance company assuming the full risk in the event that actual claims experience exceeds premiums. The insurance company retains any profit arising if premiums exceed claims plus expenses. The liability of the employer is limited to the premium paid. At the other extreme, the employer self-insures the risk, regardless of the actual claims level. The role of the insurance company is strictly to perform the administrative and claims adjudication services.

The underwriting option most appropriate for an employer depends on the benefit under consideration, the number of employees in the group and the risk tolerance of the employer. The terms being offered by the insurance company may also impact on the decision of the employer.

Each benefit has unique attributes that define its inherent risk. Two key attributes are the magnitude of potential claims and the frequency of claims. Large amount claims occurring with a low incidence will lead to a high degree of volatility in annual costs. For example, life insurance claims are relatively infrequent and each claim represents several thousand dollars. The combination of infrequent incidence and a large amount for each occurrence increases the risk of fluctuation in expected claims year-to-year. Conversely, vision care claims, for example, occur more frequently, and the benefit schedule may limit the dollar amount of any one claim to a hundred dollars. Relative to group life insurance, the combination of high incidence and low dollars per claims reduces the potential underwriting risk.

The number of individuals covered in a group is a commonly used measure of claims stability. As the number of employees increases, it becomes more likely that future claims can be projected based on the past claims of the group. The term "credibility" is used to denote the likelihood that past experience can be used reliably to project future claims. If the credibility is low, either because the group is small or the experience has been volatile, the insurance company will rely on its standard rate tables to determine the premium. If the credibility is high, the insurance company is more likely to base the premiums on the claims experience of the group, and the employer is more likely to consider some form of risk sharing.

Some organizations are more inclined towards fully pooled or pure insurance. Others have a higher tolerance for risk sharing. The same is true for employer preferences in underwriting options for the benefit plans. The insurance community has responded to employer needs by offering a wide range of underwriting options.

Underwriting Options

Fully Pooled

The insurance company assumes the full risk of a deficit in the event that actual claims experience exceeds premiums. Conversely, the insurance company profits from any surplus.

There is no annual financial accounting under a fully pooled arrangement, but the insurance company will prepare a renewal report and will normally disclose the experience of the group. Many insurers, however, have implemented strict internal policies that prohibit the disclosure of a group's detailed claims experience due to privacy concerns. Therefore, it will likely be more difficult in the future for smaller plan sponsors (i.e., under 25 lives) to view their own claims history. The renewal may reflect the overall experience of the insurance company for groups with similar characteristics. For most employer plans, the experience of the group will be factored into the renewal analysis.

Pooled funding is suitable for small employers to minimize year-to-year cost fluctuations. Pooled funding is generally appropriate for benefits with highly volatile costs, such as Accidental Death and Dismemberment (AD&D), where a single claim can represent several years of premium. Many employers elect pooled funding for life and Long-Term Disability (LTD) benefits that usually involve large amounts and low claim incidence.

Retention Accounting

Typically in a retention accounting situation, the employer receives from the insurance company an annual financial accounting of the plan, as well as some or all of the surplus arising if claims were lower than expected. The specific terms governing each refund account depend on the terms of the underwriting agreement between the insurance company and the employer.

The financial accounting takes into account the premiums paid to the insurance company, claims paid by the insurance company, changes in the reserves, administration expenses and the interest earned or charged. When premiums exceed the charges against the account, the insurance company declares a surplus. The surplus may be released to the employer, held by the insurance company on behalf of the employer in a Claims Fluctuation Reserve (CFR) or Rate Stabilization Fund (RSF) to buffer future volatility, or applied against prior deficits under the account.

Deficits arise when the premium is not sufficient to cover the claims and expenses for a given year. While the policy remains in force with the insurance company, the employer usually accepts that future surplus will be applied to reduce or eliminate the deficit. The ultimate liability for the deficit remains with the insurance company, unless liability for deficit on termination is specifically written into the terms of the underwriting agreement.

Pooling

Pooling is an arrangement whereby employers who have their group benefit plans underwritten on an ASO basis or on a retention accounting basis, are protected in situations where an individual claim exceeds a certain amount, or the total claims paid out exceeds a certain amount. An employer buys this protection from the insurer. There are three common types of pooling arrangements:

- *Large amount pooling* — provides financial protection in the event of a single catastrophic claim during the accounting period. It normally applies to health and life benefits, but it is also occasionally used for LTD benefits;

- *Duration pooling* — is a variation of large amount pooling. It is commonly used in LTD accounting and it protects the plan from individual claims that exceed a fixed duration (i.e., 2 years or 5 years, regardless of the monthly benefit payable);

- *Aggregate stop loss pooling* — provides financial protection in the event of an unexpected surge in the number of claims during the accounting period. The protection level is generally defined in terms of a percentage of the annual premium (i.e., 125% of premium).

Administrative Service Only (ASO)

An employer choosing to self-insure a benefit forgoes the risk transfer offered by insurance companies. Depending on the benefit, it may remain strategically more efficient to use the administrative services of the insurance company rather than replicate the necessary infrastructure to manage claim data and adjudicate claims. The insurance company is compensated for its services, either on a percentage of paid claims or, more recently, on a per transaction basis.

Many employers favour stop loss protection combined with their ASO arrangements. The same variations are available under an ASO plan as under an experience-rated plan, allowing the employer to protect the benefit budget for claims exceeding the acceptable level of risk.

By definition, a self-insured plan does not involve premiums. The employer has a range of payment options to replace the monthly premium flow.

A conservative employer may choose to mirror an insured arrangement, remitting monthly deposits to the insurance company based on projected claims. Deposit rates reduce the month to month fluctuation, but require annual reconciliation against actual cost.

Alternatively, the insurance company will invoice the employer based on the prior month's claims plus expenses. Monthly cost will fluctuate, but most insurance companies are prepared to offer either stop loss or some form of equalization to avoid excessive variation in cost from month to month.

A third option for a self-insured plan is to create a debit arrangement between the employer and the insurance company. The insurance company is authorized, on a daily or weekly basis, to withdraw funds equivalent to claims plus expenses from a designated account established by the employer.

Funding Disability Benefits

Employers commonly self-insure Short-Term Disability (STD) plans without pre-funding. The maximum exposure on any one claim is limited by the benefit duration. Over time, the claims experience of most groups shows a reasonable element of predictability. Insured coverage is available for smaller groups, or for employers with a lower tolerance for risk.

Long-Term Disability plans represent a significantly different risk-management challenge. A typical example of the present value of an LTD benefit that provides a 66⅔% benefit to age 65 for a 40-year-old employee with annual earnings of $45,000 could be in the order of $350,000. Many organizations are not large enough to assume a risk of this magnitude without some form of protection. Not surprisingly, LTD benefits are generally insured. Larger employers may insure the LTD benefits with some form of retention accounting. Even so, some form of pooling is generally prudent to mitigate against experience fluctuation. Pooling is also available to the very large, very solvent employer who prefers to self-insure the LTD plan.

Assets and Liabilities

The annual financial accounting from the insurance company will take into account premiums paid to the insurance company and claims paid by the insurance company. Most contracts of insurance involve obligations, which may extend beyond the end of the accounting period. Reserves held by the insurance company reflect the assets and liabilities associated with obligations for future liabilities. The ownership and accountability of each type of reserve is a matter to be negotiated between the insurance company and the employer, and documented in the underwriting agreement.

Incurred But Not Reported (IBNR)

Incurred But Not Reported (IBNR) claim reserves reflect liability for claims that are incurred during the contract year and submitted after the close of the contract year but are payable from the premiums collected during the accounting period.

The level of the IBNR reflects the claim reporting pattern associated with the benefit. For example, the IBNR for life insurance tends to reflect a reporting lag of roughly one month between the date of death and the date the claim is filed with the insurance company. If the life contract includes an insured premium waiver provision, the IBNR would tend to be a little higher. By contrast, the IBNR under an LTD contract with a six-month elimination period would be in the order of 50% to 60% of premium. The insurance company may be willing to reduce the IBNR requirements or eliminate the reserve from the annual accounting if the employer is willing to delay the financial reconciliation to allow the late-reported claims to flow through the account.

Premium Waiver

Such reserves, or waiver of premium reserves, are held under life insurance contracts in which the employer has insured the continuation of coverage for disabled lives without future payment of premium. Despite the term "premium waiver", the reserve is not based on the future value of the premiums being waived on behalf of the disabled individual. The premium waiver reserve is based on the discounted value of the death claim, taking into account the probability of recovery, termination, or death and discounting the face amount of the claim for projected interest earnings.

The insurance company remains liable for the death benefit on approved premium waiver claims beyond the termination of the contract, usually through to age 65. The premium waiver reserve allows the insurance company to reflect this obligation in the financial accounting before the death claim occurs. Each insurance company has a slightly different calculation method.

The employer may choose not to insure the premium waiver provision, in which case benefit continuation for disabled employees would be conditional on premium continuation. Self-insuring the premium waiver provision renders the employer responsible for arranging continued coverage for the disabled individuals in the event that the life insurance contract is transferred to another insurance company.

Disabled Life Reserves (DLR)

Under an income-replacement benefit, Disabled Life Reserves (DLR) reflect the obligation of the insurance company for benefit continuation beyond policy termination. Once a claim is admitted and payments commence, the insurance company becomes liable for future benefit payments, provided the individual continues to qualify under the terms of the benefit plan. The reserve reflects the present value of future benefit payments, adjusted for mortality and recovery assumptions, and discounted for projected interest earnings. Each insurance company has a slightly different calculation method for establishing its DLR.

Claims Fluctuation Reserves (CFR)

Claims Fluctuation Reserves (CFR), also known as Rate Stabilization Reserves (RSF), reflect funds that are owned by the employer and held by the insurance company. By withholding a portion of the surplus against future deficits, the insurance company is protecting itself against the contingency the employer will terminate the relationship while the account is in a deficit position. In consideration of a CFR, the employer should expect a reduction in any risk charges levied by the insurance company.

Insurance Companies

Selecting an Insurance Company

Whether the role of the insurance company is to insure the benefit or to pay claims on an ASO basis, the selection of the right insurance company and the establishment of a good ongoing relationship is a factor in the success of the benefit plan. The same applies if retaining more than one insurance company, either for different benefits or for different employee groups. Similar principles apply in the selection of a third-party administrator other than an insurance company.

An employer may have one reason, or a combination of reasons, for inviting proposals from other insurance companies. Periodically marketing a benefit program allows the employer to determine whether the costs charged by the insurance company are competitive, and to confirm that the services offered by the insurance company meet with current needs and expectations. Reasons for marketing a benefit plan may include:

- Evidence of uncompetitive rates and/or expense costs;

- Merger or acquisition;

- Consolidating two or more benefit programs;

- Introduction of flexible benefits;

- Lack of responsiveness and flexibility;

- Poor claims service by the current insurance company;

- Need to improve disability claim management;

- Need to investigate innovative services (i.e., management of prescription drug costs, administration systems, and better use of technology); and

- Mandatory tendering policy.

The reason for marketing will influence the criteria for selecting the successful quotation. Clearly articulated and prioritized selection criteria serve to streamline the analysis of quotations. Selection criteria may address any problems the employer seeks to resolve through the marketing, as well as all positive aspects of the relationship with the incumbent insurance company. Cost is generally high on the list of criteria, but it is seldom the only factor in the evaluation.

In some cases, it is readily apparent from the analysis that a single insurance company will best meet all of the selection criteria. Alternatively, it may be necessary to prioritize criteria, as several candidates excel on a few criteria, but no one candidate scores top marks on all.

The request for proposal provides the insurance company underwriters with sufficient data to assess the risk and to establish the premium required to operate the plans on a sustainable basis. It also establishes the information to be provided in the quotation for the employer or their broker/consultant to assess the competitiveness of the quotation. Information obtained as part of the proposal may be relevant in the years following to ensure that the insurance company complies with the commitments made in their proposal.

All of the information necessary to prepare the quotation should be included in the request for proposal or specifications. Plan design, employee data, open claim lists, and premium, claim and rates histories are important elements of the evaluation by the insurance company.

Within the request for proposal, the employer will often raise a series of questions to arrive at the non-financial evaluation of the proposals. Questions can be used to clarify the financial aspects, particularly when retention accounting is involved. The structure of the questions may influence the insurer response and the relative evaluation between insurance companies.

The quoted premiums or costs are usually compared using consistent assumptions of the insurance volume and the expected claims. Cost analysis includes both the gross cost and the net cost.

Service capabilities and commitments can also be compared and evaluated against the selection criteria. For example, if consistent and timely processing of health and dental claims were important selection criteria, the analysis may focus on the adjudication systems, the quality assurance programs and the claims payment capacities of the candidates.

Cost analysis will generally narrow the number of contenders to a few finalists. Interviews with finalists may be useful to probe the qualitative criteria and the acceptability of the proposed service team. Finalist interviews allow more in-depth assessment of insurance company administration and underwriting capabilities, and allow the employer to query any weak aspects of the proposal.

If the outcome of the marketing is a change of insurance companies, a checklist of transition issues and a timetable with roles and responsibilities for each task will ensure that all important details are appropriately handled in the transition. It can be helpful to review the transition plan with the new insurance company. Important transition issues vary by benefit, but may include the following:

- For all benefits, notice of termination will need to be provided to the prior insurance company as required in the policy.

- For all benefits, but particularly for life and disability benefits, all employees who are not actively at work on the transition date will need to be reported to both the old and the new insurance companies no later than 31 days after the effective date of the new policy. The CLHIA Guidelines[1] outline the protection of life insurance benefits for all plan members on transfer of insurance company.

- The change of insurance companies will need to be effectively communicated to employees. Under an insured underwriting basis, claims that occur prior to the termination date may remain the liability of the prior insurance company. Employees will need to know where to submit new claims and whether benefits are affected by the transition.

- Copies of the old policies and confirmation of any benefit plan design changes can be provided to the new insurance company. This may facilitate duplication of existing benefits.

---

[1] The Canadian Life and Health Insurance Association (CLHIA) was established in 1984 and is an association of life and health insurance companies in Canada. CLHIA sets out guidelines on various matters and members generally abide by such guidelines.

- Where appropriate, identification cards and employee booklets will need to be re-issued. For life and AD&D benefits, the new insurance company should accept existing beneficiary designations. It may be timely to encourage employees to update the beneficiary and dependant information on their files.

Partnering With An Insurance Company

An insurance company may be hired to perform any combination of the following functions relative to the management of the benefit plan:

- Adjudication, management and payment of claims;

- Administration of premiums;

- Determination of eligibility for claim purposes;

- Issuing of various documents: contracts, booklets, enrollment cards;

- Underwriting of the plan (including plan design and funding) and premium rate setting; and

- Day-to-day communication with employees.

As employers streamline their internal processes and resources, insurance companies are expected to provide a wider range of services and to show a greater degree of adaptability. Employers are becoming more demanding and informed consumers. Insurance companies are delivering more innovative and varied responses to meet the diverse and sophisticated expectations of employers and their constituents.

Underwriting Agreements

The financial terms and conditions governing an experience-rated plan are commonly documented in an underwriting agreement. For relatively uncomplicated arrangements, an informal letter of agreement may suffice. A more formal and explicit agreement is more common when the employer is accepting part of the liability normally held by the insurance company, usually in exchange for lower risk charges or for a reduction in the reserves normally required.

Performance Standards Agreements

A performance standards agreement outlines specific time and quality commitments that the insurance company promises for the payment of claims, processing of employee coverage updates, and responding to queries from the benefit administrator. There may be monetary penalties for the insurance company for failing to meet the performance standards or rewards for exceeding the performance standards.

The performance standards agreement may be verbal, or may be addressed within the Underwriting Agreement. Where the group is very large, or where service problems have been difficult to resolve, a separate written agreement may be appropriate.

Multi-Employer Issues

Although this chapter has been constructed from the perspective of a single employer, many of the same issues and considerations also govern a multi-employer benefit environment. Multi-employer benefit plans are usually, but not always, arranged through a health and welfare trust.

Quite often, the multi-employer plan provides benefits for employees of a specific industry, particularly in industries where an employee will routinely work for more than one employer at the same time, or sequentially. There are several examples in the construction trades across the country. It is not uncommon to have a single union involved in the multi-employer plan.

The trust agreement includes the terms of the benefit provisions, the level of employer contributions, and the mandate of the board of trustees. Decision-making and management decisions are generally the purview of the board of trustees. Day-to-day administration, including premium remittance, may involve individual employers but more often involves the administrators of the plan on behalf of the trust.

Trustees are elected, and may include representation from the union as well as the participating employers. If the collective agreement defines the level of employer contributions, the trustees will be responsible for determining and managing the benefits to be provided through these contributions. If the agreement defines the benefits that will be provided, the trustees will be responsible for making certain that the contributions are set at an adequate level.

The trust fund can provide a comprehensive range of benefits or a single benefit. One advantage to plan members is the ease with which benefits can be continued in the event of changing employers within the trust.

Eligibility for benefits is usually based on the number of hours worked for the participating employers. Member employment records are generally maintained by the administrator employed by the trust fund.

An hour-bank system is often used to keep track of member eligibility. In an hour-bank system, the trust defines the number of hours per month to qualify for coverage in the following month. The administrator is responsible for recording the number of hours worked each month to the hour bank and debiting the monthly benefit charge from the hour bank, for each plan member. A member can often increase the hours credited to the hour bank by working overtime or working additional shifts. The additional hours fund periods of shorter employment when the member is not working a full week, such as temporary lay-off, short weeks, or vacation.

Usually, a new member must work the equivalent of two or more months of target hours to achieve eligibility. When a member ceases employment with a participating employer, benefit coverage may be continued based on the terms of the agreement and the number of hours remaining in the hour bank.

Health and welfare trusts are not specifically mentioned in the federal *Income Tax Act*; however, Interpretation Bulletin "IT-85R2 — Health and Welfare Trusts for Employees", does attempt to explain the CCRA's opinion as to the tax treatment of such trusts. In almost all health and welfare trusts, the CCRA requires an annual tax return to be filed. The trustee also has an obligation to exercise due diligence to ensure adequate trust funding and reasonable investment decisions.

FLEXIBLE BENEFITS

Background

Flexible benefits are a natural choice for employers seeking to partner with employees in managing the cost of the benefit plan, and for employers repositioning benefits as part of the overall compensation package. This chapter reviews the evolution of flexible benefits, provides an overview of design and pricing considerations and discusses implementation steps.

History and Evolution

Flexible benefits in the 1980s were generally viewed as a product, or more correctly, a series of products. The plan design was likely to be a Canadianized version of the parent company plan, or the mirror image of the plan of a major competitor, with changes to accommodate administration and pricing objectives. The end result was sometimes more expensive and more confusing than the original plan design. Until recently, there was often more emphasis on form than on function.

For the early pioneers, flexible benefit administrative requirements were often an afterthought — and too often a barrier. For many employers, the cost associated with administration outweighed the advantages they would achieve with greater flexibility. Until the advent of affordable administration technology, flexible benefits were primarily the domain of the very large employer.

Flexible benefits programs have become more commonplace over the last 10 years. A variety of factors have led to the resurgence of the "flex benefits" popularity. One of the main reasons for the success of flexible benefits programs is the diverse employee population, whose needs in various stages of life or in differing family circumstances have prompted the need for more diverse programs. Additionally, these programs are seen as a mechanism for maximizing the cost-effectiveness of the employer's expenses for employee benefits, as rising benefit costs became a concern for employers during the 1980s and 1990s. Employers found the defined contribution aspect of a flexible benefits program to be quite appealing. Finally, the lowering of the technology barrier has meant that some form of flexible benefits can be cost effective for all but the smallest of employers.

Canadian flexible benefits plans are now at a more mature stage, having benefited from the experiences of earlier experimental approaches that often failed to provide employers with the financial integrity sought under the programs. The primary problem with these earlier designs was the multitude of choices offered under various flexible benefits plan structures, which caused anti-selection and administrative issues. As a result, changes within the flex design prompted cost-shifting to the employees through increased forms of out-of-pocket expenditure, in an effort to maintain the employer's budget objectives. Ironically, this after-tax, out-of-pocket expenditure has occurred despite the introduction of the tax-effective Health Care Spending Account available under many flex programs. We are now seeing a more streamlined, tax-effective type of design.

Elements of Flexible Benefits

A traditional benefits plan provides the same benefits, and the same level of coverage for all employees in the same class. There is little opportunity for an employee to take more or less of any benefit based on individual circumstance or preference. Plan design tends to reflect the needs of the "average" employee, and the willingness of the employer to pay for the benefits.

Flexible benefits, or flex, is now a common term for benefit practitioners. A "flexible benefits program" is commonly defined as one that allows plan members to choose some, or all of their benefits in order to meet their own personal needs.

In general terms, most flexible benefits plans are designed within four major design themes:

- Modular plans;

- Core plus option plans;
- Cafeteria plans; and
- Spending accounts.

Modular Plans

Under a modular plan, the employee may choose from a selection of pre-packaged benefit plans. Each option will contain more than one benefit. Medical and dental benefits are typically packaged together. The packages may either be fully funded by the employer on a flat-value basis, or partially by the employee on an increasing value basis, where the employee can contribute and thereby obtain increased benefits. The primary advantage of modular plans is administrative simplicity. It can also help mitigate the effects of anti-selection, especially for employers who do not employ a large number of employees. However, from the employee's perspective, this approach may not be as appealing as other flexible benefits programs. Modular plans restrict the flexibility that allows employees to choose the coverage they need under specific benefit lines. For example, an employee's need for life insurance may have nothing to do with his or her dental needs, and yet the employee must take both as part of the modular plan, if that is how it is designed.

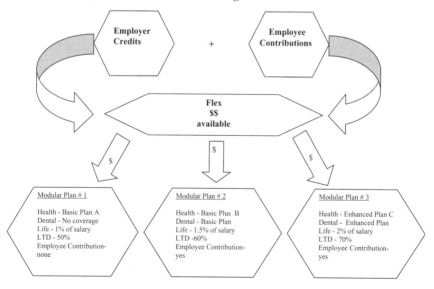

Core Plus Options Plans

There are three structural elements in a core plus options plan: core, credits and options.

The core is the minimum level of benefits that the employer requires an employee to have, and is usually fully funded by the employer. It may include a minimum level of life, disability and health coverage. However, the scope of the core will depend on the culture of the organization.

Most core plus options plans feature credits provided by the employer. The credits may be a flat dollar amount, a percentage of compensation or a combination of several factors. Employees decide how credits will be allocated according to individual need.

The options are limited only by the imagination and the ability to administer them. Options will generally include some choices within the traditional benefits, including medical, dental, life insurance and Accidental Death and Dismemberment (AD&D). In addition, the opportunity to purchase home and auto insurance or fitness and wellness options can be included.

The core plus options structure allows the employer to manage cost while giving employees a wide range of choice. The administration of a core plus options plan can be substantially more complex than modular plans.

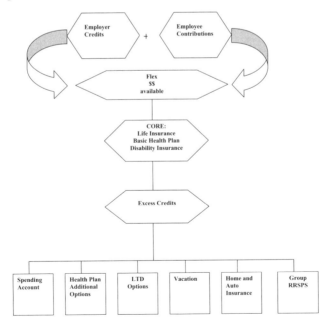

Cafeteria Plans

A cafeteria plan offers the employee a full range of options within each benefit, with no mandatory core. Employer contributions are given to employees in the form of flexible credits and employees are offered a range of benefits and benefit plan options. Each plan option has a price tag. Employees purchase benefit options with their credits. The value of one credit equals one dollar. Credits that remain following the purchase of the desired coverage are allocated to various alternate benefits, depending upon the design of the program. For example, employees may be allowed to convert their credits into cash, an RRSP contribution, or deposit credits into a Spending Account, etc.

Most employers are uncomfortable with this approach because it affords the employee an opportunity to remain without coverage. In the event of an unforeseen tragedy, such as a disability or death, the individual will be without the minimum protection. As a result, those employers who implement such a plan must be cognizant of the communication, education, and documentation issues.

Aside from the potential risks associated with a cafeteria-type plan, this program entails a significant amount of administration. It is possible that there will be hundreds of different program combinations, depending upon the size of the organization. The complexity of administering a Cafeteria approach might also have legal issues, such as a situation where errors are made in the administration process.

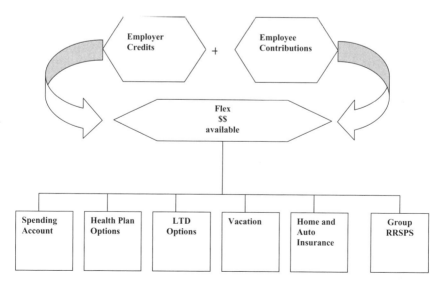

Spending Accounts

A Health Care Spending Account (HCSA) is an individual employee account into which employer credits are deposited on a pre-tax basis (subject to provincial taxes in Quebec). To be tax effective, the HCSA must be funded by employer contributions alone. The account allows for maximum flexibility with the dollars so designated, since individual choice is made at the time the expense is incurred. The employee submits his or her eligible medical and dental expenses and is reimbursed from the HCSA.

Coverage under a Health Care Spending Account must be "in respect of hospital care or expense or medical care or expense which normally would otherwise have qualified as a medical expense under the provisions of subsection 118.2(2) of the *Income Tax Act* related to the determination of the medical expense tax credit"[1].

To ensure that the payments made out of the account will be classified as non-taxable income for employees (other than employees in Quebec), the Spending Account must be established as a Private Health Services Plan (PHSP). This means that the plan must contain the following basic elements:

1. An undertaking by one person,

2. To indemnify another person,

3. For an agreed consideration,

4. From a loss or liability in respect of an event,

5. The happening of which is uncertain.

In order to satisfy the above requirements, the credits allocated to the HCSA must be made at the beginning of the plan year, at which time they are locked in. The basic principle behind a contract of insurance is the element of risk. Thus, the "use it or lose it" provisions apply. However, the employer may specify that either the HCSA balance or the unpaid benefit year expenses can be carried forward for up to one additional benefit year before they are "lost".

Flexible Benefit Choices

Any component of an employee benefit plan can be designed to allow choices in coverage. A partial menu of plan design ideas follows:

---

[1] IT-339R2 — *Meaning of "Private Health Services Plan"*

Benefit	Potential Options
Medical/Dental	buy-up or sell down using credits
Life	additional coverage for employee, spouse or child
Pension...............	contributory or non-contributory plans
Disability	taxability, percentage of income and indexation
Vacations..............	buying vacation days
Capital Accumulation	RRSP or savings plans with excess credits
Wellness...............	health promotion and fitness, stress counselling
Managed Care	open choice and preferred provider plans
Home/Auto............	offer range of plans through payroll deduction
Group Legal...........	specified services through preferred providers

The Language of Flexible Benefits

A new vocabulary has emerged to address flexible benefits. Some commonly used terms are described below.

- *Defined Benefit* — Typically associated with pension plans, "defined benefit" applies equally to any benefit where the employer's obligation is characterized in terms of benefit rather than employer cost.

- *Defined Contribution* — The term "defined contribution" describes any employee benefit for which the employer promise is characterized as a fixed cost rather than the benefit. Flexible benefit examples of defined contribution include spending accounts and credits.

- *Spending Account* — A fixed dollar account set aside by the employer per employee, the Spending Account operates under Revenue Canada's (now the CCRA) guidelines for a Private Health Services Plan. The employee may claim eligible medical and dental expenses without giving rise to income tax at the federal level.

- *Credits* — "Credits" are integral to the overall flexible benefits concept. The credits allocated by the employer can be used by the employee on a pre-tax basis to offset the price tags of benefit choices that would otherwise be paid through payroll deduction. Credit formulas vary from plan to plan.

- *Price Tag* — Because of the potential combination of credits and payroll deduction, the term "price tag" is often used to refer to employee contributions relative to a benefit or benefit option.

- *Lock-In* — Given the chance and given the information, employees will choose the coverage that best suits their needs.

To protect the plan from price volatility, the higher plan options for medical and dental benefits often require the employee to remain in that option for a fixed period of time. The "lock-in" period varies, with two to three years being the most common.

How to Flex

The process of implementing a flexible benefits plan is fundamentally the same process that an employer would apply to any major decision.

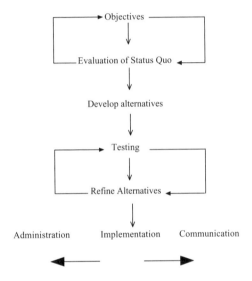

Objectives

To borrow from an adage, if you do not know where you are going, all roads are equal. Because flexible benefits represent a substantial investment of time, and an integral part of the corporate message, it is essential that objectives are clearly articulated, quantified and prioritized at the outset.

The benefit plan objectives must support the business objectives so that senior management can fully support the initiative from conception to implementation. Because flexible benefits cross many disciplines and affect many individuals, it is prudent to either seek input from the key stakeholders at the outset, or to use key stakeholders as a sounding board at various stages of the process.

Although the list of potential objectives is unlimited, six common factors shaping flexible benefit plan objectives are given below:

- The employer is faced with a diverse workforce with dissimilar benefit priorities;

- There are inequities in the current plan design;

- There is a mandate to help employees shift from entitlement to a greater sharing of accountability, and to shift corporate culture towards viewing benefits as elements in total compensation;

- After a number of mergers and acquisitions, benefit plans across the organization are being consolidated;

- The employer is struggling with low employee appreciation of a high-cost benefit plan;

- The company needs to reinforce its image as a responsive and progressive employer.

The success with which a flexible benefits plan meets any of these, or other objectives will depend on how the current plan compares with these objectives, the time frame over which the organization is willing to implement the changes, and whether the mandate for change is consistent with organizational objectives. Benefits are a fundamental part of the message of the organization to its employees.

It is feasible to design and manage a flexible benefits plan that supports the strategic objectives of the business. It is impossible to develop a sustainable flexible benefits plan that conflicts with the other objectives of the organization.

Evaluation of Status Quo

Having clearly articulated the benefit plan objectives, the current benefit plan can be weighed, benefit by benefit and objective by objective. Necessary changes should be identified and prioritized.

Evaluation of the *status quo* may include the current administration and delivery systems. Where internal recordkeeping systems and payroll interfaces are deficient, it may be necessary to revise the plan design, the timetable, or the budget to allow for required programming or upgrades. The effectiveness of current communication channels will also affect the communication strategy associated with the new plan.

Develop Alternatives

A road map should begin to emerge of where the current plans are, and where they need to be relative to the business plan and the benefit objectives. Designing the alternatives requires attention to detail and an understanding of underwriting fundamentals. Senior management needs to endorse both the objectives and the evaluation to avoid expensive and frustrating surprises at any later stage of the process.

Testing

The degree of change from the current plan will guide the timing and the level of testing required. Most employers will test the prototypes against the plan objectives, looking for improvement over the current plan.

Each employee will judge the new plan from the perspective of "What is in it for me?" Employers often conduct the testing with employees either through focus groups or using models based on actual or projected claim patterns. It would be naive to expect that all employees will respond positively. Employee testing provides the employer with an opportunity to "test market" the new plan, and to be able to stabilize the pricing strategy based on projected enrollment distribution.

Administration

Much was learned from the survivors of early flexible benefit implementations. Thorough documentation and a detailed project plan will serve the employer well during the transition and testing phases.

Communication

The successful introduction of a new flexible benefits plan requires effective communication. Employees need to be informed of the options available, as well as the consequences of their decisions. To succeed, it is necessary that the employee become an educated participant, which is a departure from the level of involvement required in a traditional benefits plan. Many employees will be faced with new terminology and concepts that are quite unfamiliar to them. As a result, it is essential that plain language be used in preparing communication materials, and that technical/legal jargon be avoided wherever possible. Timeliness is also an integral component of a successful communication strategy. Disseminating information in a timely manner assists in containing and eliminating negative employee speculations, which can sometimes sabotage the acceptance of the plan once it is actually introduced to the employee group.

Employers have a broad range of communication media available to them for the introduction of a flexible benefits plan; combining two or more of these methods will reinforce the message. The fact remains that individuals absorb information in different manners, and that they will have preferences with respect to the distribution of information. Examples of approaches that can be used when introducing employee choice or making design changes include:

- Direct Contact: focus groups, general employee meetings, individual employee meetings, information hot lines (using toll-free numbers);

- Print: newsletters, posters, booklets, workbooks, question and answer (Q & A) sheets, faxes; and

- Electronic: software programs, Web-based technology, video, voicemail, interactive voice response systems and kiosks.

Each employer's objectives are unique, as is the setting and environment in which the communication takes place. Using Web-based technology to provide information regarding a new flexible benefits program may work well for a telecommunications company, but will obviously not work as well for a manufacturing company that employs predominantly older employees with limited computer skills and access.

Paper-based communication was once the sole means of providing employees with benefit plan information, and remains a popular choice for many organizations. Portability and familiarity are two of the most compelling attributes of paper for delivering static information.

The introduction of a new benefit plan often requires an interactive approach. Face-to-face meetings continue to be the most effective means of delivering the strategic message accompanying the benefit change. It provides employees with the opportunity to ask questions and smaller groups will present better environments in which to facilitate discussion regarding the impending changes.

Technology is changing and will continue to change flexible benefits communication. While paper continues to play a very important role in the process, electronic media such as Web-based technology are becoming increasingly popular. Where employees have easy access to a PC, computers can be used for enrollment and for online access to relevant documentation. The PC is particularly valuable in allowing employees to examine their options interactively. The ability to model "what if" scenarios on screen increases employee comfort with the decisions they are being asked to make. The ability to share information with dependants is retained as employees can always print a current copy of the particular section of the document as required. Additionally, Web-based technology is a very efficient method of distributing information to all employees, no matter where they are located.

Although some employers may question the feasibility of using such media, the reality is that computers are becoming part of the fabric of our society. Statistics regarding Internet usage by teens is strongly indicative that the next generation of workers will be much more computer literate, and that the barriers that may apply to certain classes of older workers regarding PC usage may effectively be eliminated in the work force of the future.

The telephone is another medium for providing information and Interactive Voice Response systems (IVRs) are becoming increasingly popular for enrollment and the communication of flexible benefit plans. By using IVRs to record enrollment elections, the employer eliminates more cumbersome paper enrollment forms and reduces errors associated with manual entry or optical scanning. Accessibility and familiarity are two of the advantages of the telephone as a communication tool.

Communication is also discussed in Chapter 19.

Strategic Pricing

Overall cost objectives, set by the organization, drive the pricing strategy. Where employees are presented with coverage options, the relative pricing between options must "make sense" to the employee making the choices. Strategic pricing may also involve the creation of an incentive for some options to support the underlying objectives of the flexible benefits plan.

Strategic pricing may involve a deliberate investment in the first years of the plan in order to gain control of the cost curve in future years. In the long run, the benefit plan and pricing must adapt to change without major renovation.

Medical and dental pricing present unique challenges in a flexible benefits environment. Reliable claims data are basic prerequisites for flex pricing. Preferably, for each component of the medical and dental plans, the claims data will be available by individual — whether employee, spouse or dependent child. A core plus options plan with credits encompasses most strategic pricing issues for flexible benefit plans. Other plan design variations require some modification to the basic pricing methodology.

Claims data is used to develop the realistic price tag for each option, taking into account the tendency of high-end users to select the more liberal benefit options. In insurance parlance, there is an element of "anti-selection" that must be reflected in pricing.

The notion of credits is unique to flexible benefits. In most flexible benefits plans, credits are part of the employer contribution. The credit formula is as important to the pricing strategy as the determination of the price tags for each benefit option. The credit formula for medical and dental benefits tends to be a flat amount per employee. Alternatively, credits may include a salary-related portion where some of the price tags are linked to salary, or where credits have been augmented by reducing salary-related benefits. Credits linked to service may be a consideration where rewarding long-service employees forms a key objective for the benefit plan.

Pricing requires a balance between corporate objectives and employee perception. If purely realistic pricing were used, employees with families and a need for maximum coverage would find themselves materially disadvantaged relative to young single employees. Many employers use partial or temporary subsidies either directly or across plan options. A common example is to strategically lower the opt-out credit value for those who waive coverage in order to stabilize the pricing of the overall plan.

Cost management and employee satisfaction are common objectives of organizations considering flexible benefits. It is usually possible to balance these objectives, provided the real objective is cost management, not cost reduction. Where the objective is cost reduction, it is extremely difficult to achieve employee satisfaction simultaneously. It is prudent to include in the pricing not only the first year costs, but also a three-year or five-year projection to fully understand the financial impact of the flexible benefits plans relative to the current plan. A mid-term projection also helps to avoid surprises for the employer and for the employees.

Tax Issues

Income tax considerations are an important factor in the selection of benefits and in the design of the overall program. In choosing his or her benefits, an employee will be encouraged to consider which benefits are taxable upon receipt, which employer-paid premiums are considered taxable income, and which employee-paid premiums and/or expenses are tax deductible. These considerations are especially necessary in the case of a dual-income family, where both spouses have group coverage and have the opportunity to coordinate benefits.

There is no existing definition of a flexible benefits program under the *Income Tax Act* (ITA). However on February 20, 1998, IT Bulletin "IT-529 — Flexible Employee Benefit Programs" was released by the CCRA. Although it does not have the force of law, IT-529 does provide the CCRA's position regarding the taxation of flexible benefits. The following commentary touches upon some of the information provided in the bulletin. Although the ITA does not contain provisions that apply specifically to a flexible benefit plan as a whole, the design of the program must satisfy certain conditions in order to avoid adverse tax consequences for "all" of the benefits provided for under the program. The bulletin has categorized flexible benefit plans into two types:

1. Under the first type, the employer allocates a notional amount of flex credits to each eligible employee. Prior to the beginning of the plan year, the employees allocate their credits to various benefits available under the flex program. Some of these benefits may or may not result in a taxable benefit to the employee. The employer is then obligated to provide the employee with the benefits selected.

2. Under the second type, the employees are able to select a level of coverage for each benefit available under the program, ranging from no coverage to a premium level of coverage. A standard level of coverage is set out by the employer for each benefit and a dollar value is assigned to each level of coverage above or below the standard. The cost of any coverage above the standard will be withheld from the employee's salary and the difference between the standard level of coverage and the cost of coverage below the standard will be credited to the employee's account.

The employer's allocation of credits annually to its employees represents the employer's contribution to benefits. In the second type of flexible benefit program, as outlined above, all contributions that are not employee contributions are considered to be contributions by the employer.

According to the bulletin, where one part of the program is a salary deferral arrangement, a retirement compensation arrangement, an employee benefit plan or an employee trust, the ITA sections relating to those arrangements will apply to the entire flex program. However, if the employees are allowed to select the benefits and how such benefits will be funded prior to the plan year, the flex program will be segregated. As a result, the taxable benefits will not, in effect, contaminate the non-taxable benefits.

If the employee is allowed to choose which benefits are taxable and which are to be non-taxable at the beginning of the year, that decision is irrevocable unless

- There is a "life event", such as birth or death of a dependant, a change in marital status, or loss of spousal benefits; or,

- There is a change in employment status.

The change cannot be retroactive.

If an employee's negotiated salary is converted to flex credits, such converted amount will be included in the employee's taxable income. However, once the employment contract expires and the contract is renegotiated, the salary can be decreased and the new contract can include additional flex credits. These additional credits will not be included in the employee's income as part of his or her salary and wages.

Regarding HCSAs, the bulletin states there is no advantage to having the HCSA funded through payroll deductions. To be tax-effective, it must be funded by employer contributions alone. If the HCSA meets the requirements of a Private Health Services Plan (PHSP), payments made out of the account will not be taxable income to the employee (except in Quebec). However, if it does not qualify as a PHSP, the amount of any benefit received out of the plan will be taxable to the employee. See the discussion regarding HCSAs at the beginning of this chapter for further information.

Regarding disability insurance offered under a flexible benefits program, unless the entire plan is funded "solely" from employee payroll deductions, any resulting benefit paid out of the plan will be taxable in the hands of the employee. As flex credits are basically employer contributions, any usage of such credits to obtain coverage will result in the employee being taxed when any benefit is received. However, if the employer has two separate disability plans, one funded through employee contributions and the other through employer contributions, benefits received out of the plan funded by payroll deductions will not be included in the employee's income. In such cases, there can be no cross-subsidization between the employer-funded plan and the employee-funded plan.

The Bulletin also refers to vacation buying and selling. When an employee buys additional vacation with flex credits, the employee must use the vacation in the year in which it was purchased. If the vacation is carried forward to the following plan year, the arrangement may be considered to be a salary deferral arrangement. When an employee forfeits vacation to which he or she is entitled in exchange for additional flex credits, the value of the vacation foregone is considered taxable income. In this situation, the employee is considered to have purchased the extra benefits by way of additional services rendered. It is not the flex credits obtained but rather it is the trading of vacation entitlement by the employee that triggers a taxable event.

OTHER EMPLOYEE BENEFITS

Background

Change is a common theme in the current working environment. Transitions that have an impact on employee benefits include changes in workforce demographics, as well as changes in the employer's perception of "who is responsible". In response to these changes, employers are considering the merits of non-traditional benefits.

Employee Assistance Plans

Employee Assistance Plans (EAPs) were originally introduced into the workplace in the 1950's to deal with employee alcohol and drug abuse problems. Over time, EAPs have evolved and their scope of coverage has expanded to include a variety of issues. The demographics of the Canadian workforce have changed substantially over the past twenty years. There are more dual-income families, more single-parent families, and the baby boomers are ageing. These changes, in addition to other factors, have created additional stress on working individuals and their families, many of whom are struggling to balance work and their personal life. EAPs offer a confidential and professional consulting service to help employees and their families identify and resolve a wide range of personal difficulties and work-related problems. Their primary focus is to provide assessment and referral services, as well as short-term counselling to employees and their families. EAPs have evolved to become proactive in their approach, and are increasingly looked upon as a means to promote well-being, good health and problem prevention.

The business case for implementing an EAP is that providing ready access to effective help reduces the financial impact of personal and family problems on employee productivity, absence rates and turn-over levels.

The employer will have to decide how the EAP service will be provided, either externally or internally. Most employers find that out-sourcing the EAP service offers a more satisfactory arrangement than the use of in-house capabilities. The complete anonymity essential to an EAP is difficult to achieve using internal resources. Also, most employers cannot provide in-house access to a multi-disciplinary team of counselors around the clock.

EAP provider selection reflects the decision of the employer as to which services and provider capabilities are most important. Written specifications are distributed to a number of pre-qualified vendors. Objective evaluation of EAP providers takes into account:

- How access to treatment is facilitated;

- How quality service is assured;

- How confidentiality is assured;

- How patient satisfaction is assessed; and

- How plan costs are set in the first and renewal years.

Most employers monitor the performance of the EAP to ensure that corporate objectives are being met. If objectives of the program are not being achieved, the employer will want to obtain the services of another EAP provider, who will be able to meet the employer's goals.

The following chart depicts the type of EAP services generally provided by organizations.

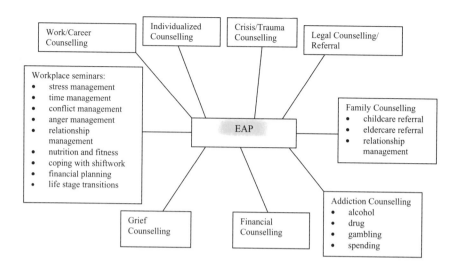

In addition to short-term counselling services, many EAPs also offer workplace seminars to employees and managers on a variety of topics (see chart above).

A recent EAP development is the provision of services via the Internet. Not only can useful information be obtained on a variety of issues that may be of interest to employees who require assistance, but employees can also join online chat groups or obtain individual cyber-counselling over the Internet. The ability to obtain assistance in the privacy of one's own home may very well be an attractive option for many employees. However, the goal of online EAP services is not to replace traditional counselling; rather, it is viewed as an enhancement to the services already offered by an EAP provider.

Wellness Programs

Wellness programs are adopted by employers to support the promotion of good health through education and the facilitation of improved health and fitness. Elements of the program may be funded by the employer, or alternatively offered on an optional basis.

The scope of wellness programs varies. A comprehensive program might encompass stress management, smoking cessation, nutrition counselling, back care, and other preventive care programs. Employer-sponsored programs may include in-house fitness opportunities or provide easy access to community facilities. A wide range of services and delivery methods makes it possible to tailor the program to the objectives, resources and budget of the employer.

Usually, the employer is seeking to reduce absence or health care costs, or to improve productivity. As with any employee benefit, quantifiable objectives are necessary to build and manage a sustainable program.

Alternative Work Arrangements

As society moves further into the Information Age, the nature of work, the workplace, and, to some extent, the worker is evolving. Technology has irreversibly and inescapably changed how and where people work. Employees themselves are re-thinking and re-prioritizing what they expect from their employers. Employers, in their quest to maintain job satisfaction and attract and retain employees, have been moving quickly to introduce measures and policies that reduce work-related stress and increase worker contentment. Alternative workplace arrangements are being tried and implemented in an attempt to promote a more satisfactory work environment.

Telecommuting

Telecommuting is one of a number of such alternative workplace arrangements. Although there is no clear consensus regarding the definition of telecommuting (also referred to as teleworking), the common principle noted in most definitions is that the employee is working at a remote site away from the normal worksite of the organization. Without a doubt, the popularity of this arrangement is growing and there are well over 1 million telecommuters in Canada today. Many businesses are able to accommodate employees, realizing that getting the work done well is more important than where the work is done. For example, transaction-based data processing can be managed as easily from a home in rural British Columbia as from an office tower in downtown Montreal.

There are a variety of advantages associated with telecommuting. Some of these potential advantages are:

- Increased employee productivity;

- Office space savings;

- Improvement in employee job satisfaction;

- Commuting time eliminated;

- Reduced absenteeism; and

- Telecommuting options act as valuable recruitment and retention tools.

Nonetheless, planning is absolutely necessary to reduce the impact of potential disadvantages, including isolation, procrastination, boredom and career/promotion concerns.

Job-Sharing

Job-sharing is where two people voluntarily share the responsibilities of one full-time job, dividing the pay, holidays and other benefits between them, according to the number of hours worked. Demographic changes are forcing employers to examine potential employees who were previously ignored in recruitment: women and men with dependants, older workers and individuals who are physically or mentally challenged.

Flexible Hours

As today's employers are facing new challenges in attracting and retaining the best employees in their field, flexible working hours are an example of another enticing mechanism that a company can utilize to attract potential employees. The term "flextime" refers to an agreement between an employer and an employee that allows the employee to work longer hours on some days and shorter hours on others. There are two common types of flextime: flex hours and the compressed work week. Under flex hours, the employer establishes the core hours required during the work week. Once this is set, the flextime is then organized around the core day. For example, the core hours may be from 9 a.m. to 3 p.m. The employee then has the option of starting anytime prior to 9 a.m. and finishing at any time after 3 p.m., so long as an eight-hour day is completed. In a compressed work week arrangement, the employee must complete a minimum number of hours per week; however, they may work those hours in less than five days, by working longer hours over the four days.

Sabbaticals

Sabbaticals, as a form of alternative work arrangement, were traditionally associated with the academic environment. Other employers are considering sabbaticals and periods of unpaid leave as a mechanism to regenerate those in "mid-career" and to motivate employees in general. Outside of the academic environment, sabbaticals are not typically funded by the employer. Some employers allow employees to budget for a sabbatical by voluntarily reducing salary for a fixed period in order to accrue income for the sabbatical period.

Educational Leaves

A leave of absence for educational purposes can either be short-term or long-term in duration. In general, such leaves can benefit both the individual employee and the employer. A short-term leave arrangement enables employees to successfully complete courses for continuing education programs that are approved by the employer. This enables employees to take ongoing, part-time studies towards completion of a certification or degree while maintaining their jobs. In general, employers combine these leave arrangements with tuition refund programs, which reimburse employees for course fees. Supplementary expenses for textbooks and other course materials may or may not be paid by the employer. Some employers will pay course-related fees in advance, while others may require successful completion before fees are reimbursed. Educational leaves can also be longer in duration, allowing employees to pursue advanced, post-graduate education that will have a direct benefit to their job and the employer. Full-time education is often taken in the form of extended leaves of absence from work, and can be an unpaid leave, or the employee can be paid through a salary deferral arrangement.

Dependant Care

Eldercare

The senior population in Canada is increasing. Seniors are living longer, hospital stays are shorter and they are experiencing more difficulty in obtaining accommodations in retirement and nursing homes. As a result of these factors, the responsibility for the seniors' well-being is more frequently resting on the shoulders of their children, many of whom are full-time employees. While it is clearly not the responsibility of the employer to look after the parents of their employees, employers are certainly becoming more aware of the impact that this issue is having on productivity in the workplace. In fact, there are a variety of potential problems that might arise as a result of eldercare responsibilities, including: absenteeism, tardiness, frequent distractions, depression, inability to work overtime, and turnover, just to name a few. There are a number of approaches that employers can take to provide eldercare assistance to employees who are caregivers. It may include direct assistance (i.e., financial assistance) or indirect assistance (i.e., flexible work arrangements)

Child Care

The increasing number of households with a single parent, or in which both parents work outside the home, leads to additional challenges for the employer. Child care is becoming an increasingly valuable benefit for employees with children, particularly those who are required to travel as part of their job.

Some employers have been able to accommodate on-site child care centres. More often, the employer will provide day-care subsidies to employees to defray the cost of child care expenses.

Further creative solutions are beginning to emerge. To provide for the contingency of sick children, a few property and casualty insurers have added "child-sitting" services to their standard homeowner and tenant policies. For example, one plan provides up to 10 hours a day for three consecutive days with an overall maximum of 15 days per year. Another innovative response brings temporary child-minding services to the home as part of a service subscribed to by the employer. During the next few years, employers will be directing their attention to the issue to help employees find affordable day care solutions from reliable sources that suit work schedules.

Long-Term Care (LTC)

As people age, their disabling conditions change from mild to severe, requiring appropriate changes in their level of care. Generally, LTC is associated with medical or custodial care for the elderly.

Given the choice, most people want to remain in their home as long as they can. In fact, statistics indicate that most seniors with disabling conditions continue to live in the community as compared to those that live in institutions. It is estimated that by 2011, there will be more than 1.5 million disabled Canadian seniors living in the community as compared to the 312,000 who will live in institutions. Even though the number of seniors living in long-term care facilities will increase 60% between 1986 to 2011, the fact remains that by far, the majority of elders with disabling conditions will be treated in the community before they enter a facility.

Home care is made possible when there is assistance available from professional and paraprofessional home services to support the assistance being provided by the family member who has taken on the role of caregiver. While the government provides some financial assistance with home care and home health care, there are limits to the number of hours they will cover. Eventually, it becomes cost-prohibitive for the individual to remain at home, and the decision must be made to move to a facility with full time nursing care. This makes it very important that any LTC policy considered contains a combination of both home care benefits and facility care benefits.

Group Critical Illness Insurance

Critical illness insurance is a relatively new product, offered in Canada by a few carriers since the mid-1990s, and designed to fill needs where gaps exist between life insurance and disability insurance. Group critical illness insurance first became available in 1997, and is often described by insurers as a tax-free, lump-sum payment, which is usually paid out within 30 days of diagnosis of a critical condition. A critical condition may cover such items as a heart attack, stroke, cancer, bypass surgery, kidney failure, blindness, deafness, organ transplants, multiple sclerosis and paralysis.

With advances in medical science, people now survive many illnesses that might previously have been fatal. However, people who survive can place added burdens, including financial ones, on their caregivers. Critical illness insurance differs from disability insurance. Disability insurance typically pays a portion of an employee's income if a doctor declares that person unable to work within the meaning of the insurance company's policy. The definition of disability under many disability insurance policies could force someone who has suffered a mild heart attack, has undergone heart surgery or who has been diagnosed with cancer, to work through financial necessity, although this may not be practical. With critical illness insurance, the policyholder gets the payout regardless.

Cost is one of the main reasons why employers are unwilling to provide critical illness insurance as a benefit. However, if it is offered as an optional benefit or as part of a flexible benefits plan, such concerns should be eliminated. The issue surrounding the tax implications of group critical illness insurance payments are also the subject of some debate. However, the reality may be that as the quality of government-sponsored health care continues to decline, the CCRA may be reluctant to impose a tax on critical illness insurance payments. The CCRA has yet to officially confirm that group (or non-group) critical illness insurance actually qualifies under the *Income Tax Act* as a "sickness or accident insurance plan", the issue being that in some cases, the critical illness policy may not agree with the widely accepted definition of sickness insurance as being compensation for loss or a reimbursement of expenses. This is due to the fact that a payment under such a policy could be made without the insured actually incurring a specific loss.

Individual Financial Planning

In the past, individual financial counselling was provided primarily to highly compensated executives in the belief that advice on large capital accumulation, investments, tax and estate planning applied only to them. Increasingly, employers are aware that there are consequences for all employees if they do not plan properly for retirement.

Employer pension plans are designed to supplement — not replace — government benefits and personal savings. Employers are now turning to individual financial planning for executives, for employees who are close to retirement and for employees who are being offered termination packages.

The trend towards a broader audience for individual financial planning reflects the increasing use of defined contribution pension plans, savings plans and flexible benefit plans that require choices, as well as downsizings and early retirements. Chapter 4 outlines the components of employer-provided financial counselling.

In addition to financial counselling, many employers offer retirement counselling for employees approaching retirement. Counselling sessions can be conducted for individuals or on a group basis. The focus of the session is to help the individual anticipate the lifestyle changes associated with retirement, and the decisions that may need to be made in respect of retirement income. From a tax position, the fees paid by an employer for retirement counselling do not produce taxable income for the employee. It should be noted that benefits relating to financial counselling provided by virtue of employment are included as income from employment.

Group Legal Insurance

The spread of group legal plans in Canada as an employee benefit has been limited and those plans that do exist are most often found in a union setting. Group legal plans provide a specified range of legal services that do not compromise the relationship between the employer and the employee. Services generally include the following:

- Purchase or sale of residential housing;
- Landlord and tenant issues;
- Motor vehicle offences;
- Separation;
- Adoption;

- Divorce; and

- Wills and estate issues.

The employer may contract with those who provide the legal services, either a closed group of qualified lawyers or internal counsel, to provide the services for a fixed annual fee per person. Alternatively, the employer may agree to pay a fixed amount towards the cost of the specified services, allowing the employee to choose the lawyer.

Generally speaking, subject to Section 248 of the *Income Tax Act*, employer contributions are tax-deductible to the employer but taxable in the hands of employees.

By contrast with the lack of growth of group legal plans, an increasing number of Employee Assistance Plan (EAP) providers include legal referral services as a component of the overall service package. A referral to qualified lawyers may adequately meet the needs of most employee groups.

Domestic Partner Benefits

Today's family bears little resemblance to the traditional family of a few decades ago. It is no longer composed of the working father, stay-at-home mother and 2.5 children. In fact, the traditional model only applies to a relatively small percentage of today's society. We now see a variety of familial relationships, ranging from single-parent families to grandparents raising grandchildren. As a result of the Supreme Court decision in *M. v. H.*, an entirely new dimension has also been added to the contemporary definition of family — same-sex partnerships. Domestic partner benefits have arisen out of the need to accommodate unmarried opposite-sex and same-sex partners, and to put them on the same footing as married spouses.

Nova Scotia now recognizes conjugal domestic partnerships whereby same-sex or opposite-sex unmarried couples can file a declaration with the Nova Scotia Registry of Vital Statistics. Registration provides the domestic partners with the same legal privileges that married spouses are entitled to, in relation to various rights, such as division of pensions upon the death or dissolution of the relationship. On June 7, 2002, the Quebec National Assembly passed Bill 84, "An Act instituting civil unions and establishing new rules of filiation". The intent of the Act is to enable the solemnization of gay and lesbian civil unions, but it is not limited to same-sex couples. The legislation defines a civil union as "a commitment between two persons eighteen years of age or over who express their free and enlightened consent to live together and to uphold the rights and obligations that derive from that status". Individuals in a civil union must be unmarried, and cannot be parties to another civil union, nor may the parties be siblings, ascendants or descendants. The Bill affects a variety of other legislation in Quebec, including employment and pension legislation.

By 1999, all federal and provincial human rights legislation had been voluntarily amended, or governments were forced to include sexual orientation as a protected ground. Although some employers may be reluctant to offer domestic partner benefits, inevitably they will be required to provide domestic partners with coverage or risk claims of discrimination. For example, the 1992 decision, *Leshner v. Ontario*, involved a complaint of discrimination on the basis of sexual orientation stemming from the denial of benefits under a group supplementary health insurance and pension plan. The complainant wanted to claim his partner as his spouse under his employee group benefits. However, the plans were administered on the basis that only opposite-sex spouses qualified for dependant coverage, and same-sex, common-law relationships were not recognized for the purposes of providing family benefits. The Ontario Human Rights Board of Inquiry determined that the employer had discriminated against the complainant, and it was ordered to amend its benefit programs to provide same-sex couples with the same benefits as those provided to opposite-sex couples.

For some time, employers were dealing with mixed messages. On the one hand they were being told that denying benefits to same-sex partners was a violation of human rights legislation, and on the other hand the *Income Tax Act* (ITA) and pension standards legislation did not recognize same-sex spouses. The ITA did not include same-sex partners in the definition of "spouse" (as it had with common-law, opposite-sex partners since 1993). It did not permit pension plan registration that purported to offer benefits to same-sex couples, and pension standards legislation defined a spouse as being someone of the opposite sex. Revenue Canada (now the CCRA) also stated that health and dental plans providing same-sex spousal benefits would not qualify as Private Health Service Plans (PHSPs). That left employers with the choice of either non-compliance with the ITA, or the provision of different benefits that would not be eligible for advantageous tax treatment. In the Ontario Court of Appeal *Rosenberg* decision, the Court held that provisions in the ITA did in fact discriminate against same-sex couples. The Court of Appeal effectively changed the definition of spouse to permit the registration of pension plans that provided for the payment of spousal survivor benefits to same-sex partners. Effective September 9, 1996, the CCRA changed its position regarding

PHSPs and stated that a PHSP providing same-sex partner coverage would be considered a qualified plan. The ITA was amended in 2001 and same-sex partners were incorporated into the new definition of common-law partner included in the Act.

Eligibility

Employers will have to determine how they are going to define who is eligible for domestic partner benefits. Unlike a marriage, there is no specific and universal definition of domestic partnerships. However, certain elements are normally included in most definitions. Basically the partners, either opposite or same sex, must reside together in a committed relationship. Employers need to establish criteria that domestic partners need to meet in order to be eligible for benefits, and such criteria typically include the following:

- Cohabitation for a specific period of time (usually between 1 and 3 years);

- Minimum age requirements; and

- Shared financial responsibilities.

The employer will require certification from the employee that the person named as their domestic partner actually meets the eligibility requirements as set out by the company. Other documentation may also be required to establish that the employee actually meets the outlined prerequisites, such as the cohabitation element.

Scope of Benefits and Costs

The employer will need to determine what benefits will be made available to domestic partners. Although some employers fear that domestic partnership benefits will substantially increase costs, there has been no evidence that costs will increase rapidly because of the addition of such benefits.

Executive Benefits

Many organizations provide additional life insurance coverage and enhanced medical and dental benefits for executives. Over and above the traditional benefits provided to employees, a number of organizations provide additional non-cash benefits to designated executives.

As with all benefits, executive benefits assist in attracting and retaining key people. Appropriately designed executive benefits can set the tone for executive performance and reinforce the value system of the organization.

The following are some of the principal reasons that organizations provide executive benefits, and the corresponding benefits that meet the objectives.

- *Business needs* — Company cars, expense accounts, membership dues in professional associations, and certain club memberships are often considered a part of doing business. To the extent that they facilitate client service, maintain key competence and reinforce client relationships, these additional benefits are seen to contribute to the success of the organization.

- *Recognition* — First-class travel, reserved parking and personal assistants are sometimes granted in recognition of the value of the executive to the organization. Also included in this category would be conference and convention expenses, which may include an accompanying spouse and feature attractive locations. Benefits based on recognition are viewed as status symbols and reinforce the perceived contribution of the individual to the organization.

- *Image* — Corporate jets, spacious offices and special furnishings create an image of prestige and status for both the executive and the organization. To the extent that these appropriately reinforce credibility and market dominance, they are viewed to support the corporate image.

- *Financial planning* — Personal financial planning for executives can cover financial planning, estate planning and legal counselling, together with tax preparation services. The rationale is to allow the executive to focus on the business of the employer. Formal guarantees of compensation arrangements with regard to termination following a merger, acquisition or any other "change of control" may also form part of the financial planning for executives.

- *Stress management* — To encourage executives to maintain their physical fitness, executives may be provided with memberships to health clubs. Additionally, in recognition of the demands of the job, executives tend to be provided with more vacation days.

- *Tax effectiveness* — Once a driving force in executive compensation, there are relatively few avenues for tax-effective applications remaining. Although tax consequences are no longer the primary rationale for providing non-cash compensation, taxation remains an issue to be considered in evaluating the alternatives.

PART III
EMERGING ISSUES

RECENT ISSUES AND TRENDS

This chapter is a brief outline of some the recent issues and trends that have occurred and are occurring in the pension and employment benefits sector. It was compiled to provide some context and direction for managers thinking about the role of pensions and benefits within their particular organizations.

The chapter begins with some general observations about prevailing conditions that will influence pensions and benefits: economics, demographics, government policy and the globalization of business. Next are some comments on issues specific to pension plans and benefit programs, dealing with strategic decisions that are being made as the environments for these programs are changing. The chapter ends with a note on the need for human resources managers to ensure that employee programs are responsive to employer priorities — which are also changing.

General

The preceding chapters of this *Handbook* have covered the world of employer-sponsored pensions and benefits in some detail. A recurring theme is that, over the years, pensions and benefits have become more complex to design and administer, and generally more expensive to deliver. Employers are experiencing an accelerated pace of change in pensions and benefits.

Ideally, an employer's pension and benefits policies should be driven by corporate philosophy and aligned with the broad strategic objectives of the enterprise. An effective benefits policy is not designed solely around cost or tax considerations — that would be a case of the "tail wagging the dog". But practical pension and benefits design and ongoing administration must also take into account the realities of economics, demographics, government policy, globalization and technology.

After the tragedy of September 11, 2001, many economists were concerned about the possibility of a global recession. Prior to the September 11 events, the North American economy had already been suffering from an economic slowdown and some believed that the market's response to these terrorists' attacks would seal the world economy's fate. However, the Canadian economy actually rebounded quite well from this downturn and its economic growth exceeded expectations at the beginning of 2002. On the other hand, the economic reaction for other nations throughout the summer of 2002 has not been so positive and even Canada has not been immune to the uncertainties in the financial markets. Adding fuel to the fire is the ongoing threat of terrorist attacks, the crisis in the Middle East and the unrelenting wave of corporate scandals, which have continued to plague corporate America.

The historical use of benefits packages to "attract and retain" the desired employee profile has also shifted towards using benefits to help employees address their own needs while containing the costs to the employer. This dual purpose presents potential for conflict and confusion. The purpose of a program must therefore be carefully defined before it is designed, and the intention must be clearly communicated to employees.

Many employers, accustomed to long service employment, have cultivated an environment of paternalism that encouraged some employees to develop an entitlement mentality; a transition to more employee responsibility does not come easily. Both the objectives and the message to employees needs to be clear.

The demographics of the workforce present a further challenge. The Canadian population is ageing. Older employees are more interested in pensions and are, on average, heavier users of health benefits. The 2001 census shows that the median age of Canadians reached an all-time high of 37.6, an increase of 2.3 per cent since the last census in 1996[1]. Logically, the workforce is therefore ageing as well. According to the census, the median age in the workforce is 41.3 years, in comparison to 38.1 in 1991. Statistics Canada stated that this has been the largest increase since 1921. Changes in composition of

---

[1] The median age means that half the population is older than that age and half the population is younger than that age.

the workforce will drive changes in pensions and benefits design. There are more women in the workforce and there are more dual income families. In fact, today's family bears little resemblance to the traditional family of a few decades ago. The traditional family consisted of a lawfully wedded heterosexual couple who were of the same age, colour and religion and who parented 2.5 children, most likely born of the same parents. The husband worked and the wife was a homemaker. Today, this structure constitutes only a small percentage of Canadian families. A benefits program designed specifically to meet the needs of a working husband supporting a wife working in the home and supporting two or three children no longer makes sense for most employers. The needs of employees, like the strategies of employers, have become more diverse.

The Canadian workforce has also become, on average, more educated — a trend that will support the growing focus on employee education in benefits programs.

With respect to government policies, we have experienced some changes that required considered responses by employers:

- Beginning in the 1990's the Federal Government began reducing transfer payments to the provinces. In turn, to reduce costs, the provinces began delisting health services that were previously provided. Because most employer health benefits were designed to wrap around government programs, employers are particularly vulnerable to cost downloading as governments delist services and drugs.

- The freeze on the ceiling on tax-assisted retirement savings to employees making approximately $86,000 in 2002. The freeze until 2005 means that the need for supplementary non-registered plans is reaching much farther down the pay scale, into the ranks of middle management in many enterprises.

Human resources managers are faced with the need to create valued benefits programs to meet diverse needs — with sharp budget constraints and often with reduced staff!

The globalization of business is another development that is shaping the pensions and benefits policies of some Canadian companies. There are two different directions in which human resources management in companies with international operations can move. The choice is usually dictated in part by the industry, as well as by management's desire, as part of a drive to world-scale operations, to see that specific compensation and benefit principles are extended globally. One is to have policies of operations in different countries reflect to a large extent local practices and expectations. The other direction is to plan human resources policies, including total compensation and benefits, centrally and then adapt the central model to fit local competition and the legislative environment.

Technology is the tool, or support structure that allows modern benefit managers to adapt to change. Benefit managers can design, introduce and deliver innovative benefits packages that would have been too expensive and cumbersome using traditional administration and communication tools. Technology is often an essential support to current and contemplated changes in pensions and benefits; some uses are outlined in the "Applications of Technology" section later in this chapter.

The outsourcing of administration functions — especially pension and flexible benefits — is another well-established trend. From an employee perspective, probably its most significant implication is for greater sophistication in the methods used to educate employees and communicate entitlements.

These are times of economic uncertainties, an ageing workforce and increasing health care costs. There will be significant challenges facing employers in the future. How to strike a balance between providing employees with the benefits they need and at the same time managing the escalating costs of such benefits will be the challenge that lies ahead. A well-thought-out benefits policy makes sense to all stakeholders — beneficiaries and payers — and can be effectively communicated to them.

Issues For Pension Plan Sponsors

A retirement planning change that needs to be seriously considered by government is phased-in retirement. Phased retirement generally refers to the gradual reduction of work by older employees transitioning into full retirement. A well-designed phased retirement program can be beneficial for both the employer and the employee. The employees are able to gradually reduce their hours and yet maintain an adequate level of income, while the employer meets its staffing objectives. As noted above, current trends in Canadian demographics indicate that as the baby boomer generation nears retirement, employers will be faced with labour shortages in key areas. To compound the problem, with the baby boom generation tending to occupy many of the more attractive positions, many workers of the next generation are under-employed or not qualified to fill the positions left behind. A phased retirement program might indirectly assist an employer in developing a qualified workforce for the future by allowing older employees to reduce their work hours, and reassigning those hours to younger employees. This allows for the transfer of skills and knowledge from older to younger employees during the phased retirement period.

The design of a phased retirement program may take a number of forms. This may include the use of accumulated sick days or leave of absence provisions, as well as payments from a company's registered pension plan. Each design may have cost implications for a company, as well as income replacement consequences to an employee.

Certain restrictions under the *Income Tax Act* constrain the ability of an employer to implement the best phased retirement program possible for the employee who is a member of a defined benefit plan. An employee, for example, is prohibited by regulations from both accruing and receiving a defined benefit pension at the same time. The *Income Tax Act* also specifies that lifetime pensions must be paid in equal periodic payments for both defined benefit and defined contribution plans. In other words, an employee will not be able to receive increasing pension benefits as the employee decreases his or her working hours. Quebec was the first province to arrive at a solution, which effectively skirted around these two barriers by amending its pension benefits legislation to permit employees to withdraw lump-sum amounts from their pensions during the phased retirement period. Alberta has also subsequently amended its legislation. Conflict with the *Income Tax Act* has been avoided as a result of regulations under the *Income Tax Act*, which permit a lump-sum distribution from a registered pension plan. Although these phased retirement options exist, they are certainly not a panacea, and due to certain restrictions in relation to these options, their popularity has been limited.

Another concern pertaining to phased retirement is in relation to the restrictions on obtaining CPP and QPP benefits during a phased-retirement period. Quebec has addressed such concerns by amending its legislation so that employees can reduce their hours of work without suffering a corresponding reduction to their QPP entitlement. Additionally if the employee's salary is reduced by at least 20% as a result of the phased retirement agreement, the employee is entitled to receive an early QPP pension while continuing to work on a reduced basis. There have been no corresponding amendments to the CPP. As it stands, an employee who wants to receive early retirement benefits from the CPP from the age of 60 must have "wholly or substantially" ceased working, meaning that the employee must have annual earnings of less than $9,775 in 2002 (25% of the YMPE).

Both the federal and provincial governments will have to reconsider their existing legislation as we enter into a predicted period of labour shortage. Phased retirement appears to be a much-needed solution for both employees and employers, if only the legislation existed to support the ideal program — a program that does not financially penalize the employee.

The fact that contribution limits to RRSPs and the upper limits on benefits that can be paid from a registered pension plan have been frozen for some time has resulted in a shrinking amount of retirement income from tax-preferred sources for many plan members. These cut-offs have come to affect a large number of employees who are professional, skilled tradespeople and upper-middle management. Employers have come to recognize such limitations, and in an attempt to attract and retain valued employees have had to embrace other options to satisfy employee needs for more retirement income. The options have included:

- Opting out of employer-sponsored pensions altogether to allow employees to save using the tax advantages of RRSPs;

- Encouraging further personal savings through supplemental savings plans;

- Share purchase and stock option plans;

- Financial planning advice; and

- Provision of Supplemental Executive Retirement Plans (SERPs) to all employees affected.

With respect to SERPs, a recent Morneau Sobeco survey indicates that 55% of the organizations polled offered some form of a SERP. The larger the employer, the more likely a SERP will be provided.

> . . .the prevalence of SERPs increases significantly with the size of the organization — over 90% of organizations with revenues in excess of $1B offer a SERP.[2]

A fundamental factor affecting an employer's ability to attract and retain productive, committed employees is the type of pension plan the employer has to offer. Traditionally, pension plans have provided employees with little flexibility or opportunity to customize their options, or to meet their unique retirement needs and objectives. Choices have also been limited to those concerning employee participation and/or contribution levels. However, during recent years, greater consideration has been given to providing employees with

---

[2] *Are You on Top of Your "Top Hat"?*, Richard Béliveau, *Vision*, February 2002 Volume 6 Number 1. This article can be viewed at Morneau Sobeco's Web site at **www.morneausobeco.com**.

more flexible pension options. This trend is expected to become even more significant in years to come.

One of the main reasons for the interest in flexible pension plans is the diversity of the employee population, whose needs in various stages of life, or in differing family and financial circumstances, prompt the desire for differing programs. The unprecedented high investment returns of the 1990s generated employee interest in defined contribution plans. Also, employees today are experiencing a greater degree of job mobility and have demonstrated a greater willingness to take responsibility for their retirement income and, hence, moved away from defined benefit plans, which provide greater rewards to retiring, long-service employees. Moreover, changes to the *Income Tax Act* led to an increased demand for plan revisions, as those changes were perceived to be unfair.

Flexible pension plans are still at a relatively early stage of development. Plan sponsors are contemplating changes, but governing legislation is still in development, and the regulatory framework is not harmonized across jurisdictions. The administrative systems needed to handle more flexible plans are also still being developed.

An alternative way to achieve flexibility, which is often overlooked, is offering employees the right to opt out: allowing them to refuse to join the plan, or to postpone joining. If they have already joined the plan, they could be given the right to opt out at that particular point in time.

The "opt-out" option gives employees the additional flexibility needed to tie their period of plan membership more closely to their perceived need for retirement income, and to their pension plan's role in meeting that objective.

Not all supervisory authorities will accept such provisions, however. For example, in Manitoba, pension enrollment is compulsory once certain eligibility conditions are met, and opting out is not permitted, except under certain prescribed circumstances.

A flexible pension plan as defined in the CAPSA Communiqué is "a plan that allows members to make voluntary defined benefit contributions (called 'optional ancillary contributions' in the Revenue Canada Newsletter) to a flexible component of the plan". These contributions can then be used to purchase ancillary benefits. A front-end flex plan requires the employee to choose the ancillary benefits in advance in exchange for his or her contributions. Under a back-end flex plan, the employee makes his or her contributions, which accumulate, and the employee may then choose the ancillary benefits he or she desires upon termination or retirement.

Another noticeable trend with respect to registered pension plans is the shift from defined benefit plans to defined contribution arrangements, such as defined contribution registered pension plans and group RRSPs. These defined contribution arrangements have grown significantly in popularity. There are various reasons cited for this shift. One of the most obvious reasons cited is the fact that defined benefit plans are more complex to administer from a regulatory point of view. Furthermore, the risk of unfunded liabilities associated with such plans is naturally an obvious drawback for employers. On the other hand, even when a defined benefit plan surplus exists, if ownership rights have not been clearly outlined, costly disputes may arise in order to determine surplus entitlement.

Defined contribution arrangements provide a growing balance of pension savings that employees can see, understand and direct for investment. From the employer's perspective they are appealing because they are less regulated than defined benefit plans. Furthermore, under a defined contribution arrangement, employers are not obligated to provide guaranteed benefit payments; rather, they are only obligated to make their promised contributions. The reduction in administrative costs associated with such plans as compared to those associated with defined benefit plans is another attractive feature for employers.

Although there has been a shift, this is not to intimate that defined contribution arrangements are without their drawbacks. In the article *Our Inaugural DC Survey Results: Plan Members Speak Out*[3], Morneau Sobeco surveyed individual plan members about their knowledge of retirement concepts and the perceived effectiveness of their employers' communication and educational undertakings. Overall, the survey illustrated that the members did not display a high level of investment knowledge. In fact, only 8% of members correctly answered five or more of six knowledge-assessment questions — less than half answered three or more correctly. This dismal showing was especially surprising given that the respondent group was slightly older, had more formal education and a higher average income than that of the general workforce. As the authors of the article noted, the level of investment knowledge was "mediocre at best". Furthermore, plan sponsors and their advisors had a tendency to overestimate employees' basic investment knowledge. Compounding this problem

---

[3] *Vision*, March 2001, Volume 5, Number 1. This article can be viewed at Morneau Sobeco's Web site at **www.morneausobeco.com**.

was the fact that the educational materials provided to members presumed greater knowledge and comprehension of basic investment and retirement concepts than was actually the case. The article also provided interesting insight into the range of investment options provided and its impact on members:

> Beyond developing an effective communication strategy, the survey findings suggest that plan members may place a premium on clearer investment choices. Recent trends have been to add more and more investment funds. This has generally been driven by a vocal minority of plan members. We may be doing the majority a disservice.

> Over two decades of experience with flexible benefit plans has proven the wisdom of offering fewer, and more compelling choices. This perhaps sets the stage for greater adoption of "goof-proof" investment options, like life-cycle funds. Is the pendulum starting to swing back towards offering a restricted number of funds which address the needs of the majority?

Employees must be educated about the range and impact of different investment options. Many employees with defined contribution accounts such as group RRSPs may be overly conservative investors and rely on accumulated savings that will not provide sufficient retirement income to meet their expectations. Employee education programs are becoming more prevalent, not only because they are a useful employee benefit, but also because employers are becoming increasingly concerned about their fiduciary risk. Unlike defined benefit plan members, the burden of risk is shifted to the participants in defined contribution arrangements. Employers might suffer potential litigation if employees suffer investment losses or poor investment performance.

On April 27, 2001, the Joint Forum of Financial Market Regulators released a paper titled *Proposed Regulation Principles for Capital Accumulation Plans* (CAPs). As defined in the paper, CAPs refer to "investment vehicles established by employers for the benefit of their employees that permit those employees to make investment decisions". The paper was designed to address, among other issues, the fact that employees need to have sufficient information and tools to make investment decisions and that plan sponsors need to have their duties clearly defined.

The Joint Forum outlined the four principles that could form the regulatory model for CAPs. These principles were mainly derived from the current securities, pension and insurance models and the U.S. ERISA (*Employee Retirement Income Security Act of 1974*) model. The principles outline the plan sponsor's obligations with respect to the establishment and maintenance of a CAP (i.e., prudent selection and monitoring of investment managers); the plan sponsor's duties with regards to providing a minimum level of disclosure to new members, as well as continuous disclosure obligations; the plan sponsor's duty to ensure that the CAP members rely on advice provided by appropriate individuals; and that investment products must comply with minimum standards.

The proposed principles regarding the plan sponsor's duty to monitor the investment managers and investments funds are *somewhat* similar to the Safe Harbour Rules under section 404(*c*) of ERISA. When certain requirements have been met, the ERISA Safe Harbour Rules protect plan sponsors from liability. Under the Joint Forum's paper, Canadian plan sponsors are obligated to meet certain requirements as is the case with ERISA; however, there is no associated "safe harbour" for Canadian plan sponsors. In other words, there is no provision in the proposed regulations that would shield the employer from legal actions brought by employees.

Another recent issue has been with respect to electronic communication in the pension industry. As technology progresses, inevitably electronic communication will become a more acceptable and more efficient form of communication. Nonetheless, many issues need to be resolved before the electronic communication becomes mainstream. In February 2002, the Canadian Association of Pension Supervisory Authorities (CAPSA) released its *Guideline No. 2 — Electronic Communication in the Pension Industry*. In the Guideline, CAPSA states that the benefits of electronic communication are readily identifiable: namely, reduced administrative costs, improved service for members and enhanced fiduciary monitoring. The Guideline's stated purpose is to help administrators and members "apply the provisions of applicable electronic commerce legislation to pension communications required under the pension benefits legislation in each jurisdiction." Legislative clarification regarding the status of electronic pension plan communications would resolve some of the current anxiety, thereby enabling administrators to forge ahead and to make use of a more efficient communication medium. As it is still in its infancy, electronic communications in the pension industry will, without a doubt, be a topic of discussion in the future.

Canadians have become more and more concerned about the companies they invest in and whether or not such companies are involved in activities that they consider to be socially or environmentally undesirable. Individual investors are empowered and capable of factoring certain social, economic, or environmental criteria into their investment decision-making process. They can partake in what is referred to as socially responsible investing (SRI).

The question is whether such investing is permissible in the pension plan context, which is subject to certain investment constraints (i.e., "prudent person" rule). Of course, there is no clear answer. It appears as if the basic statements from regulators is that SRI is not in and of itself imprudent, so long as its usage does not compromise the plan sponsor's obligations.

In her article *Ethics and Prudence in Canada: An Uneasy Co-existence*[4], Bethune Whiston of Morneau Sobeco stated:

> Some pension funds, however, are investing in accordance with social or environmental goals, and studies show SRI returns have been favourable. If social responsibility implies progressive management, this should not be surprising. Increased opportunity coupled with pressure from plan members may encourage more socially responsible investment of pension funds in the future. These factors and others make SRI a less risky activity in Canada today, than it was 25 years ago.

Furthermore, Whiston outlines some recommended steps that a pension trustee should take if considering participating in SRI:

- review alternative approaches and select one that is suitable for the particular pension plan and its environment;

- ensure that the ethical investment mandate is incorporated in the plan documents;

- make full disclosure to plan members and regulators; and

- analyze the impact of the investment activity on a regular basis.

Another recently emerging trend in the pension industry is with respect to the unlocking of pension benefits. The question is, does this recent trend conflict with the purpose behind pension benefits legislation, which is to promote savings for retirement? The concern of regulators is that if members are allowed to access their benefits prior to retirement, they may not have adequate income for retirement and an additional burden will be placed on government programs. However, the stringent locking-in requirements have been subject to erosion as members are gaining greater access to their pensions. Some jurisdictions have granted access to such assets where:

- The terminating employee's life expectancy is shortened;

- The member is a non-resident for a specific period;

- The value of the pension is "small" (the amount defined as "small" has increased in some jurisdictions, thereby granting access to larger amounts); and

---

[4] *International Pension Lawyer*, Sept 2001, No. 37.

- In Ontario, the member is suffering from financial hardship.

In 2002, Saskatchewan introduced a new portability option giving employees access to their formerly locked-in pension money. This new option, a RRIF, is only locked-in until age 55, and replaces LIFs and LRIFs in Saskatchewan. The New Brunswick government is following Saskatchewan's lead by introducing a provision that, when proclaimed into force, will permit a member upon termination of employment to have the administrator of the plan transfer up to 25% of the member's pension to a RRIF.

Employee activism is also making pension plan governance a more prominent issue. Since a pension entitlement can be the largest personal asset of an employee, an employer's administration and general governance of the investment of the funds are likely to come under increasing scrutiny. Pension plan governance will also grow in importance as the power of employees and employers as "pension fund capitalists" increases. The assets of trusteed pension funds now represent one of the largest pools of capital in Canada.

Various guidelines and reports have been published on the subject of good governance. For example, on May 25, 2001, CAPSA issued its draft *Pension Governance Guideline and Implementation Tool*, which identifies various principles of good governance. The Guideline outlines 13 principles in relation to good governance, under five main headings: namely, pension plan objectives, governance structure, communication, internal controls and performance measures and assessment. The Implementation Tool is designed to assist administrators adopt the pension governance principles set out in the guideline. Although governance issues will continue to evolve over time, the Guideline has provided a detailed approach to pension plan governance and is a logical progression forward.

The entitlement to pension and employment benefits for same-sex partners has undergone a significant transformation over the last decade. Same-sex partners have finally been recognized under the *Income Tax Act*, and most minimum standards jurisdictions include them under either their definition of "spouse" or "common-law partner". Full equality has still not been achieved, but we have definitely seen some progression. Both Nova Scotia and Quebec have gone a step further than other jurisdictions. In Nova Scotia, same-sex partners can file domestic partnership declarations with the province. Once registered, such domestic partners are entitled to all the same rights and obligations as married couples, including entitlement to pension benefits. In Quebec, the government has created a new legal institution — the civil union — which is as close to a conventional marriage as the law will currently allow.

On July 12, 2002, the Ontario Superior Court stated that the definition of marriage, which excludes gay couples, is a violation of the *Canadian Charter of Rights and Freedoms*. The Federal Government is currently appealing this decision to the Ontario Court of Appeal. It is fully expected that the resolution of this issue will ultimately rest with the Supreme Court of Canada.

Same-sex conjugal relationships are not the only relationships to come under scrutiny. The Law Commission of Canada recently released its report *Beyond Conjugality*. In its Strategic Agenda, the Law Commission observed that:

> Canadian law rests on a number of assumptions about how people organize their private lives, and how they relate to their parents, partners, children, and those with whom they make a home. These assumptions are frequently out of touch with the facts.

The Report suggests that adults in economically interdependent and close personal relationships should be entitled to certain benefits, which are currently only available to married spouses, common-law opposite-sex partners and same-sex partners. The report recommends that individuals in economically interdependent and close personal relationships have the option to register and that such registration would not be based upon whether the relationship was conjugal. Examples of non-conjugal relationships that would be permitted to register include disabled individuals and their caregivers, adult children and their parents, and adult siblings. Upon registration, such individuals would be entitled to certain employment, tax and other benefits.

The Alberta government is currently reviewing its existing provincial family law to determine whether the legislation can be updated and improved. The *Public Workbook Alberta Family Law Reform 2002* was released on January 10, 2002. The Workbook canvasses a variety of issues, and also refers to the possibility of according special legal rights to individuals in "interdependent" relationships. According to the Workbook, under an interdependent relationship model, the emphasis would be placed on economic interdependency, although emotional interdependency would exist. An important measure of whether the relationship is interdependent would be the intermingling of finances and property to a degree where economic interdependency is present.

Whether the suggestions to create rights for economically and emotionally interdependent adult relationships will go beyond these reports remains to be seen.

It is difficult to ascertain how serious federal and Alberta policymakers are about moving forward with this initiative. While society may benefit from extending recognition to non-conjugal relationships, it is clear that there will be a high cost to pay for those benefits.

The price of implementing the recommendations in the Report and the Workbook will likely require both the federal and provincial governments to increase business and personal income taxes in an attempt to offset the cost. In addition, . . . extending benefits to individuals in non-conjugal relationships will dramatically increase benefit and pension plan costs. Therefore, whether in the form of increased taxes or staggering, skyrocketing benefit costs, employers will pick up much of the tab if governments decide to provide benefits to non-conjugal partners.

Given the tremendous impact these proposals will have on employers, they must be given a seat at the negotiating table before any final decisions are made about extending benefits to Canadians in non-conjugal relationships. Otherwise, it will be another case of governments downloading expenses to employers without understanding the potentially far-reaching consequences of their actions.[5]

Issues For Benefit Plan Sponsors

In the context of employee benefits, change is the only constant. The composition of the workforce, and therefore its needs, is changing and will continue to change. Beginning on January 1, 2000, the accounting method used by Canadian employers (private sector) for post-retirement benefits changed. Prior to that date, these benefits were calculated on a pay-as-you go basis, and now must be accounted for on an accrual basis. This new accounting requirement was an enlightening process for some employers, who suddenly became aware of how expensive post-retirement benefits were and the impact on their financial statements of providing these benefits. Employers are becoming more interested in reducing or eliminating their obligations to provide post-retirement benefits to retired employees. Similar accounting methods for public sector employers will come into effect in 2004.

The ongoing cost shift from provincial health plans to employer plans and to the consumer, coupled with the intrinsic and rising cost of the products and services, will cause employers to seek new answers to the challenge of managing benefit costs.

---

[5] *Benefits for One and All?*, by Karen DeBortoli, LL.B., CCH Canadian Limited's *Canadian Employment Benefits and Pension Newsletter* April 2002, Issue #497.

Some employers are already looking to managed care options. While there is no standard definition of managed care in the Canadian environment, it is generally accepted that the term refers to a change in the delivery and funding of medical and dental services. An employer may negotiate preferred terms with a group of health care providers and structure the benefit plan to create an incentive to use the preferred providers. Instead of traditional "fee for service" compensation for services rendered, the employer may arrange to pay a fixed fee per employee based on anticipated usage. Alternatively, the employer may define the benefit amount instead of the benefits covered. More variations of managed care will emerge in response to the need to balance cost and value in the benefit equation.

The diversity of benefit needs and employment relationships suggests a continuation in the trend towards more flexible benefit plans. Employers will need to provide a benefit structure that allows employees to select from among different types or levels of benefits and to revise the choice on a periodic basis. The role of the employer will shift from providing all benefits to providing some benefits and creating access to others. Concurrently, the employee will accept more responsibility for choices made regarding benefits, and health care in general. Transferring responsibility from the employer to the employee will in turn increase the need for education and communication to allow employees to become informed consumers.

Adding more complexity to the benefit administrator's responsibilities is the introduction of new privacy legislation. The federal *Personal Information Protection and Electronic Documents Act* (PIPEDA) came into force on January 1, 2001 for federal works, undertakings and businesses. Effective January 1, 2002, PIPEDA is applicable to personal health information of these organizations. Any organization covered by the Act must obtain the consent of an individual when they collect, use or disclose the personal information of that individual, including personal health information. On January 1, 2004, the Act will apply to all organizations regarding the collection, use and disclosure of personal information in the course of "commercial activity" within a province, unless the province has adopted "substantially similar" privacy legislation. Most provinces will likely enact their own privacy legislation.

Will PIPEDA affect the benefit sponsor's benefits programs?

The answer is yes and no. While the principles underlying PIPEDA will undoubtedly affect your pension and benefits programs, the nuts and bolts of compliance will likely be left up to one or more pending provincial privacy statutes. Unfortunately, it appears that a patchwork of privacy protection legislation is developing in Canada, and that employers will need to develop a good understanding of both the principles underlying privacy legislation and their various permutations in order to implement an effective privacy program.[6]

The future relationship of government-sponsored and employer-sponsored benefits is an enigma because the cost picture for health care and disability costs is not yet fully visible. To cope with unacceptable costs, some employers will make decisions that reduce benefit costs but increase the cost to the overall system. For example, not covering a more expensive advanced drug formulation may help keep down the medical plan cost, but it may result in greater absenteeism and higher hospital costs in the longer term. Employers will need more data, and more incentive, to develop more creative solutions.

Outsourcing

There has been a trend towards outsourcing the administration of both pension and group benefits. There are a number of reasons:

- To remain competitive, many employers are focusing on their core businesses and expertise. This may lead to strategic alliances or outsourcing some generic functions to suppliers who specialize in them. In the case of pensions and benefits, employers will outsource some functions of administration and communication, while retaining control of the strategic components that are most important to the individual employee/employer relationships.

- The complexities of administration, and exposure to litigation are increasing, and employers will not want, or cannot afford, to retain sufficient expertise in-house.

- The increasing cost of investments in technology to administer pensions and benefits means that more employers will not be able to justify the investment for in-house use only.

Applications of Technology

Even with constraints on budgets and limited staff, employers will underscore the value of the employer benefits by communicating more directly with individual employees. While personal communication will always be preferred by most people, there will be increased take-up of

---

[6] *How Will the Privacy Patchwork Cover Benefits?* by Deric Jacklin, LL.B. and Karen DeBortoli, LL.B., CCH Canadian Limited's Canadian Employment Benefits and Pension Newsletter, July 2002, Issue #500.

the opportunities technology now provides for messages targeted to individual employees. For example:

- Toll-free numbers allow employees in defined contribution pension plans to check their savings levels and register new investment options.

- Pension plan options and savings choices can be effectively demonstrated to employees through software using "what-if" scenarios on PC-based programs. The employee enters his or her income, expectations for retirement and assumptions about interest rates and inflation. The program, automatically including CPP/QPP and employer-provided benefits, will demonstrate how much personal savings are needed under various scenarios. (The results are usually a shock.)

- An employer introducing a flexible benefits plan can do so through interactive voice technology. Using a touch tone telephone, the employee can choose the various options, find out what the costs and benefits will be, and then register for the choice of options. Confirmation is given through a printed statement.

- Another recent development in benefits administration is the trend toward self-service Web sites for employees. Not only can employees obtain information about their benefits via the Internet, but they can also enroll in flexible benefits plans and print off forms and information that they require. Statistics demonstrate that Internet access and usage is definitely increasing.

- Some Canadian employers are using the Internet to communicate benefit changes and smart benefits shopping tips to retirees.

- Using an Intranet connection, a Canadian employer has provided all employees with personalized records of their pensions and benefits. The program also allows employees to perform "what-if" scenarios for both flex benefits and savings plans, and register changes.

In benefits communication and design, as in many other communications industries, narrowcasting is complementing broadcasting. Employers will be designing and communicating their benefits programs for and to individuals, rather than the workforce as a whole.

Shifting Focus

The focus of pensions and benefits managers is shifting with increased emphasis on communication, education and responsiveness to change. The reasons are not only the extensive communications requirements of arrangements such as defined contribution pension plans and flexible benefits, but also the leverage from more communication, as well as the availability of communications technology. The shift is also due to new factors in the workplace: continuous learning, flexible and fluid business strategies that require a quick response, and more mobile workforces, at least in the larger metropolitan centres. Within a strategically oriented human resources policy, these factors also influence design and delivery of pension and benefits.

CASE TABLE

(References are to Pages)

WEB SITES

GOVERNMENT AND NON-GOVERNMENT ORGANIZATIONS REFERRED TO IN PENSION HANDBOOK

Organization	Role/Stated Objectives	Web Site Address
Statistics Canada	Statistics Canada provides Canadian social and economic statistics and products	**www.statcan.ca**
Canada Customs and Revenue Agency (CCRA)	CCRA promotes compliance with Canada's tax legislation	**www.ccra-adrc.gc.ca**
Human Resources Development Canada (HRDC)	EI, CPP, OAS and GIS	**www.hrdc-drhc.gc.ca**
Régie des Rentes	QPP	**www.rrq.gouv.qc.ca**
CPP Investment Board	Crown Corporation responsible for managing CPP funds	**www.cppib.ca**
Canadian Association of Pension Supervisory Authorities (CAPSA)	Association of senior government officials whose mission is to facilitate an efficient and effective pension regulatory system in Canada	**www.capsa-acor.org**
Association of Canadian Pension Management (ACPM)	ACPM's mission is to advocate the growth and health of the retirement income system in Canada	**www.acpm.com**
Canadian Institute of Actuaries (CIA)	National Organization of Canadian Actuarial profession, which promotes advancement of actuarial sciences and sponsors programs for the education and qualification of members and prospective members	**www.actuaries.ca**

Pension and Benefit Plans

Organization	Role/Stated Objectives	Web Site Address
Canadian Institute of Chartered Accountants (CICA)	CICA represents CAs in Canada. It conducts research into current business issues and sets accounting and assurance standards for business, not-for-profit organizations and government	www.cica.ca
Canadian Life and Health Insurance Association (CLHIA)	CLHIA is a voluntary trade association that represents the collective interests of its member life and health insurers	www.clhia.ca
Law Commission of Canada	The Law Commission of Canada is an independent federal law reform agency that advises Parliament on how to improve and modernize Canada's laws	www.lcc.gc.ca
Morneau Sobeco	Morneau Sobeco provides benefits, investment, communication, compensation and retirement consulting, as well as administrative solutions for clients	www.morneausobeco.com
Watson Wyatt (Canada)	Watson Wyatt is a global consulting firm and its practice includes benefits consulting and eHR Technologies	www.watsonwyatt.com/canada
FEDERAL AND PROVINCIAL PENSION REGULATORS		
Federal	Office of the Superintendent of Financial Institutions	www.osfi-bsif.ca
Alberta	Alberta Finance	www.finance.gov.ab.ca/business/pensions
British Columbia	Pension Standards Branch	www.labour.gov.bc.ca/psb
Manitoba	Manitoba Pension Commission	www.gov.mb.ca/labour/pen
New Brunswick	Office of the Superintendent of Pensions	www.gnb.ca/0307/001e.htm

Organization	Role/Stated Objectives	Web Site Address
Newfoundland and Labrador	Insurance and Pensions Division	www.gov.nf.ca/gsl/cca/ip
Nova Scotia	Pension Regulation Division	www.gov.ns.ca/ enla/pensions
Ontario	Financial Services Commission of Ontario	www.fsco.gov.on.ca
Quebec	Régie des rentes du Quebec	www.rrq.gouv.qc.ca
Saskatchewan	Pension Benefits Branch	www.saskjustice.gov.sk.ca/ Pensions/default.shtml
PENSION AND INVESTMENT ONLINE MAGAZINE AND INFORMATIONAL RESOURCES		
Canadian Investment Review	Investment Magazine online	www.investmentreview.com
Benefits Canada	Pension & Benefits Magazine Online	www.benefitscanada.com
Canadian Healthcare Manager	Healthcare Magazine online	www.chmonline.ca
BenefitsWorld.com™	Employee Benefits and Compensation Information	www.benefitsworld.com
InnoVisions Canada/ Canadian Telework Association (IVC/CTA)	Site provides great information on teleworking and flexible work programs	www.ivc.ca

TOPICAL INDEX

(References are to Pages)